IRD LO
F

SAMS
Teach Yourself

Microsoft®

Windows® Server
2003

in 24 Hours

Joe Habraken

SAMS   800 East 96th St., Indianapolis, Indiana 46240 USA

Sams Teach Yourself Microsoft® Windows® Server 2003 in 24 Hour

Copyright © 2003 by Sams Publishing

International Standard Book Number: 0-672-32494-6

Library of Congress Catalog Card Number: 2002112347

Printed in the United States of America

First Printing: April 2003

06   05   04   4   3

Trademarks

All terms mentioned in this book that are known to be trademarks or service
marks have been appropriately capitalized. Sams Publishing cannot attest to the
accuracy of this information. Use of a term in this book should not be regarded
as affecting the validity of any trademark or service mark.

Warning and Disclaimer

Every effort has been made to make this book as complete and as accurate as
possible, but no warranty or fitness is implied. The information provided is on
an "as is" basis. The author and the publisher shall have neither liability nor
responsibility to any person or entity with respect to any loss or damages aris-
ing from the information contained in this book or from the use of the CD or
programs accompanying it.

Bulk Sales

Sams Publishing offers excellent discounts on this book when ordered in quan-
tity for bulk purchases or special sales. For more information, please contact

U.S. Corporate and Government Sales
1-800-382-3419
corpsales@pearsontechgroup.com

For sales outside of the U.S., please contact

International Sales
1-317-428-3341
international@pearsontechgroup.com

PUBLISHER
el Stephens

IONS EDITOR
Rowe

LOPMENT EDITOR
Mark Renfrow

MANAGING EDITOR
Charlotte Clapp

PROJECT EDITOR
Matthew Purcell

COPY EDITOR
Krista Hansing

INDEXER
Mandie Frank

PROOFREADER
Leslie Joseph

TECHNICAL EDITOR
Philip Bocko

TEAM COORDINATOR
Cindy Teeters

INTERIOR DESIGNER
Gary Adair

COVER DESIGNER
Alan Clements

PAGE LAYOUT
Stacey Richwine-DeRome

GRAPHICS
Tammy Graham
Laura Robbins

Contents at a Glance

Contents

About the Author

Joe Habraken is a computer technology professional and best-selling author with more than 15 years of experience in the information technology field. His recent publications include *Microsoft Office XP 8-in-1*, *The Absolute Beginner's Guide to Networking (3rd Edition)*, and *Practical Cisco Routers*. Joe currently serves as an assistant professor at the University of New England in Biddeford, ME, where he heads up the Information Technology program offered by the Business Administration Department. Joe is a Microsoft Certified Professional and a Cisco Certified Network Associate.

Dedication

To my wonderful wife, Kim; thanks for making my life so great and loving me. I love you too!

Acknowledgments

Creating a book that covers a topic such as Microsoft Windows Server 2003 takes a team of dedicated professionals; information technology experts, highly skilled editors, proofreaders, and desktop publishers. First of all, I would certainly like to thank all the folks at Sams Publishing who were involved in the creation of this book. I would also like to specifically thank some of the folks who have made this book a reality.

First of all, I would like to thank the very hard-working Neil Rowe, my acquisitions editor, who assembled the team that worked on this project. Neil showed great enthusiasm for the project and also great patience during the writing of the book. He also provided some very insightful thoughts on the subject matter for the book. Neil, thanks for making my continued association with Sams a pleasant and productive one.

A big thanks goes out to Mark Renfrow, the Development Editor, who worked extremely hard to make sure this was the best book possible. I would also like to thank Krista Hansing, our copy editor, for cleaning up the text and finally, a big thanks to the Project Editor, Matt Purcell, who ran the last leg of the race and made sure this book got into print (and into your local bookstore). Thank you all very much!

We Want to Hear from You!

As the reader of this book, *you* are our most important critic and commentator. We value your opinion and want to know what we're doing right, what we could do better, what areas you'd like to see us publish in, and any other words of wisdom you're willing to pass our way.

As an associate publisher for Sams, I welcome your comments. You can email or write me directly to let me know what you did or didn't like about this book—as well as what we can do to make our books better.

Please note that I cannot help you with technical problems related to the *topic* of this book. We do have a User Services group, however, where I will forward specific technical questions related to the book.

When you write, please be sure to include this book's title and author as well as your name, email address, and phone number. I will carefully review your comments and share them with the author and editors who worked on the book.

Email: feedback@samspublishing.com

Mail: Michael Stephens
           Sams Publishing
           800 East 96th Street
           Indianapolis, IN 46240 USA

For more information about this book or another Sams title, visit our Web site at www.samspublishing.com. Type the ISBN (excluding hyphens) or the title of a book in the Search field to find the page you're looking for.

Introduction

Selecting and deploying a network operating system is one of the most important tasks shouldered by a network administrator. In this book, I wanted to put together a body of information related to the newest version of Microsoft's powerful network operating system platform—Microsoft Windows Server 2003—that would not only highlight the functions and capabilities of the network server software, but also provide a hands-on approach to deploying the product. The *SAMS Teach Yourself in 24 Hours* format provides for both the subject matter coverage and a practical step-by-step look at important server features and tools.

Microsoft has spent a great deal of time and effort (and development money) to improve both the security and scalability of Windows Server 2003. *SAMS Teach Yourself Windows Server 2003 in 24 Hours* provides you with all the information you need to get a Windows domain up and running. Coverage of network services and the ins and outs of supporting users on the network is also provided.

Material in the book is approached in a straightforward, step-by-step manner that makes it easy to digest the information. The hours in the book are arranged so that there is a building of information as you move from Hour 1 to Hour 24.

Who Should Use This Book?

This book is designed for people who have a basic knowledge of computer networking. The book is arranged in 24 self-contained hours. Each hour helps build your knowledge base of Windows Server 2003. Coverage includes many important Windows Server 2003 network services such as WINS, Routing and Remote Access, DHCP, DNS, and file and print services. A hands-on approach, coupled with easy-to-read background information, will help you quickly raise your knowledge base of Microsoft's powerful network operating system platform.

The book is also divided into four parts. Each part provides a grouping of hours that share a common theme.

Part I, "Server Installation and Configuration," includes hours that provide you with information on installing the Windows Server 2003 operating system and configuring a server running this network operating system for a variety of possible roles. Part I also provides you with insight into network security issues, the Windows Server 2003 administrative tools, and how to configure hard drives and volumes on your servers.

Part II, "Network Users, Resources, and Special Server Roles," includes hours that help you expand your knowledge of data communications on the network through a discussion of network protocols and securing resources using share and NTFS permissions. You also learn how to use the different Active Directory snap-ins and how to provide file and printing services to your network users.

Part III, "Advanced Networking," provides information on a number of Windows Server 2003 services, such as DNS, DHCP, WINS, Routing and Remote Access, and Windows Terminal Services. The hours in Part III help you get all these services up and running in your Windows Server 2003 domains and provide insight into how to fine-tune a complex network configuration that requires specialized domain servers.

Part IV, "Performance Monitoring, Security, and Web Services," provides hours that help you fine-tune server performance on the network and tackle security and services related to data traffic on the Internet and that help you provide Web Services to your user base. Tools such as the System Monitor, Event Viewer, and Network Monitor are explored in the context of keeping important domain servers up and running at peak performance. Securing IP data packets using IPSec on both private and public networks and using virtual private networks to move data securely across public networks are discussed as well. Part IV also provides information on installing and configuring a Web server using Internet Information Server 6.0.

Conventions Used in This Book

Certain conventions have been followed in this book to help you digest all the material. For example, at the beginning of each hour, you'll find a list of the major topics that will be covered in that particular hour. You will also find that icons are used throughout this book. These icons either are accompanied by additional information on a subject or supply you with shortcuts or optional ways to perform a task. These icons are as follows:

> Notes include additional information related to the current topic, such as asides and comments.

> Tips contain shortcuts and hints on performing a particular task.

At the end of each hour, you will find both a Summary section and a Q&A section. The Summary section provides a brief encapsulation of the core information covered in the hour. The Q&A section provides a series of questions and answers that help cement important facts and concepts covered in the hour.

PART I

Server Installation and Configuration

Hour

HOUR 1

Introducing Microsoft Windows Server 2003

With the release of Microsoft Windows 2000 Server, Microsoft dramatically changed the way network administrators plan and configure the logical hierarchy for a network that deploys servers running Microsoft network operating systems (NOS). The Active Directory provided a tree structure not available in the domain-centric networks in earlier versions of the Windows server operating system.

In this hour, you are introduced to the latest version of Microsoft's network operating system platform: Microsoft Windows Server 2003. We look at the features that Windows Server 2003 has inherited from its predecessors and some of the new features provided by this NOS. We also look at the different editions of Windows Server 2003.

In this hour, the following topics are covered:

- Improvements and features added to Windows Server 2003
- The different editions of Windows Server 2003
- Windows Server 2003 compatibility with other Windows operating systems

What Is Windows Server 2003?

Microsoft Windows Server 2003 is the latest version of Microsoft's network operating system. Windows Server 2003 builds on the features found in the Windows 2000 Server family and also offers a number of enhancements. Windows Server 2003 provides a scalable enterprise networking platform that can be easily expanded as a company or organization grows.

All the features and tools made available in Windows 2000 Server are also found in Windows Server 2003, including these:

- **The Active Directory**—The directory service for the 2003 server platform provides a hierarchical directory of objects on the network (such as users, computers, and printers).
- **The Microsoft Management Console (MMC)**—The MMC allows a common interface for managing services and utilities as MMC snap-ins.
- **Plug-and-play hardware support**—A system of wizards and the operating system's capability to scan for new hardware makes installing hardware components a very straightforward task.
- **Web server capabilities**—.NET Server ships with the newest version of Microsoft's Internet Information Server (Version 6), which supplies a robust Web server foundation for the Internet or a corporate intranet.
- **Group Policy**—Group Policy provides a way to control the user and computer environment found on the network. Application deployment, client desktop settings, and policies related to administrative controls such as auditing can all be configured in Group Policy.
- **High-level security**—Windows 2000 Server introduced data encryption, smart cards, certificates, and a number of other security enhancements, such as the IP Security Protocol. Windows Server 2003 builds on these security features and offers even greater security than its predecessor.

Windows Server 2003 builds on the security that was provided by Windows 2000 Server. Because security is such an issue in today's networking world, an overview of Windows Server 2003 security features is provided in Hour 2, "Windows Server 2003 Security Overview."

In addition to these inclusions, Windows Server 2003 adds functionality by including new features discussed in this next section.

Improvements to Windows Server 2003

A number of improvements and additions have been made to this newest version of the Microsoft Windows network operating system. Although many of the improvements to Windows Server 2003 are not as radical as those faced by network administrators who upgraded from Windows NT Server to the Windows 2000 family of servers (remember switching from the domain model to the directory services model?), some changes deserve discussion.

One of the first things that you might find different is the look and feel of the Windows Server 2003 environment. It will be different for those of you upgrading from the Windows NT or Windows 2000 network operating systems. Windows Server 2003 has adopted the Microsoft XP desktop, which has a more minimal approach to accessing tools and services than either the NT or Windows 2000 environments you have been working in (see Figure 1.1).

FIGURE 1.1
Windows Server 2003 has the look and feel of Windows XP.

The desktop environment is certainly not the only new feature you will find in Windows Server 2003. As mentioned in the previous section, it provides a platform for XML services and other new features, including new network and security enhancements. Another important new feature is Windows Server 2003 support of Internet Protocol Version 6; with IP addresses at a premium, IPv6 will solve the problem of IP addressing (and other issues related to the IPv4 protocol).

A number of other enhancements have been made to the Windows Server 2003 platform. Some of these improvements you will see; others are improvements to security or services that operate behind the scenes.

Probably the most spectacular change in how Windows networks were designed and managed came when Active Directory was introduced with Windows 2000 Server. In Windows Server 2003, enhancements to the Active Directory include Health Monitoring (which allows administrators to check the replication of the Active Directory database between domain controllers), a credential manager (which speeds remote user access to the network), forest trusts (a new way to implement trust relationships between different Active Directory forests), and an enhanced user interface that supports drag and drop and selection of multiple objects.

Another area in which Windows Server 2003 has improved over Windows Sever 2000 is in new commands (see Figure 1.2), including DiskPart, which allows you to manage drives and volumes from the command prompt. Other new commands include the dfscmd Distributed File System utility that enables you to create DFS roots from the command line.

FIGURE 1.2

Windows Server 2003 has beefed up the number of command-line utilities, such as the DiskPart utility, for server administration.

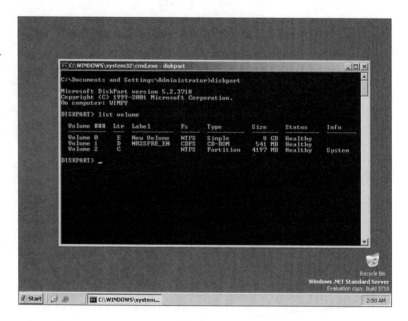

Windows Server 2003 has also improved on file and print services. The new remote document-sharing feature makes it easier for users to access content held in Web repositories by using "typical" file-access tools. The distributed file system has also been tweaked so that data is pulled from the closest DFS server when files are requested by a user. Windows Server 2003 also supports wireless printing, allowing remote user computers to automatically download the needed drivers to print to a network print server.

One of the biggest headaches related to administering Windows 2000 domains was the implementation of Group Policy. Windows Server 2003 provides a Group Policy Management snap-in. This console provides one-stop shopping for configuration of your server and network policies. Figure 1.3 shows the Group Policy Management snap-in.

FIGURE 1.3

The new Group Policy Management snap-in makes it easier to control group policy at different levels in the Active Directory hierarchy.

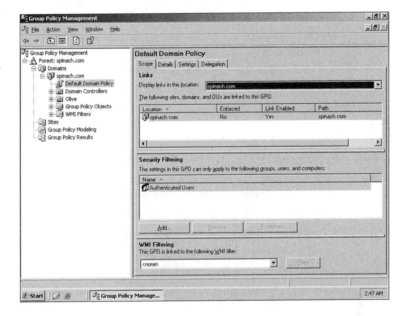

 Group Policy and the new Group Policy Management snap-in are discussed in Hour 11, "Group Policy and User Profiles."

Because deploying a Web site has become imperative for companies (both large and small), the Windows Server version, Internet Information Server (version 6), has a number of new enhancements to bring it online as part of the Microsoft Framework. IIS has been integrated with ASP.NET (Active Server Pages that treat all elements of the page as separate objects), and the metabase for IIS is now a simple XML-formatted plain-text file, making it easier to troubleshoot file-corruption problems or edit the file with a text editor.

Windows Server 2003 is also Microsoft's delivery platform for data exchange and Web applications. Windows offers support for XML; Universal Description, Discovery, and Integration (UDDI); Simple Object Access Protocol (SOAP); and the Web Services Description (WSDL) language. The server software provides specific tools for deploying these Web services, including the Microsoft Framework wizards.

The discussion here only scratches the surface of new features found in and the improvements made to the Windows Server 2003 platform. Other improvements include a new Terminal Services client (Terminal Services is discussed in Hour 19, "Windows Terminal Services"), the Remote Desktop Connection, a new firewall feature that can be used with the Internet Connection Sharing feature, and shadow copies, which allow you to create copies of different versions of files on a file server that can then be accessed by your users. The lists that follow provide a quick look at some of the most important new features and the improvements found in the Windows Server 2003 network operating system platform.

New features:

- **Remote Desktop for Administration**—This feature provides the capability to administer a server from any workstation.

- **Internet Information Services 6.0**—Rebuilt from the ground up, IIS 6 provides a secure platform for serving Web content on an intranet or the Internet.

- **Store Usernames and Password applet**—This new Control Panel applet enables you to store usernames and passwords for accessing resources on secured sites and computers.

- **Shadow copy of shared folders**—Different versions of files in shared folders are maintained.

- **Internet Protocol Version 6 support**—Windows Server 2003 supports the use of IPV6.

Improved features:

- **Group Policy**—The new Group Policy Management tool makes it easier to create policies at the tree, domain, and server levels.

- **Command-line tools**—A number of new command-line tools, including disk-management tools, have been added at the command prompt.

- **The Distributed File System**—DFS has been improved so that resources requested by users are pulled from the nearest DFS server on the network.

1

- **Active Directory improvements**—Health-monitoring and forest trusts, as well as the capability to rename domain and domain controllers, make the Active Directory hierarchy a more flexible environment.

We will be working with a number of the new features and improvements found in the Windows Server 2003 operating system. These features are discussed throughout the book in the context of the appropriate subject matter.

The Different Flavors of Windows Server 2003

The Windows Server 2003 family consists of several different network operating systems that are designed to serve businesses of different sizes and different needs.

The members of the Windows Server 2003 family are listed here and discussed next:

- Standard Edition
- Enterprise Edition
- Datacenter Edition
- Web Edition

Standard Edition

Standard Server is considered the entry-level version of Windows Sever 2003 (if there is such a thing as "entry-level" with server platforms). It is suitable for smaller businesses and organizations ("smaller" meaning users in the hundreds, not thousands, although multiple standard servers in a tree or trees would certainly accommodate even the largest of companies).

Standard Server supplies all the print- and file-sharing capabilities and the Active Directory and Group Policy features contained in the higher-end versions of Windows Server. In reference to Standard Server as a small business networking solution, Standard Server supplies the Internet Connection Service and firewall capabilities that would allow multiple network clients to share the same Internet connection in a small business setting.

Standard Server supports multiple processors and up to 4GB of RAM. This version of Windows Server is comparable to the entry-level server OS provided by the Windows 2000 Server Standard Edition.

Because this book is an introduction to and survey of installing and administering a Windows network environment, we will be covering the tools and features found in Windows Server 2003 Standard Edition. The features found in the Standard Edition are also available in the "advanced" versions of the product. However, the Web edition is intended as a Web server product and does not contain many of the standard features for deploying a domain.

Enterprise Edition

The Enterprise Edition supplies all the features and tools provided by the Standard Edition. The major difference is that the Enterprise Edition is considered a work-horse platform for very large enterprise-wide networks.

To provide the processing power needed for larger networks, the Enterprise Edition can support up to eight processors and also supports server clustering (up to eight cluster nodes, meaning that eight servers can be tied together using the clustering feature and thus can act as one megaserver). The Enterprise Edition also allows for up to 32GB of RAM.

The Enterprise Edition was built for 64-bit computing and will run on servers outfitted with the new Intel Itanium processors. In the 64-bit environment, the Enterprise Edition will support up to 64GB of RAM. Microsoft claims that the Enterprise Edition will be available in a version that supports 32 processors and 128GB of RAM in the 64-bit environment.

Datacenter Edition

The Datacenter Edition provides all the features found in the other editions and provides the same support for multiple processors found in the Enterprise Edition. The Datacenter will also be available for the 64-bit environment and will support 32 processors and 128GB of RAM. Datacenter has more advanced clustering services than the other editions of Windows Server 2003 (these capabilities greatly exceed those found in the Windows 2000 version of the Datacenter Server).

Datacenter is available only through Microsoft's Windows Datacenter program, which means that you can get it only on certain hardware configurations from certain vendors who have worked in conjunction with Microsoft. This means that a server running Datacenter would be highly reliable because all the drivers and hardware configurations have been rigorously tested.

1

The Datacenter Edition is considered the appropriate platform for very large-scale networks requiring access to large databases and real-time transaction validation. Datacenter also has enhancements built in that guard against malicious code.

The Web Edition

The Web Edition is a new product in the Windows server line and is considered the ideal platform for Web hosting; it is a scaled-down version of Windows Server and does not provide tools for deploying a domain-based network, so it is best used as a Web server. The Web Edition uses IIS6 as its Web platform. It is intended for those who want to deploy IIS6 Web services and who do not need the full-featured network operating system platform found in the other versions of Windows Server 2003.

Microsoft Windows Server 2003 Compatibility with Other Versions of Windows

Microsoft Windows Server 2003 supports the use of earlier versions of the Windows desktop operating systems as network clients. This means that network client computers can be running any version of Windows, such as Windows 3x, Windows 9x, Windows 2000, and Windows XP.

> Configuring client computers for the Windows Server network is discussed in Hour 10, "Client Computers and the Domain."

You can deploy Windows Server 2003 servers on networks that still use Windows NT and Windows 2000 servers. In the case of Windows NT networks, you can use Windows Server 2003 only for member servers. In a Windows 2000 domain, you can deploy Windows Server 2003 domain controllers.

The fact that Windows Server 2003 can operate at different levels of functionality makes it compatible with the earlier versions of the Windows network operating system. On networks in which Windows NT 4 Server is running concurrently with Windows Server 2003 or Windows 2000 Server, the network is considered a mixed environment.

Running a mixed network does not allow you to deploy Universal groups, which are provided by the Active Directory when you run Windows Server 2003 in native mode (which can include Windows 2000 servers). If you run a pure network with only

Windows Server 2003 servers, you can raise the functional level to Windows Server. This allows increased functionality in the Active Directory and provides for the renaming of domains and domain controllers. Domain functional levels are discussed in Hour 9, "Active Directory Groups and Organizational Units."

So, here's the bottom line: No matter what you are running on your network in terms of both client operating systems and network operating systems, you can still deploy a Windows Server 2003 to take advantage of its new features and tools. With this in mind, move on to Hour 2 for an overview of Windows Server 2003 security features.

Summary

In this hour, we discussed the latest version of Microsoft's network operating system: Windows Server 2003.

Windows Server 2003 includes the tools and features first offered in Microsoft Windows 2000 Server, including the Active Directory, the Microsoft Management Console, and other features such as plug-and-play capabilities. Windows Server 2003 offers a number of enhancements of these features and provides new features related to server administration, Web hosting, and network security.

The Windows Server 2003 family consists of the Standard, Enterprise, Datacenter, and Web editions. The Standard Edition is considered the entry-level version of this powerful server platform.

Q&A

Q What are some of the new tools and features provided by Windows Server 2003?

A Windows Server 2003 now provides a desktop environment similar to Microsoft Windows XP and includes the remote Desktop for Administration feature. It also provides a new version of Internet Information Server, a number of new command-line utilities, and the Group Policy Management snap-in for managing domain Group Policy. Windows Server 2003 also is compliant with the Microsoft .NET Framework and provides tools for deploying XML and other services.

Q What are the different editions of Windows Server 2003?

A The entry-level version of Windows Server 2003 is the Standard Edition. The Enterprise Edition provides a platform for large enterprise-wide networks. The Datacenter Edition provides support for 64-bit processing and advanced clustering services. The Web Edition is a scaled-down version of Windows Server 2003 intended for use as a dedicated Web server.

HOUR 2

Windows Server 2003 Security Overview

Network security was once a very company-centric pursuit that revolved around securing resources and information on an isolated network. Today, because most networks are connected to the Internet and many companies maintain a Web presence in the form of a Web site, network security focuses on attacks from the outside. In this hour, we look at network security and how to employ security features provided by Windows Server 2003.

In this hour, the following topics are covered:

- Creating a network security plan
- Understanding access control
- Configuring logon options and secure passwords
- Understanding Kerberos authentication
- Assigning permission levels
- Understanding the Encrypting File System

- Using IP Security
- Understanding the public key infrastructure and certificates
- Using the Windows Server 2003 firewall

 This hour provides an overview of Windows Server 2003 security. A number of the security features discussed in this hour are discussed in greater detail in other hours.

Creating a Network Security Plan

Before we look at the different security strategies and tools provided by Windows Server 2003, a few words should be said in support of developing a security plan for your corporate network. Every network needs a security plan that catalogs the possible threats to the network and lists the measures you plan to take to negate these identified threats.

And although much of the industry "buzz" related to security revolves around protecting networks from *malware* (short for "malicious software"), such as viruses, Trojan horse programs, and worms and direct hacker attacks from the outside, your security plan must also include policies and procedures for protecting network data and resources from the inside (meaning your user base). And although most attacks from the inside do not have malicious intent, simple user error or an inappropriate access level to an important database (which is basically administrator error) can wreak as much havoc as a hacker trying to bring down your network from the outside.

 When you create network security policies that provide an action plan against misuse and abuse of your network resources, you must consider the human resources side of protecting the network. Without buy-in from company officers (and the HR department), your security plan and its relation to employee misuse of the network (and potential penalties for misuse) will be impossible to enforce.

Network security plans, then, must include policies that provide the rules for how your end users behave on the network. The plan also needs to include policies that dictate how your network administrative team behaves and that deals with security issues that originate from your user base or outside network. Not only must the plan identify protection mechanisms (firewalls and proxy servers), but it also must state how the network team will deal with network intrusions when they occur. So, the plan must contain "rules of engagement" that dictate the procedures for identifying and blocking security breaches.

An old sports adage goes something like, "The best defense is a strong offense." But in the case of networks, the best defense is a good defense, plain and simple. This means that configuring the network to have very few potential security gaps is your best defense against security breaches.

Windows Server 2003 provides a number of security tools for configuring, auditing, and controlling user access to the network and important network resources. Windows Server 2003 also provides data encryption, IP Security, virtual private networking (VPN and IP Security are discussed in Hour 21, "Working with Virtual Private Networking and IP Security"), and other defense mechanisms, such as a built-in firewall. Let's look at some of the basics related to how you can secure your Windows server network, beginning with access control, the most fundamental aspect of securing your network.

2

 If you are new to developing security plans and policies, a very good place to start as you explore network security issues is the SANS (System Administration, Networking, and Security) Institute Web site. SANS, a security information clearinghouse and educational site, can be found at www.sans.org.

Using Access Control Settings

An important "front-line" security issue that network administrators (especially those dealing with large numbers of network clients) face daily is access control. Really two different aspects are involved in controlling user access to network resources: user authentication and access permissions. User authentication is handled by assigning a user a logon name and a password. Other parameters, such as when a user can log on and whether a user can log on using a remote connection, are configured by the administrator when the user's account is created.

Access permission involves the level of access or rights that an administrator assigns a user in relation to a particular resource on a network. For example, a user might have the capability to open and read files in a particular share on the network, but not to edit (or delete) those files.

Configuring User Logon

The level of authentication afforded a user account determines the resources that a user can and cannot access on the network. Therefore, managing user accounts appropriately is really the network administrator's first line of defense in securing the network.

When you create a new user account in the Active Directory Users and Computers snap-in, a security identifier (SID) is created for the account. Windows actually uses the SID to identify the account (in internal processes) instead of the username. The SID is unique for every user account and includes information on the user's group memberships and security settings.

When a user logs on to the network from a client computer, the username and password are used to validate or authenticate the user to the domain. (Kerberos authentication is discussed later in the hour.) The user account also dictates the access level that the user will have to resources on the network. (Permissions are discussed briefly in this hour and in more detail in Hour 13, "Understanding Share and NTFS Permissions.")

When you create a user account in the Active Directory Users and Computers snap-in (user accounts and the Active Directory are discussed in detail in Hour 8, "Introducing Active Directory"), you are provided with several options to help increase the security related to user logins. Some of these user account options are listed here:

- **Logon Hours**— You can control when a user can log on to the network (see Figure 2.1). For example, you might choose to allow the user access to the network from 9 a.m. to 5 p.m. on workdays (meaning, during those times when you know the person is at work and needs to access the network). Weekend access or late-night access both could be denied.

FIGURE 2.1

You can limit the logon hours for users.

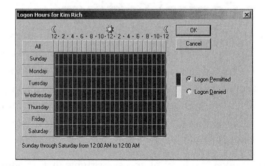

- **Specify Computers for Logon**— You can also specify the computers that a user can use to log on to the network. This limits the particular account to certain physical locations on the network. NetBIOS must be enabled on all the computers that have been specified for use by the user.
- **Specify Users with Dial-Up and VPN Connection Rights**—You can specify which users can log on to the network remotely using dial-up or VPN connections. (Remote access is discussed in Hour 18, "Using Routing and Remote Access," and VPN connections are discussed in Hour 21, "Working with Virtual Private Networking and IP Security.")
- **Disabling User Accounts**—As a last resort, you can right-click any account in Active Directory Users and Computers and immediately disable the account.

Although these account options do not provide a foolproof security shield, they do provide you with some control over when, where, and how your users log on to the network. Additional control over user "behavior" can be configured using Group Policy settings and user profiles, both of which are discussed in Hour 11, "Group Policy and User Profiles."

The default network access security policy for Windows Server 2003 has been strengthened so that any users (or hackers) who somehow gain access to a server running Windows Server 2003 are afforded only guest-level privileges. This protects the server from someone gaining administrative privileges and hacking the system.

Securing Passwords

Windows Server 2003 has strengthened password protection for user accounts. Earlier versions of Windows Server (even Windows 2000 Server) allowed the use of blank passwords and other simple passwords that were a security liability. In the Windows Server 2003 environment, users who attempt to use blank passwords in a domain (when given the option of selecting their own account password, they basically choose not to have a password) are not given access to network resources in the domain. Their blank password allows them only to log on to the local computer.

Windows Server 2003 also provides guidelines for creating passwords that afford a greater level of protection. For example, when you create the Administrator's password during the installation of Windows Server 2003, you are advised to use a combination of alphanumeric and numeric characters (at least seven characters) to create a "strong" password for the key administrative account on the server.

Microsoft defines strong passwords as passwords that contain at least seven characters; that do not contain user, real, or company names; that do not contain complete dictionary words; and that contain a combination of numeric, alphanumeric, and nonalphanumeric characters.

You can, in fact, invoke a password policy (through Group Policy) that requires passwords to meet strong or complex password requirements (this can be configured for the local computer or a domain). Setting the policy at the Domain level enables the policy throughout the domain, affecting all client computers and servers in the domain (Group Policy is discussed in Hour 11). This password security setting requires that passwords be created using the following rules:

If this policy is enabled, passwords must meet the following minimum requirements:

- Cannot contain the login name or a part of the login name
- Must be at least six characters (although Microsoft suggests that at least seven characters be used).
- Must contain characters from at least three character groups: English uppercase, English lowercase, numeric (0–9), and nonalphanumeric characters (such as %% and $)

To enable the password policy for the domain (using Group Policy) from your domain controller, follow these steps:

Before you invoke the default password policy on a computer or the domain, you might want to get a better feel for how Group Policy affects objects up and down the Active Directory tree. This is discussed in Hour 11.

1. Group Policies are accessed via the new Group Policy Management snap-in (discussed in Hour 11). Select Start, Administrative Tasks, Group Policy Management. The Group Policy Management snap-in opens

2. In the snap-in tree, expand the Domains node and then expand the specific domain node that contains the policy that you want to work with.

3. Expand the Group Policy Objects node, shown in Figure 2.2 (note that Default Domain Policy object is listed among the objects), and then select the Default Domain Policy object.

4. Right-click the Default Domain Policy object and then click Edit. The Group Policy Object Editor opens (it is an MMC snap-in, as are most of the Windows Server 2003 management tools).

5. Under the Default Domain Policy object, expand the Computer Configuration node and then expand the Windows Settings node.

6. Under the Windows Settings node, expand the Security Settings node, followed by the Account Policies node and then the Password Policy node. If you expanded the appropriate nodes, the default password policies for the domain will appear in the Details pane of the Group Policy Object Editor (see Figure 2.3) .

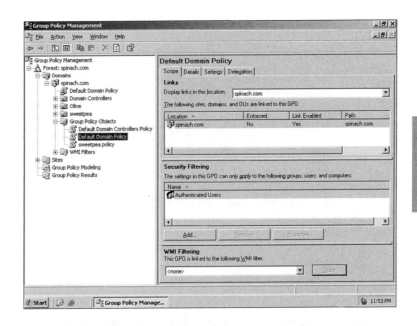

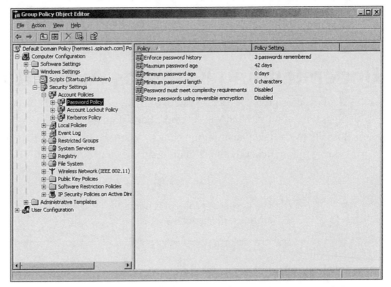

7. The policy that you want to enable is Password must meet complexity requirements. Right-click this policy in the Details pane and select Properties from the
   shortcut menu.

8. The Password must meet complexity requirements Properties dialog box appears
   (see Figure 2.4).

FIGURE 2.4

Enable the policy by selecting the Enabled option button.

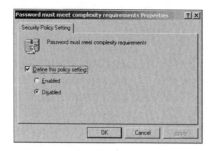

9. Select the Enabled option button to enable the policy. Then click OK. You can close the Group Policy Object Editor and the Active Directory (if you want) .

The Password must meet complexity requirements policy is now in force in your domain. This means that users who have the ability (and are required to periodically change their passwords) must be trained on the strong password parameters. You will find that user training can be as effective of a security measure as firewalls or data encryption. Informed users make fewer fatal errors on the network.

After a valid username and password are provided, the user is authenticated to the domain. In the Windows Server 2003 environment, the default authentication protocol is Kerberos Version 5.

Understanding Kerberos Authentication

The Kerberos protocol uses a system of tickets to authenticate users logging on and requesting services on the Windows network. Each domain controller in the Windows Server 2003 domain acts as a key distribution center. When the user logs on, that user is provided a ticket-granting ticket by the domain controller that authenticates the client account.

The Kerberos protocol is named after the three-headed dog that guards the entrance to Hades.

When the client wants to access a particular resource on the network, such as a file server, the client presents its ticket-granting ticket to a key distribution center (any of the domain controllers) and requests that it be provided a ticket-granting service ticket to access a particular resource.

After the ticket-granting service ticket has been provided to the client by the key distribution center, the client supplies the ticket-granting service ticket to the resource server that it wants to access. The resource server then grants access to the resource. All of this ticket action, of course, is at the machine level and is not something that users or administrators actually see taking place (unless the administrator is monitoring the network, which is discussed in Hour 20, "Monitoring Server and Network Performance").

As with other features (such as password security, discussed in the previous section), even Kerberos functions can be fine-tuned for greater security using the Group Policy Manager. Although editing Kerberos policies is certainly not for everyone and requires an advanced knowledge of both Group Policy and authentication and service issues, let's take a look at some of the default Group Policy settings for Kerberos.

To view the Kerberos default policies, follow these steps:

1. Open the Group Policy Management snap-in (select Start, Administrative Tools, Group Policy Management).

2. Expand the Domains node followed by the specific domain node that contains the policy that you want to view.

3. Expand the Group Policy Objects node to locate the Default Domain Policy object.

4. Right-click the Default Domain Policy object in the snap-in tree, and then click Edit. The Group Policy Object Editor opens.

5. Expand the Computer Configuration node, and then expand the Windows Settings node, the Security Settings node, and the Account Policies node. Then select the Kerberos Policy node (see Figure 2.5).

FIGURE 2.5

Kerberos security can be fine-tuned.

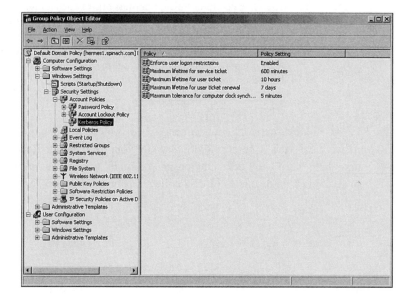

6. The default Kerberos policies appear in the Details pane. To view any of the policies, double-click a particular policy in the Details pane.

7. When you are finished viewing the Kerberos policies, you can close the Group Policy Object Editor and the domain Properties dialog box.

As you can see, a great deal of the security provided by Windows Server 2003 revolves around the policies set for particular features (such as passwords and Kerberos, which have both been discussed in this hour). Group Policy is certainly an important part of your overall network security, and we discuss it in Hour 11.

Security and Permissions

Another of the "basic" security structures that we mentioned at the outset of this hour is the rights that users have to access resources on the network (rights to local resources on a computer can also be regulated). In the Windows Server 2003 environment, a user's rights to access network resources are dictated by permissions. A *permission* is the access level for a resource that you assign to a user or group of users (we talk about Active Directory groups in Chapter 9, "Creating Active Directory Groups, Organizational Units, and Sites"). Because you can potentially assign a different permission level to each user for every resource on the network, you can really fine-tune the access security for important information on the network.

> You typically do not assign permissions to each individual user. It is best to create groups that have certain permission levels to resources and then add users who are to be assigned a particular permission level to the appropriate group. This actually conserves network bandwidth because you don't have multiple permission credentials being checked per user; instead, this is controlled on the group level.

In the Windows network environment, when you create a new share, any users on the network can view it because the Everyone group is given the Read permission for the new share (see Figure 2.6). Obviously, you might not want to allow Everyone to be able to access certain resources or data collections on the network, even with just the Read permission.

FIGURE 2.6

New shares can be read by the Everyone group.

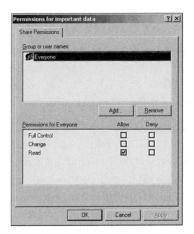

This means that the network administrator must determine whether the share's security needs to be "upgraded" in terms of allowing all the network users the Read permission. Any and all permissions for the Everyone group can be deselected, if necessary (meaning that you could remove the Read permission). Greater levels of access to the share, such as Full Control or Change, could be assigned to certain user groups. For individual users to have these different levels of permissions, they must be added to the group that has the appropriate access level.

When a user has been assigned permissions to a particular resource on the network (such as a folder), those permissions dictate how the user can interact with that resource. For example, if the user has been assigned only the Read permission for a folder on a server, he can't add any files to that folder or delete items in that folder.

Not only do you have different share permissions available to you as you design the access structure for the network, but you also have NT File System (NTFS) permissions as another method of securing resources. NTFS can secure resources right down to the file level and can be used in combination with share permissions. Both share permissions and NTFS permissions (and how a user's permission level is determined when both types of permissions are used) are discussed in Hour 13.

The Everyone group can include users who are not necessarily known to the domain, which can be a potential back door for hackers. It is advised that permission levels for resources be assigned using the Authenticated Users group rather than the Everyone group. The Authenticated Users group includes only users who are validated by the domain.

The Encrypting File System

When share and NTFS permissions don't provide the level of security required for certain folders or files, the next step to raise security is to use the Encrypting File System (EFS). EFS was introduced with Windows 2000 Server; Windows Server 2003 has an updated version of EFS that allows for the encryption of offline or cached files.

EFS is built into the Windows Server 2003 operating system kernel and uses a system of randomly generated keys to encrypt files. Both folders and files can be encrypted using EFS. EFS protects folders and files only at their location (on the storage device). When an encrypted file is opened over the network, it again becomes vulnerable. Other measures, such as IP Security (IPSec) must be used to protect the data as it travels on the network wire. IPSec is discussed briefly in the next section. The Encrypting File System is discussed in more detail in Hour 12, "Working with Network Shares and the Distributed File System."

EFS was developed by Microsoft to combat utilities that can be used to mount NTFS volumes offline and ignore the permissions assigned to files on the volume. EFS encrypts the data, making it inaccessible.

IPSec

Because IP Version 4 (which all of us use, until the day comes when we move to IPv6) does not include any built-in security mechanisms, the need for authentication and data protection has become increasingly apparent as Internet use and IP addressing have become more prevalent (this is now the rule rather than the exception). This is where IPSec comes in.

IPSec, short for IP Security, is a suite of cryptography-based protection services and security protocols that can be used to secure internal networks, networks that use WAN solutions for connectivity, and networks that take advantage of remote access solutions such as virtual private networking.

IPSec embraces an end-to-end security model; this means that only the sending and receiving computers are aware that the data has been secured. IPSec secures the data even if the routers and other devices involved in moving the data from sender to receiver do not support IPSec.

IPSec is implemented on the network using IPSec policies. Because IPSec policies can be integrated with Group Policy, IPSec policies can be assigned to individual computers, Organizational Units, and domains. Windows Server 2003 provides default IPSec policies that you can use to implement IPSec in your domain (see Figure 2.7). IPSec (including IPSec configuration) is discussed in more detail in Hour 21.

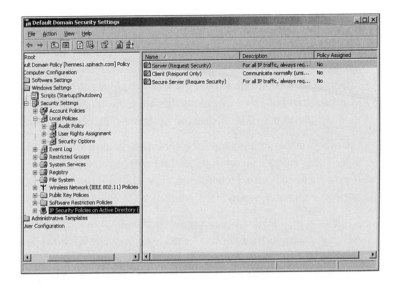

FIGURE 2.7
Default IPSec policies are provided by Windows Server 2003.

The Public Key Infrastructure and Certificates

Private keys (basically access tokens provided to users to access particular features or services) are used by a number of Windows Server 2003 security features, such as the Kerberos protocol, the Encryption File System, and IPSec. The public key infrastructure provided by Windows Server 2003 is a validation system that provides public keys to users outside the network. These public keys are used in conjunction with a user's private key to access data on the network.

Public keys actually come in the form of certificates (the certificate holds the public key and other information about the user, such as username and email address). The public key infrastructure has become a necessity in recent years because many companies are directly connected to the Internet and often provide services or resources to users and customers that access the corporate network through the Internet (many e-commerce sites featuring online stores use the public key infrastructure for secure transactions). The public key infrastructure enables you to implement public key cryptography, which ensures data privacy even on public networks.

Microsoft Windows Server 2003 provides you with the tools to configure a Certificate Authority and grant certificates to specific users. Configuring a Certificate Authority and working with Certificate Services is covered in Hour 23, "Working with Certificate Services."

Firewall Security

Firewalls are designed to sit between your network and the Internet, to protect the internal network from outside attack. Microsoft Server contains a software firewall called Internet Connection Firewall that you can implement. The Internet Connection Firewall keeps track of connection requests that come from outside your network, meaning the Internet. If an internal computer did not request this connection, the request is denied.

Internet Connection Firewall is best used on small networks, particularly when you are using the Windows Server 2003 as the Internet connection for the clients on the network. If you are already using a hardware firewall or a proxy server on your network, you do not need Windows Server 2003's software firewall.

Because some outside requests must be allowed into the internal network, you can configure the settings for Internet Connection Firewall. Windows Server 2003's firewall can be used in conjunction with the Internet Connection Service and Network Address Translation. See Hour 22, "Using Internet Connection Sharing and Network Address Translation," for a discussion of the firewall, Internet connection-sharing, and Network Address Translation features.

Other Windows Server 2003 Security Features

Windows Server 2003 provides a number of other security enhancements related to specific features or services. For example, dial-in remote access can be secured using the Internet Authentication Service (IAS), which is Microsoft's implementation of the Remote Authentication Dial-in User Service (RADIUS). Remote access and the IAS are discussed in Hour 18.

Users can also attach to network resources using the Internet by taking advantage of a secure connection via a virtual private network (VPN). Virtual private networking is discussed in Hour 21.

When you are planning your Windows Server 2003 network infrastructure and are configuring the roles for the various servers on your network (discussed in Hour 5, "Configuring a Windows Server"), you should try to take advantage of the various security features available for each network service. Making security integral to the overall Windows Server 2003 rollout on the network will save you a lot of potential headaches by blocking many security holes long before anyone tries to exploit them.

Summary

No matter how small the network is being overseen, every network administrator should have a network security plan. This plan should work in conjunction with management-approved policies that dictate user behavior on the corporate network.

Access control settings such as user logins and access permissions are really your first line of security. User passwords really build the security into the logon process, and Windows Server 2003 provides password policies for enforcing strict password rules.

Users are authenticated to the Windows Server 2003 network by the Kerberos protocol, which uses a system of tickets to provide users authentication on the network and access to various network resources.

Passwords, Kerberos authentication, and a number of the other security features and services provided by Windows Server 2003 are manipulated using Group Policy.

You can protect stored files on your servers and other computers using the Encrypting File System. EFS uses a system of randomly generated keys to encrypt folders and files.

IPSec is an IP-related security suite that provides protection for IP packets on internal and external networks. IPSec policies are implemented via Group Policy.

For securing traffic on public portions of the corporate network, Windows Server 2003 provides the public key infrastructure. This system allows you to set up a Certificate Authority that grants certificates to users or customers who are external to the main corporate network.

Microsoft Windows Server 2003 provides a new Internet Connection Firewall that can be used to secure small networks that are using Internet Connection Sharing. Other security features included in Windows Server 2003 are the Internet Authentication Service and virtual private networking.

Q&A

Q What settings related to user accounts can help you create a more secure network environment?

A User account options that specify when a user can log on and that also specify the computers that a user can log on to help to create a more secure network by limiting the possibilities for a hacker who has stolen a user account name. Other options, such as whether a user can log in remotely, can also help secure the network from attack using a stolen user account name.

Q How can you strengthen the rules in your domain for creating user account passwords?

A When you enable the domain password policy, which is a part of the Group Policy for the domain, a set of rules related to creating passwords is invoked. For example, the password policy negates passwords from containing the user's logon name and requires that passwords use a variety of characters, such as uppercase, lowercase, and numeric characters.

Q What two permission systems can be used to secure shared file resources in a domain?

A Resources on the network that have been shared can be secured using share permissions. File resources stored on server volumes that are formatted with the NTFS file system can also be secured using NTFS permissions.

Q What two Windows Server 2003 security systems can be used to protect data stored on network volumes and protect data as it moves from private to public networks, respectively?

A The Encrypting File System can be used to encrypt data that is stored on NTFS volumes on your servers. When data is shared between the private internal network and a public network such as the Internet, IPSec can be used to secure the IP data packets.

Q What purpose do certificates play in the public key infrastructure?

A Certificates are used to identify a user who must be authenticated to a network or other resource such as an e-commerce site that uses the public key infrastructure. The user's certificate holds the public key and other information related to the user.

HOUR 3

Installing Windows Server 2003

In this hour, we discuss the different types of Windows Server 2003 installations, such as upgrading an existing server or making a clean install on a server that is not currently configured with a network operating system. We also look at the Windows Server 2003 hardware requirements, server licensing issues, and server activation.

In this hour, the following topics are covered:

- Planning Windows Server 2003 installations
- Windows Server 2003 hardware requirements
- How to check Windows Server 2003 hardware and software compatibility on a serve to be upgraded
- Working with server licensing
- Installing Windows Server 2003
- Upgrading a server to Windows Server 2003

Planning the Server Installation

Before you install Windows Server 2003 on a computer, particularly in cases when you are creating a new network infrastructure, you should create a map of what your network will look like. In particular, you should outline the servers and other resource devices, such as printers, that will provide your network clients with services. The role that a particular server will fill on the network should be determined long before you install the network operating system. The server's role, such as acting as a domain controller or a multihomed router (a Windows Server 2003 configured with more than one network interface card) or a NAT server, dictates not only the server's hardware configuration, but also the configuration of that server (and the services that it provides).

 Hour 5, "Configuring a Windows Server," provides an overview on how to configure the various roles for a server, including such services as DNS, the file server, and the print server. Other hours in the book look at the specifics of configuring these various services. Hour 8, "Introduction to Active Directory," looks at the Active Directory namespace and provides the steps for making a Windows Server 2003 a domain controller.

Other issues related to the installation of Windows Server 2003 on a computer have to do with the computer's hardware configuration and its compatibility with Windows Server 2003. You must also be aware (before installation) of how you will configure client licensing on your network. Let's look at the Windows Server 2003 hardware requirements; then we can look at a quick way to check an existing server's upgrade compatibility and discuss server licensing issues.

Server Hardware Requirements

Windows Server 2003 requires a minimum hardware configuration to run. As with all software—particularly network operating systems—the more you exceed the minimum requirements in areas such as RAM, processor speed, and hard drive space, the faster the server supplies services to network users and the greater the number of roles one server can fill on the network. (For example, a server could be a domain controller and could provide the DNS and DHCP services.)

Microsoft's suggested minimum hardware requirements (and some Microsoft recommendations) for Windows Server 2003 (Standard) are listed here:

- CPU speed: 133MHz (550MHz recommended)
- RAM: 128MB (256MB recommended; 4GB maximum on Standard Server)
- Disk space for setup: 1.5GB
- CD-ROM drive: 12X
- Monitor: Super VGA capable of providing 800 × 600 resolution

Not only must you meet the minimum hardware requirements to successfully install and run Windows Server 2003, but you also must have a server that provides hardware that is proven to be compatible with the network operating system. If you will use the server in a true production environment where you must supply mission-critical services to network users, your server hardware must come right off the Microsoft Windows Server 2003 Hardware Compatibility List. A copy of the list is available at

www.microsoft.com/hwdq/hcl/scnet.asp.

3

> In my humble opinion, a good middle-of-the-road but somewhat "beefy" hardware configuration for a computer running Windows Server 2003 is a processor in excess of 900MHz, with 512MB of RAM and a SCSI drive array with at least three 20GB drives. Any server hardware configuration must address the capacity that will be required by the services that you run on the server and any server-side applications that you will deploy, such as Microsoft SQL Server or Microsoft Exchange Server.

Checking Hardware and Software Compatibility

If you plan to upgrade a server that is running Windows NT 4 or Windows 2000 Server, you should probably run the hardware and software compatibility test provided on the Windows Server 2003 installation CD. This text lets you know if the server is configured with hardware that is not on the Windows Server 2003 Hardware Compatibility List, and it provides a list of any software running on the server that is not compatible with Windows Server 2003.

1. To run the Check System Compatibility utility, place the Windows Server 2003 CD in the CD-ROM driver of a currently running server.
2. The Welcome screen for the Windows Server 2003 family opens. Click the Check System Compatibility button on the screen.

3. On the next screen, you are given the option of checking the compatibility of the server's software and hardware automatically. A link is also provided to take you to the Windows Server 2003 Compatibility Web site, where you can check the hardware compatibility list. Select the option Check My System Automatically.

4. A Get Updated Files dialog box opens. This downloads additions to the hardware compatibility list from Microsoft (see Figure 3.1). Make sure the Download Updated Files option is selected, and then click Next.

Figure 3.1

Allow the dynamic update from Microsoft.

5. After the compatibility utility is upgraded dynamically, a screen appears listing any software or hardware compatibility issues on the server that you will want to upgrade. Drivers are software, so any driver that is found to be incompatible will be removed from the system when you upgrade to Windows Server 2003. This means that some legacy devices (such as an old modem) might not operate on the server. If there are also hardware issues, you should consider replacing the hardware component with a device on the hardware compatibility list.

Understanding Server Licensing Issues

Another aspect of planning your Windows Server 2003 installation is determining whether you will license the clients that log on to your network servers. There are two licensing modes: per server and per seat. It's important that you choose the licensing mode that best suits your networking plan and the potential growth of your user base.

In *per server* mode, you are licensed for a certain number of concurrent connections to the server. If you have 50 licenses, 50 clients can connect to the server. Per server mode is the best choice when you have a small network consisting of only one domain (and one domain controller). It also works best for networks when only part of your client base is connected to the server at any one time. For example, if you run different shifts at your company, you need only a per server license that covers the number of users connected to the server at any one time (not your entire employee population).

In *per seat* mode, you purchase a license for each network user on the network. Each of these users can connect to any and all the servers on the network. As far as large networks go, per seat mode is probably the best licensing strategy, especially if network resources are spread across a number of Windows Server 2003 servers.

You must select your licensing mode during Windows Server 2003 installation. So, it is important to consider licensing in terms of network growth and usage.

However, if you select to use the per server licensing and then determine that it would make more sense to change to per seat licensing, you have one opportunity to switch licensing modes. This switch is done using the Licensing snap-in.

3

1. To open the Licensing snap-in, select Start, then Administrative Tools, and then Licensing. The Licensing snap-in opens in the Microsoft Management Console (see Figure 3.2).

FIGURE 3.2

The Licensing snap-in is used to record the various licenses for products that you use in your network environment.

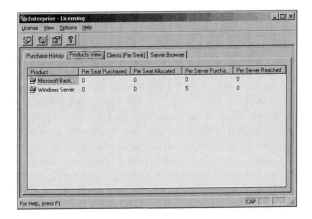

2. In the Licensing snap-in, select the Server Browser tab in the snap-in window. Then expand the domain (or workgroup) node. Right-click the Server icon (the local server) and select Properties. The Properties dialog box opens for the server and shows the current licensing mode for the server (and the number of licenses purchased).

3. To change the licensing mode from a server that is currently in per server mode, click the Edit button. The Choose Licensing Mode dialog box opens (see Figure 3.3) .

FIGURE 3.3

Change the licensing mode to Per Seat.

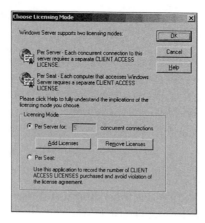

4. Select Per Seat and then click OK.

5. When you are using the per seat licensing mode, new licenses are added using the Licensing snap-in. Use the License command and then the New License command to record licenses for your Windows domain client licenses and other network products.

Microsoft has created some new licensing schemes for Microsoft Windows Server 2003. A new User Client Access license enables a user to connect to network services using any device, including computers and devices such as PDAs (this does not replace the Device Client Access licensing scheme currently in use in Windows 2000 and Windows Server 2003). External Connector licenses are also new and can be used by customers or partners to connect to license network services in the domain. Whatever licensing you use, the License snap-in provides you with a way of recording and tracking licensing on the network. For more information on Microsoft licensing, check out www.microsoft.com/licensing/Default.asp.

Choosing to Upgrade or Make a Clean Installation

A major consideration related to a Windows Server 2003 installation is whether to upgrade in-place servers or do a clean install on a replacement server that will take over the role of a server or servers already on the network. For example, you might be running Windows 2000 Server on a computer that you want to replace (it might have seen better days hardware-wise). You can install Windows Server 2003 on a new server and make it a domain controller in the Windows 2000 domain that already exists. This will allow the new server to replicate all the information in the Active Directory on the Windows 2000 Server (the Windows 2000 Server should have the latest service packs installed). You can then "retire" the Windows 2000 Server and use the Windows Server 2003 as the domain controller for the domain.

Whatever your strategy is for bringing new servers online on an existing network, you must deal with issues related to earlier versions of the Windows network operating system, such as Windows 2000 and Windows NT. The next two sections discuss issues related to upgrading these two versions of Windows server.

Planning for a Windows 2000 Upgrade

3

Upgrading a server (even a domain controller) from Windows 2000 to Windows Server 2003 is a fairly easy process. Because Windows 2000 and Windows Server 2003 both embrace the Active Directory hierarchy and DNS namespace, the notion of forests, trees, and domains is common to both network operating systems. This means that a radical redesign of the network domain structure is not necessary.

However, you need to keep some things in mind when upgrading Windows 2000 Server to Windows Server 2003. First, you must make sure that the server's hardware is compatible with Windows Server 2003 (as you would for a server that will get a clean installation). It is also important that you have installed Windows 2000 Server Service Pack 2 (or later, if available) on the server to upgrade the files in the Windows 2000 Server installation.

Finally, you must prepare the forest and the domain for the upgrade to Windows Server 2003. This is done using the adprep command-line utility found in the i386 folder on the Windows Server 2003 CD-ROM. You actually have to run this upgrade program on the Schema Master and the Infrastructure Master on the domain. The *schema* is the database template for the Active Directory and defines the objects that can exist in the Active Directory (such as users, groups, and so on).

> On smaller domains with a limited number of domain controllers, the Schema Master and the Infrastructure Master are the same Windows 2000 domain controller.

The Schema Master is typically the first server you brought online using Windows 2000 Server. It is the Schema Master because it defines the Active Directory schema for the domain (the schema being the actual definition of the objects contained in the Active Directory). There is only one Schema Master per Windows 2000 forest (which can be many domains).

The Infrastructure Master is charged with the task of upgrading group and user associations. It keeps track of what groups users belong to. If group membership changes, the Infrastructure Master records this and then replicates it to the other domain controllers in the domain. When you create the first domain in a Windows 2000 forest, that domain controller is assigned the Infrastructure Master status.

> To locate the Schema Master in your Windows 2000 domain, install the Active Directory Schema snap-in. It is part of the adminpak tools found in the i386 folder on the Windows 2000 Server CD (it is also in the same place on the Windows Server 2003 CD, but do not install the adminpak.msi file from the 2003 CD on the Windows 2000 server). After installation, open the Active Directory Schema snap-in. In the console tree, right-click Active Directory Schema and then click Operations Master. The name of the current domain-naming master (the Schema Master) appears in Current Operations Master.

Before you upgrade the Schema Master, back up the server and then disconnect this server from the network. Place the Windows Server 2003 CD in the server's CD-ROM drive. Open a command prompt and then switch to the CD's i386 folder. At the prompt, type **adprep /forestprep**. Then press Enter. If no errors are reported when the utility has completed running, you can hook the Schema Master back up to the network. It then replicates with the Infrastructure Master. (This can take a number of hours or even a day or so on a large network, so be patient.)

When you are ready to upgrade the Infrastructure Master, run the `adprep /forestprep` command, as outlined for the Schema Master. After giving the Infrastructure Master time to replicate with the other domain controllers on the network, you can then begin upgrading the domain controllers running Windows 2000 Server with Windows Server 2003.

Planning for a Windows NT Upgrade

You can also upgrade a Windows NT domain (or domains) to a Windows Server 2003 domain. The first thing you should do is install NT Service Pack 5 to the servers running Windows NT 4 (also install any service packs on the server that have become available after Service Pack 5). You should also back up domain controllers and other specialized servers before performing the upgrades. In addition, you should check the server hardware to see if it meets the requirements for Windows Server 2003, including hardware compatibility.

In the Windows NT networking environment, one primary domain controller is configured for each domain. The primary domain controller is aided by backup domain controllers that contain a copy of the primary domain controller's database.

You might want to upgrade member servers in the domain first. This enables you to bring services such as the Windows Server 2003 versions of DNS and DHCP online. The first domain controller that must be upgraded in the NT domain is the primary domain controller. You can then upgrade the backup domain controllers (which in the Windows Server 2003 environment are domain controllers because there is no such thing as a backup domain controller).

During the upgrade from Windows NT to Windows Server 2003, you will also want to allow the installation software to upgrade the system partition on your server to NTFS 5. Windows Server 2003 requires it for the Active Directory.

3

A lengthy discussion of transforming a Windows NT multidomain network into a Windows Server 2003 Active Directory hierarchy is beyond the scope of this book. However, one approach to upgrading multiple NT domains is to set up the Windows Server 2003 network that will replace it and then transfer user accounts and other domain information using a tool called the Active Directory Migration Tool (ADMT). This tool is available with the Windows Server 2003 Resource Kit.

Using Supported File Systems

Windows Server 2003 supports the entire range of file systems supported by Microsoft operating systems. This ability was first introduced with Windows 2000 Server.

You can have FAT, FAT32, and NTFS partitions or volumes on your server's hard drives. A description of each file system follows:

- **FAT**—FAT volumes use a file allocation table that provides the name of the file and the location of the actual clusters that make up the file on the hard drive. FAT is a holdover from the days of DOS. I see no compelling reason to use FAT volumes on your servers.
- **FAT32**—FAT32 is an extension of the FAT file system. It uses disk space on a drive more efficiently than FAT and was designed for Windows 95/98.

- **NTFS**—NTFS 5 is the newest version of the NT file system (NTFS 5 was first introduced with Windows 2000 Server). It provides increased security for files on NTFS volumes and supports more robust file system recovery. Microsoft recommends that you use NTFS as your file system on your Windows servers. It is also required if you want to install Active Directory on a server to make it a domain controller.

It really makes sense to use NTFS volumes on your servers unless you need to create a dual-boot server on which a legacy operating system requires a FAT or FAT32 partition to run on the server. Actually, in most cases, it doesn't make sense to deploy a server on a network that was configured for dual-boot. NTFS provides the stability, the security, and other bells and whistles that makes it the appropriate choice for your server drive implementations.

> Even the Home edition of Windows XP now supports NTFS volumes. FAT is definitely a file system antique. Although FAT32 is still recommended for home users, we might see its demise as newer desktop versions of Windows are released.

Performing a Clean Installation

To install Windows Server 2003 on a server that is not configured with a previous operating system, set up the system so that it boots to the CD-ROM drive (using the computer's BIOS settings utility). The clean installation consists of two different phases: a text phase and then a Windows phase. During the text phase, you specify (and create, if necessary) the partition that will be used as the target for the Windows Server 2003 installation.

When the text phase is complete. The system reboots into a pre-Windows environment. The Windows phase of the installation consists of a series of Windows-based screens that enable you to select configuration items such as the computer's name, the time zone and time for the computer, and the password for the computer's Administrator account.

Text Mode Installation Phase

1. Place the Microsoft Windows Server 2003 CD in the server's CD-ROM drive. Reboot the system, if necessary.

2. The server boots to the CD. After loading some initial setup files, the server provides you with the Setup Notification screen. To continue the installation process, press the Enter key.

3. The next screen (the Setup screen) provides you with the options of starting a new installation or repairing a previous installation. To continue with the "fresh" installation, press Enter.

4. The Windows Licensing Agreement appears. After reading the licensing information, press F8 to continue. (This means that you agree to abide by the agreement provided.)

5. On the next installation screen, you are asked to specify a partition that will be used as the target for the Windows Server 2003 installation. You can create a new partition or use an existing partition on the server. To create a new partition, select a drive (containing free space) on the server and then press C. You then must provide the amount of the free space on the selected drive that you want to use for the partition. Specify the space to use (in megabytes) and then press Enter.

> You can also select an existing partition and delete the partition (or partitions). This enables you to "reconfigure" all the drives on the server and divide up the storage space on the server's drives as you see fit.

6. The new partition is listed in the partition box. To install Windows Server 2003 on the partition (make sure the partition is selected), press Enter.

7. You are asked to format the new partition. You are provided with a choice of NTFS or FAT. Because domain controllers require an NTFS partition to run the Active Directory, you typically want to select NTFS. (If you will configure the server as a member server, such as a file server or an extra DNS server, FAT is okay, but NTFS is still preferred for all Windows servers because it provides a greater level of security.) Select the file format (using the error keys) and then press Enter.

8. The setup program formats the partition and then copies installation files to the server. After the appropriate files are copied, the server reboots. This ends the command-line portion of the Windows Server 2003 setup.

Windows Installation/Configuration Phase

After the system reboots, the system runs the Windows configuration phase of your Windows Server 2003 installation.

1. The first screen asks you to customize language and regional settings for Windows. By default, the standards settings are set to English. The default location is set to the United States. You can use the Customize button to change the language or regional settings. To continue with the installation, click Next.

The Regional and Language options screen also allows you to change the
input language for the server installation and the input device you use. The
default is the U.S. keyboard layout.

2. On the next screen, provide your name and organization. Then click Next to continue.

3. Next you must provide your product key, which is on the back of your Windows
   CD case. After you enter the product key, press Next to continue.

4. The next screen asks you to select your licensing method. You can license your
   network either per server or per seat (see the discussion of the differences between
   the licensing modes found earlier in this hour). If you select Per Server (the
   default), specify the number of concurrent connections using the spin box. After
   you select the licensing mode, click Next.

5. You then are asked to supply a unique name for the computer and to enter the
   Administrator's password for the local computer. Type the computer name. Then
   enter and then re-enter the Administrator account password. Windows Server 2003
   stresses the use of strong passwords. A strong password contains at least six characters; does not contain user, real, or company names; does not contain complete
   dictionary words; and contains a combination of numeric, alphanumeric, and nonalphanumeric characters. (More about passwords and Windows Server 2003 security is discussed in Hour 2, "Windows Server 2003 Security Overview.") After you
   enter the computer name and password, click Next.

If you enter a password that Windows Server 2003 does not consider strong,
a message box appears letting you know what a strong password is. If you
want to continue with your current password, click Yes. If you want to
choose a new stronger password, click No.

6. The next screen enables you to set the time zone for your computer and the current
   date and time (if necessary). After you set these parameters, click Next to continue.

7. Next you are asked to configure the network settings for the computer. You can go
   with the default of the client for Microsoft Networks, File and Print Sharing, and
   the TCP/IP protocol. If you want to change this configuration, you can click the
   Custom settings option button on this screen. In most cases, it is probably easier to

install additional network protocols such as NWlink (the Microsoft IPX/SXP–compatible program) after the serving is up and running. Click Next to continue.

8. You can choose whether this server belongs to a workgroup or a domain. The default setting is that the computer is not on a network or is on a network with a workgroup instead of a domain. The default workgroup name is WORKGROUP. Whether you will use the server in a workgroup or a domain, at this point it is best to go with the default and complete the Windows Server 2003 installation and configuration. Changing the workgroup name or making the server a member server of an existing domain is covered later in the hour. Press Next to continue.

9. After you click Next, the installation program copies and installs files to your new Windows Server 2003 as it completes the installation process and configures your server's hardware and peripherals. After the installation is complete, the server reboots. After the server restarts, press Ctrl+Alt+Del. At the password prompt, supply the password you set for the Administrator account during the installation process. You will be logged on to the server.

When you are logged onto the server, the Manage Your Server Window appears. This provides you with the capability to add roles to your server and also provides links to Help information on the various roles that your server can play. For an overview of server roles, see Hour 5.

Performing an Upgrade

If you are not in a position to do a clean install of Windows Server 2003, you can also upgrade an existing network operating system, such as Windows NT and Windows 2000. The actual upgrade process is very straightforward. But as already mentioned in this hour, the upgrade of a domain controller has consequences for the entire domain. Running mixed environments in which Windows NT servers must interact with servers running Windows Server 2003 (and perhaps even some Windows 2000 servers) makes supplying important network resources in the domain more difficult (and quite confusing at times). In an ideal situation, you will be able to upgrade all servers on the network to Windows Server 2003.

1. To perform an upgrade on a Windows NT or Windows 2000 Server, insert the Windows Server 2003 CD in the server's CD-ROM drive. Then click the Install Windows Server 2003 button on the Welcome screen that opens.

2. The Welcome to Windows Setup window appears. The Installation Type is set to Upgrade (see Figure 3.4). Click Next to continue.

3

FIGURE 3.4

Select Upgrade as the
installation type.

3. The Licensing Agreement screen appears. Select I Accept This Agreement (after reading the agreement) and then click Next to continue.

4. On the next screen, provide your Windows Server product key. Then click Next to continue.

5. The next screen provides you with the option of downloading any new setup files that have changed for Windows Server 2003 since you purchased the installation CD. The default is set to Yes, Download the Updated Setup Files. Click Next to continue.

You can now move through the screens provided by the Windows Server 2003 installation software to complete the upgrade of the server's current network operating system. These screens are many of the same ones provided in the "Performing a Clean Installation" section. Windows Server preserves settings on your upgraded server, such as domain controller settings and other services.

You can also install multiple Windows Server installations using the Remote Installation Services. This enables you to install Windows Server on several computers from an image of the server software. Remote Installation Services is discussed in Hour 10, "Client Computers and the Domain." You also can begin an installation on any Windows desktop software from the command prompt by using the winnt.exe executable file in the I386 folder on the Windows Server CD-ROM. To do an installation on a server running Windows NT or Windows 2000, use the winnt32.exe file in the I386 folder.

Understanding Windows Product Activation

One of the first things that you will want to do after installing the server software is activate the product. To combat software piracy, Microsoft has developed a product activation strategy for its network operating systems, client operating systems, and applications such as Microsoft Office. You can activate your Windows Server 2003 software either over the Internet or by telephone. When you install Windows Server 2003, you might want to have the server hooked up to an Internet connection, even though the server might not be connected to the Internet when you actually put it into service on the network or in your Active Directory domain.

1. To activate Windows Server 2003, select the Activation word balloon (it appears as soon as you log on to the server for the first time), or click on the Activation icon in the system tray. The Activate Windows window opens (see Figure 3.5).

FIGURE 3.5

Select the option Activate Windows over the Internet.

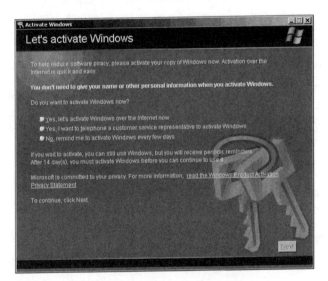

2. The easiest way to activate the network operating system is to use the option Activate Windows over the Internet. Select this option and then click Next.

3. The next screen provides you with the option of registering your Windows Server 2003 with Microsoft as you activate the product. Choose the appropriate option button (either to register and activate or to activate only) and then click Next. If you select to register, the next screen requests registration information. Complete the form and then click Next (this screen is bypassed if you chose to activate only).

4. A connection is made to the Internet (and Microsoft), and your product is activated. Click OK to complete the process.

Windows Server 2003 is now activated, and you can configure the server for its various roles on the network.

Choosing Between a Workgroup and a Domain

One aspect of a server's configuration that you should have determined long before installing Windows Server 2003 is whether the server will be part of a workgroup or domain.

In a workgroup setting, a Windows server 2003 can supply services such as the Internet Connection Sharing feature, the Internet Connection Firewall, and file and print services.

In a domain, a server can be a domain controller, can supply services such as DNS and DHCP, or can serve as a router or remote access server. Windows Server 2003 is built to provide services on a domain, so deploying this server software on a domain really gives you more bang for your buck (instead of running a workgroup using the services that can be deployed by Windows desktop operating systems over an expensive server).

1. To make a server part of a workgroup or to add it as a member server to an existing domain, first select Start. Then right-click My Computer and select Properties. The System Properties dialog box opens. Select the Computer Name tab on the System Properties dialog box (see Figure 3.6).

FIGURE 3.6

You can view the server's current membership on the Computer Name tab.

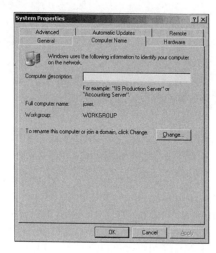

2. To change the workgroup membership or to add the server to a domain, click the Change button. The Computer Name Changes dialog box opens (see Figure 3.7). You can change the computer's name and its domain or workgroup affiliation.

FIGURE 3.7

You can change the server's name or membership.

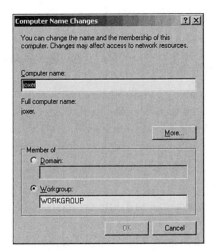

3. To add the server to an existing domain, select the Domain option button and then type in the name of the domain (you need to provide the Fully Qualified Domain Name of the domain, which includes prefix and suffix). Or, to add the server to a different workgroup, select the Workgroup option button and type in the name of the workgroup. When you complete either choice, click OK. It might take a moment, but you then are welcomed to the domain or the workgroup that you have specified.

Summary

In this hour, we looked at installing Windows Server 2003. It is important to keep in mind that Windows Server 2003 requires a minimum hardware configuration and to ensure that your server uses server hardware on the Windows Server 2003 Hardware Compatibility List. Windows Server 2003 licensing can be done either per server or per seat. With per server mode, the server is licensed for a certain number of connections. With per seat mode, each connecting client has a license of its own. Licensing is managed in the Licensing snap-in.

To upgrade previous versions of the Windows server software to Windows Server 2003, make sure that you have installed the latest service packs for that version of Windows.

Also be sure to back up any servers that you will then upgrade. Upgrading Windows 2000 Server domains requires that the adprep utility be used to upgrade the Schema Master and Infrastructure Master on the domain.

Q&A

Q What two hardware considerations should be an important part of the planning process for a Windows Server 2003 deployment?

A Any server on which you will install Windows Server 2003 should have at least the minimum hardware requirement for running the network operating system. Server hardware should also be on the Windows Server 2003 Hardware Compatibility List to avoid the possibility of hardware and network operating system incompatibility.

Q What are the possibilities for licensing clients in relations to your servers running Windows Server 2003?

A Client licenses can be handled in two different modes. The per-server mode provides a license for a definite number of concurrent connections to the server. The per-seat mode requires a license for each network user on the network. Recording and managing licensing is handled by the Licensing snap-in.

Q What are the options for installing Windows Server 2003?

A You can install Windows Server 2003 on a server not currently configured with a NOS, or you can upgrade existing servers running Windows 2000 Server and Windows NT 4.

Q What are the options for file systems on a new Windows Server 2003?

A Windows Server 2003 supports NTFS, FAT, and FAT32 partitions. It is a best practice to use NTFS on system volumes and any other volumes on which you want to have the added security provided by NTFS permissions. NTFS is required if you want to install the Active Directory to make the server a domain controller.

HOUR 4

The Windows Server 2003 Administrative Environment

Windows Server 2003 sports a slightly different look than previous versions of Microsoft's network operating systems. It now embraces the "minimalist" desktop found in the Windows XP desktop operating systems.

And although accessing administrative features might require a slight learning curve, all the tools needed to manage the local computer, its peripherals, and the various network functions of the server are easily accessed. In this hour, we look at the overall administrative environment for Windows Server 2003.

In this hour, the following topics are covered:

- Becoming familiar with the Windows Server 2003 desktop
- Using Automatic Updates
- Working with the Windows Control Panel

- Configuring virtual memory settings
- Configuring a WINS server
- Becoming familiar with the Microsoft Management Console
- Working with local user accounts and groups

Working with the Server Desktop

Windows Server 2003 began as part of Microsoft's Whistler project that also developed the Microsoft Windows XP Desktop products. The Windows Server 2003 development cycle has gone on long after the release of Windows XP, but Windows Server 2003 and Windows XP are considered complementary server and desktop environments. This means that Windows Server has many things in common with the XP, particularly the Professional version of the desktop operating system (such as the support of multiple processors, automatic product updates, and support of FAT, FAT32, and NTFS file systems). One of these similarities is the Windows Server 2003 desktop.

The new desktop (labeled by Microsoft as the "user experience" desktop) provides a less cluttered approach to the Windows desktop and has clustered access to many features (such as My Computer and Windows Explorer) on the Start menu. The Start menu now consists of a double-column format.

In the first column, quick access icons to Manage Your Server, the command prompt, and Windows Explorer are provided. Programs that you have used recently (the last six) also are listed in this first tier of the Start menu. In addition, the first column of the Start menu provides access to all the programs on your computer via All Programs.

The second column provides access to other important tools, such as My Computer, the Control Panel, Administrative Tools, Printer and Faxes, Help and Support (which also has a new look when compared to how Help was accessed in Windows 2000 Server), Search, and Run (see Figure 4.1).

If you want to retrofit the Start menu so that it appears as it did in earlier versions of Windows (such as Windows 2000), open the Control Panel and then open the Taskbar and Start Menu applet. On the Start Menu tab, select the Classic Start menu option.

FIGURE 4.1

The Windows Server 2003 desktop and Start menu have been given a makeover.

The taskbar has also undergone a subtle change (again, a new feature we see in Windows XP). When you have multiple applications running, which crowds the taskbar with application icons, any concurrent sessions of a particular application are condensed into a single cascading icon for that application. For example, if you are running Windows Explorer sessions in multiple windows, all windows are accessed by selecting the single Windows Explorer icon on the taskbar (see Figure 4.2).

If you want to close all the sessions of a particular application, right-click the icon on the taskbar and select Close Group.

FIGURE 4.2

Multiple sessions of the same application are accessed by a single tiered icon.

When you run a number of different administrative tool snap-ins, they all are found on the taskbar under the Microsoft Management Console (because they all run within this one utility).

Understanding Automatic Updates

The Windows Server 2003 software can be updated automatically using the Automatic Update feature (this feature is not new and is available in a number of versions of the Windows desktop software versions and Windows 2000 Server). After you install the Windows Server 2003 software on your server, you will find that every time you boot up the server, you are reminded about the Automatic Update feature.

1. To configure this feature, click the reminder message or the Automatic Update icon in the System Tray. The Automatic Updates Setup Wizard appears. Click Next to move past the introductory screen.

2. The only parameters that you have to set for the automatic updates relate to when you want the updates downloaded and installed. These options appear in Figure 4.3. You can choose to have Automatic Update notify you when updates are available for downloading and again before these updates are installed. Or, you can go with the default and have the updates downloaded automatically; you then are notified that they are ready to install. Because servers can't necessarily be rebooted any time of the day, the third option allows updates to be downloaded automatically but provides Automatic Update with a set schedule (using the drop-down lists in the Wizard window).

FIGURE 4.3

Set the download and install parameters for the Automatic Update feature.

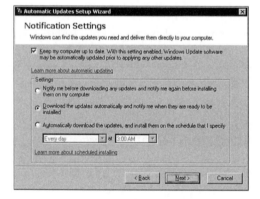

3. When you have made your selections related to Automatic Update scheduling, click Next. On the Summary wizard screen, click Finish.

4. If you find that you want to change the Automatic Update settings that you chose, you can edit them in the System Properties dialog box. Click the Start menu and then right-click My Computer. Select Properties from the shortcut menu. The System Properties dialog box opens. Select the Automatic Update tab on the dialog box to change the download and install settings.

Although automatic updates can be annoying and can mean that you might have to reboot the server, keeping Windows Server 2003 up-to-date can only enhance your possibilities of plugging security leaks and fixing bugs in the software code. A number of hacker attacks on Microsoft systems, which affected large numbers of users, happened because client and server software were not updated on a regular basis.

Using the Control Panel

If you have worked with any version of Windows since the 95 desktop, you are familiar with the types of control utilities that are provided in the Windows Control Panel. Windows Server 2003 is no different. To access utilities (applets) that provide you with control over your computer's peripherals (and other hardware devices), installed software, and a number of other local computer and server settings, all you have to do is access the Control Panel.

To access the Control Panel's utilities in Windows Server 2003, select the Start button, point at the Control Panel, and then select any of the items that appear on the Control Panel menu. If you want to open the Control Panel in a window (as was done with previous versions of the Windows server software), select the Start menu, right-click the Control Panel, and select Open from the shortcut menu. Figure 4.4 shows the Control Panel.

4

FIGURE 4.4

The Windows Server 2003 Control Panel.

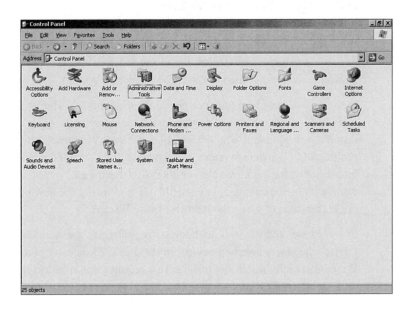

The Control Panel is populated by a number of different applets, and many of these applets also are found in the Control Panel of Windows desktop operating systems such as Windows XP. For example, you can access display properties by opening the Display applet, change your mouse from right-handed to left-handed using the Mouse applet, or install a new printer using the Printers and Faxes applet (we look at printing issues in Hour 14, "Working with Network Printing").

To access any applet, double-click the icon. If you want to return to the Control Panel from a particular applet, click the Back button on the toolbar.

Because a server typically sits in a server closet and is not tweaked and fine-tuned as often as a desktop workstation would be (for example, you probably shouldn't be adding a game controller to a production server's hardware configuration), you will probably not access the Control Panel applets with such careless abandon. Let's take a look at the applets that you will probably use related to your server administration.

 If you are upgrading from Windows 2000 Server to Windows Server 2003, you might find that some of the new Start menu, Control Panel, and Taskbar settings don't seem any different or don't appear as described in this hour. This is because preferences set in Windows 2000 Server are preserved in the upgrade.

Adding New Hardware

The Add Hardware Wizard opens when you access the Add Hardware applet. Because Windows Server 2003 supports plug-and-play technology, in many cases all you will have to do to add a new device to a server (such as a tape backup drive or a printer) is attach the device and then run the Add Hardware Wizard.

In the case of plug-and-play peripheral devices, the Add Hardware Wizard typically identifies the new device and helps you install the appropriate drive for the device. If you install a new plug-and-play device when the server is turned off, you won't even have to run the Add Hardware Wizard: The device will be installed when you boot the system. Interestingly, the Windows Server 2003 Add Hardware Wizard advises that if software came with the new device, you should use it to install the new hardware (and appropriate drivers) instead of using the Add Hardware Wizard.

In some cases (particularly with legacy peripherals), the Add Hardware Wizard does not "sense" the newly attached device. In these cases, you can opt to have the Add Hardware Wizard manually install the device. This requires you to select the appropriate device name (which selects the appropriate driver) from a hardware list. We make use of the Add Hardware Wizard in Hour 18, "Routing and Remote Access," when a modem is installed on a RAS server.

Adding or Removing Programs

The Add or Remove Programs applet is used to install new software on your server or to remove software that you no longer need. The Add or Remove Programs applet can also be used to install Windows components and services such as WINS, DHCP, DNS, and other tools such as the Network Monitor. The Add or Remove Programs applet (use the Add/Remove Windows Components utility) crops up in a number of different hours throughout the book.

Viewing Network Connections

The Network Connection applet enables you to view all the network connections of your Windows server (which means that you can access the properties for these connection in the Network Connection window). This includes remote access dial-up and virtual private network connections. The Network Connection applet also provides the New Connection Wizard, which enables you to create new connections to the Internet or other networks. Figure 4.5 shows an active connection that was accessed via the Network Connection applet.

FIGURE 4.5

The Network Connection applet enables you to view your server's connections.

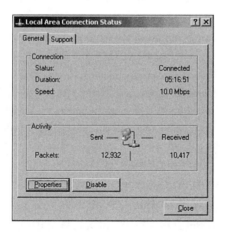

Scheduling Tasks

The Scheduled Tasks applet enables you to schedule and automate the launching of applications or utilities on your server. For example, you could schedule the Backup utility to run at a specific time or to have the Disk Defragmenter run late at night, when clients hits on the server are at a bare minimum.

To schedule a task using the Scheduled Tasks applet, follow these steps:

1. In the Control Panel, double-click the Scheduled Tasks applet. The Scheduled Tasks window opens.

2. To schedule a new task, double-click the Add Scheduled Task icon. The Scheduled Task Wizard opens. Click Next to bypass the wizard's introductory screen.

3. On the next screen, select the application or utility that you want to specify as the task (see Figure 4.6). Then click Next.

FIGURE 4.6

You can automatically launch tools using the Scheduled Task applet.

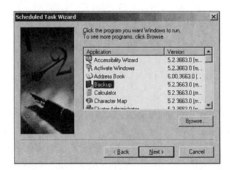

4. On the next screen, supply a name for the scheduled task and then select when to perform this task (daily, weekly, monthly, and so on). After making a selection, click Next.

5. The next wizard screen asks you to set the start time and the start date for the automatic launching of the selected application. Set the time and the date, and then click Next.

6. The next screen asks you to supply a username and a password to specify the user running the application (that will start automatically). Use the Administrator account or some other account that has administrative privileges on the server, or the application might not run when scheduled. After supplying the username and password (and verifying the password), click Next.

7. The last screen asks you to click Finish.

Your new scheduled task appears in the Scheduled Tasks window. You can change the settings for a particular scheduled task by double-clicking the task. Its properties box opens, providing you with the ability to edit the settings. You can delete any task that you create by selecting the task and then pressing the Delete key.

Accessing System Properties

The System applet opens the System Properties dialog box. This dialog box enables you to configure and control system-level features of your server. These settings include virtual memory usage and processor performance. The System Properties dialog box also enables you to create hardware profiles for your server and provides you with access to the Device Manager, which lists all the hardware devices on the computer (and their status) and settings related to Automatic Update.

Figure 4.7 shows the General tab of the System Properties dialog box. This tab provides information on the operating system installed on the computer and the processor speed and RAM installed on the computer.

FIGURE 4.7

The System Properties dialog box provides access to system settings and system information.

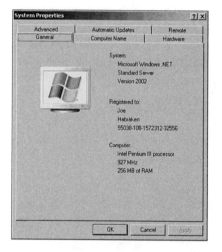

We take a look at three items accessed through the System Properties dialog box in the sections that follow. These items are hardware profiles, the Device Manager, and virtual memory settings.

It goes without saying that you will use the various applets and services found in the Administrative Tools applet. However, you will probably more often access these various tools from the Start menu.

Creating Hardware Profiles

When you install Windows Server 2003, a *hardware profile* is created for your computer. This hardware profile contains your hardware settings (the hardware devices on the computer when Windows Server 2003 was installed) and the services related to the hardware components.

You can create additional hardware profiles for your server. This is useful when you have a portable tape backup drive or other device that is not always connected to the server (such as a CD burner). You can create an alternative hardware profile that includes the device. Then when you boot the server, you can select the hardware profile that is appropriate at that moment (either the special device is connected or it is not).

To create a new hardware profile, follow these steps:

1. Open the System Properties dialog box (double-click the applet in the Control Panel).

2. Select the Hardware tab and then click the Hardware Profiles button. The Hardware Profiles box opens (see Figure 4.8).

FIGURE **4.8**

*You can create alterna-
tive hardware profiles
for your server.*

3. To create a new hardware profile, select Profile 1 (the current profile) and then click Copy. The Copy Profile box appears. Supply a name for the new profile and then click OK. The new profile appears in the profile list.

4. Select the Wait until I select a hardware profile option button in the Hardware Profiles dialog box. This means that when you restart the server, a menu appears before Windows is loaded that enables you to specify the hardware profile that should be loaded. Click OK to close the Hardware Profiles box, and click OK again to close the System Properties dialog box.

That completes the creation process. Now you must reboot the server. When you are asked to select the hardware profile, select the new profile that you created. When the server is up and running, install the special hardware that you want to include in this hardware profile.

Now when you boot the server, you can select Profile 1 when the device is not attached and select the profile that you created when the device is attached.

Using the Device Manager

The Device Manager can be used to verify whether a device is working properly, to change the driver used by a device, and to view the resources used by a particular device. To start the Device Manager, open the System Properties dialog box and then select the Hardware tab; click the Device Manager button on the tab.

> The Device Manager is one of a number of Microsoft Management Console snap-ins discussed in this book. The Management Console snap-ins provide administrators with a common management interface.

The default view in the Device Manager provides a category list of the devices on the computer. Expand any of the category nodes to view the devices in that category. For example, you can expand the Network Adapter node to view the network cards installed on the server (see Figure 4.9)

4

FIGURE 4.9

The Device Manager provides a look at the devices installed on the server.

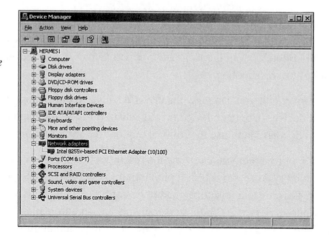

A device flagged with a exclamation point is not working correctly. Devices that are having problems (particularly with a driver) can also be flagged with a question mark.

To view the status of a particular device, right-click the device icon and select Properties from the shortcut menu. This opens the properties dialog box for the particular device. Figure 4.10 shows the Properties dialog box for a network card that is functioning normally.

FIGURE 4.10

You can view the status of a particular device.

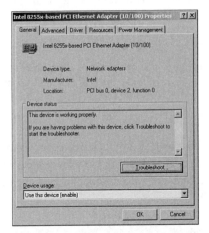

If you are having trouble with a particular device, you can troubleshoot the device. Click the Troubleshoot button; the Help and Support Center opens and walks you through a number of troubleshooting steps.

On the Driver tab, you can view the driver details and either upgrade or roll back the driver for a device. (Upgrade device drivers whenever they are available; if a new driver proves to be a problem, use the rollback option to reinstall the previous driver.)

On the Resources tab, you can view the resources that the device is using. These include Direct Memory Access (DMA), Input/Output (I/O), Interrupt Request (IRQ), and Memory. These resource settings had to be configured manually in the good old days. With Windows Server 2003, these parameters are set automatically and negate many of the problems faced in the past, such as IRQ conflicts (although you can choose to change the settings for a device that is involved in a resource conflict).

To close the Device Manager, click its Close button. This returns you to the System Properties dialog box (click OK or Cancel to close it).

Changes that you make in the Device Manager, such as disabling a device, can be saved as part of the current hardware profile or a new hardware profile.

Configuring Virtual Memory Settings

Virtual memory is fixed disk space that is reserved for the temporary store of items that can no longer be held in the server's RAM. In the Windows Server 2003 environment, the virtual memory is referred to as the paging file (we take a look at monitoring page file use in Hour 20, "Monitoring Server and Network Performance").

Microsoft recommends that the virtual memory or paging file be equivalent to 1.5 times the RAM installed on the server (you will find that this is actually the default setting for your paging file). If you use programs that use large amounts of memory, you can increase the paging file size beyond the recommendation.

1. To view the paging file settings, open the System Properties dialog box, select the Advanced tab, and then click the Performance Settings button. The Performance Settings dialog box appears.

2. You will notice in this dialog box that the option Let Windows choose what's best for my computer is selected. In most cases, this is a good idea when concerned with performance settings. To view the virtual memory settings, select the Advanced tab (see Figure 4.11). You can increase (or decrease) the virtual memory setting.

3. Click the Change button. The Virtual Memory dialog box appears. Provide an initial size and a maximum size. If you want to have Windows determine the size of the paging file, select the System Managed Size option button. After making your changes (or leaving everything as it was), click the OK button. You can close the other open dialog boxes by clicking OK on each.

It is probably a good idea to run your server with the default performance settings. If over time you see some performance problems using the System Monitor, you can attempt to tweak the settings. But remember that mission-critical servers on a network shouldn't be tweaked to the point of bringing down the network.

4

FIGURE 4.11

Virtual memory settings are on the Advanced tab.

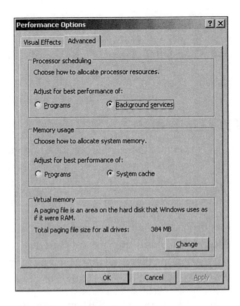

Using Other Control Panel Applets

Although the Windows Control Panel contents have remained somewhat consistent as the Windows desktop and server operating systems have evolved (up to Windows XP and Windows Server), some additional Control Panel tools deserve mention. We can probably forgo discussion of some applets, such as the Mouse and Keyboard applets, because of their extreme familiarity. We also can ignore others, such as the Game Controllers applet, because they are rather ridiculous options for a server.

- **Administrative Tools**—This applet provides quick access to administrative tools such as the Computer Management snap-in and other installed services utilities, such as the Active Directory, DNS, DHCP, and other snap-ins. These can also be accessed via the Start menu.

- **Folder Options**—This applet allows you to configure how folders open and the file types that are shown when a folder is opened. Information related to files and folders on the server can also be configured in the Folder Options dialog box.

- **Fonts**—This applet enables you to manage the fonts available on the server. You can delete fonts or add new fonts.

- **Power Options**—This applet opens the Power Options Properties dialog box, which enables you to set the power schemes for the server and enable hibernation. It is also used to configure uninterruptible power supplies that you connect to the server (the dialog box provides a UPS tab for the installation and configuration of a UPS).

- **Network Connections**—This applet provides access to the local area connections on the server. It also provides the New Connection Wizard that can be used to create a connection to the Internet or a connection to a network through a VPN or other connection.

- **Printers and Faxes**—This applet enables you to manage and configure printers and faxes on the server. It also provides the Add Printer Wizard, which can be used to add local or network printers to the server.

- **Scanners and Cameras**—This applet provides the Add Device Wizard, which can be used to add a scanner or digital camera to the server.

- **Taskbar and Start Menu**—This applet enables you to control the look and feel of the Windows taskbar and the Start menu. You can choose to use the classic Start menu provided by earlier versions of Windows.

- **Stored Usernames and Passwords**—This new applet enables you to store the usernames and passwords that are used to connect to other networks (such as the Internet) or computers that reside outside the domain. You can store the username and password associated with any connection resource, making it unnecessary to enter this information every time you seek to make the connection.

Using the Microsoft Management Console

Any discussion of the Windows Server 2003 administrative environment must include a look at the Microsoft Management Console (MMC). The MMC provides a common interface for a number of the services and tools that you will be working with as you manage your server. The MMC provides the container, and each service or tool operates as a snap-in within the console. Group Policy is managed as an MMC snap-in, as is DNS, DHCP, WINS, and a number of other services and utilities. Figure 4.12 shows the Computer Management snap-in, which enables you to access a number of local computer tools, such as the Event Viewer, the Performance Monitor, the Device Manager, and storage-related tools.

The left pane in the MMC window is referred to as the console tree, and the right pane is referred to as the Details pane. When you select a particular item in the tree, its contents are displayed in the Details pane.

We look at a number of MMC snap-ins throughout this book. In the next section, we look at local user accounts and groups in the Computer Management snap-in.

FIGURE 4.12

*The Microsoft
Management Console
provides the common
interface for Windows
Server tools.*

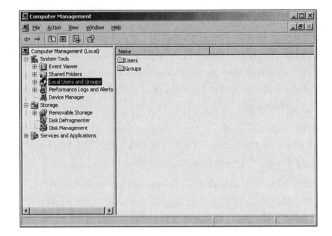

Local User Accounts and Groups

When you install Windows Server 2003 on a computer (as discussed in Hour 3, "Installing Windows Server 2003"), an Administrator account is automatically created (you had to provide the password for the account). This account is used to configure and administer the server. It is considered a local account (however, after you install Active Directory on the server, this account also has domain access privileges).

You can create additional local user accounts that have varying degrees of access to the settings and service on the local machine. This is in contrast to the domain user accounts that you will create in Hour 8, "Introduction to Active Directory." These types of accounts are designed to allow users to access different resources throughout the domain.

When you install Active Directory on a server, there will be no local accounts available. When you are upgrading an existing domain controller to Windows Server, there will be no local accounts.

The default local user accounts are Administrator, Guest, and Support (used by Microsoft for support purposes). The Guest and Support accounts are also disabled by default.

So, in a nutshell, local user accounts on a server are designed for people who will help maintain and administer the server. Local groups also exist on the local server and can be used to provide different access levels to your local users. (A large number of different domain groups will be discussed in Hour 9, "Active Directory Groups Organizational Units.")

Creating local users and groups on a Windows Server 2003 such as a member is really no different than creating local users on a shared office computer running an operating system such as Windows XP Professional. You are creating the local accounts so that these users can access local resources on the computer.

Local user accounts are created using the Computer Management console on the local computer. To open the Computer Management window, follow these steps:

1. Select the Start menu, point at Administrative Tools, and then select Computer Management. The Computer Management Console opens.

2. Expand the System Tools node in the tree and then expand the Local Users and Groups node. To view the current local users, click the Users folder (see Figure 4.13) .

FIGURE 4.13

You can view the current list of local users.

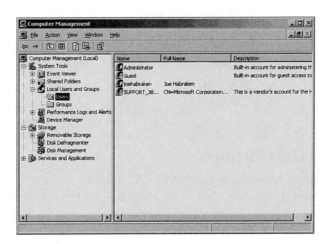

Adding Local Users

To add a local user to the computer with the list of local users showing, follow these steps:

1. Right-click in an empty portion of the Details pane and select New User from the shortcut menu. The New User dialog box appears (see Figure 4.14).

2. Enter a username, a full name, a description, and a password for the new account. You can also use the check boxes to set the following password options:

    • User must change password at next logon

- User cannot change password
- Password never expires
- Account is disabled

FIGURE 4.14

Set the username and password for the new local user.

3. After entering the various parameters, click the Create button. You can add other local user accounts if you want. Then click Close to close the dialog box. The new user (or users) appears in the user list.

The new user can now log on to the local computer. After you create a user, you can edit any settings related to the user, such as renaming the user and changing the user's password.

Local User Groups

On Windows Server 2003, computer local groups are typically used to impart certain access levels to the local users on the computer. For example, adding a local user to the Administrator group (a default group) grants that user all the administrative privileges on the local machine. This is also how you can create security equivalences for multiple users.

When you click the Groups folder in the tree, a list of all the default local groups (this is before you make the computer a domain controller) appears in the Details pane (see Figure 4.15). The built-in groups provide special access levels and capabilities that make it easier to assign a user certain privileges without making the user a local Administrator. The number of local groups shown depends on the services that you have installed. For example, if you have installed DHCP on the local computer, a DHCP Administrators group is added to the default group list.

FIGURE **4.15**

Default local groups can be used to provide access levels to local users.

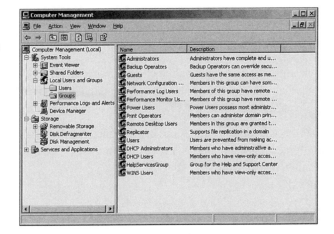

To add users to a local group, follow these steps:

1. Right-click a particular group (let's say you want to add users to the Administrator group). Then select Add to Group from the shortcut menu. The group's properties dialog box appears (see Figure 4.16). The current user members of the groups are listed.

FIGURE **4.16**

You can add local users to your local groups.

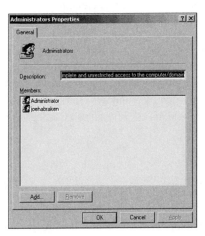

2. To add users to the group, click the Add button. The Select Users dialog box opens. Type the user names that you want to add to the group in the Enter the Object Names box, and then click OK. The username (or names) is added to the group's list. Click OK to close the dialog box.

4

You can also create local groups, if you want. It probably makes sense to take advantage of the different access levels provided by the built-in local groups before you go to the trouble of creating special local groups.

To add a new group, right click on the Groups folder and then select New Group. The New Group dialog box opens. Enter a name for the new group. To complete the process, click the Create button. Your new group appears in the group list.

Remember that local users and groups are designed for the local server environment. Domain user accounts and groups are a different animal; we discuss them in detail in Hours 8 and 9, respectively.

Summary

In this hour, we looked at the Windows Server 2003 desktop, which embraces the user experience model pioneered by Windows XP. As with previous versions of Windows, the Control Panel (either the menu or the window) provides access to a number of system utilities and applets, such as the Add Hardware, Add or Remove Software, and Network Connections applets.

You can create different hardware profiles that reflect hardware configurations of your server that use different peripheral devices. You can choose the appropriate hardware configuration when you boot up the system.

Local user accounts are used to grant users access to the local computer. You can create local user accounts in the Computer Management snap-in. Local groups are used to provide access levels to the local users. A number of default local groups, such as the Administrator's group, are provided by Windows Server 2003. Adding users to a group provides these users with the local access privileges afforded by the group.

Q&A

Q Which Control Panel applet enables you to automate the running of server utilities and other applications?

A The Scheduled Tasks applet enables you to schedule the launching of tools such as Windows Backup and Disk Defragmenter.

Q What are some of the items that can be accessed via the System Properties dialog box?

A You can access hardware profiles, the virtual memory settings, and the Device Manager via the System Properties dialog box.

Q What Windows Server utility provides the common interface for tools such as the Active Directory Users and Computers snap-in and other snap-ins used to manage DNS, DHCP, and others?

A The Microsoft Management Console provides the interface for a large number of the utilities and tools that you will access as you manage your Windows server.

Q How are local user accounts and groups created?

A Local user accounts and groups are managed using the Local Users and Group node in the Computer Management snap-in. Local user accounts and groups are used to provide local access to a server. If the Active Directory is added to the server, making it a domain controller, local users and groups are no longer available.

4

HOUR 5

Configuring a Windows Server

After you have installed Windows Server 2003 on a computer, the next step is to configure the server to fulfill its role on your network. A single server can actually serve a number of different roles and offer a variety of services. However, the number of specialized servers that you will need depends not only on the services required by your users, but also by the size of the network and amount of traffic the network experiences. In this hour, we define different server roles and look at how services are managed on the network.

In this hour, the following topics are covered:

- Becoming familiar with Microsoft's Networking Model
- Determining roles for domain servers
- Managing server's roles
- Understanding Network Services
- Using the Services snap-in

Understanding the Microsoft Networking Model

The Microsoft Networking model (going as far back as Microsoft LAN Manager and including the Windows NT environment) has always embraced the domain as the basic administrative container for the network. A *domain* is a logical grouping of computers and other devices that are managed as objects by a Windows domain controller. The domain maintains its own directory database of user accounts and controls all published resources within the domain, such as printers and shared files.

> Microsoft operating systems, including the network operating systems such as Windows Server 2003, enable you to share resources between computers without creating a domain. You can set up a workgroup and share resources between computers in what is termed a peer-to-peer network. Workgroups do not provide the security or scalability of the domain model and should be used only in very small office settings or for home networks.

Although a domain could potentially serve thousand of users, there is often the need to go beyond the limitations provided by a single domain and expand the scale of the network. The directory services provided by Windows Server 2003's Active Directory provide you with a hierarchical structure in which domains can be nested within other domains.

Let's look at the domain hierarchy of the Windows Server 2003. As already mentioned, the basic unit is the domain. The next largest unit is the tree. A *tree* is a collection of child domains. The tree itself is defined by a root domain, which serves as the parent domain for the child domains that branch from the domain root.

The largest administrative structure provided by the domain hierarchy is the forest. A *forest* is a collection of domain trees.

To truly understand how domains interact within trees and forests, you need to understand trust relationships. A *trust* is an electronic security agreement between domains. Users can log on to their domain but still get at resources in another domain if that domain "trusts" the user's domain.

When you create child domains within a domain tree using Windows Server, the child domains and the parent domain all are assigned transitive trusts. A *transitive trust* is a two-way street between the domains.

The domains trust each other, so they share each other's resources. This means that all the domains in a tree trust the other domains in the tree to use their resources (such as printers and DNS server). So, the transitive trust relationships provide a reciprocating resource-sharing environment that flows down through the tree.

 This notion of a hierarchical directory services structure and how the Active Directory provides the infrastructure is discussed in more detail in Chapter 8, "Introduction to Active Directory."

You create a domain in the Windows Server 2003 environment by bringing the first domain controller online. Domain controllers are created by installing the Active Directory Services on a server running Windows Server 2003 (or Windows 2000 Server). So, you will have to deploy on your network at least one domain controller. Let's take a look at other server roles that often need to be filled on a network.

Determining Server Roles

The whole point of networking computers is to provide users with the capability to connect to network resources (and to each other). For resources to be available, a computer running a network operating system must be available to "serve up" the resource to the requesting client. A number of server roles exist, such as that of a file, print, database, or application server. Let's look at some of the common server types you might have to deploy in your network.

Understanding Domain Controllers

As already mentioned, a Windows Server 2003 domain requires a domain controller. The domain controller authenticates users to the Active Directory as they attempt to log on to the network. The domain controller also provides the Global Catalog for the domain, which is a listing of all the objects in the domain, such as users, groups, and printers.

Because domain controllers must validate users, additional domain controllers are often deployed on a very large network. This enables user accounts to be validated more quickly because any domain controller in the domain can handle the authentication.

On large networks that consist of multiple forests or sites, a domain controller or controllers can serve as Global Catalog servers. These servers contain information on resources that span the forests or sites, making it easier for users to find the resources that they need.

Working with File Servers

A file server's job is to serve as a repository for the files that are needed by users on the network. These files are typically held in what is called a public folder, which can include private folders that are specific for a particular user.

Windows Server 2003 actually makes it easy for you to package file resources that are held on any number of file servers in a way that users are not aware of the actual location of the resource files. This system is called the Distributed File System (DFS). DFS and the creation of network shares on a Windows Server 2003 file server are discussed in Chapter 12, "Network Shares, Files, and the Distributed File System."

Deploying Print Servers

A print server is used to host a network printer. It is basically the control conduit for the printer. Because print jobs need to be spooled (placed on the computer before they are sent to the printer) before they are printed, the print server supplies the hard-drive space needed.

The print server also queues up all the print jobs being directed to the printer. The network administrator can delete print jobs and change the queue order of print jobs by accessing the print server. Providing print resources in the Windows Server 2003 environment is discussed in Chapter 14, "Working with Network Printing."

Running a Web Server

Web servers provide you with the capability to create a Web site that can be accessed by the general public via the World Wide Web. Web servers can also be used to create private Webs called intranets that allow employees to use Web browsers to access internal company information.

Microsoft Windows Server 2003 provides Internet Information Service (IIS) 6.0, a full-featured Web server platform that also provides other services such as FTP sites and NNTP newsgroups. IIS is discussed in Chapter 24, "Internet Information Service."

Understanding Application Servers

Application servers host various applications, such as specialized databases. Even typical desktop applications such as word processors and spreadsheet software can be stored on an application server. This makes updating software applications much easier because the software doesn't actually reside on every client workstation; users start these applications from their local computers, but the application software is actually stored on the server.

Although we typically look at the Internet Information Service provided by Windows Server as a Web service, the addition of XML applications and other platforms for Web applications (such as ASP.NET) has prompted Microsoft to consider IIS an application-server platform.

Understanding Messaging Servers

A messaging server runs specialized software that enables users on the network to communicate and collaborate. It provides services such as electronic mail and discussion groups. Microsoft Exchange is an example of a communication server software package. It is installed on a server that is already running one of the Microsoft network operating systems, such as Windows Server 2003.

Using the Manage Your Server Tool

Windows Server 2003 makes it very easy for you to configure a particular server for a role or roles. For example, on a small network, a domain controller could also function as a file server and a print server. The number of specialized servers that you will have to deploy really depends on the size of your network (based on the number of users you must serve).

The Manage Your Server Tool, which resides in its own window, provides you with the capability to quickly assign a particular role to your server. You will notice that as soon as you install Windows Server 2003 on your computer, the Manage Your Server window opens automatically when you reboot or start up the server.

This window (see Figure 5.1) also shows you the roles that have been assigned to your server. This window provides easy access to background information on server roles and configuration help.

Adding a Server Role

Server roles can be added to a server directly from the Manage Your Server window.

1. Click Add or Remove Role near the top of the window. The Configure Your Server Wizard opens. To bypass the initial wizard screen, click Next.

If you want, you can bypass the Manage Your Server window when you want to install new server roles or services. Select Start, Administrative Tools, and then Configure Your Server Wizard.

FIGURE **5.1**

Manage Your Server makes it easy to configure your server for various roles.

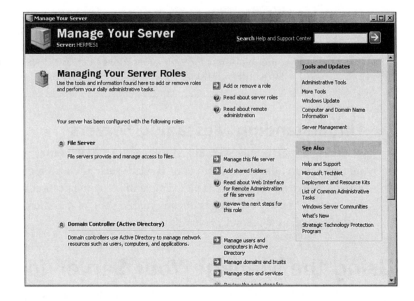

2. The next screen reminds you to connect your network medium and modems, and to turn on peripherals such as printers. In most cases, you should have all these devices and peripherals active when you install Windows Server 2003 on the computer. This allows the operating system to identify and install most devices. After making sure all devices are connected, click Next.

3. The next screen provides a list of server roles (services provided by Windows Server 2003 are also listed—see Figure 5.2). Roles that have already been assigned to the server are so noted by Yes in the configuration column. To add a particular server role, such as a Web application server, click the appropriate server role in the list provided by the wizard and then click Next.

FIGURE **5.2**

Select the server role that you want to add to the server.

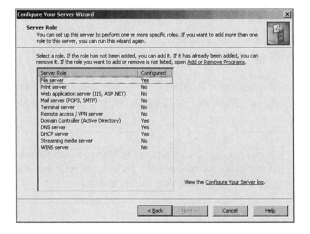

The wizard walks you through a number of screens that are specific to the server role that you selected for installation. The Configure Your Server Wizard is discussed in a number of chapters in this book related to the installation of a specific server role or service.

After you have completed the steps provided by the Configure Your Server Wizard, the new server role is listed in the Manage Your Server window.

Managing a Server's Role

The Manage Your Server window also provides quick access to the management tools that are provided for the various roles your server has assumed. For example, let's say that your server is a domain controller and that you want to add users to the domain. Open the Manage Your Server window (Start, Administrative Tools, Manage Your Server) and locate the Domain Controller (Active Directory) role in the window.

Figure 5.3 shows the Manage Your Server window and the Domain Controller (Active Directory) management area. You can launch any of the Active Directory tools (the Active Directory Users and Computers snap-in, the Active Directory Domains and Trusts snap-in, and the Active Directory Sites and Services snap-in) from this area.

FIGURE 5.3

Tools for managing server roles can be launched from the Manage Your Server window.

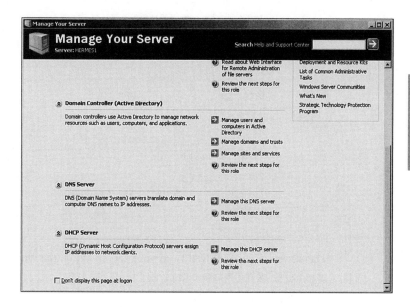

For example, to launch the Active Directory Users and Computer snap-in (which is the Active Directory tool employed to add new users), click the Manage Users and Computers in the Active Directory link provided by the Manage Your Server window.

The Active Directory is discussed in Chapter 8, "Introduction to Active Directory," and in Chapter 9, "Active Directory Groups and Organizational Units."

Removing a Server Role

Server roles can also be removed from your Windows Server 2003.

1. Start the Configure Your Server Wizard (either from the Manage Your Server window or by selecting Start, Administrative Tools, Configure Your Server Wizard).

2. After bypassing the initial screen and the screen that reminds you to connect your network media and other devices, you will be provided with a list of all the potential server roles (and services). Select any installed server role and then click the Next button.

3. The next screen advises you that the selected server role will be removed (see Figure 5.4). You must select the appropriate check box to remove the role. Then click Next.

FIGURE 5.4

Specify that you want the server role to be removed.

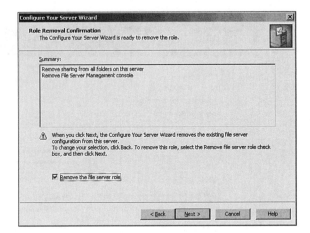

4. The server role is removed from your server. When the wizard has completed the process, click the Finish button.

Many of the Windows Server 2003 services can also be installed using the Add/Remove Windows Component Wizard that is provided in the Add or Remove Application window (which is reached via the Control Panel). In some cases, this enables you to add a service faster than when using the Configure Your Server Wizard. Be advised, however, that the wizard also often helps you configure the service, whereas the Component wizard only adds it to the server's configuration.

The Manage Your Server window provides you with an excellent way to keep track of the roles that you have assigned a particular server. It also provides you with the capability to launch the management tool for each of the roles that you have assigned to the server.

Seasoned Windows network administrators will probably find the Manage Your Server window more of an annoyance than a help. The overview that it provides of installed server roles and services, and its quick access to management tools makes it a useful launching pad for administrators new to the Windows server environment.

Understanding Network Services

A number of services can also be provided by the servers on your Windows Server 2003 network. And although a service such as DHCP is run on a server called a DHCP server, which would really connote a server role, we will look at things such as DHCP and DNS as network services instead of server roles.

- The Domain Name Service (DNS) is used to resolve "friendly" fully qualified domain names to IP addresses. DNS is the naming service used in the Windows Server 2003 environment. It must be deployed on the network for the Active Directory to function. DNS is discussed in detail in Chapter 15, "Domain Name Service."

- The Dynamic Host Configuration Protocol (DHCP) dynamically provides IP addresses, subnet masks, and other IP configuration options (such as the primary DNS server) to DHCP clients on the network. DHCP provides much more flexibility than static IP addresses, and it also negates the possibility of assigning the same IP address to two different nodes on the network. DHCP is discussed in Chapter 16, "Dynamic Host Configuration Protocol."

5

- The Windows Internet Naming Service (WINS) resolves NetBIOS names to IP addresses. This allows down-level client operating systems such as Windows 9x to use the WINS service to help them identify resources on the network. In a network running all Windows 2000 or XP clients and Windows 2000 Server or Windows Server 2003, the WINS service would not be needed. Because many networks still use older client software, it is still often necessary to deploy WINS on the network. WINS is discussed in Chapter 17, "Understanding WINS."

- Remote access enables your users to access network resources from a remote computer (a computer not directly connected to the physical network). Users can log in remotely using dial-in accounts and virtual private networking. Configuring Windows Server 2003 for remote access and setting up dial-in accounts are discussed in Chapter 18, "Routing and Remote Access." Virtual private networking is discussed in Chapter 21, "Virtual Private Networking and IP Security."

- Routing provides a method of breaking a large network into logical IP subnets and connecting network subnets across WAN connections. Routing is typically handled by a dedicated hardware device called a router (routers also have their own proprietary operating systems). However, a Windows Server 2003 configured with two or more network cards can be configured as a router. Routing is discussed in Chapter 18.

- Terminal Services allows a client computer to remotely connect to a terminal server and access Windows-based applications. The client computer actually functions as a terminal, and the terminal server provides the application and operating system environment. Terminal Services is discussed in Chapter 19, "Windows Terminal Services."

- Network Address Translation (NAT) enables you to connect your network to the Internet using one public IP address (an IP address supplied by an Internet service provider). The computers on the internal network using NAT are assigned IP addresses from a private range (that do not conflict with outside IP addresses). Network Address Translation is discussed in Chapter 22, "Internet Connection Sharing and Network Address Translation."

- Certificate Services provides you with the capability to issue certificates that authenticate users and data from outside your network. Certificates can also be used to encrypt data, making information from inside your network safe as it travels on a public network such as the Internet. A certificate can enable a Web user to be authenticated to your network, or a certificate can be used to authenticate email from a customer. Certificate services and creating a Certificate Authority on a Windows Server are discussed in Hour 23, "Working with Certificate Services." An introduction to the public key infrastructure and how it relates to certificates is also presented in Hour 23.

The number of services that you will want to run on any one server greatly depends on the size of your network. A server burdened with a number of services such as DHCP, DNS, and WINS on a large network might soon become a performance bottleneck for these services.

One way to test how well a server will run when providing multiple services is to run a test server, enabling you to monitor server performance before deploying the server on the network. Information on creating server performance baselines is discussed in Chapter 20, "Monitoring Server and Network Performance."

Adding Services to the Server

The most straightforward way to add services to a Windows Server 2003 is with the Configure Your Server Wizard (Start, Administrative Tools, Configure Your Server Wizard). Services not available in the Configure Your Server Wizard can be added to the server using the Add or Remove Programs applet found in the Windows Control Panel.

1. Open the Add or Remove Programs applet window (Start, Control Panel, Add or Remove Programs). Then click Add/Remove Windows Components to open the Windows Components window (see Figure 5.5).

FIGURE 5.5

Use the Add/Remove Windows Components applet to add or remove Windows Server 2003 services.

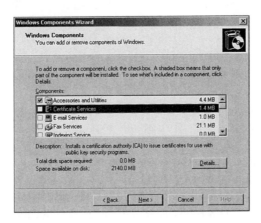

2. Locate the service you want to add in the Add/Remove Windows Components window, and then select the service (click the check box next to service). Then click Next to add the service. The service is added to your server's configuration. Click Finish to complete the process.

Using the Services Snap-In

The services that you add to your Windows Server 2003 are managed using specific Microsoft Management Console snap-ins (such as the DNS or DHCP snap-ins). You can also view a list of the services running on your server using the Services snap-in, which provides a list of all the Windows Server 2003 services installed on a server and shows which services are currently running and which are not.

To open the Services snap-in, select Start, Administrative Tools; then select Services. The Services snap-in opens in the Microsoft Management Console (see Figure 5.6).

FIGURE 5.6

The Services snap-in enables you to view and manage services on the server.

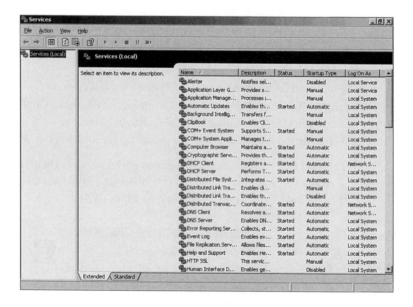

The Services snap-in is useful because you can view all the services installed on a server and quickly check whether they are currently running (a service that is not running but that should be is not providing any resources or performing the necessary tasks for your users). Services can be stopped or started from the Services snap-in. Stopping a service is usually a troubleshooting measure. For example, you would have to stop the WINS service to restore the WINS database if you felt that database corruption was causing WINS resolution problems (WINS is discussed in Chapter 17, "Understanding WINS").

You can start, stop, restart, and pause services in the Services snap-in. Right-click a particular service in the Details pane (see Figure 5.7). Select an option, such as Stop, from the shortcut menu. The status of the service changes to Automatic (if it is a service loaded when the server boots up) or Stopped.

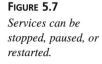

FIGURE 5.7

Services can be stopped, paused, or restarted.

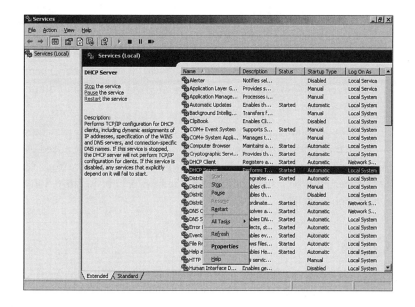

The Services snap-in also provides you with a good way to familiarize yourself with the services that your Windows Server 2003 is running. Click any service in the Details pane, and a description of the service appears in the tree pane of the snap-in.

Summary

In this hour, we took a look at the Microsoft domain model and the different roles that can be filled by a server running Windows Server 2003. The administrative container for Microsoft server-based networks is the domain. A collection of domains resides in a tree. Each tree has a root domain; the other domains in the tree are child domains of the root. All the domains in a tree share transitive trusts, meaning that resources in any of the tree's domains are available to the users in the tree. A group of domain trees is called a forest.

Servers on the network serve specific roles. For example, the domain requires at least one domain controller. Files are made available to users by a file server, and print services are provided by a print server. A single server can serve multiple roles, but this greatly depends on the size of the network and the number of roles a single server is required to fill.

5

The Manage Your Server window provides an easy-to-use platform for viewing the roles currently installed on a server. Server roles can also be added or removed using links on the Manage Your Server window. Role addition or deletion is actually handled by the Configure Your Server Wizard, which can be started independently of the Manage Your Server window (the wizard can be started via Start, Administrative Tools, Configure Your Server Wizard).

Network servers can also run a number of services that provide specialized resources such as DNS, DHCP, and WINS. Many services can be added using the Manage Your Server window (or more directly by using the Configure Your Server Wizard). Some services must be installed using the Windows Add or Remove Software applet in the Control Panel.

Q&A

Q When a child domain is created in the domain tree, what type of trust relationship exists between the new child domain and the tree's root domain?

A Child domains and the root domain of a tree are assigned transitive trusts. This means that the root domain and child domain trust each other and allow resources in any domain in the tree to be accessed by users in any domain in the tree.

Q What is the primary function of domain controllers?

A The primary function of domain controllers is to validate users to the network. However, domain controllers also provide the catalog of Active Directory objects to users on the network.

Q What are some of the other roles that a server running Windows Server 2003 could fill on the network?

A A server running Windows Server 2003 can be configured as a domain controller, a file server, a print server, a Web server, and an application server. Windows servers can also provide services such as DNS, DHCP, and routing and remote access.

Q Which Windows Server 2003 tools make it easy to manage and configure a server's roles?

A The Manage Your Server window enables you to view the roles installed on a server and also to quickly access the different snap-ins that are used to manage these various roles. The Configure Your Server Wizard can be used to add and remove roles from a server.

HOUR 6

Managing Hard Drives and Volumes

In Hour 3, "Installing Windows Server 2003," the basic formatting and partitioning tasks related to setting up a hard disk for a Windows Server 2003 installation were discussed. In this hour, we look at managing server drives using the Disk Manager snap-in/console. We also look at some of the ways you can protect data on your server's hard drives. Strategies for protecting important files and your server configuration include building redundancy in your server's disk arrays using RAID (Redundant Array of Independent Disks) and the backing up important data. We also discuss keeping your drives healthy by scanning for disk errors and using the Disk Defragmenter tool.

In this hour, the following topics are covered:

- Managing server disk drives
- Understanding the Virtual Disk Service
- Basic drives versus dynamic drives

- Creating RAID implementations
- Working with DiskPart
- Using the Disk Defragmenter
- Backing up and restoring data

Managing Your Disk Drives Using Windows Server 2003

After you have completed a basic installation of Windows Server 2003 on a server computer (discussed in Hour 3), the next step is to configure the server for the particular role that it will serve on the network (such as a domain controller or a file server, as discussed in Hour 5, "Configuring a Windows Server"). Another important aspect of configuring a server is setting up the hard drive or drives on the server so that the computer can successfully fulfill its role on the network. For example, a file server on the network needs appropriate storage capacity to supply data to users on the network. As the number of users on the network and the data on the server grow, it might be necessary to configure unused space on the drive or to add additional drives to the server.

Windows Server 2003 provides you with the Disk Manager tool, which is used to configure and manage your drives. You can format drives and create drive volumes. More advanced drive configurations such as RAID arrays can also be configured using the Disk Manager. RAID arrays can be used to add redundancy to network data storage, helping protect valuable network information and server configurations.

Although server disk management is one aspect of protecting important network data, how data is shared and the level of access given to users are other important parts of your overall network resources plan. Working with network shares and permissions related to shared data are discussed in Hour 12, "Working with Network Shares and the Distributed File System." Share permissions and NTFS permissions are discussed in Hour 13, "Share and NTFS Permissions."

Windows Server 2003 Virtual Disk Service

As with all computer hardware, each component is available from different manufacturers. Hard drives and drive controllers are no different. Managing drives on different servers often has necessitated using a number of different utilities, with each utility specific to a particular drive array and its manufacturer.

In an attempt to provide a consistent approach to drive management, a new service has been added to Windows Server 2003 called the Virtual Disk Service (VDS). VDS is a set of application programming interfaces (APIs) that enable you to manage the configuration of different manufacturers' hard disks using the same Windows tools (the Windows Server 2003 Disk Manager and the command-line DiskPart—we discuss DiskPart later in the hour).

> The burden of making disks manageable using the Windows disk tools is really on the manufacturer of the drives that you use in your servers. Each manufacturer must supply APIs to Microsoft that makes the Virtual Disk Service a reality. So, there might be a time lag before all vendors' drive configurations can be managed directly from Windows Server 2003.

Basic Drive Versus Dynamic Drives

Computers running Windows (even servers running Windows NT) have long embraced the MS-DOS model of disk configuration in which drives were partitioned and the various partitions were then formatted. Not until advances provided with the release of Windows 2000 Server were network administrators provided with an alternative way to divide, combine, and configure the storage capacity of hard drives.

Windows Server 2003 embraces two types of disk storage strategies (which originated with 2000 Server): basic storage and dynamic storage. These storage strategies are also available in Windows Server 2003.

Basic storage is the traditional standard for how hard drives are formatted and configured, and it is based on the way drives were configured using MS-DOS. A *basic disk* is a physical disk that contains a primary partition and possibly extended partitions that contain logical drives. A *partition* is a logical portion of a hard drive that is actually read by the computer's operating system as a separate drive. Basic storage is the default for Windows Server 2003. Basic disks can be divided into a maximum of four partitions.

Dynamic storage allows for the creation of dynamic disks. A *dynamic disk* consists of one partition that can be divided into any number of volumes. A *volume* is a portion of an entire drive or parts of several drives that are assigned a single drive letter. Dynamic disks can be sized and resized without having to restart Windows Server 2003. Dynamic disks do not contain logical drives, as do basic disks; each volume can be potentially configured as a discrete drive with its own drive letter.

6

You can use only one storage type (basic or dynamic) on a physical disk.

The use of dynamic disks allows for the creation of disk arrays that use RAID implementations. As mentioned earlier, the use of RAID allows for redundancy and fault tolerance on network drives, which helps to protect network data. Because basic drives are the default for Windows Server 2003, you must convert a drive or drives to dynamic. Converting a basic drive to a dynamic drive is discussed later in the hour.

Using the Disk Management Tool

Disk management (both basic and dynamic) is handled by the Disk Manager snap-in, which is found in the Computer Management console. To open the Disk Manager, click the Start button, point at Administrative Tools, and then click Computer Management. The Computer Management console opens. To open the Disk Management tool, click the Disk Management node. The disks on your computer (and their current configurations) appear in the Details pane (see Figure 6.1).

FIGURE 6.1

The Disk Manager is found in the Computer Management console.

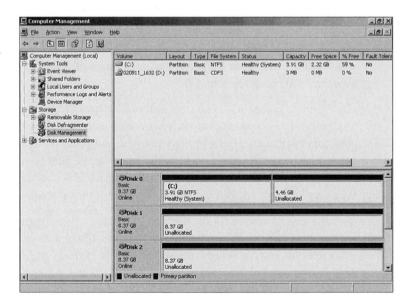

The Disk Manager provides you with a great deal of information on each of the physical drives installed on your computer. The upper portion of the Details pane (the right side of the Disk Manager window) lists volumes or partitions that have been assigned a drive letter (including CD-ROMs). Additional information, such as the file system used on the partition or volume, the capacity and free space, and whether the volume or partition is part of a fault tolerance array (RAID), is also provided.

> Make sure that you are logged on to the sever using a user account that has administrative privileges.

The lower portion of the Details pane lists each physical drive, including any CD-ROM drives (this would include any CD-writeable or DVD drives on the system). This lower area of the Details pane is the easiest place to access commands related to drive management. You can change drives from basic to dynamic, and you can create and format partitions or volumes (depending on whether the disk is basic or dynamic).

> Physical drives are numbered starting with 0. So, a server configured with three hard drives would list drives 0, 1, and 2 in the Disk Manager Details pane. Partitions are numbered, as in 1, 2, and 3.

Creating a Partition on a Basic Disk

Basic disks enable you to create partitions and logical drives (a legacy from the days of DOS and earlier versions of Windows NT). You can create partitions on unused space on basic disks using the Disk Manager.

1. Right-click the unallocated space of a basic disk (the space is marked unallocated), and select Create Partition from the shortcut menu. The Create Partition Wizard appears. Click Next to move past the wizard's introductory screen.

2. The next screen (see Figure 6.2) asks you to select the type of partition you are creating on the drive. Select either the Primary partition or Extended partition option button. (If this is the first partition on the drive, select Primary; otherwise, select Extended.) Then click Next.

6

> The primary partition of a basic disk (again, a legacy of DOS) is typically the boot and system partitions of the drive.

FIGURE 6.2

Partitioning basic drives requires that you select either a primary or an extended partition.

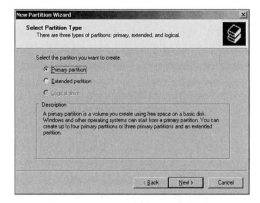

3. The next screen asks you to select the size for the partition, as shown in Figure 6.3. Use the Partition size in MB box to set the size of the partition. By default, the entire space available on the partition is listed. Click Next.

FIGURE 6.3

Designate the amount of free space available on the drive that should be used in the new partition.

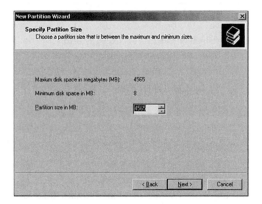

4. If you are creating a primary partition, the wizard assigns a drive letter to the partition. (For extended partitions, you must create a logical drive to assign a drive letter, as detailed in the next section of the hour.) To select the default drive letter assigned, click Next.

5. The next screen (which, again, you will see only if you are working with a primary partition) enables you to select the file system that you want to use to format the partition (see Figure 6.4). This screen also enables you to set the allocation unit size for the partition and assign a volume name to the partition.

FIGURE 6.4

Select the file system for the partition.

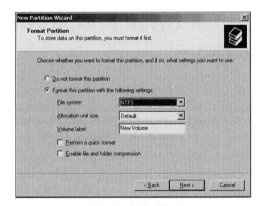

You can format drives on your Windows servers as FAT, FAT32, and NTFS. Microsoft recommends NTFS as the best choice for your server drives. This makes sense because NTFS partitions can be as large as nearly 16exabytes (EB) (a FAT32 partition has a maximum of 2terabytes [TB]), NTFS volumes allow file compression, and NTFS permissions provide additional security to resources on the network.

Select the file system using the wizard's File system drop-down box. Use the Allocation unit size drop-down box to select the *allocation unit size* you want to use on the drive. The allocation unit size selected determines the cluster size used on the partition (which holds the sectors, the basic unit of disk space). Using an allocation unit size of 4096MB creates a cluster size no greater than 4KB, which is the limit for NTFS compressions. In most cases, the default allocation unit size will suffice for your partition.

6. After selecting the file system and allocation unit size (optional) and providing a volume name for the partition (also optional), click the Next button. The last wizard screen appears, providing a summary of the options you chose for the new partition. When you click Finish, the new partition is created (and formatted, in the case of primary partitions).

The Disk Manager uses a color scheme in the Details pane to designate primary and extended partitions. Primary partitions are blue, and extended partitions are green. Unallocated drive space is black.

To delete a partition, right-click the partition and select Delete Partition. Remember that any data on the partition will be lost if you delete it.

Creating a Logical Drive and Formatting an Extended Partition

Extended partitions that you create must be assigned a drive letter and formatted as a logical drive.

1. To begin the process, right-click the partition that you have created and select New Logical Drive from the shortcut menu. The New Partition Wizard appears. This might seem confusing because you already used this wizard to create the extended partition, but it will now help you designate the extended partition as a logical drive, select a drive letter, and format the partition (as was done automatically when a primary partition was created, as detailed in the last section).

2. Click Next to bypass the introductory screen of the New Partition Wizard. The next screen is used to select the partition type. Logical Drive is the only option available (and rightly so). Click Next to continue.

3. The wizard now asks you to specify the partition size. This screen is the same as in Figure 6.3. Specify the size in megabytes for the logical drive and click Next.

4. The next screen asks you to assign a drive letter to the logical drive (you can go with the default). Click Next to continue. The next screen enables you to format the logical drive, select the allocation unit size, and optionally name the volume (the same screen as shown in Figure 6.4).

5. Click Next after selecting the file system and allocation unit size (optional) and naming the volume (optional). This takes you to the wizard's summary screen. Click Finish to complete the process. Your new logical drive appears in the lower-right pane of the Disk Manager.

> You might want to convert FAT or FAT32 drives to NTFS when they already contain data or software. This conversion can be done without disrupting the information on the drive and is accomplished at the command prompt. The command is convert x: /fs:/ntfs, where x is the drive letter. If you are converting the system volume, the conversion will not occur until you reboot the system.

Converting a Basic Drive to a Dynamic Drive

Basic disks are somewhat limited in terms of what you can do with them in the Windows Server 2003 environment. Think of them as legacy DOS or NT 4.0 disks: They can be partitioned and formatted, and that's about it. If you want to build any fault tolerance into your disk arrays using RAID, you will need to convert basic drives to dynamic drives.

> If you use a DOS-based boot disk (DOS, Windows ME/XP) and fdisk to con-
> figure the drives on a new server (or a server on which you have deleted all
> the drive partitions or volumes), you must leave a megabyte of unparti-
> tioned space on any drive that you want to later convert from a basic disk to
> a dynamic disk.

To convert a basic disk to a dynamic disk, right-click the disk in the Details pane (on the disk's designation box, such as Disk 1 or Disk 2). Then select Convert to Dynamic Disk from the shortcut menu that appears. The Convert to Dynamic Disk dialog box opens, as shown in Figure 6.5.

FIGURE 6.5

Designate the drives that you want to convert from basic to dynamic.

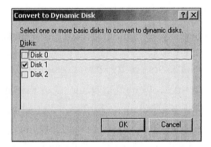

All the physical drives on your server are listed in the Convert to Dynamic Disk dialog box. You may select any and all drives (that are currently online) using this dialog box to mark them for conversion. After making your selection, click OK. Quite quickly you will notice that drive designation changes from Basic to Dynamic.

Converting basic drives to dynamic drives is imperative when you want to build fault tolerance into a drive array. However, you should keep in mind some things related to converting drives:

- You cannot convert removable media such as Jazz, ZIP, and other disk types considered "nonfixed" drives from basic to dynamic.
- If you upgrade a basic disk that is part of a volume that spans several different physical drives, you must convert all the disks in the volume from basic to dynamic.

6

- If you convert a disk that contains another operating system (on a server that offers a dual-boot environment) from basic to dynamic, the other operating system will no longer function or boot. This includes Microsoft Windows NT Server.
- You can upgrade a basic disk containing the boot and system partitions to a dynamic disk. However, you cannot reverse the conversion from dynamic to basic as you can on drives that do not contain boot and system information.

If you plan on implementing Windows Server 2003, it makes sense to take advantage of dynamic disks. Dynamic disks provide many more configuration possibilities when compared to basic disks. The next section discusses the different types of volumes that can be created on a dynamic disk.

Creating a Volume

After you have converted a disk from basic to dynamic, you can create volumes on that drive. Different types of volumes can be created:

- **Simple volume**—A portion of a dynamic disk that functions as an independent drive and is assigned a drive letter. Simple volumes can be expanded using additional disk space on the same disk or by spanning the volume to multiple disks.
- **Spanned volume**—A simple volume that spans more than one physical disk.
- **Striped volume**—A volume on which data is striped across multiple disks, speeding up the write and read processes to and from the volume. At least two drives are needed to create a striped volume. A striped volume is also known as RAID 0.
- **Mirrored volume**—A volume on one drive is mirrored (duplicated) on a volume on another drive. This is RAID 1, which is discussed later in the hour. When the drives are on separate drive controllers, you are actually implementing disk duplexing.
- **Striped volume with parity**—A volume that spans multiple drives. Data is striped across the multiple drives with parity information written to the drives, allowing for the regeneration of the whole data set if one of the drives fails. A minimum of three drives is required for this type of volume. This is RAID 5, which is discussed later in the hour.

The New Volume Wizard manages volume creation on a Windows server. To create a simple volume, perform the following steps:

1. In the Disk Management Details area, right-click a dynamic disk that contains unallocated disk space.
2. Select New Volume from the shortcut menu.

3. When the New Volume Wizard appears, click Next to bypass the opening wizard screen.

4. Select the type of volume that you want to create on the disk, as shown in Figure 6.6. In the case of a simple volume, select the Simple option button (which is the default).

FIGURE 6.6

The New Volume Wizard is used to create volumes on a dynamic disk or disks.

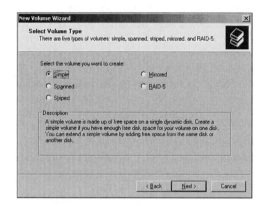

5. Click Next to continue.

6. The next screen asks you to select the disks that will be included in the volume (only disks with available space are listed). In the case of a simple volume, the drive you right-clicked to begin the process is included in the Selected box (see Figure 6.7). Other drives are listed in the Available box. To include additional disks (other than the default), select the disk or disks in the Available box and then click Add.

FIGURE 6.7

Specify the drive or drives for the volume and set the size of the new volume.

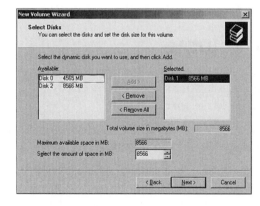

6

7. This wizard screen also provides you with the capability to set the size for the new volume. The maximum amount of space available on the selected drive or drives is shown in the Select the amount of space in MB box. Use the spinner box to change the space to be used if this is different from the maximum. Then click Next to continue.

8. The next screen provides a default drive letter for the new volume. Use the Drive drop-down box to select a drive letter other than the default. Then click Next to continue.

8. On this wizard screen, select the file system for the new volume. You can use FAT, FAT32, or NTFS (NTFS is the default). You can also add a volume name. After choosing the file format, click Next to continue the process.

9. A summary screen appears detailing the selections that you made for the new volume; click Finish. The new volume appears in the Details area of the Disk Manager. Depending on the size of the volume, formatting of the drive might take a few minutes.

> To delete a volume, right-click the volume and select Delete Volume. Remember that any data on the volume will be lost if you delete it.

Creating any of the other volume types, such as the spanned volume, is just a matter of working through the various screens of the New Volume Wizard and making the appropriate selections. For a spanned volume, you would select Spanned Volume as the volume type. You would then specify more than one drive as the disks involved in the spanned volume.

Extending a Volume

Dynamic volumes can easily be extended. And as was the case when creating volumes, a volume can be extended using free space on the same physical drive or space available on other physical drives on the server.

1. Right-click the volume that you want to extend, and then select Extend Volume. The Extend Volume Wizard appears. Click Next to continue.

2. A wizard screen appears (see Figure 6.7). Here you can select more free space on the physical drive to extend the partition, or you can select additional physical drives that contain free space. After selecting additional space, click Next.

3. A summary screen appears. Click Finish to end the process.

When a simple volume extends across more than one disk, the failure of any of the disks will make the volume unusable.

Understanding RAID

Redundant Array of Independent Disks (RAID) is a collection of strategies designed to provide fault tolerance for files stored on hard drives (it can be used to protect boot and system files as well). In general, using RAID means that you are placing data on more than one disk. If a disk in the RAID set goes down, you still recover your data because you either have a complete copy of that data (on the other disk in the RAID 1 mirror set) or can regenerate the data on the failed disk from the data and parity information (discussed when we look at RAID 5) on the remaining disks in the array.

In the simplest terms, RAID enables you to combine volumes on more than one drive into a volume set (or array) that functions as a single logical drive.

There are eight different levels of RAID, numbered from 0 to 7. Windows Server 2003 supports software versions of RAID 0, 1, and 5.

RAID can be either hardware or software supported. A number of RAID controllers are available for network servers. We discuss the software RAID levels embraced by Windows Server 2003. RAID configurations can even be expanded beyond a single server. Windows Server 2003 also supports server clustering. This enables you to tie a number of servers into a cluster, producing extremely powerful processing and a high-storage capacity environment.

Table 6.1 provides a listing and description of each of the eight RAID levels.

TABLE 6.1 Description of RAID Levels

Level	Name	Description
0	Striping without parity	Data is written across the disks in the array. RAID 0 is not a fault-tolerance method; it's actually used to speed disk access.
1	Mirroring	Two drives (such as partitions or volumes) are mirrored so that each disk in the array is an exact copy of the other disk.

continues

TABLE 6.1 Continued

Level	Name	Description
2	A proprietary disk striping method using Hamming code error detection	Data is striped across a disk set and parity information is written on a set of parity drives.
3	Disk striping with a single-parity disk	Data is written across multiple disks in a stripe with the parity information stored on a single drive that is not part of the data set.
4	Disk striping with a single-parity disk using block parity	The same as RAID 3. However, the parity information is arranged in defined data blocks.
5	Disk striping with distributed parity	Data is written across a stripe set of multiple disks, with the parity information distributed across the disk array.
6	Disk striping with distributed parity and double-parity bytes	Very similar to RAID 5. Two sets of parity blocks are created for each block of data stored on the array. It is slower than RAID 5.
7	Disk striping with a single-parity disk and disk caching	Another proprietary system similar to RAID 3 and 4. It requires additional hardware and software. This level is patented by Storage Computer Corporation.

Let's take a look at implementing software RAID levels in the Windows Server 2003 environment that build fault tolerance into the network.

Implementing RAID 1

RAID 1 requires two disks and is often referred to as mirroring (if these disks are on different drive controllers, it is called duplexing). Mirror sets can be very useful for protecting the boot and system volume of your server. You can mirror this volume using unallocated space on another dynamic disk. Then, if the primary boot drive on the server goes down, you can reconfigure the boot.ini file so that the server boots from the mirror.

The volumes used in the mirror must have an equal amount of free space, or there must be more space on the volume that will be used to create the mirror (meaning that you need another drive on the server that has an equal amount of free space or more free space than the volume that you will mirror).

To create a mirror set, follow these steps:

1. In the Disk Management Details area, right-click the dynamic volume that you want to mirror. Select Add Mirror from the shortcut menu.

2. The Add Mirror dialog box appears (see Figure 6.8). Select the drive that will supply the mirror volume.

FIGURE 6.8

Select the drive that will supply the mirror volume.

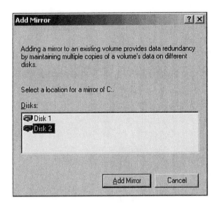

The mirror volume is created and formatted, and the data on the original drive is mirrored onto it. The two drives in the mirror set share the same drive letter and always contain the same files; data is synchronized between the original volume and the mirror partner.

Breaking a Mirror Set

You can break a mirror if it doesn't fit into your overall fault-tolerance scheme.

1. Right-click either volume in the mirror set and select Remove Mirror.

2. You are asked to specify which of the volumes in the mirror you want to remove. Select the volume that served as the mirror (not your original disk, or your server might not boot). Then click Remove Mirror.

3. You are asked to verify the process; click Yes.

Booting the Server When a Mirror Volume Fails

When you are mirroring the volume that contains the Windows Server 2003 boot and system files, and the drive containing this volume fails (meaning the drive that boots up the server), you can use a boot disk to boot the server and reconfigure the server so that it boots from the mirror drive.

6

First, you must create a book disk for the server. It is best to do this as a failsafe measure as soon as you get the server up and running; don't wait for the drive to crash before you make the disk.

To create a boot disk, follow these steps:

1. Format a disk using the Windows Explorer (or My Computer, the disk must be created on the Windows server).
2. Right-click the Drive A icon and then select Format from the shortcut menu.
3. The Formatting dialog box appears. Click Start to format the disk.

After the disk is formatted, copy the following files to the disk:

Ntldr

Ntdetect.com

Boot.ini

Bootsect.dos (if the file exists)

Ntbootdd.sys (if the file exists)

After the files have been copied to the disk, you should be able to boot the system from the disk. Now you need to edit the boot.ini file on the disk. The boot.ini file on your server determines the drive from which the system boots. It is a text file and can be edited. You can use a text editor such as Windows Notepad, or you can use the `bootcfg` command at the command prompt. Executing `bootcfg` without any switches shows you the current boot parameters for the server.

Drives on your computers are designated in the boot.ini file by their Advanced RISC Computing, or *ARC*, name. Using the ARC naming conventions, SCSI drives (with the BIOS enabled) and IDE drives are referred to as multidrives. For example, the first SCSI or IDE drive on a computer would have the following ARC name:

multi(0)disk(0)rdisk(0)partition(1)

Multi (short for multifunctional controller) gives the disk controller number (in this case, 0), which would be the first disk controller on the computer's motherboard (they start numbering at 0). Ignore the "disk" designation for multi drives (more about it in a moment). `rdisk` tells you the actual drive number (with 0 being the first drive on the controller). The partition tells you which partition the boot files are on (partitions start with 1).

SCSI drives without the BIOS enabled are designated by the ARC name scsi. So, the first BIOS-disabled SCSI drive on a system would have this ARC name:

scsi(0)disk(0)rdisk(0)partition(1)

The scsi number is the controller. The disk number tells you which drive you are looking at; for example, disk(0) would be the first BIOS-disabled SCSI drive on a particular controller, which is designated by scsi (controller number). In the case of SCSI drives, you ignore the disk number (it tells you nothing); the partition again tells you which partition the boot files are on.

When you have two drives on your system (both on the mirror set), the actual boot drive would have this ARC name:

multi(0)disk(0)rdisk(0)partition(1)

The mirror of the boot disk would be this:

multi(0)disk(0)rdisk(1)partition(1)

Notice that only the rdisk number differs.

This means that all you have to do is edit the boot.ini file on the floppy disk so that it points to the mirror drive—in this case, multi(0)disk(0)rdisk(1)partition(1).

Figure 6.9 shows the boot.ini file. Use Notepad to edit the boot.ini file that you copied to the disk.

FIGURE 6.9

The boot.ini file on the disk can be edited.

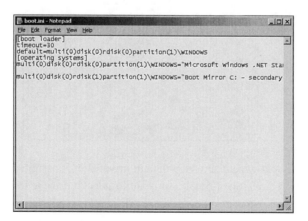

You can then use the disk to boot the server (because it points at the mirror of your boot volume). After you replace the failed drive, you can break the mirror set using the Disk Manager, install a new drive, and re-establish the mirror.

Implementing RAID 5

RAID 5, disk striping with parity, provides you with faster access time than a single-disk volume and also enables you to rebuild the stripe set if one of the disks in the set goes down. RAID 5 is an excellent choice for file servers, when you want to improve access time but also want to build some fault tolerance into the system.

RAID 5 requires at least 3 disks and can be deployed on up to 32 disks. Disks in the stripe set must have either an equal amount or a greater amount of disk space compared to the drive that you select when you initiate the creation of the stripe set.

1. In the Disk Management Details pane, right-click any dynamic disk that contains unallocated disk space. The amount of unused disk space on this disk dictates the amount of space on the other drives that are in the stripe set. Select Create Volume from the shortcut menu. The Create Volume Wizard appears.

2. Click Next to bypass the wizard's introductory screen.

3. On the next screen, click the RAID 5 option button. Then click Next to continue.

4. The next screen enables you to select the drives that will be part of the RAID 5 stripe set, as shown in Figure 6.10. Select two drives in the Available box, and add them to the Selected box. Then click Next.

FIGURE 6.10

Select the drives that will be in the stripe set.

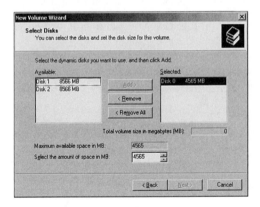

5. On the next wizard screen, a default drive letter is assigned to the stripe set. Use the drop-down drive box if you want to select a drive letter other than the default. Then click Next.

6. The next screen asks you to select the file system for the RAID 5 volume; NTFS is the default. You can also set the allocation unit size for the stripe set and give the new volume a volume name (the latter two are both options, as they were for creating a simple volume discussed earlier) .

7. Click Next. The wizard's summary screen appears. Click Finish to complete the process.

Figure 6.11 shows a RAID 5 stripe set in the Disk Management Details pane.

FIGURE 6.11

A three-drive RAID 5 stripe set.

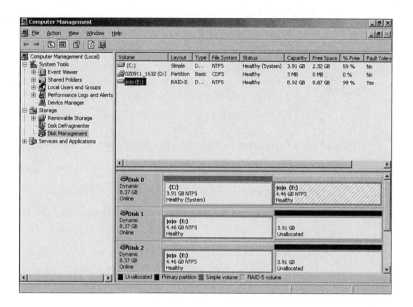

If one of the drives fails in the stripe set, you can regenerate the whole RAID 5 array. All you have to do is replace the bad drive and then use the Regenerate command in the Disk Management window to get your stripe set up and running again (right-click any of the stripe set volumes to access the Regenerate command). If you decide not to use the stripe set, you can delete it as you would a simple volume.

The Event Viewer can help to track problems with RAID sets. Sometimes RAID 5 arrays will fail because of bad disk controllers. Look for events in the system log that might provide hints on whether a drive or a controller associated with the RAID set is having problems. We discuss the Event Viewer in Hour 20, "Monitoring Server and Network Performance."

6

Working with DiskPart

Before we complete our discussion of the Disk Management tool and turn to disk properties, disk defragmentation, and strategies for backing up data, we need to take a look at a new feature provided by Windows Server 2003 called DiskPart. DiskPart, or diskpart.exe, is a command-line program that provides all the functionality of the Disk Management tool found in the Management console. As we mentioned in Hour 1, "Introducing Microsoft Windows Server 2003," Microsoft has made a concerted effort to provide more command-line functionality to server management (something that many network administrators have asked for).

 Providing a complete reference to DiskPart is beyond the scope of this book. However, we take a look at this command-line program and discuss common commands for creating such things as partitions and simple volumes.

To start DiskPart, open a command-line window and follow these steps:

1. Click Start and then Run.

2. Type **command** in the Run dialog box, and then click OK.

3. The command-line window opens. Type **diskpart** at the command line and press Enter .

A useful DiskPart command is the list volume command, which provides you with a list of volumes on the server. Note in Figure 6.12 that the volumes have been numbered 0–2. This number becomes important when you want to see details related to a particular volume.

FIGURE 6.12

The result of the list volume *command.*

Now that you know that your RAID 5 stripe set is volume number 1, you can use DiskPart to get more specific information about this volume. For example, you might want to see which physical drives are used for this stripe set.

1. First you must use the select volume 1 command to select the volume that will be the focus of your drive inquiry. Type **select volume 1** at the DiskPart command line and then press Enter. Diskpart responds with the message "Volume 1 is the selected volume."

2. Now you can use the `detail volume` command to see the disks that have been used in this stripe set. Type **detail volume** and press Enter.

Figure 6.13 shows the results of the DiskPart `select volume` and `detail volume` commands.

FIGURE 6.13

You can use DiskPart to view the disks used for a particular volume.

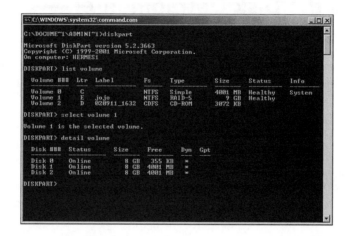

DiskPart provides commands that enable you to manage your drives and volumes as you did using the Disk Manager (discussed in a number of sections in this hour). You can convert basic disks to dynamic disks, create simple volumes, and create RAID 5 stripe sets.

For example, let's take a look at creating a simple volume using DiskPart. At the DiskPart command line type:

list disk

Then press Enter. This lists the drives on the server (numbered beginning with 0) and shows the amount of free space on the drive.

Let's say that your Disk 2 (a dynamic disk) has 4004MB of free space. To create a simple volume you would use the following command

create volume simple size=4004 drive=2

After typing the command, press Enter. DiskPart creates the volume and returns the message "DiskPart successfully created the volume." You can then use the `list volume` command to view the new volume (and the other volumes on the server).

DiskPart is not just a command-line alternative to the Disk Manager; it also enables administrators to create scripts that automatically perform disk- and volume-related

6

commands. The Windows Server 2003 Help and Support system provides an overview of many of the DiskPart commands and can help you get started with this command-line utility.

Using the Disk Defragmenter

Another way to keep your drives operating optimally is to use the Disk Defragmenter. The Disk Defragmenter moves fragmented files and folders to one location on the drive. This cleans up the drive and increases drive performance. Consolidating the folders and files on the drive also decreases the likelihood that new files will be written to the free space on the drive becoming fragmented.

The Disk Defragmenter can defragment FAT, FAT32, and NTFS volumes. The time that it takes to defragment a particular volume depends on the size of the volume, the number of files it contains, and the degree to which the drive is fragmented.

Select the Start menu, point at All Programs, and then point at Accessories. On the Accessories menu, point at System tools and then select Disk Defragmenter. The Disk Defragmenter window opens (see Figure 6.14).

FIGURE 6.14

The Disk Defragmenter enables you to defragment drive volumes.

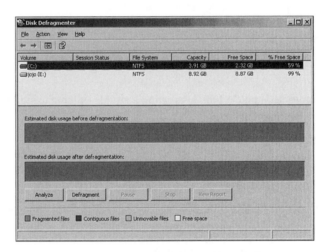

In many cases, you might want to analyze a particular volume to see if it actually needs defragmentation. To analyze a drive, select the drive letter and then click Analyze. A box appears when the analysis is complete, letting you know whether the drive needs to be defragmented.

To defragment the drive after the analysis, click the Defragment button in the Analysis Complete dialog box. A Defragmentation display appears in the Disk Defragmenter window. These windows use a color-coded scheme shown at the bottom of the application window, to show you the fragmented files, contiguous files, and free space as the defragmentation process proceeds.

When the process is complete, the Disk Defragmenter dialog box appears. To view a report associated with the defragmentation, click the View Report button as seen in Figure 6.14. Figure 6.15 shows you the report. After viewing the report, click the Close button (you can also print the report). You can then close the Disk Defragmenter or analyze or defragment another volume.

FIGURE 6.15

You can view or print a report generated by the Disk Defragmenter.

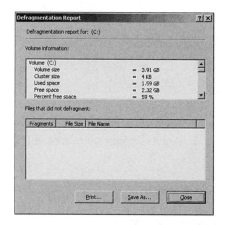

 Windows Server also provides a defrag command-line utility. Type `defrag` followed by the drive letter to be defragmented.

Viewing Drive Properties

6

You can access the detailed properties of any of the volumes on your server in the Disk Management window, in the My Computer window (where the volumes are represented as drives with drive letters), or through Windows Explorer.

Open any of these tools (Disk Management, My Computer, or Windows Explorer) and right-click a particular drive letter. Select Properties from the shortcut menu.

The Properties dialog box provides information such as the file system used on the volume, the free and used space, and the capacity of the volume (see Figure 6.16).

FIGURE **6.16**

The Properties dialog box provides specific information on a selected volume.

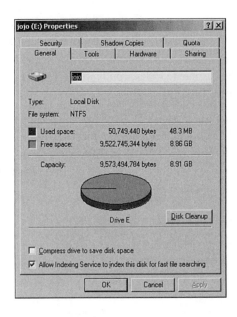

The Properties dialog box also contains a number of tabs that give you access to drive tools, hardware information, disk quota settings (discussed in Hour 12), and local security options.

Drive-sharing parameters are also found on the Properties dialog box (the Sharing tab), as is the new Windows Server 2003 Shadow Copy feature. Both of these features are discussed in Hour 12.

Let's take a look at the Tools tab and the options it provides. Figure 6.17 shows the Tools tab.

One of the options on the Tools tab of the Properties dialog box is Error-checking, a utility that checks the volume for any errors. To start the process, click the Check Now button.

The Check Disk dialog box opens, providing two check box options:

- Automatically Fix File System Errors
- Scan and Attempt Recovery of Bad Sectors

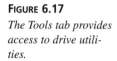

FIGURE 6.17

The Tools tab provides access to drive utilities.

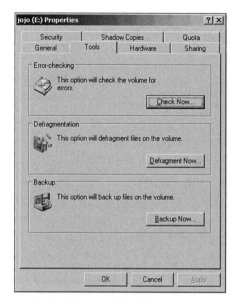

You can select either option (or both) and then click Start. When the scanning of the volume is complete, the Disk Check Complete dialog box appears. Click OK to close it.

The Tools tab also provides access to the Disk Defragmenter (discussed in the previous section) and the Backup utility. We discuss backups in the next section.

Planning Your Server Backups

The best way to protect data on the network and important configuration files is to perform scheduled backups on mission-critical servers. Installing a backup device such as an internal or external tape backup drive on your domain controller or a file server not only enables you to back up the registry on a particular server (backing up the registry cannot be done over the network), but it also does not add to network traffic by moving the backup files over the network medium.

Backup devices are available from a number of manufacturers, as is specialized backup software. In this section, we take a look at server backup using the Windows Server 2003 Backup utility.

6

A large number of backup devices using different media types are available—everything from DAT tape to 8mm tape to CD-RW jukeboxes. No matter what type of device you choose, you must make sure that the device is listed on the Windows Server 2003 compatibility list, available at www.microsoft.com.

Although the media and backup software that you use for your backups should be sufficient for your needs, another important aspect of backing up data is to have a backup plan. Your backup plan must revolve around the data that must be backed up and how often you decide to back up that particular information.

Before determining your backup plan, some basic issues related to backups should be discussed, including the different types of backups that can be made. First, Windows uses file markers (or tags) to specify whether a file has been backed up.

When you create a new file, one of the file's attributes is that the file has not been backed up since changes were made to it last (the changes here are its creation).

When you back up the file, the "never been backed up" tag is removed. In effect, this marks the file as having been backed up. Then when you make new changes to the file, the file is again marked as having not been backed up since recent changes were made. Markers are important because you can use them to your advantage during the backup process.

The fact that files are tagged based on their backup status enables you to use three different types of backups:

- **Normal**—A *normal backup* backs up all the files and folders you select (no matter how the files are currently marked). The files' attributes are changed to denote that they have been backed up. Windows Server 2003 Backup also provides a daily backup that operates like a normal backup: It backs up all the files, no matter what the marker attribute says.

- **Differential**—A *differential backup* backs up files that have been marked as having changed since their last backup. However, the differential backup does not change the marker attribute indicating that the file has been backed up. It leaves the marker alone, so the file will still read as if it has not been backed up.

- **Incremental**—An *incremental backup* backs up only the files that have been changed since the last backup (using the marker attribute on the files to identify those that have been modified). The incremental backup changes the archive marker to identify that the file has been backed up.

So, a possible strategy for a backup plan would be to do a normal backup the first time you run a backup on the server. You can then run an incremental backup on a daily basis to back up any changes made to the files. This speeds up the daily backup process because you are backing up only files that have been modified since the previous backup. Differential backups can be run once a week, to back up all the data that changed since the last differential backup (giving you a week's worth of changes).

Using the backup plan discussed, if the server goes down on Tuesday, you have to restore only the differential backup that you ran on Friday and the incremental backup that you ran on Monday evening. This should restore all the files to the state they were in before the crash.

 You should also have a backup plan for keeping a copy of backup tapes or other media offsite. This enables you to restore the company data even if a major disaster such as a fire hits the business.

Backing Up Files

To start the Windows Server 2003 Backup utility, follow these steps:

1. Click the Start menu, point at All Programs, point at Accessories, and then point at System Tools. To launch the application, click Backup.

2. The Backup or Restore Wizard appears. Click Next to bypass the introductory screen.

3. The Next screen provides two options: Backup Files and Settings, and Restore Files and Settings. Select Backup Files and Settings to continue with the backup process. Then click Next.

4. The next screen gives you the option of backing up the entire server or choosing the folders and files to back up. To back up the entire server, select the All Information on This Computer option. To select specific items to back up, select Let Me Choose What to Back Up. Click Next to continue.

5. If you choose the option Let Me Choose What to Back Up, the next screen (see Figure 6.18) provides a tree view of your computer contents. Double-click an area of the computer in the left pane to see its contents in the right pane. To select a folder or files to back up, place a check mark in the box to the left of the folder or filename. Click Next after making your selection.

6

FIGURE **6.18**

*You can select the files
to back up.*

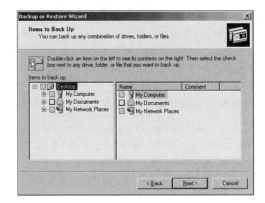

6. The next screen (which you see if you selected to back up the entire server) enables you to select the backup device and type a name for the backup. Backup devices attached to the server are listed in the Choose a Place to Save Your Backup drop-down list. Or, you can use the Browse button to specify another target location for the backup. Click Next to continue.

7. A summary screen appears. Before you click Finish, however, you might want to set the type of backup (Normal is the default). Click the Advanced button. The Type of Backup screen appears.

8. Use the Backup Type drop-down list, and select the type of backup. After making your choice, click Next. The next screen enables you to specify that the data should be verified after the backup. There is also a check box that disables the volume shadow copy feature (we discuss shadow copy in Hour 12). Check the Verify After Backup check box if you want to have the data verified. Then click Next.

9. The next screen (see Figure 6.19) enables you to append the current backup to the previous backups on your backup drive, or you can erase and replace the previous backups. Select the appropriate check box and then click Next to continue.

10. The next screen enables you to back up immediately or set a specific start date for the backup. If you select to specify a start date, you can use the Set Schedule button to specify a particular day and time. After selecting the When to Backup options, click Next. The summary screen appears. Click Finish to run the backup (or to close the wizard, in the case of a scheduled backup).

If you run the backup immediately, the Backup Progress dialog box appears and provides you with details related to the in-progress backup. When the backup is complete, the Backup Progress dialog box notifies you. It provides details of the backup and also provides a Report button that you can click to view a report associated with the backup.

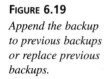

FIGURE 6.19

Append the backup to previous backups or replace previous backups.

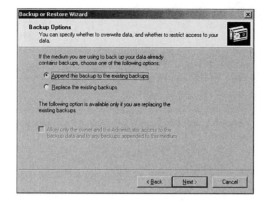

Restoring Files

The flip side of backing up data is restoring data. Although the entire backup process might seem to border a little on paranoia, regular backups are really the only complete way to protect valuable information. If a server fails or a user with specific file permissions inadvertently destroys important data, your backup can quickly restore the information to the network.

The restore process is very similar to the backup process. The Backup or Restore Wizard is used to specify the files that should be restored and the location that they should be restored to.

1. Start the Backup utility by clicking the Start menu, pointing at All Programs, pointing at Accessories, and then pointing at System Tools. To launch the application, click Backup. Click Next to move past the opening wizard screen.

2. On the next screen, select the Restore Files and Setting option button. Then click Next.

3. Select the drive, folders, or files that should be restored (see Figure 6.20). Double-click any of the drives or folders to view their contents. Then place a check mark next to the items that you want to restore. Click Next when you are ready to continue.

4. A summary screen for the restore appears. When you are ready to restore the data, click Finish. The Restore Progress dialog box appears and keeps you apprised of the restore status. When the restore is complete, you can view a report related to the restore by clicking Report.

6

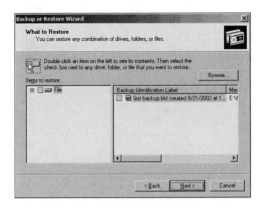

FIGURE 6.20

Select the data to be restored.

Summary

In this hour, you learned how to manage server drives and create partitions and volumes. Windows Server 2003 provides two tools for configuring and managing your server drives: the Disk Management tool (also known as the Disk Manager) and DiskPart, a new command-line utility. Windows Server 2003 supports two drive types: basic and dynamic. A basic disk follows the legacy partitioning and logical drive scheme that originated with MS-DOS. Dynamic drives can be divided into any number of volumes and can be included in RAID implementations such as mirror sets and RAID 5 arrays. All drives are basic when you first install the server software; however, you can convert your basic drives to dynamic drives at any time.

Both the Disk Manager and DiskPart use Windows Server 2003's new Virtual Disk Service. This enables you to use these tools (as the appropriate APIs are built) to manage any drive types, no matter who the manufacturer is.

Disk Manager, which is found in the Windows Management console, can be used to create partitions, format basic disks, and create volumes and RAID arrays on dynamic disks. A RAID 1 array is also known as a mirror set. RAID 5 requires three separate drives with the same amount of disk space to create a disk stripe set.

DiskPart is a new command-line utility that enables you to do all the disk and volume manipulations provided by the Disk Manager. DiskPart also provides advanced scripting features that can be used by the administrator to automate certain drive-related tasks.

RAID, or Redundant Array of Independent Disks, enables you to build redundancy and fault tolerance into your servers. RAID 1 is a mirror set, in which two drives mirror each other, supplying a complete copy of a particular drive. When the files change on one drive in the mirror set, they are also changed in the other mirror drive.

RAID 5 enables you to strip data across three or more drives. This not only speeds up write and access time to the drive set, but because parity data is collected on the array, the data on a stripe set drive that fails can be rebuilt from the information held on the other drives.

Another way to build fault tolerance into your network is to regularly back up your server drives. Windows Server 2003 provides a Backup utility that can be used to back up and restore drives, folders, and files. It is important to develop a backup plan that will protect your data in any situation.

Q&A

Q What utility is provided by Windows Server 2003 for managing disk drives, partitions, and volumes?

A The Disk Manager provides all the tools for formatting, creating, and managing drive volumes and partitions. Disk Manager functionality can also be accessed using DiskPart at the command line.

Q What is the difference between a basic and a dynamic drive in the Windows Server 2003 network operating system environment?

A A basic disk embraces the MS-DOS disk structure; a basic disk can be divided into partitions (a maximum of four) with extended partitions that hold logical drives. Dynamic disks consist of a single partition that can be divided into any number of volumes. Dynamic disks also support Windows Server 2003 RAID implementations.

Q What is RAID?

A Redundant Array of Independent Disks (RAID) is a strategy for building fault tolerance into your file servers. RAID enable you to combine one or more volumes on separate drives so that they are accessed by a single drive letter. Windows Server 2003 enables you to configure RAID 1 (a mirror set) and RAID 5 (disk striping with parity).

Q What file formats can be defragmented by the Disk Defragmenter?

A The Windows Server 2003 Disk Defragmenter can defragment FAT, FAT32, and NTFS volumes.

Q What is the most foolproof strategy for protecting data on the network?

A Regular backups of network data provide the best method of protecting you from data loss.

6

PART II

Network Users, Resources, and Special Server Roles

Hour

HOUR 7

Working with Network Protocols

In this hour, we take a look at the ins and outs of local area network (LAN) protocols. We look at the different protocol stack possibilities, such as TCP/IP and IPX/SPX. Because the IP protocol and addressing scheme is the default for Windows Server 2003 and is used by most computers on networks worldwide, much of our discussion centers on TCP/IP. We also look at the basics of IP subnetting (which provide for a better understanding of the material in Hour 18, "Routing and Remote Access"). Our discussion also includes configuring protocols on your Windows server and the OSI model, which is the conceptual model for network communication.

In this hour, the following topics are covered:

- Working with LAN protocols
- Understanding the OSI model
- Using NWlink

- Understanding the TCP/IP protocol stack
- Understanding IP subnetting
- Configuring TCP/IP

Understanding Network Protocols

LAN protocols provide the rules for how computers communicate on a network. Most network protocols are not actually single protocols, but a stack of specialized protocols that work together. Some of these member protocols in the stack are responsible for the user interface and network connections necessary to move the data. Other member protocols in a stack actually address the data (to get it to the right destination). Still others provide the mechanism for transporting the data to and from places on the network.

A number of different protocol stacks, such as TCP/IP and SPX/IPX, exist. To understand how the different protocols in the stack work (moving data through different formats as it is sent from sending computer to receiving computer), a conceptual model called the OSI model was developed. Let's take a brief look at how this model works.

Understanding the OSI Model

In the late 1970s, the International Standards Organization (ISO) began to develop a conceptual model for networking called the Open Systems Interconnect Reference Model. This is now commonly abbreviated as the OSI model. In 1983, the model became the international standard for network communications, providing a conceptual framework that helps explain how data gets from one place to another on a network.

The OSI model describes network communication as a series of seven layers; each layer is responsible for a different part of the overall process of moving data. This framework of a layered stack, while conceptual, can then be used to understand how actual protocol stacks work when data moves from a sending computer to a receiving computer. So, don't think of the model as a series of layers, but rather as a stack of protocols, with each protocol handing off the data to the next protocol in the stack.

Table 7.1 provides a list of the OSI model layers from the top of the stack to the bottom, with a brief description of each layer. The layers are actually numbered from bottom to top and are often referred to by the layer number (in discussions related to the OSI model). Data moves from the sending computer down the OSI model stack. Then, when it is received by the receiving computer as a bit stream, the data moves back up the model until it is in a form that can be understood by the receiving user (such as an email message).

TABLE 7.1 The OSI Layers

Layer Number	Layer	Function
7	Application	Provides the interface and services that support user applications and provides general access to the network.
6	Presentation	The translator of the OSI model. Responsible for the conversion of data into a generic format and the coding of data using various encryption methods.
5	Session	Establishes and maintains the communication link between communicating computers (sending and receiving).
4	Transport	Responsible for end-to-end data transmission, flow control, error checking, and recovery.
3	Network	Provides the logical addressing system that is used to route data from one node to another, meaning that it is responsible for path determination.
2	Data Link	Responsible for framing of data packets and the data movement across the physical link between two nodes.
1	Physical	Manages the process of sending and receiving bits over the physical network media (the wire and other physical devices) .

Real-world protocols are often mapped to the OSI model. For example, the protocols that make up the TCP/IP protocol would be mapped to the layers of the OSI model (this mapping is provided later in the chapter). This enables you to understand the general purpose of each protocol in the TCP/IP stack.

The TCP/IP protocol suite was actually developed before the OSI model was created. In fact, a model known as the Department of Defense (DOD) model was used in the development of TCP/IP. Despite these facts, the OSI model is still used today to explain how the different protocols in the TCP/IP stack function in the sending and receiving of data on a network.

Selecting Protocols for Your Windows Network

7

Windows Server 2003 provides two core LAN protocols: TCP/IP (and TCP/IP V6) and NWlink (Microsoft's implementation of Novell's IPX/SPX stack). Both of these LAN protocols are routable and can be used on small or large subnetted networks.

If you have used Microsoft networking software for a number of years, you are probably wondering what happened to NetBEUI. NetBEUI is no longer a supported protocol on the latest versions of the desktop and server operating systems. (This began with the launch of Windows XP. NetBEUI is also not a supported protocol on Windows Server 2003.) NetBEUI is not a routable protocol, and it also had limitations related to the number of addressable devices. It is certainly not a transport protocol suitable for enterprise-wide networking since it is not scalable.

> AppleTalk is still supported by Windows Server 2003 when communication is required with PCs running the MAC OS and using AppleTalk instead of TCP/IP as their transport protocol.

Let's take a closer look at NWlink (IPX/SPX) and TCP/IP.

Working with NWlink (IPX/SPX)

IPX/SPX (which stands for Internetwork Packet Exchange/Sequenced Packet Exchange) is a network protocol stack developed by Novell for use on networks running the Novell NetWare network operating system. NWlink is Microsoft's implementation of IPX/SPX, and it provides you with the capability to connect Windows clients and servers to network resources located on NetWare networks. It can also be used to connect Windows networks that formally have used NetBEUI and do not require the TCP/IP stack, such as a Windows workgroup.

IPX/SPX, like TCP/IP, is actually a stack of protocols that perform different functions in the overall network communication process. Figure 7.1 shows a mapping of IPX/SPX stack protocols to the OSI conceptual model. Table 7.2 provides definitions of some of the more important protocols in the IPX/SPX stack.

TABLE 7.2   IPX/SPX Protocol Stack Members

Protocol	Job
NCP	The NetWare Core Protocol handles network functions at the application, presentation, and session layers. It is responsible for providing the connection between clients and servers. It also handles packet creation when the sending of data is initiated by a computer on the network.
SAP	The Service Advertising Protocol is used by NetWare servers to announce the addresses of file and print servers on the network, as well as other application services. This is how NetWare clients know how to find network resources.
SPX	The Sequenced Packet Exchange protocol is a connection-oriented protocol that operates at the transport layer of the OSI model.
IPX	The Internetwork Packet Exchange protocol is a connectionless transport protocol that handles the addressing of nodes on an IPX/SPX network.

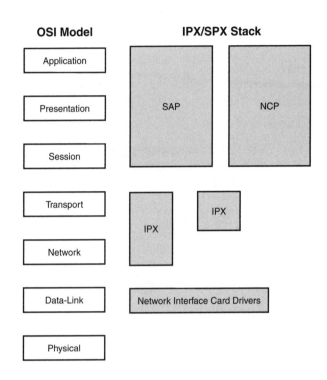

FIGURE 7.1

The IPX/SPX stack mapped to the OSI model.

The logical addressing system used by IPX/SPX is created by the first NetWare server that is installed on the network. It generates a network number. This network number, along with the MAC hardware address of a computer (the address on its NIC card), determines the network address for the computer. When you view IPX/SPX packets using a packet sniffer or other network-monitoring protocol, you will find that these 80-bit addresses are expressed as a hexadecimal number.

NWlink (IPX/SPX) is a supported protocol on Windows Server 2003 because many networks still support legacy NetWare file servers or new implements of NetWare on the enterprise network. NWlink allows connectivity between Windows servers and clients to resources on IPX/SPX networks. NWlink also provides a method for connecting legacy Microsoft computers because it still contains the NWlink/NetBIOS component.

7

Installing NWlink

To install NWlink on your Windows server, follow these steps:

1. Select the Start menu, point at the Control Panel, and then right-click Network Connections and select Open. The Network Connections window opens (see Figure 7.2).

FIGURE 7.2

The Network Connections window.

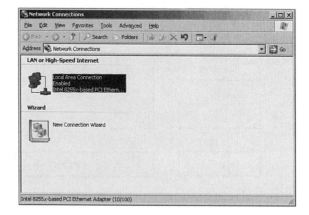

2. Right-click the local area network connection that you want to configure with NWlink, and select Properties on the shortcut menu. The Local Area Connection Properties dialog box opens (see Figure 7.3).

FIGURE 7.3

The Local Area Connection Properties dialog box is used to add clients and proto-cols to the network configuration of the server.

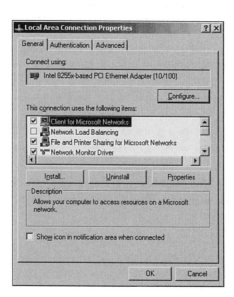

3. By default, the Client for Microsoft Networks is installed, as is the File and Print Sharing for Microsoft Networks service. (TCP/IP is also installed by default.) To add NWlink to the configuration, click the Install button.

4. The Select Network Component Type dialog box opens. Select Protocol and then click Add. The Select Network Protocol dialog box appears (see Figure 7.4).

FIGURE 7.4

Select the protocol to be installed.

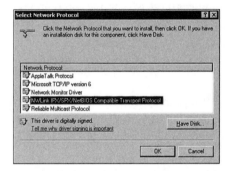

5. Select the NWlink IPX/SPX/NetBIOS Compatible Transport Protocol. Then click OK. The NWlink protocol is added to the Local Area Connection Properties dialog box.

After you have installed NWlink on the server, you should also configure options related to the protocol. Select NWlink IPXS/SPX in the Local Area Connection Properties dialog box, and then select Properties.

Two settings can be configured for NWlink: the Internal network number and the frame type (both are optional, however):

- **Internal network number**—This number is used to uniquely identify all the connections on a server (such as a server with multiple network cards) that provide NetWare services that rely on the SAP Agent (SAP is the Service Advertisement Protocol and is used to advertise resources on a network running IPX/SPX). The Internal network number takes the form of an eight-digit hexadecimal number. If you are configuring only one server for NWlink, the default of 00000000 will work.

- **Frame type**—Novell NetWare has supported different Ethernet frame types in various versions of NetWare. This can lead to compatibility problems if different frame types are present on the network (when you are integrating NetWare servers with a Windows domain). By default, the frame type is detected automatically. If you want to configure the frame types manually (when multiple frame types are present), select the Manual Frame Type Detection option button and then use the Add button to add the various frame types.

7

Understanding TCP/IP

The TCP/IP protocol suite is often referred to as the Internet protocol suite because it was created during the development of the Internet. As it later became integrated into all UNIX servers, TCP/IP entered wide use with large networks (often referred to as enterprise networks). TCP/IP's scalability from small to large networks and the current heavy interest in connecting LANs to the Internet has enabled TCP/IP to evolve into the most widely used network protocol today. TCP/IP is installed by default on your server running Windows Server 2003. TCP/IP is actually required by the Active Directory and the access protocols that are used to access Active Directory information.

Figure 7.5 shows the TCP/IP stack mapped to the OSI model (it doesn't map exactly to the seven layers, but it does provide some insight into what the TCP/IP protocols do). The list that follows describes a number of the protocols in the TCP/IP stack.

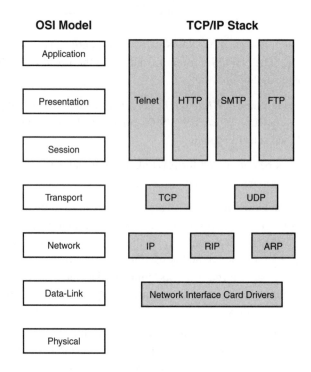

Figure 7.5

The TCP/IP protocol mapped to the OSI model.

- **File Transfer Protocol (FTP)**—FTP provides a method for transferring files between computers.

- **Telnet**—With Telnet, users can log on to remote systems across a network.

- **Simple Mail Transport Protocol (SMTP)**—SMTP defines the standard for all email sent across the Internet.

- **Simple Network Management Protocol (SNMP)**—SNMP provides the ability to collect network information. SNMP uses agents that collect data on network performance. SNMP is discussed in more detail later in the chapter.

- **Transmission Control Protocol (TCP)**—TCP is the primary transport-layer protocol used within TCP/IP. It provides a reliable, connection-oriented data transportation service in conjunction with IP (defined in the following section). When establishing a connection, TCP uses a port address to determine which connection a packet is destined for. TCP also provides the capability to fragment messages and reassemble packets through sequencing.

- **User Datagram Protocol (UDP)**—UDP provides a connectionless transportation service on top of IP.

- **Internet Protocol (IP)**—All network addressing and routing in TCP/IP network is handled by IP. IP provides a connectionless datagram service for fast but unreliable communication between network nodes.

- **Address Resolution Protocol (ARP)**—ARP is a network-layer protocol that maps hardware addresses to IP addresses for delivery of packets on the local network segment.

- **Internet Control Message Protocol (ICMP)**—ICMP is a messaging service and management protocol for IP. ICMP messages are actually carried as IP datagrams. ICMP messages are used for a variety of purposes. The ping, for example, uses ICMP echo packets.

- **Routing Information Protocol (RIP)**—RIP is a distance-vector routing protocol that determines the shortest path between two locations by counting the number of *hops* that a packet has to make. It is similar but not identical to the RIP protocol used in IPX/SPX networks.

- **Open Shortest Path First (OSPF)**—OSPF is a newer link-state routing protocol that is more efficient and needs less overhead than RIP.

7

IP Addressing

Within TCP/IP networks, each computer is assigned a 32-bit *IP address* that resembles the following:

192.168.24.123

The 32-bit address is divided into four groups of eight bits, called octets, with each octet written as a decimal number from 0 to 255 separated by a period (referred to as a *dot*). Part of the IP address defines the *network ID* of your network (which is assigned to you when you purchase a range of public IP addresses); the remainder of the address provides the *host ID* of the individual computer. For instance, 24.123 in the preceding address might identify a specific computer within the TCP/IP network that has the address 192.168. Note that within TCP/IP networking, the term *host* is used to refer to a computer on the network.

Three address classes are used for IP addressing:

- Class A is used for very large networks. The default mask is 255.0.0.0. Class A networks range from 1.0.0.0 through 126.0.0.0. Class A networks provide 16,777,214 host addresses. This is because the second, third, and fourth octets are available for host addressing. ARPANET is an example of a Class A network. Class A addresses (that are not submitted) provide network and host information in the format network.host.host.host.

- Class B is used for networks that still need a lot of node addresses, such as a large company or institution. Class B ranges from 128.0.0.0 to 191.0.0.0. The default subnet mask is 255.255.0.0. There are 16,384 Class B network addresses, with each Class B supplying 65,534 host addresses. The third and fourth octets are available for host addressing. Class B addresses provide network and host information in the format network.network.host.host.

- Class C is used for small networks. There are 2,097,152 Class C networks. Class C addresses range from 192.0.0.0 to 223.0.0.0. The default subnet mask is 255.255.255.0. Class C networks provide 254 host addresses per network. This is because only the fourth octet is reserved for host addressing. Class C addresses provide the network and host information in the format network.network.network.host.

- Two other classes of IP addresses should also be mentioned: Class D and Class E. Class D network addresses are used by multicast groups receiving data from a particular application or server service. An example of a multicast use of Class D addresses is Microsoft NetShow, which can broadcast the same content to a group of users at one time. Class E addresses belong to an experimental class, which is not used for public IP addressing.

> The IP addressing scheme discussed in this section is for IP Version 4. A new version of IP, IP Version 6, is just on the horizon of implementation (Windows Server 2003 provides support for IPv6 now) and provides a greater number of IP addresses. IPv6 is not in general use as of the writing of this book. It is discussed briefly at the end of this chapter.

Understanding what part of the IP address refers to the network and what part refers to the host is a very important aspect of working with IP addresses. And you can't really determine either without seeing the subnet mask that goes with the IP address.

Subnet masks are also represented as four dotted-decimal octets. There is a standard subnet mask for each of the IP address classes. For example, the IP address 10.1.1.1 (a Class A address) would have the standard Class A subnet mask of 255.0.0.0.

This combination of the IP address and subnet mask provides you with the ability to determine what portion of the address is the network address and which portion provides the host address. Because the 255 (all ones in binary) "ands" out the network portion of the address, only the first octet of the address 10.1.1.1 specifies the network address (10.0.0.0). The second, third, and fourth octets provide the host addressing (0.1.1.1). Table 7.3 provides the default subnet masks for Class A, B, and C networks.

TABLE 7.3   Typical Subnet Masks

Subnet Mask	IP Address Class
255.0.0.0	Class A
255.255.0.0	Class B
255.255.255.0	Class C

Understanding IP Subnetting

IP subnetting is as much art as it is math. When you subnet a range of IP addresses, you are dividing the available addresses into logical subunits. Subnetting enables you to place subnets or logical groupings (in terms of IP addresses) of computers on different router interfaces. This enables you to connect disparate groups of users (at different worksites) into one large IP network.

Subnetting is a two-part process. First, you must determine the subnet mask for the network (it will be different than the default subnet masks shown in Table 7.3). Then you must compute the range of IP addresses that will be in each subnet. One way to subnet is to refer to subnetting charts. Tables 7.4, 7.5, and 7.6 show Class A, Class B, and Class C subnetting, respectively.

7

TABLE 7.4   Class A Subnetting

Bits Used	Subnet Mask	# of Subnets	Hosts/Subnet
2	255.192.0.0	2	4,194,302
3	255.224.0.0	6	2,097,150
4	255.240.0.0	14	1,048,574
5	255.248.0.0	30	524,286
6	255.252.0.0	62	262,142
7	255.254.0.0	126	131,070
8	255.255.0.0	254	65,534

TABLE 7.5   Class B Subnetting

Bits Used	Subnet Mask	# of Subnets	Hosts/Subnet
2	255.255.192.0	2	16,382
3	255.255.224.0	6	8,190
4	255.255.240.0	14	4,094
5	255.255.248.0	30	2,046
6	255.255.252.0	62	1,022
7	255.255.254.0	126	510
8	255.255.255.0	254	254

TABLE 7.6   Class C Subnetting

Bits Used	Subnet Mask	# of Subnets	Hosts/Subnet
2	255.255.255.192	2	62
3	255.255.255.224	6	30
4	255.255.255.240	14	14
5	255.255.255.248	30	6
6	255.255.255.252	62	2

Converting Decimal to Binary

Now the question is, what do these charts mean? IP addresses are actually seen by the computers on the network as a bit stream (a collection of ones and zeros). The address 130.1.16.1 would be represented in binary as this:

10000010 00000001 00010000 00000001

Notice that the bits have been divided into four groups of eight, or octets, just as the dotted-decimal version of the address was (130.1.16.1).

This is how you convert dotted-decimal numbers to binary (bits). Each octet has 8 bits. The decimal value of the bits in an octet, from left to right, is as follows:

128 64 32 16 8 4 2 1

So, the decimal number 130 in the first octet of our address is determined by 128 + 2. This means that the first bit (the 128 bit) and the seventh bit (the 2 bit) are both turned on (they are represented by ones in the binary format). To convert the decimal to the binary, you mark the bits that are turned on with ones and the rest with zeros. You get 10000010 (which is what you saw previously in the binary format of the IP address).

Now about subnetting: Because the network ID portion of IP addresses is fixed (it is provided by your Internet service provider or another provider of IP address ranges), you will actually borrow some bits from the leftmost portion of the host ID of the address to create subnets (remember, you can't mess with the network ID portion of the IP address because it is assigned to you). Let's walk through an example of subnetting.

Let's say that you want to divide the Class B network of 191.1.0.0 (this is the network address you were assigned by your IP address provider) into 30 subnets.

You can't touch the first or second octets because they have been assigned. But you can borrow bits starting from the leftmost portion of the third octet. So, you have to determine how may bits you must borrow from the third octet to create 30 subnets. The number of bits that you borrow will determine the new subnet mask for your network (which lets all devices on the network know that the network has been divided into 30 logical subnets). The bits you borrow will also help you determine the range of IP addresses that will be in each subnet.

Borrowing Bits

First you borrow the bits; you use the decimal values of the bits in the third octet to do this. You want to come up with 30 subnets. The formula that you use to do this is the sum of lower-order bits −1.

Look at the bit values again (shown next). The lower-order bits are the ones on the right (1, 2, 4, and so on). So, you add 1 + 2 + 4 + 8 + 16, which equals 31. Then you subtract 1. You get 30. So, you used the 1, 2, 4, 8, and 16 bits; you borrowed 5 bits.

128 64 32 16 8 4 2 1 < low-order bits

7

You have to subtract the 1 because you cannot use subnet 0, which is what you derive when you steal only the first lower-order bit (the 1).

The next thing you need to do is determine the subnet mask for the subnetted network. The bits on the left of the decimal values (128, 64, 32, 16, and so on) are referred to as the higher-order bits. You now add the first 5 higher-order bits:

High-order bits> 128 64 32 16 8 4 2 1

$128 + 64 + 32 + 16 + 8 = 248$

The default subnet mask for a Class B network is 255.255.0.0.

You borrowed 5 bits from the third octet, so your new subnet mask is 255.255.248.0. Check Table 7.5; when you borrow 5 bits from a Class B network, you get the subnet mask that you derived.

Computing the number of host addresses available per subnet is very straightforward. The formula you use is $2^x - 2$, where X is the number of bits left for host addresses after bits have been borrowed for subnetting.

Computing the Host Addresses in a Subnet

You have 30 subnets (remember, that's what you decided to divide the IP address range into at the outset of this problem). Now you can find out how many addresses you will get for each of the 30 subnets. Normally, on a Class B network two octets are reserved for host addresses. The network address in this case is 191.1.0.0, so originally two full octets (the third and fourth) were available for node addresses. This was 16 bits total (8 bits from each octet). Then you borrowed 5 bits from the third octet, so 16–5 = 11. You have 11 bits left for node addresses after borrowing 5 bits to create the 30 subnets.

Use the formula $2^x - 2$. You can see that $2^{11} - 2$ is 2,048–2, which equals 2,046 (just as Table 7.3 shows). You get 2,046 addresses per subnet.

Computing Host Ranges

You now have 30 subnets with 2,046 addresses each. Next you need to determine the starting and ending IP addresses for each subnet. This is rather easy, compared to what you've done so far. What was the lowest of the high-order bits used to create the new subnet mask for the subnetted network? You used 128, 64, 32, 16, and 8. The lowest of the high-order bits is 8, which becomes the increment for your subnet address ranges.

The network address is 191.1.0.0, so the first subnet would start with the address 191.1.8.1 (you can't have a zero in the last position of the address). This subnet would end with 191.1.15.254 (you can't end an address with 255 in the last octet).

Table 7.7 shows the range of addresses for the first 5 subnets (of 30) using the network address of 191.1.0.0.

TABLE 7.7 Address Ranges for First Six Subnets

Subnet	Address Range
1	191.1.8.1 to 191.1.15.254
2	191.1.16.1 to 191.1.23.254
3	191.1.24.1 to 191.1.31.254
4	191.1.32.1 to 191.1.39.254
5	191.1.40.1 to 191.1.47.254

Notice that you can easily come up with the start of each subnet range by adding 8 to the third octet. The end of range addresses are just one less (in the third octet) than the start of the next subnet. You could easily continue this table to show all 30 subnets.

Class A and C network addresses can be subnetted in a like manner. Just remember that Class A networks provide you three octets of node address space (the second, third, and fourth), whereas a Class C network address supplies only one octet (the fourth).

> Another way to do subnetting calculations is to download a subnet calculator on the Web. Several free ones can be found by doing a search for subnet calculator in any search engine. You can then tell the calculator how many subnets you want for a specific network address, and it will give the subnet mask and the range of addresses for each subnet. It's easy, but it requires that you at least understand what subnetting is so that you know what the calculator is telling you.

Configuring TCP/IP

TCP/IP is installed by default on your Windows server (if it has been removed, you can install it via the Network Connection Properties dialog box, as discussed for NWlink). Configuring TCP/IP settings in the TCP/IP Properties box is very straightforward—much more straightforward than subnetting.

7

Open the Local Area Connection Properties dialog box for your server. Click the Internet Protocol (TCP/IP) and then select Properties. The Internet Protocol (TCP/IP) Properties dialog box opens (see Figure 7.6).

FIGURE 7.6

Supply the IP address and the Subnet mask for the server.

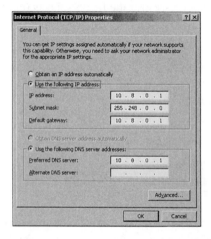

To set a static IP address for the server, type the IP address, the subnet mask, the default gateway, and the preferred DNS server (and the secondary DNS server, if available).

You can also set additional IP settings by clicking the Advanced button on the Properties dialog box. This opens the Advanced TCP/IP Settings dialog box (see Figure 7.7).

FIGURE 7.7

The Advanced TCP/IP Settings dialog box.

This dialog box includes the following tabs:

- **IP Settings**—Enables you to add, edit, or remove IP addresses and default gateways. (Yes, you can assign multiple IP addresses to a single network adapter.)

- **DNS**—Enables you to add multiple DNS servers to the TCP/IP configuration and register this computer with the DNS server.

- **WINS**—Enables you to specify WINS servers (also known as NetBIOS name servers) to be included in the TCP/IP configuration.

After making changes to the Advanced TCP/IP Settings, click OK to close the dialog box. You can also close the Internet Protocol (TCP/IP) Properties dialog box and the Local Area Connection Properties dialog box.

Checking IP Configurations and Server Connectivity

Windows Server 2003 provides a set of tools that can help you check IP configurations and connectivity. For example, ipconfig can be used to both check and renew the IP configuration on a Windows server. ping is used to check a computer's connection to any device on a network that is configured with an IP address.

Commands such as ipconfig and ping are executed at the command prompt. To open a command prompt, select Start and then select Command prompt.

Using `ipconfig`

You can check IP configurations on your Windows Server 2003 from the command line using the ipconfig command. ipconfig/all shows the information for all network interfaces on the server and provides more details than ipconfig. Figure 7.8 shows the results of the ipconfig/all command.

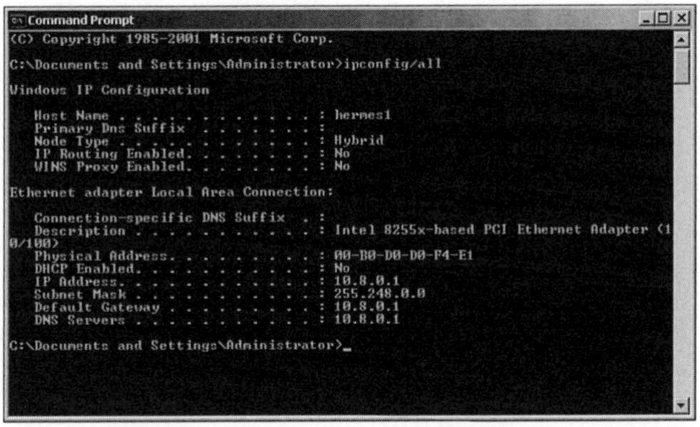

FIGURE 7.8

The ipconfig/all *command.*

On servers or clients that receive IP addresses dynamically, you can use the
ipconfig command to release and renew the IP address assignment. Use
ipconfig/release when you want to release the old address lease. Use
ipconfig/renew to renew an IP address lease. Dynamic assignment of IP
addresses is discussed in Chapter 16, "Dynamic Host Configuration Protocol."

Using Netstat

Netstat displays a list of the active TCP connections on your server (TCP is the Transport
Control Protocol and the *TCP* in TCP/IP). At the command prompt, type **netstat/a** and
press Enter. Figure 7.9 shows the results of this command.

FIGURE 7.9

*Netstat shows the TCP
connection on the
server.*

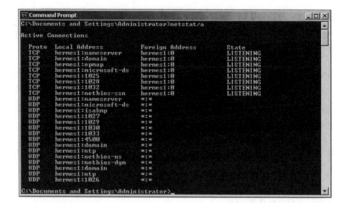

The netstat command provides a number of switches. For example, the -s switch displays statistics by protocol in the TCP/IP stack, including TCP, UDP, and IP. The -e
switch (which can be combined with the -s switch) displays ethernet statistics, including
the number of bytes and packets sent and received by the computer.

Using ping

Another useful command is ping. It can be used at the command line to send a data
packet to any IP address on the network to check connectivity. For example, to see if
your server is connecting to a computer with an IP address 192.5.6.1, you would type
this command:

```
ping 192.5.6.1
```

If the ping packet reaches the other computer, you will get an echo response letting you
know that the computer is out there. If it does not reach the computer, you will get a
request time out.

The `ping` command also provides options that you can specify, such as the number of echo packets to send and the time to wait for a reply. For example, `ping -n count` is used to specify the number of echo requests that are sent, where `count` is the number of requests.

Commands such as `netstat` and `ping` provide a number of different switches and options. To view the switches for a particular command, type the command followed by `-h` (or `-?`). A list of the different options then is provided in the command window.

Introducing IP Version 6

Before leaving the subject of network protocols, we should discuss IP Version 6 briefly. IP Version 4, as discussed earlier, provides a 32-bit addressing system. This supplies more than 2,290,865,642,415,000,000 addresses.

The problem with IP Version 4 is that the IP address pool has been nearly exhausted. This is amazing, considering that even as little as 10 years ago, no one would have imagined the possibility of running out of unique IP addresses.

IP Version 6, which will become more prevalent as time goes by, uses a 128-bit addressing system that provides 340,282,366,920,938,463,463,374,607,431,768,211,456 addresses. This is a very large number of IP addresses, and it will be difficult to exhaust this pool.

The IP Version 6 address is a hexadecimal address that consists of eight 16-bit parts. A sample address is FEDC:BA98:7654:3210:FEDC:BA98:7654:3210.

Windows Server 2003 supports IP Version 6 and provides you with the protocol in the Add Protocol dialog box (you can add it to your server's network configuration settings). IP Version 6 is also compatible with Version 4, and the two can cohabitate on the server and network with no problems.

While the Internet Engineering Task Force (IETF) has had specifications for IP Version 6 in place since the late 1990s, there has not yet been a stampede to adopt this new IP addressing scheme. It should be phased in over the next couple of years, which means that subnetting and addressing concerns will change dramatically to accommodate the new address format.

7

Understanding and configuring TCP/IP is essential to implementing a Windows Server 2003 domain. Additional information related to the TCP/IP protocol stack and network services such as DNS, DHCP, NetBIOS to IP address resolution with WINS, routing and remote access, IP security, and Internet connection sharing and Network Address Translation is covered in Hour 15, "Understanding the Domain Name Service," through Hour 22, "Internet Connection Sharing and Network Address Translation."

Summary

In this hour, you learned the basics of LAN protocols. Local area network protocols define how computers communicate on a network. The OSI model was created to provide a conceptual model for how networks work; it consists of seven layers.

NWlink is the Microsoft implementation of Novell's IPX/SPX protocol. NWlink is used on a Microsoft network to communicate with NetWare servers on the network.

TCP/IP is the most used LAN protocol in the world. An IP address consists of a 32-bit address in the form of a four-octet dotted-decimal number. TCP/IP is installed (if necessary) via the Local Area Connection Properties dialog box. TCP/IP properties such as the IP address, subnet mask, default gateway, and DNS server address are configured in the Internet Protocol (TCP/IP) Properties dialog box.

IP subnetting enables you to subnet your network IP addresses into logical groupings or subnets. Because dotted-decimal IP addresses can be converted to binary, subnetting consists of using bits from the node address octets of the network address and creating subnets.

Windows Server 2003 is compatible with IP Version 6. This protocol can be installed via the Local Area Connection Properties dialog box. At this time, IP Version 6 has still not reached any large-scale implementations.

Q&A

Q What conceptual model helps provide an understanding of how network protocol stacks such as TCP/IP and IPX/SPX work?

A The OSI Model consisting of the application, presentation, session, transport, network, data link, and physical layers, helps describe how data is sent and received on the network by protocol stacks.

Q What protocol must be installed on a Windows Server (or client) to communicate with NetWare servers?

A The Microsoft implementation of IPX/SPX is NWlink. It must be installed and configured on a Windows server or a client that will communicate with a NetWare server.

Q What protocol stack is installed by default when you install Windows Server 2003 on a network server?

A TCP/IP is the default protocol for Windows Server 2003. It is required for Active Directory implementations and provides for connectivity on heterogeneous networks.

Q When TCP/IP is configured on a Windows server (or domain client), what information is required?

A You must provide at least the IP address and the subnet mask to configure a TCP/IP client. Other parameters, such as the default gateway and DNS server for the computer, can also be provided in the TCP/IP Properties dialog box.

Q How can a range of IP addresses be divided into logical subsets or segments?

A IP subnetting enables you to "segment" a range of IP addresses into logical subnets. Subnetting requires that you borrow host bits for the subnets. A range of addresses for each subnet must be calculated in addition to the subnet mask for the subnetted network.

Q What are two command-line utilities that can be used to check TCP/IP configurations and IP connectivity, respectively?

A The `ipconfig` command can be used to check the IP configuration of a computer and also renew the IP address of the client if it is provided by a DHCP server. `ping` can be used to check the connection between the local computer and any computer on the network using the destination computer's IP address.

7

HOUR 8

Introducing Active Directory

With the introduction of Windows 2000 Server, Microsoft radically changed how an administrator structures a Microsoft network. Such concepts as resource domains, account domains, and the master domain model were pushed to the wayside by a true hierarchical directory services structure called Active Directory. Windows Server 2003 also embraces Active Directory as its directory service. In this hour, we look at the basics of Active Directory, its installation, its use, and the different Active Directory snap-ins.

In this hour, the following topics are covered:

- Understanding the Active Directory hierarchy
- Creating a root domain
- Creating a child domain
- Working with the Active Directory snap-ins
- Working with domain user accounts
- Searching for objects in the Active Directory

Understanding Active Directory

Active Directory is the directory service (a directory service is a database of information that is arranged in a top-down hierarchical manner) for your Windows network; it provides a hierarchical structure for domain management and implementation. The Active Directory provides the namespace for your domains and catalogs users, groups of users, computers, printers, and even security policies in a centralized database that is replicated among domain controllers on the network. Each item, such as a user or a group, is referred to as an *Active Directory object*.

Because Active Directory provides a hierarchical, treelike structure for your domains, sharing resources throughout the domain structure is made easier. And adding new domains to the tree is very straightforward, making the directory service provided by Active Directory highly scaleable.

Planning the Active Directory Hierarchy

While it doesn't hurt to oversimplify the Active Directory domain hierarchy and characterize it as a branching tree, it is also useful to look at the different levels in the Active Directory hierarchy as administrative containers. This would make the domain the most basic container available. (This is not to ignore the existence of the Organizational Unit, however, which is a very useful Active Directory container; Organizational Units are discussed in Hour 9, "Creating Active Directory Groups, Organizational Units, and Sites.")

The tree, then, (in terms of the Active Directory) is a collection of domains. All these domains share the same Global Catalog, which is the central repository for all the objects in a domain (or domain tree). This means that all the domains in the tree can get at the same set of resources, no matter which of the domains in the tree is actually hosting that resource.

When you create a new tree, you are creating a domain that will serve as the root of the tree. Other domains added to the tree will actually be child domains of the root domain (the initial domain that you create is the root—we discuss creating the root in the next section). Figure 8.1 shows a tree root domain called spinach.com. Notice that a number of child domains (such as popeye.spinach.com and wimpy.spinach.com) exist as "subdomains" of the tree root (spinach.com).

Child domains in the tree are in the same namespace as the root domain (the root supplying the root name). The child domains actually take on the root domain name as part of their complete name. This naming convention is also seen in DNS, and child domains in a DNS tree are named in a similar fashion (using the root name as part of their complete name). For more about DNS (which you might want to read before designing your Active Directory tree structure), see Hour 15, "Understanding the Domain Name Service."

FIGURE 8.1

*A Windows Server
2003 Active Directory
domain tree.*

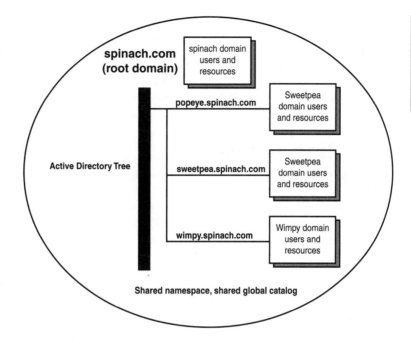

While the tree provides an extremely large administrative and security container (you can place a large number of child domains in a tree), there is actually a larger container called a forest. A *forest* is a collection of trees. For example, spinach.com, a tree, could be in a forest with carrot.com, another tree.

Although these trees are managed separately and operate in their own namespaces, they can belong to the same forest; this allows the different domains in these separate trees to share the same Global Catalog. This means that trees in the same forest can share resources (and will be able to locate resources by virtue of sharing the same Global Catalog).

An important aspect of sharing the Global Catalog by domains in the same tree is the replication of this database of Active Directory objects. Global Catalog replication is discussed in Hour 9.

When you create your first Windows Server 2003 domain, you are creating both a new forest and a new tree. The next section discusses installing Active Directory and creating these administrative and security containers.

A single Windows Server 2003 domain can serve thousands of users and provide many resources to those users (particularly when a number of specialized servers are used to provide these services). Only very large corporations will require a root domain that has child domains in the Active Directory tree. Only the largest of organizations or corporations would require a forest of multiple trees.

Installing Active Directory and Creating the Root Domain

Active Directory can be installed using the Configure Your Server Wizard. The wizard can be started by selecting Start, Administrative Tools and then selecting Configure Your Server Wizard. Or, you can start the wizard from the Manage Your Server window by selecting Add or Remove Role.

To install Active Directory, you must have an NTFS volume on your server.

After opening the Configure Your Server Wizard, click Next to bypass the opening wizard screen. The next screen asks you to make sure that modems, network cards, and other devices have been connected to the server. After looking over the checklist of devices (and making sure you have them all connected), click Next.

The wizard detects the settings for your local area connection (or connections, in the case of a server with multiple network cards). After the local area connections have been detected, the wizard supplies the Configuration Options screen (see Figure 8.2).

FIGURE 8.2

The wizard provides configuration options for your server.

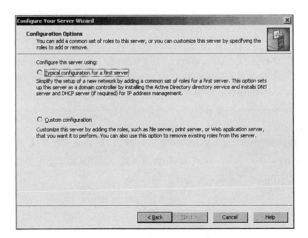

The wizard provides two configuration options:

- **Typical Configuration for a First Server**—This option enables you to configure your server as a domain controller. The installation includes Active Directory, DNS, and DHCP. This option is appropriate for cases when you are bringing the first server (which will be a domain controller and will provide DNS and DHCP services) online in the domain.

- **Custom Configuration**—This option enables you to select the server role components that you install on the server, such as Active Directory, the file server, and the WINS server. This option is ideal when you are expanding your server's roles (adding roles) or removing roles. If DNS and DHCP servers already exist on the network, this is also the route you would want to take to add domain controllers to the domain. We discussed server roles and configuration options in Hour 5, "Configuring a Windows Server."

Let's assume that you are bringing the first domain controller online for the domain. Select Typical Configuration for a First Server (otherwise, you would select Custom Configuration) and then click Next.

On the next screen, you are asked to provide the full DNS name of your domain, as shown in Figure 8.3 (the Active Directory hierarchy is discussed in the previous section of this hour, and DNS naming conventions and the DNS hierarchy are discussed in Hour 15). If your Active Directory tree will mirror your DNS tree, supply the domain name that will serve as the tree for your Windows network (for example, you might use the tree or top-level domain name spinach.com, to follow the earlier example).

FIGURE 8.3

Provide the domain name for the Active Directory.

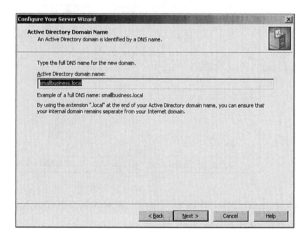

If you are creating a Directory Services tree for your network that does not mirror your DNS structure (the network is separate from your Internet/DNS domain), you can use the suffix .local. After entering the domain name, click Next to continue.

On the next screen, the DNS domain name that you provided appears along with the NetBIOS version of this name (it drops the .com or other suffix and uses the first 20 characters of the DNS name you provided). You have the option to change the NetBIOS name, if you want. In most cases, you will want to use the default (the shortened version of the DNS name). Click Next to continue.

> The NetBIOS name is typically used by network clients who are not running Windows Server 2003, Windows XP, or Windows 2000 (although these operating systems can also be enabled for NetBIOS). Using legacy clients who use NetBIOS names also might require that you set up WINS on the network. WINS is discussed in Hour 17, "Understanding WINS."

Because you are configuring this server as the first domain controller in the domain and the DNS and DHCP server for the domain, the next screen asks if you want to configure this DNS server (which it will become during the Active Directory installation process) to forward DNS queries that it cannot resolve. To enable this DNS query forwarding, supply the IP address of another DNS server on the network (perhaps in another domain in the tree) or the IP address of the DNS server provided by your Internet service provider (see Figure 8.4).

FIGURE 8.4

Supply the IP address for DNS query forwarding.

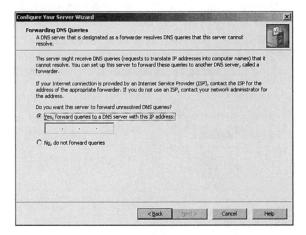

If you do not want to forward these queries, select No, do not forward queries. After making your selection, click Next.

Much more about DNS and how to configure your DNS servers is discussed in Hour 15.

The summary screen appears for the Configure Your Server Wizard, listing the server components that will be installed. These include DHCP (if no other DHCP server is currently available in the domain), Active Directory, and DNS. You can now move to the last step in the process of adding Active Directory: Click Next.

The Active Directory and other server components are installed. Your computer reboots during this process. After the system reboots and you log on to the system, the Configure Your Server Wizard displays the Server Configuration Process screen, a summary screen of the installed components and configuration choices (see Figure 8.5) .

FIGURE 8.5

After the system reboots, the Server Configuration Process screen provides a summary of the component installations.

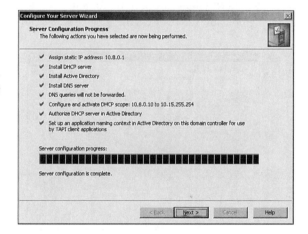

To complete the process of installing Active Directory (and other components), click Next. You are taken to the final wizard screen; click Finish to complete the process.

You can start the Active Directory Wizard (to either create a domain controller or demote a domain controller to a member server) by using dcpromo.exe. Click Start, Run, and type **dcpromo** in the Run window. Then click OK to start the wizard.

Adding a Child Domain

After the root domain has been created, any number of child domains can be added to the domain tree. You add a child domain to the root using the Configure Your Server Wizard. The procedure for adding a child domain to the root domain is very similar to creating the root domain itself. Follow these steps:

1. Start the Configure Your Server Wizard (select Start, Administrative Tools, Configure Your Server). Click Next to bypass the initial wizard screen. The Preliminary Steps screen reminds you to connect network cables and modems; click Next to continue. After network connections are detected the wizard's Server Role screen appears.

2. On the Server Role screen, select Domain Controller (Active Directory) and then click Next. The next screen asks you to select the type of domain controller you want to create: either a domain controller for a new domain or a domain controller for an existing domain (see Figure 8.6).

FIGURE 8.6

Select the domain con-troller for a new domain option.

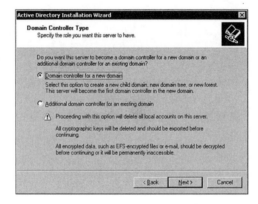

3. To create a child domain (which will be nested in the existing root domain), select the Domain Controller for a New Domain option and then click Next.

Adding an additional domain controller for an existing domain is handled in a similar fashion as creating a root domain or a child domain. Use the Configure Your Server Wizard to configure any Windows Server 2003 as a domain controller.

8

4. On the next wizard screen, you are provided with three options related to the type of new domain you will create; select one of the following:

- **Domain in a New Forest**—This option creates a new forest, with the new domain controller serving as the root of the first tree in the forest.

- **Child Domain in an Existing Domain Tree**—This enables you to place a child domain within an existing tree (this is the option you will choose to create a child domain).

- **Domain Tree in an Existing Forest**—This option enables you to create a domain in an existing forest, but not make it a child of any existing domain in the forest, such as the root of a tree.

5. For sake of discussion, select the Child Domain in an Existing Domain Tree option (in the previous step). Click Next to continue.

6. On the next screen, you must provide a username and a password for an account that has the administrative rights to install Active Directory on this computer and make it a child domain within an existing tree (see Figure 8.7). Typically, you will supply the Administrator account's name and password that exist on the root domain controller.

FIGURE 8.7

Provide a username and a password that will allow this sever to become a child domain controller in the tree.

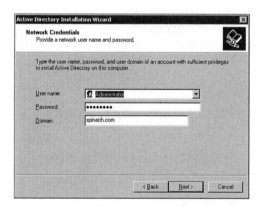

7. Click Next to continue. On the next screen, supply the name for the child name (the parent domain, the tree root, appears in the Parent Domain box). As you type the child name into the Child Domain box, the complete DNS for the new child will be shown at the bottom of the wizard screen. After you supply the child domain name, click Next.

8. On the next screen, the NetBIOS name for the new child domain appears (it will be what you typed into the Child Domain box on the previous screen). In almost all cases, you will not want to change the default NetBIOS name for the domain

(unless you know that it conflicts with another computer already on the network—the NetBIOS name is only 15 characters of the domain name that you typed). Click Next to continue.

9. On the next screen, you are notified that an Active Directory database and log folder will be created on the new domain controller that you are creating. Use the default file names for these folders. Click Next to continue.

10. The next screen asks you to supply a location to keep the SYSVOL folder. This folder contains information that is replicated among the domain controllers in the namespace (that is, this information will be in the Global Catalog for the tree). Again, it is best to go with the default location. Click Next to continue.

11. The next screen lets you know that DNS registration diagnostics have been run and that the DNS service has been found on the network (remember that to install Active Directory on the tree's root server, DNS had to be available, so it would certainly be available when you install child domains). Click Next to continue.

12. On the next wizard screen (see Figure 8.8), you are asked to select the permission levels that you will use in the domain. If you will be running Windows 2000 and Windows Server 2003 on your servers in the domain, you can select the option Permissions compatible only with Windows 2000 or Windows Server 2003 operating systems. This permission option provides greater security. If you will still have some Windows NT Server computers on the network, you must choose the option Permissions compatible with Pre–Windows 2000 server operating systems. This allows the servers running Windows Server 2003 to operate with the Windows NT Servers. After you make your selection, click Next.

FIGURE 8.8

Select the permission level for the domain.

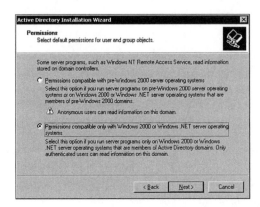

13. The next screen asks you to supply the restore mode password. This password is used only when the server is started in the Directory Services restore mode. Type in the password (it does not have to be the same as the default Administrator account's password). Then click Next.

8

14. A summary screen appears, providing a list of the options that you chose for the new domain controller. Click Next. The wizard configures the Active Directory for this child domain controller.

15. When the final wizard screen appears, click Finish. The server must be restarted; click Restart Now.

When the server reboots, you are notified that the server is now a domain controller. Click Finish. Figure 8.9 shows a domain root (spinach.com) and a child domain (popeye.spinach.com) in the Active Directory Domains and Trusts snap-in (discussed later in this hour).

FIGURE 8.9

The domain tree can be viewed in the Active Directory Domains and Trusts snap-in.

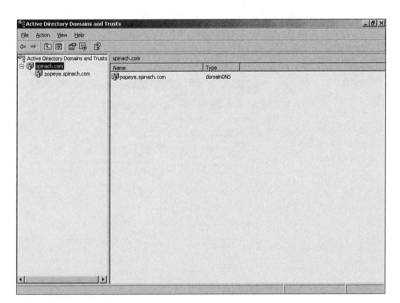

Using the Active Directory Management Tools

After Active Directory is installed on a domain controller (along with DNS and DHCP, if necessary), you are provided with a set of Active Directory Management tools. These tools enable you to add users and computers to the domain, manage the trusts among your various domains, and deal with wide area network sites on the network.

The Active Directory tools come in the form of three Microsoft Management Console snap-ins: Active Directory Users and Computers, Active Directory Domains and Trusts, and Active Directory Sites and Services. We will take a quick look at each of these snap-ins in a moment. The remainder of the hour then focuses on the Active Directory Users and Computers snap-in (as does the beginning of Hour 9). Active Directory Domains and Trusts and Active Directory Sites and Services are also discussed in Hour 9.

To launch one of the Active Directory snap-ins, select Start, point at Administrative Tools, and then select the appropriate Active Directory snap-in on the menu that appears.

Active Directory Users and Computers

The Active Directory Users and Computers snap-in is used to manage user accounts, computers, groups, and Organizational Units. It is the management tool for all the logical Active Directory objects residing in your Windows Server 2003 domains. It will also, no doubt, be the Active Directory snap-in that you use the most often as you manage your domain or domains and the various domain controllers. Figure 8.10 shows the Active Directory users and Computers snap-in.

FIGURE 8.10

The Active Directory Users and Computers snap-in is used to manage objects such as users and groups.

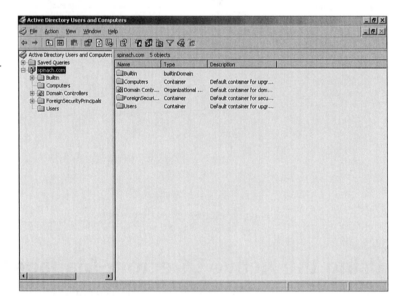

Active Directory Domains and Trusts

The Active Directory Domains and Trusts snap-in is used to manage trusts between your domains (see Figure 8.9 for a look at the Active Directory Domains and Trusts snap-in). Because transitive trusts are assigned to domains in the same domain tree, Active Directory Domains and Trusts typically is used to manage trust relationships between different domain forests.

The Active Directory Domains and Trusts snap-in is also important in another respect: It provides you with the ability to raise a domain's functional level. The domain functional level that you select determines what type of domain controllers (based on the Microsoft network operating system they are running) are supported within your domain. By default, the domain functional level is set to Windows 2000 Mixed, which supports Windows NT 4, Windows 2000, and Windows Server 2003 domain controllers. We will discuss raising the domain functional level in Hour 9.

> The functional level of a domain can affect a number of features, such as the domain groups available, the ability to nest groups in the Active Directory, and the ability to rename the domain.

Active Directory Sites and Services

The Active Directory Sites and Services snap-in is used to manage the physical and logical structure of your Windows Server 2003 network. A *site*, which can be a subnet or a collection of subnets, is typically one physical location. Active Directory Sites and Services enables you to create multiple sites, which consist of different physical locations connected by WAN connections. Figure 8.11 shows the Active Directory Sites and Services snap-in.

FIGURE 8.11

The Active Directory Sites and Services snap-in is used to manage sites and subnets on your network.

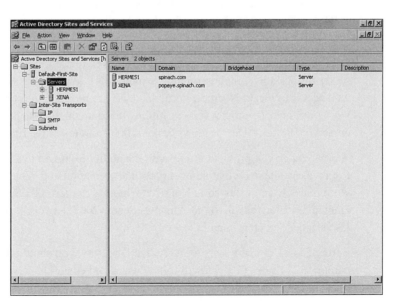

Creating sites enables you to control the amount of replication (for the Global Catalog and domain controllers) that takes place between parts of your network that are connected by slower WAN connections as well as internal LAN replication. The Active Directory Sites and Services snap-in also enables you to specify the IP subnets on your network, which also helps control the efficiency of replication between domain controllers. Sites and subnets are discussed in Hour 9.

 Another Active Directory tool, the Active Directory Schema snap-in, is not installed by default when you install Active Directory on a Windows Server 2003. The schema of the Active Directory is the naming conventions used to refer to the Active Directory objects. You can use the Active Directory Schema snap-in to edit the schema or add objects to the schema. This is not typically required of most network administrators.

Working with Domain User Accounts

Microsoft operating systems, particularly network operating systems, can make user accounts a little confusing, particularly for the novice administrator. Two different types of user accounts exist: local accounts and domain accounts. Two different account types are necessary because two different security systems pervade computers running Microsoft operating systems and network operating systems such as Windows Server 2003: local security and domain-level security.

A *local account* is used to gain access to the local machine and its resources. Having a local account means that the user can be validated to the local security database on the server (or desktop computer running Windows NT, Windows 2000, or Windows XP) and gain access to local resources. Local accounts are more of an issue on computers in workgroups or on member servers within your domain. Creating local accounts is discussed in Hour 4, "The Windows Server 2003 Administrative Environment."

A *domain account* provides a user with the ability to log on to a domain and access the resources available on that domain (user authentication and Windows Server 2003 password issues were discussed in Hour 2, "Windows Server 2003 Security Overview"). Domain users are added to the Windows Server 2003 network using the Active Directory Users and Computers snap-in.

Before adding domain users to the Active Directory, you should determine the set of parameters or rules that you will follow when you create the usernames for your domain (or domains). For example, you might determine that you will use the first initial and

8

then the last name of employees at your company to create each username. Keep the following in mind as you determine your set of rules for naming your users' accounts:

- Usernames must be unique. So, the convention of using the first initial followed by the last name will not work when you have users with the same last name and the same first initial. Networks running Windows Server 2003 or Windows 2000 on the domain controllers provide you with 256 characters to create the username, which provides more than enough possibilities.

- User logon names can be a combination of numeric and alphanumeric characters. You can use names and even floor locations, such as marysmithfloor2, to help define unique and descriptive usernames. Although logon names are not case sensitive, the case in which you create the logon name is preserved.

- You cannot end a username with a period or use the reserved characters *, /, |, :, ;, =, <, and >.

> Windows Server 2003 (and Windows 2000 Server) domain usernames are also referred to as user principal names. These names consist of two parts: the user's name and the user principal name suffix. You create the username; the suffix consists of the @ sign followed by the domain where the user resides.

Adding Users to the Domain

User accounts are added to the domain using the Active Director Users and Computers snap-in. To add a user to your domain, follow these steps:

1. Open the Active Directory Users and Computer snap-in (click Start, Administrative Tools, and then Active Directory Users and Computers).

2. Expand the domain node in the snap-in tree. Then select the Users folder in the tree. A list of the default groups and users in your domain appears in the Details pane.

3. To create a new user, click the Create a New User in the Current Container button on the Active Directory toolbar. The New Object–User dialog box opens (see Figure 8.12).

4. Enter a first name, initials, and a last name for the user (this is actually the name that will appear in the Active Directory).

5. In the User Logon Name box, type the username that the user will use to log on to the domain.

FIGURE 8.12

The New Object–User dialog box is used to create the new user account.

>
> When you create the domain user account, note that a pre–Windows 2000 version of the user account is also created for the user, truncating the user-name that you have created at 20 characters.

6. When you have entered the appropriate information (see steps 4 and 5), click Next to continue.

7. On the next screen (see Figure 8.13), you are asked to provide a password for the user (and confirm it) and to set properties related to the user's password. The password possibilities are as follows:

   - **User must change password at next logon**—If you want to let the users have control over the password that they assigned themselves, check this check box. You can then enter something generic, such as password, as the user's password. At the first logon, the user will be required to change the default password.

   - **User cannot change password**—If you want to assign passwords to your users and not allow them to change passwords, click this check box.

   - **Password never expires**—This makes the password selected by you or the user a lifelong password; it has no expiration time limit. When you do not use this option, passwords are good for a month (31 days), by default.

   - **Account is disabled**—This check box allows you to disable the current account without actually deleting the account.

8. After supplying the password and setting password options, click Next. A summary screen for the new user account appears. Click Finish.

The new user account appears in the Details pane of the Active Directory Users and Computers snap-in.

FIGURE 8.13

Enter a password for the user and set password properties.

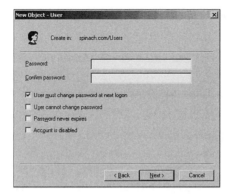

How passwords are determined and managed is an important aspect of securing your domain and its important resources. For some thoughts on passwords, see Hour 2.

Setting User Account Properties

After you create a user account, you can access a number of properties related to the account. These properties range from when the user can log on to the domain, to the user's business information, such as phone number and address.

To access a user account's properties, right-click a user account in the Active Directory Users and Computers snap-in, and select Properties from the shortcut menu. The Properties dialog box for that user account opens (see Figure 8.14).

FIGURE 8.14

User properties are set in the account's Properties dialog box.

The various user properties are set using the tabs of the dialog box. The user Properties dialog box includes the following tabs:

- **General**—Enables you to edit the user's display name. You can also enter optional information, such as the user's office (location) telephone number, email address, and Web page URL. This information will be available to other users on the network when they search the Active Directory.

- **Address**—Provides the option of entering address information related to the user.

- **Account**—Enables you to edit the username or the password options set for the account (see Figure 8.15). This tab also provides access to logon hour and computer logon settings (discussed in Hour 2). You can also use this tab to set an expiration date for a user account.

FIGURE 8.15

You can change user-names and password options and also control when and where a user can log on to the network.

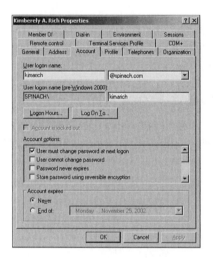

- **Profile**—Enables you to specify the location of a user's profile and any logon scripts that should run when the user logs on to the network. You can also set the path for a user's home folder (typically on a file server). We discuss user's profiles in Hour 11, "Understanding Group Policy and User Profiles." Setting a home folder is discussed later in this hour.

- **Telephones**—Gives you the option of entering telephone numbers related to the user, such as home number, pager number, mobile phone number, and fax number.

- **Member Of**—Used to view (and add or remove) the group memberships for the user. Domain groups are discussed in Hour 9.

- **Dial-In**—Used to enable the user account to take advantage of remote access dial-in or network access via virtual private networking. Dial-in remote access is

8

discussed in Hour 18, "Using Routing and Remote Access," and virtual private networking is discussed in Hour 21, "Working with Virtual Private Networking and IP Security."

- **Terminal Services Profile**—Used to set the path for the user's Terminal Services profile. Terminal Services is discussed in Hour 19, "Implementing Windows Terminal Services."

- **Sessions**—This tab is used to set Terminal Services timeout and reconnect options.

- **Environment**—Also associated with Terminal Services. It is used to start a certain program upon logon, and it also controls the client devices that are connected upon user login.

- **Remote Control**—Used to enable (or disable) the Terminal Services remote control feature that allows an administrator to view a user's client session or take control of the client computer.

- **Organization**—Enables you to enter the user's title and department and company-related information, such as the user's direct reports.

- **COM+**—Used to specify the COM+ partition that the user belongs to. COM+ partitions are used to assign applications provided by an application server to users, groups, or Organizational Units.

As noted in this list, a number of these tabs are discussed in more detail in later hours of this book. Before we end our discussion of user account options, let's take a look at setting the logon hours for users and the computers that they can log on to and access domain resources.

Setting Logon Hours and Computers

The Account tab is used to set the logon hours for a user and the computers on which that user can log on to the domain. To set the logon hours for the user, follow these steps:

1. Right-click the user's account in the Active Directory Users and Computers Details pane, and select Properties from the shortcut menu that appears. Then select the Account tab on the Properties dialog box (if necessary).

2. On the Account tab, select the Logon Hours button. The Logon Hours dialog box for the user appears (see Figure 8.16).

3. All hours are allowed by default (all hours are in blue). To disallow certain hours (such as Saturdays) for logon, click and drag to select the time range. Then click the Logon Denied option button. The time frame that you selected will turn white. This time frame is no longer allowed for user logon. When you have finished specifying the time frames for logon (and logon denial), click the OK button. You are returned to the Account tab of the Properties dialog box.

FIGURE **8.16**

You can change user-names and password options and also control when and where a user can log on to the network.

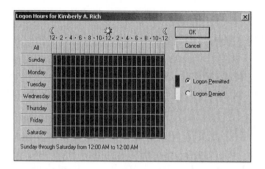

4. You can also specify the computers that a user can use to log on to the network. On the Account tab, select the Log On To button. The Logon Workstations dialog box opens (see Figure 8.17).

FIGURE **8.17**

You can specify the computers that a user can use to log on to the network.

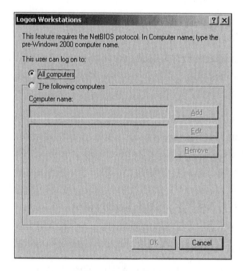

5. Select The following computers option button. To add a computer to the list, type the computer's NetBIOS name into the Computer name box (the NetBIOS name is the first 15 characters of a computer's name and does not include the domain name suffix).

6. After typing in the computer name, click the Add button. You can add a number of computers to the list (computers can also be removed from the list using the Remove button). After entering the computers for the user, click OK. You are returned to the Account tab of the Properties dialog box. Click OK to close the dialog box.

Renaming Users

You can rename domain user accounts. When you rename an account, the account keeps all its group affiliations and permissions.

In the Active Directory Users and Computers snap-in, right-click on a username in the Details pane. Select Rename for the shortcut menu. The name is highlighted. Edit the name as needed, and then click anywhere in the Active Directory window. The Rename User dialog box appears, showing the changes that you made to the user name (see Figure 8.18).

FIGURE 8.18

You can rename domain user accounts.

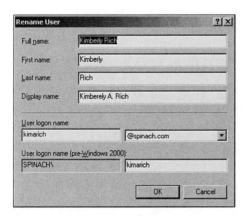

You can make additional changes to the account name or the user logon name using the Rename User dialog box. When you have completed the changes you want to make to the account's name, click OK. The new name appears in the Active Directory.

Working with Active Directory Objects

Thus far, we have discussed only one type of Active Directory object: the user account object. However, in our discussion of user accounts, we have looked at some of the basic possibilities for manipulating other Active Directory objects, such as computer accounts and domain printers.

This is because the ways in which you manipulate objects in the Active Directory is fairly uniform across the various object types in the Active Directory schema. We look at additional Active Directory objects in Hour 9, "Creating Active Directory Groups, and Organizational Units, and Sites"; Hour 10, "Adding Client Computers and Member Servers to the Domain"; and Hour 14, "Working with Network Printing" (we will discuss how to publish a printer to the Active Directory).

A new feature worth noting is that the Windows Server 2003 Active Directory Users and Computers snap-in now enables you to select multiple objects in the Snap-In Details window. This allows you to manipulate a number of user accounts at once or nest multiple user groups in a particular Organizational Unit.

For example, you might want to quickly disable a number of domain user accounts because of some type of security issue. In the Active Directory Users and Computers snap-in, you would expand the Domain node in the snap-in tree and then select the Users node. A list of your users would appear in the Details pane. You then would select the first with a click of the mouse and then hold down the Ctrl key when selecting other users. After selecting the users, you would right-click (see Figure 8.19). Notice that you can select Disable from the shortcut menu (as well as Delete).

FIGURE 8.19

You can select multiple objects in the Active Directory.

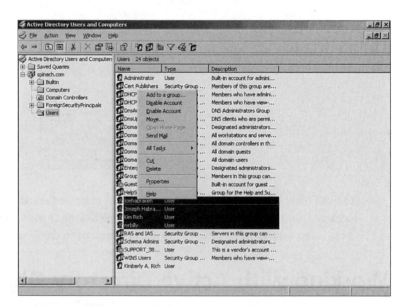

Selecting multiple users is extremely useful when you want to add users to a particular group or groups. Users can be identified, selected, and then added to the group or groups en masse.

Searching for Objects in the Active Directory

The Active Directory Users and Computers snap-in makes it easy for you to find objects in the Active Directory. The Find feature provides a number of built-in queries for searching for particular objects (such as users who have passwords that never expire), and it also provides you with the ability to set up search queries and then save them for later use.

To use the Find feature, select a particular node in the snap-in tree (such as Users) and then select the Action menu; then select Find. The Find dialog box appears (see Figure 8.20).

FIGURE 8.20

The Find feature enables you to select the object and location for a search.

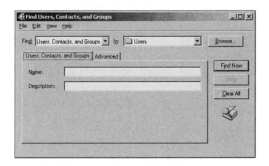

Use the Find drop-down list to specify the object type you want to find, such as Users, Contacts, and Groups; Computers; or Printers. After specifying the object type, use the In drop-down box to specify the container for the search, such as a particular Active Directory node or another location such as an Organizational Unit.

> You can change the container for the search by clicking the Browse button and selecting a node, folder, or other container from the list provided.

After specifying the object and the location for the search, you can provide additional search parameters, such as a particular username or name of a printer. You then click Find Now to complete the search.

Creating Your Own Queries

Although the Find feature provides a fast way to locate particular user accounts or other Active Directory objects, you might want to create specific queries that locate certain objects. You can then save these queries and reuse them when needed.

1. Select the Saved Query folder in the Active Directory tree. Then select the Action menu, point at New, and select Query. The New Query dialog box opens (see Figure 8.21).

2. Type a name and a description (optional) for the new query. Then click the Define Query button. The Find Common Queries dialog box opens. Tabs are provided for Users, Computers, and Groups. Use any of these tabs to specify the parameters for the query.

FIGURE 8.21

Search queries can be
created and saved.

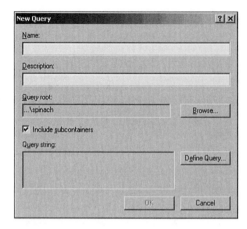

3. Define the variables for your query (on either the Users, Computers, or Groups tabs) using the Name and Description drop-down boxes. These enable you to specify that the query find names or descriptions that start (or end) with a particular character string.

4. Check boxes are also included on the Users, Computers, and Groups tabs. For example, on the Users tab, two check boxes are provided that enable you to search for disabled accounts or accounts that have nonexpiring passwords. A drop-down box is also provided that enables you to search based on the last time the user logged on (see Figure 8.22).

FIGURE 8.22

Set the criteria for the
query.

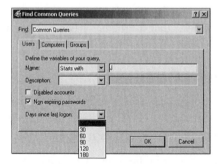

After setting the criteria, click OK. Click OK again to close the dialog box.

5. The new query is displayed in the Saved Queries folder. To see the results of the query in the Details pane, select the query in the snap-in tree (see Figure 8.23).

FIGURE 8.23

Query results are displayed in the Details pane.

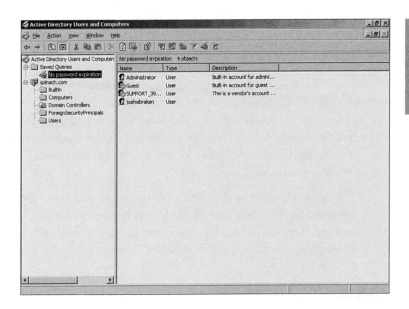

Saving various queries enables you to quickly filter information in the Active Directory. After you click the query in the tree, results are immediately displayed in the Details pane.

Deleting Objects in the Active Directory

Any object that you create in the Active Directory Users and Computers snap-in can be deleted from the Active Directory. You might need to delete certain user accounts, or you might have decided certain user groups are not needed or that you need to remove other objects, such as a printer from the Active Directory.

To delete an object from the Active Directory, right-click the object (such as a user account) and select Delete from the shortcut menu. You are asked if you are sure that you want to delete the object. Click Yes to delete the object from the Active Directory.

Summary

The Active Directory is the directory service for the Windows Server 2003 networking environment. It provides the hierarchical structure for the domain and the objects within the domain. The domain is the basic administrative container for a Microsoft network. Domains that share the same Global Catalog are in the same domain tree. A forest is a collection of domain trees.

A domain controller for a domain is created by installing Active Directory on the server. The first domain created for your organization is the root domain of your domain tree (it also is the root of a forest).

Child domains reside inside the domain tree container (they could also be considered branches on the domain tree). Root and child domains in the same tree can share services and resources because they are configured with transitive trusts, by default. This means that these trusts flow up through the tree and child domains on the network, allowing users in any domain on the tree to access resources anywhere in the tree (including the root and child directories.

The Active Directory is managed using three snap-ins: Active Directory Users and Computers, Active Directory Domains and Trusts, and Active Directory Sites and Services. The Active Directory Users and Computers snap-in is used to manage your user accounts, Active Directory groups, and Organizational Units.

Q&A

Q What term is used to refer to the first domain created in a new Active Directory tree?

A The first domain created in a tree is referred to as the root domain. Child domains created in the tree share the same namespace as the root domain.

Q How is a server running Windows Server 2003 configured as a domain controller, such as the domain controller for the root domain or a child domain?

A Installing the Active Directory on a server running Windows Server 2003 provides you with the option of creating a root domain for a domain tree or of creating child domains in an existing tree. Installing Active Directory on the server makes the server a domain controller.

Q What are some of the tools used to manage Active Directory objects in a Windows Server 2003 domain?

A When the Active Directory is installed on a server (making it a domain controller), a set of Active Directory snap-ins is provided. The Active Directory Users and Computers snap-in is used to manage Active Directory objects such as user accounts, computers, and groups. The Active Directory Domains and Trusts snap-in enables you to manage the trusts that are defined between domains. The Active Directory Sites and Services snap-in provides for the management of domain sites and subnets.

Q How are domain user accounts created and managed?

A The Active Directory Users and Computers snap-in provides the tools necessary for creating user accounts and managing account properties. Properties for user accounts include settings related to logon hours, the computers a user can log on to, and settings related to the user's password.

HOUR **9**

Creating Active Directory Groups, Organizational Units, and Sites

In Hour 8, "Introducing Active Directory," we discussed how the Active Directory and the logical hierarchy that it provides have dramatically changed how administrators design and implement their Windows Server 2003 networks. We also took a "first" look at the Active Directory and discussed domain user accounts.

In this hour, we examine two other Active Directory objects: groups and Organizational Units. We also discuss the use of Active Directory sites and issues related to Active Directory replication and the Global Catalog.

In this hour, the following topics are covered:

- Understanding Active Directory groups and group scopes
- Working with group nesting
- Using default and built-in groups

- Creating groups
- Adding users and groups to a group
- Raising domain functional levels
- Using Organizational Units
- Working with Active Directory sites

Understanding Active Directory Groups

The Active Directory Users and Computers snap-in is used to manage Active Directory objects such as users, computers, and groups. A *group* is a collection of user accounts (which can include nested groups—more about these later in the hour). The primary purpose of a group is to enable you to group users and define permissions based on group membership. This is a much easier strategy for determining the access levels that users have to domain resources when compared to the alternative of assigning permissions on a per-user basis.

A number of default Active Directory groups are available for the administrator to work with. New groups can also be created using the Active Directory Users and Computers snap-in. Before we look at the default Active Directory groups provided, we should expand our definition of Windows Server 2003 groups. There are actually two different group types: security and distribution.

A *security group* is a group that defines permissions related to resources and objects in the domain. Members of a security group (such as users) are assigned a security token when they log on to the domain, which provides them with the necessary permissions to files, printers, and other resources.

The second type of Windows Server 2003 group is the *distribution group*. A distribution group is really nothing more than a list of users, such as a grouping of contacts that you would send an email to. Distribution groups cannot be used to assign permissions to the users in the group. Microsoft Exchange Server is an example of a platform that uses distribution groups.

We discus security groups in this hour and use them throughout the book as we assign permissions related to various Windows Server 2003 services. Before we look at using or creating groups, however, we need to look at how security groups operate at the different levels in the Active Directory hierarchy (especially when you are working with enterprise networks that contain a number of domains).

Windows Server 2003 Group Scopes

A security group always has a particular scope. The group *scope* refers to the level at which the group operates within the Microsoft network (and within the Active Directory hierarchy). It also refers to the types of objects that can be actually contained in the object. Remember that you are potentially working with a network that not only can consist of a single domain, but that also could span a domain tree, or even a forest. The three group scopes are universal, global, and domain local.

- **Universal group**—A group that spans multiple domains and can have users (or groups) from any of these domains as members. Permissions assigned to a universal group can allow group members to access resources across domain boundaries. Universal groups are designed to contain objects that remain fairly static (such as global groups, which are discussed in a moment). These groups are best used in multidomain networks, where you want to group sets of users and other objects at a higher level in the Active Directory container.

> By default, Windows Server 2003 domain controllers operate in what is called mixed mode (this is discussed in more detail later in the hour). Mixed mode accommodates Windows NT domain controllers on the network. Universal groups cannot be created in mixed mode. You must raise the domain functional level to either Windows 2000 native or Windows Server 2003 levels to take advantage of advanced domain-wide Active Directory features such as universal groups. Functional levels are discussed in more detail later in the hour.

- **Global group**—A group used to organize users in one domain. Membership to the global group is limited to the domain where the global group is created. However, a global group can access resources in any domain in the Active Directory tree.

- **Domain local group**—A group created at the domain level and used to provide users with permissions to local resources (within the domain). So, the domain local group members have permissions only to resources that are in the domain where the domain local group was created. However, group membership in a domain local group is not restricted to the domain that actually contains the domain local group. The domain local group can have members from any domain in the tree.

> Do not confuse domain local groups with the local groups that you can create on computers running Windows XP and Windows Server 2003 to provide rights to local resources on a particular computer. Local groups are discussed in Hour 4, "The Windows Server 2003 Administrative Environment."

Whether you actually use all these different types of groups depends on the size of your network. If your network consists of only one domain, you would typically use global groups to organize your users into security subsets, with each group assigned a particular level of permissions to resources within the domain.

Universal groups come into play only if your network is of greater scope, meaning that your Windows Server 2003 network is big enough to embrace multiple domains. For example, your company might be made up of several divisions, with each division its own domain.

Domain local groups are most often used to assign users permissions to specific resources within a domain (where the group has been created). The fact that other group scopes can be nested (discussed in the next section) within domain local groups means that you can use the domain local group to specify the permissions for domain resources and then add users to groups from the domain tree (or forest) as required.

Nesting Groups and Group Membership

You can actually create a group hierarchy by nesting groups inside other groups. Nesting simply means placing a group inside another group. For example, you can add a global group (which provides a way to organize a group of users in a particular domain) to a domain local group. The global group provides the list of users, and the domain local group actually provides the permission level that will be assigned to members of the domain local group; in this case, that includes the global group you've nested.

The nesting of groups is controlled by the group membership rules for each group scope. In Windows 2000 native mode or Windows Server 2003 mode (these domain functional levels are discussed later in the hour), the group scopes allow the following memberships:

- **Universal**—Members can include users, global groups from any domain, and other universal groups.
- **Global**—Members can include users and global groups from the same domain.
- **Domain local**—Members can include users, global groups from any domain, domain local groups from the same domain, and universal groups.

In mixed mode, global groups can contain only users from the same domain, and domain local groups can contain only user accounts and global groups from any domain. In this functional level mode, universal groups don't exist.

Using Default Groups

Default, or predefined, groups are found in the Active Directory (meaning, on a Server 2003 domain controller). These groups have been assigned user rights so that members of a particular default group can perform specific actions in the domain. Not only are these groups created automatically when you set up your domain controller, but some of them add members automatically (these groups are considered global groups). These groups are listed here:

- **Domain Users**—This is a broad-based group that, by default, contains all your users. The Administrator account is a member, and any new users you create also are added to the group automatically. This group is automatically added to the Users domain local group on your server.

- **Domain Admins**—This group provides its members with the capability to perform administrative tasks on any computer in the domain. It is automatically added to the Administrators domain local group. The Administrator account is automatically made a member of the Domain Admins group.

- **Enterprise Admins**—This group is for users who have the capability to administer the entire network (this means all the domains in the network). However, for the members of this group to actually have the management abilities they need, you must manually add this group to each of the Administrators domain local groups (that means for all the domains in the network). By default, the Administrator account is added to the Enterprise Admins group.

Although three default groups are discussed here, you might have other predefined groups on your server, depending on the services that have been installed. For example, if your domain controller is also a DNS server, there will be a predefined DNS Admins group. This group serves as the administrator for the Domain Name Service (DNS is discussed in Hour 15, "Understanding the Domain Name Service").

Built-in Groups

Windows Server 2003 also provides built-in domain local groups. For the most part, these groups provide users with the permissions needed to perform certain tasks on your domain controllers and in the Active Directory. Remember, domain local groups are usually used to secure resources on the network, such as files or printers.

A number of built-in domain local groups exist. Figure 9.1 shows the Builtin container, which contains the built-in domain local groups.

FIGURE 9.1

*The built-in domain
local groups.*

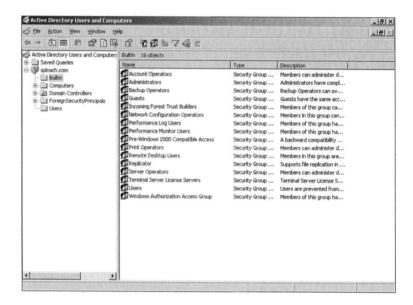

The Guests group is used to grant limited permissions to nonpermanent users on your network. Some of the other built-in domain local groups are as follows:

- **Account Operators**—This group provides its members with the capability to create, modify, and delete user accounts and groups, which means that it gives its users access to the Active Directory. However, members do not have the capability to change properties or membership related to the Operators groups or the Administrators group.

- **Server Operators**—Members of this group can create shares on a server and back up and restore files on the domain controller.

- **Print Operators**—This group is for users who need to set up and manage printers on your domain controllers that will be available on the network.

- **Backup Operators**—Members of this group can back up and restore files on your domain controllers.

- **Administrators**—This group is for users who need to perform all the administrative tasks required on your domain controllers. Members are provided with the capabilities of all the Operator groups. Your Administrator account is automatically added to this group, as is the Domain Admins and Enterprise Admins global groups.

- **Users**—This group is used to control the access of all your users to resources. It contains the Domain Users global group by default (which, if you remember, contains all your users by default).

Although you aren't required to use these groups, be advised that they have already been assigned permissions that relate to getting certain jobs done in the domain. Adding a user to the Print Operators group, for example, immediately gives that user the capability to set up printers in the domain. Using the group's predefined permissions saves you from having to assign these same permissions to individual users or creating a group of your own and assigning the permissions to the group.

Creating Groups

Domain-level groups are created on the domain controller using the Active Directory Users and Computers snap-in.

After groups are created, you can add users or other groups to them.

Open the Active Directory Users and Computers snap-in (select Start, point at Administrative Tools, and then select Active Directory Users and Computers). To view the default domain user groups, expand the domain node and then select the Users container. The default global groups (and users) appear in the Details pane (see Figure 9.2).

FIGURE 9.2

The default global groups.

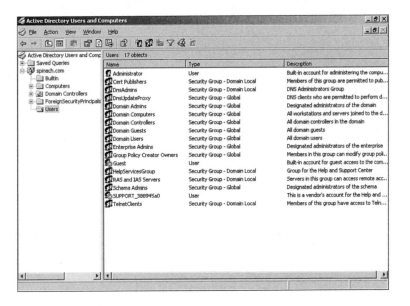

To create a new group, follow these steps:

1. Click the icon Create a New Group in the Current Container, on the snap-in toolbar (or right-click in an empty space in the Details pane and select New. The Create New Object (Group) dialog box appears (see Figure 9.3).

FIGURE 9.3

FIGURE 9.3

The New Object Group dialog box.

2. Type a name for the new group. This name is duplicated (or shortened) and placed in the pre–Windows 2000 name box automatically.

3. Choose the group type, security or distribution, by clicking the appropriate option button (you will probably be working exclusively with security group types).

4. Choose the scope for the new group by clicking the appropriate option button: Domain Local, Global, or Universal. Click OK to close the dialog box and complete the creation of the new group.

The new group appears in the Users container (you can see it in the Details pane). You can create groups in other containers. For example, you might want to create a group that is in an Organizational Unit container. We discuss Organizational Units later in the hour.

You can just as easily delete groups. Deleting is actually easier. Right-click a group in the Details pane, and select Delete from the shortcut menu. Click OK to go ahead with the deletion. When you delete the group, users who were members of the group are not deleted, but those users lose any privileges that they were afforded to resources as a result of their membership in that particular group.

Adding Users and Groups to a Group

Users and groups can be added to the groups that you create (membership depends on the scope of the group, as discussed earlier in the hour). To add users (or other groups) to a group, follow these steps:

1. Double-click the group in the Details pane to open the group's Properties dialog box. On the group's Properties dialog box, select the Member tab (see Figure 9.4).

FIGURE 9.4

Users are added to the Members tab.

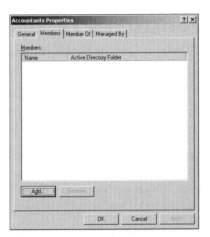

9

2. Click the Add button on the Members tab. The Select Users, Contacts, Computer, or Groups dialog box opens. To specify a user or group to add to the group, type the name of the user or group in the Enter the Object Names to Select box (you can type the first few letters of the user or group and then use the Check Names button to place the object in the box).

   If you add multiple users or groups to the dialog box, separate each object name with a semicolon.

3. When you have completed adding users or groups, click OK. The users or groups are added to the Members tab list. If you decide to remove any of the users or groups from the Members list, select the user or group and then click the Remove button. When you have finished working in the group's Properties dialog box, click OK to return to the Active Directory Users and Computer snap-in.

An alternative to adding the users to the group using the group's Properties dialog box is to select the users in the Details pane (select the first with a click and then Ctrl+click to select additional users). Right-click any of the selected users and select Add to a Group on the shortcut menu. The Select Group dialog box opens. Enter the name of the group (or the first couple of letters in the group's name) and then select Check Names. When you have specified the group, click OK. All the selected users are added to the group.

Raising Domain Functional Levels

Windows 2000 Server introduced the concept of domain functional levels. A domain could operate in either *mixed mode* or *native mode* (in the Windows Server 2003 environment, this is now called Windows 2000 native mode).

Windows Server 2003 takes domain functional levels one step further by offering an additional level: Windows Server 2003. So what do these different levels provide?

Mixed mode is designed for domains in which you will still have Windows NT domain controllers. This mode enables Windows 2000 and Windows Server 2003 domain controllers to interact with Windows NT domain controllers. Universal groups are not available in mixed mode.

Windows 2000 native mode provides an environment that supports universal groups in the Active Directory. This mode also ceases support for replication to previous versions of Windows server, meaning that you cannot add Windows NT 4 domain controllers to a domain that has been raised to the native mode. You can deploy both Windows 2000 and Windows Server 2003 in native mode.

Windows Server 2003 mode provides an environment in which only Windows Server 2003 can be run as a domain controller. This mode also provides you with the capability to rename domain controllers and to fully nest groups (the native mode also enables you to nest groups).

> Other features provided by the Windows 2000 native and the Windows Server 2003 modes include the capability to change security groups to distribution groups (and vice versa) and to migrate security principals from one domain to another.

Forest functional levels can also be raised to either native mode or Windows Server 2003 mode. Be advised that raising the domain or forest functional level is a one-way process. After you raise the functional level, you cannot change it. Raising the root domain functional level of any tree in a forest also raises the functional level of all the child domains in the tree.

To raise the domain functional level, follow these steps:

1. Open the Active Directory Domains and Trusts snap-in (click Start, Administrative Tools, and then Active Directory Domains and Trusts). Right-click the domain icon in the snap-in tree. Select Raise Domain Functional Level from the shortcut menu. The Raise Domain Functional Level dialog box opens (see Figure 9.5).

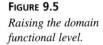

FIGURE 9.5

Raising the domain functional level.

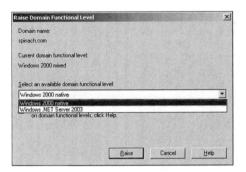

2. Click the Select an available domain functional level drop-down list. Select either Windows 2000 native or Windows Server 2003. Then click the Raise button. A message box appears letting you know that you cannot reverse this action. Click OK to complete the process.

3. A message appears letting you know that the functional level was raised. The new functional level will be replicated to the domain controllers in your domain. Click OK. You can close the Domains and Trusts snap-in if you want.

Using Organizational Units

In Hour 8, we discussed the logical hierarchy provided by the Active Directory when working in networking environments that embrace multiple domains in trees or forests. You can actually add additional compartmentalization to your Windows Server 2003 domains using Organizational Units. An *Organizational Unit* (OU) is an Active Directory object that serves as a domain container. This container can be used to hold users, groups, computers, and other OUs.

OUs basically provide a container environment that enables you to refine the logical grouping of Active Directory objects (such as users or groups) within the domain. You can apply Group Policy settings to OUs, enabling you to refine policies and security settings at a level below the domain level. OUs provide you with a domain container that can be used to mimic the hierarchical structure of your business. For example, within the domain, you could create an OU for each company department, such as accounting, receiving, and so on. Policies and security settings could then be applied on the OU level. This also provides you with a way to logically group employees (at a higher level than with actual groups).

Creating OUs is very straightforward:

1. In the Active Directory Users and Computers snap-in tree, right-click the domain node (or other object that you want to place the OU in, such as another OU). Then point at New on the shortcut menu and select Organizational Unit. The New Object–Organizational Unit dialog box opens (see Figure 9.6).

FIGURE 9.6

Create an
Organizational Unit.

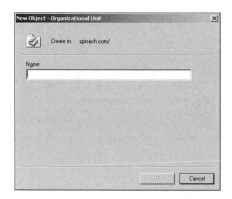

2. Supply a name for the OU and then click OK. The new OU appears in the snap-in
   tree.

3. To add users, groups, or other Active Directory objects to the OU, drag the items
   from their current location (such as the Users node). Remember that you can select
   and drag multiple items from one location to another (use Ctrl+click for objects
   that are not adjacent). A mouse click and then Shift+click allows you to select a
   series of adjacent objects.

4. You also control the properties associated with an OU. OU properties include
   information such as the OU's location, description, and group policies that have
   been set for the OU. To open the Properties dialog box for an OU, right-click the
   OU and then click Properties. The Properties dialog box opens (see Figure 9.7) .

FIGURE 9.7

The OU's Properties
dialog box.

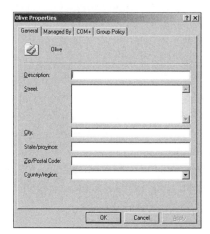

The OU's Properties dialog box consists of four tabs:

- **General**—Used to enter a description and location for the OU.
- **Manage By**—Enables you to select a user account (or accounts) to serve as manager for the OU.
- **Group Policy**—Enables you to specify the Group Policy objects in force for the OU. You can also turn off policy inheritance using this tab (Group Policy is discussed in Hour 11, "Understanding Group Policy and User Profiles").
- **COM+**—Enables you to specify the COM+ partition that is member of the COM + Partition set. COM + partitions are used to synchronize information between the Active Directory and an application server.

When you have completed setting the properties for the OU, click OK. You are returned to the Active Directory Users and Computers snap-in.

You can also view additional tabs on the OU Properties dialog box. Select the View menu and then Advanced Features. Two additional tabs, Object and Security, are provided. The Security tab can be used to step through the permissions for the OU. Use the Security permissions only if you want to delegate control of the OU to another user or group.

Using Active Directory Sites

Much of the discussion related to the Active Directory thus far (in this hour and Hour 8) has revolved around the Active Directory's logical hierarchy (domains, OUs, and so on). Sites, on the other hand, are physical entities (having an actual physical location) and determine your network's physical topology. Sites are contained in Active Directory and represent IP subnets that are connected by LAN or other reliable, high-speed connections. So, in a nutshell, an *Active Directory site* is typically a physical location on the network that represents one or more IP subnets. Subnets on the network and sites are separated by IP routers (IP subnetting is discussed in Hour 7, "Working with Network Protocols," and configuring Windows Server 2003 for routing is discussed in Hour 18, "Using Routing and Remote Access").

Your site structure should really help you keep local IP traffic on the subnet and minimize the need for a lot of data transfer between the different sites. For example, it makes sense to have a domain controller within a site so that users on that subnet can log on using a local (to the site) domain controller.

9

When you configure sites, you can also determine how often domain controllers in the different sites replicate the Active Directory (discussed later in the hour). You can minimize the amount of time that replication takes place between the sites, conserving network bandwidth.

Creating a Site

Sites are created using the Active Directory Sites and Services snap-in (select Start, Administrative Tools, Active Directory Sites and Services). To create a new site, follow these steps:

1. Right-click the Sites folder and then select New Site. The New Object–Site dialog box opens (see Figure 9.8).

FIGURE 9.8

The New Object–Site dialog box.

2. Type a name for the new site. You must also select a site link object for this site. By default, there is only the DEFAULTIPSITELINK object. This object type is stored in the Active Directory (and is part of the schema). After you supply the site name and select the site link object, click OK.

3. A message box appears letting you know that the new site has been created. A list of tasks that need to be performed related to the site, such as linking the site to other sites and adding a subnet or subnets to the new subnet container, is also provided. Click OK to close the information box.

By default, you are provided with a site named the Default-First-Site-Name. You can rename this site and use it as one of your sites. Right-click the site icon and select Rename. Then you can type a new name for the site.

Configuring a Site

To configure a site, you must associate a subnet (or subnets) to the site and connect the site to other sites using an Active Directory connection (this takes care of replication between the sites). To associate a subnet to the site, follow these steps:

1. Right-click the Subnets folder in the snap-in tree and select New Subnet. The New Object–Subnet dialog box appears (see Figure 9.9).

FIGURE 9.9

Associate a subnet with a site.

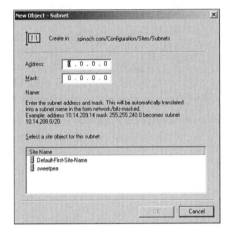

2. Enter an IP address in the subnet range that you are associating with the site, and also enter the subnet mask for the subnet. A subnet name is created using the IP address and subnet mask.

3. In the Site Name box, select the site that will be associated with this subnet (you can add additional subnets later). Click OK. The new subnet appears in the Subnets folder.

For replication to occur between the sites in your network, you must create a site link between the sites. To create a site link, follow these steps:

1. Click the Inter-Site Transports folder in the Active Directory Sites and Services tree. To create an IP link, right-click the IP folder in the snap-in Details pane and click New Site Link. The New Object–Site Link dialog box opens (see Figure 9.10).

2. Enter a name for the site link. Then add two or more sites to the Site in this site link box (select the site and then click Add). When you have entered the information required, click OK. The new site link is stored in the IP folder (or the SMTP folder, if you created the new site link in that protocol container) .

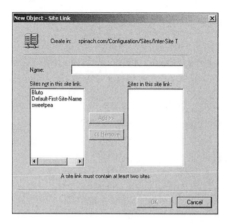

FIGURE 9.10

The New Object–Site Link dialog box.

You can also create site links using the SMTP protocol. However, this requires that you have an Enterprise Certificate Authority server available and that SMTP has been installed on all domain controllers that will use the link. Typically your site links will be of the IP variety.

3. You can also add sites to an existing site link. Right-click the site link icon and select Properties. Make sure the General tab is selected.

4. Select site names listed and then add them to the site link as needed using the Add button. Click OK when you have finished adding sites to the site link.

Active Directory Replication and Sites

Replication is the process that allows domain controllers to keep Active Directory data consistent throughout the network. The Active Directory uses remote procedure calls to replicate data between domain controllers over IP (another reason why TCP/IP is the default transport protocol installed when you install Windows Server 2003 on a computer).

In terms of replication between sites, you can control intersite replication by the site links that you create. You can also specify the schedule for replication between sites that are linked by a site link.

1. Right-click a site link in the IP or SMTP folders in the Active Directory Sites and Services snap-in. Select Properties from the shortcut menu. Select the General tab on the Properties dialog box, if necessary (see Figure 9.11).

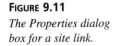

FIGURE 9.11

The Properties dialog box for a site link.

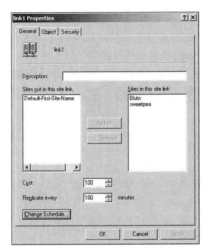

2. To change the replication interval, use the Replicate every spin box to set the minutes between replication events. To actually change the schedule for replication, click the Change Schedule button.

3. The schedule for the link opens. By default, replication is available every day of the week. To remove certain days and time periods from the schedule, use the mouse to select the day and time frame, and then select the Replication Not Available option button. Repeat as necessary. Then click OK to close the Schedule box.

4. When you have finished working with the links Properties dialog box, click OK to close the dialog box.

Understanding Delegation

Every action that we have discussed related to the Active Directory requires that a user be a member of the Domain Admins or Enterprise Admins groups. Otherwise, a user must be delegated the appropriate authority to make changes to the Active Directory, such as adding OUs or sites. So what is delegation? It is the assignment of administrative responsibility to a user or group (it can also be assigned to a computer). Delegation can be handled using group memberships or Group Policy settings. The Delegation of Control Wizard also can be used to delegate the control of Active Directory objects such as OUs or sites.

1. To start the Delegation of Control Wizard for an Active Directory OU or site, right-click the object and select Delegate Control. The Delegation of Control Wizard opens. Click Next to bypass the initial wizard screen.

2. On the next wizard screen, you are asked to select users or groups that will be delegated control for the object. Click the Add button. The Select Users, Computers, or Groups dialog box opens.

3. Specify the object names in the Object Name box (you can type key letters in an object name and then click Check Names to see a list of objects that begin with those characters).

4. After specifying the users or groups for delegation, click OK. Then click Next. The next wizard screen asks you to specify the tasks to be delegated (see Figure 9.12).

FIGURE 9.12

Group Policy links or custom tasks can be delegated.

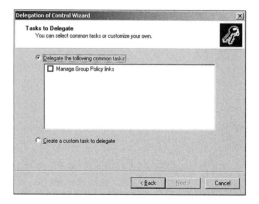

5. You can delegate common tasks, such as the capability to manage Group Policy links, or you can create custom tasks to delegate. Custom tasks enable you to manage objects in the container and specify control based on object permissions. Select the Group Policy links or Create a Custom Task to Delegate. Then click Next. If you selected Manage Group Policy links, the wizard takes you to the final screen, where you can click Finish.

6. If you choose to create a custom task to delegate, the next screen provides you with the capability to delegate control of all the objects in the current object folder (such as an OU or site) or to specify objects from a list (such as only account objects or computer objects). After making your selection, click Next.

7. A permissions list is provided on the next screen that enables you to specify the permissions that you will delegate for the object. Select the permissions using the appropriate check boxes, and then click Next.

8. The wizard provides a summary screen; click Finish.

Summary

Active Directory groups come in two types: security and distribution. Security groups are used to determine the access levels that users (members of the group) have to resources on the network.

Domain group scopes consist of universal, global, and domain local. Universal groups are available only if the domain functional level has been raised to Windows 2000 native mode or Windows Server 2003 mode. Groups can be nested within groups. For example, you can nest global and universal groups in domain local groups.

Groups are created using the Active Directory Users and Computer snap-in. You can add users to the group using the Member tab of the group's Properties dialog box.

Domain functional levels are raised using the Active Directory Domains and Trusts snap-in. By default, the functional level is set to mixed mode. You can raise the level to either Windows 2000 native mode or Windows Server 2003 mode.

An Organizational Unit (OU) provides a security container that can be used to hold users, groups, computers, and other OUs. OUs can be used to define logical groupings of users or other objects in the Active Directory, specify security settings, and assign policies to the OU.

Active Directory sites define the IP topology of your Windows Server 2003 network. A site can consist of a subnet or subnets. Sites and associated subnets are created using the Active Directory Sites and Services snap-in. Sites are linked using site links, which determine the replication paths on your network.

Delegation is used to assign an object such as a user or group a certain level of control over an object, such as a Active Directory OU or site. Delegation can be set using the Delegation of Control Wizard.

Q&A

Q What type of Active Directory objects can be contained in a group?

A A group can contain users and other nested groups.

Q What snap-in is used to create and populate groups?

A The Active Directory Users and Computers snap-in is used to create and manage groups. Default groups such as Domain Users and Domain Admins can also be accessed in the snap-in.

Q What is the purpose of the mixed-mode domain functional level?

A It is a functional level available for servers running Windows Server 2003 (and servers running Windows 2000 Server) so that they can communicate and replicate with Windows NT domain controllers.

Q What type of group is not available in a domain that is running at the mixed-mode functional level?

A Universal groups are not available in a mixed-mode domain. The functional level must be raised to Windows 2000 or Windows 2003 to make these groups available.

Q What types of Active Directory objects can be contained in an Organizational Unit?

A Organizational Units can hold users, groups, computers, and other OUs. The Organizational Unit provides you with a container directly below the domain level that enables you to refine the logical hierarchy of how your users and other resources are arranged in the Active Directory.

Q What are Active Directory sites?

A Active Directory sites are physical locations on the network's physical topology. They represent one or more IP subnets that are connected using IP routers. Because sites are separated from each other by a router, the domain controllers on each site periodically replicate the Active Directory to update the Global Catalog on each site segment.

HOUR 10

Adding Client Computers and Member Servers to the Domain

In this hour, you learn about the variety of network clients that can be used in a Windows Server 2003 domain or workgroup. We also discuss adding member servers to the domain.

In this hour, the following topics are covered:

- Adding Windows clients to the domain
- Using the Active Directory to add domain clients
- Managing computer accounts
- Adding Windows XP clients
- Adding Windows 2000 clients
- Configuring Windows 9x/ME clients
- Using Remote Installation
- Adding member servers to the domain

Adding Client Computers to the Domain

Windows Server 2003 supports a variety of client computer operating systems, including DOS, Windows 3.11, Windows 9x/ME, Windows NT Workstation, Windows 2000 Professional, and Windows XP (both the Home and Professional versions). It even provides connectivity for computers running the Macintosh operating system.

> Not only does Windows Server 2003 provide a "typical" network environment for a variety of operating systems, but it also can provide an "enhanced" remote connection for older computers running legacy versions of Windows (or the Macintosh OS). Check out the Terminal Server possibilities discussed in Hour 19, "Implementing Windows Terminal Services."

In an ideal situation (although this might not exist in the networking world), you will have to install and connect only one or two types of the possible client operating systems. In any case, try to standardize your client OS as much as possible. This keeps you from having to configure (and troubleshoot) many different client platforms.

Another aspect of standardizing client computers is standardizing their hardware configurations. If you have the luxury (the budget, in most cases) of configuring your client computers with a consistent hardware configuration, it will be easier to select and configure a particular client operating system.

A network client must be configured so that a user (or users) can log on to the domain. However, the computer must also be configured with the appropriate network protocol or protocols so that it can "talk" to the domain controller that grants a user access to the domain and the other servers on the network that provide services such as file and print services. Hour 7, "Working with Network Protocols," provides an overview of selecting and installing network protocols on the computers running Windows Server 2003. In this hour, we discuss the basic aspects of configuring network clients with the appropriate network protocols.

Setting up and configuring client computers is a somewhat consistent task when you are working with Microsoft operating systems such as Windows 9x/ME and later versions of the Windows operating system, such as Windows 2000 and Windows XP. However, a major difference exists between configuring the Windows 9x/ME computers and configuring the Windows NT, Windows 2000, and Windows XP clients. Computers running Windows NT, 2000, and XP must be added to the domain before the user can log on to the domain controller (or one of the domain controllers in the domain) using a username and password. The Windows 9x/ME computers do not require that the computer itself be added to the domain.

The fact that Windows NT, 2000, and XP must be added to the domain means that these operating systems provide a more secure user environment. Windows 9x/ME does not provide the local or network security that the "professional" Windows client operating systems afford. You should keep this in mind as you plan your network and future upgrades of client operating systems and hardware.

Client computers can be added to the domain when the computer is configured as a domain client (configured as the client), or the computer can be added by an administrator from a domain controller. Let's take a look at how a computer can be added to the domain using the Active Directory for Users and Computers snap-in.

Using Active Directory to Add Computers to the Domain

10

As you already know from the discussion in Hour 8, "Introducing Active Directory," a user needs a domain user account to log on to a domain. If the user will use a client computer that is running Windows NT, 2000, or XP, the computer itself also must be added to the domain.

As already mentioned, one way to add computers to the domain is to use the Active Directory:

1. Open the Active Directory Users and Computers snap-in on your Windows Server 2003 domain controller by selecting Start, Administrative Tools, Active Directory Users and Computers.

2. In the snap-in tree, click the Computers node (see Figure 10.1). To add a new computer to the domain, right-click the Details pane, point at New, and then select Computer. The New Object–Computer dialog box opens.

> If you have multiple domains in the domain tree, expand the domain node that you will add the computer to before selecting the computers node. You want to make sure that you place the new computer in the appropriate domain container.

3. In the Computer Name box, type the name of the computer that you are adding to the domain (see Figure 10.2). Because DNS is the default name-resolution mechanism for the Windows Server 2003 environment, the computer name can be up to 63 characters. (The Fully Qualified Domain Name of the computer can be up to 255 characters, including all the suffixes.)

FIGURE **10.1**

Select the Computers node.

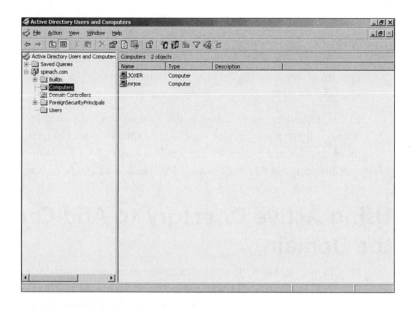

FIGURE **10.2**

Enter the name of the computer being added to the domain.

In some cases, you might also want to truncate the name to a NetBIOS length (15 characters) if you have NetBIOS clients (those using WINS for name resolution) on the network. This NetBIOS name is typed in the Computer name (Pre-Windows 2000) box.

4. You can also change the group membership required to join the computer to the domain. Select the Change button. Then use the Select User or Group dialog box to specify the groups (or specific users) who can join the computer to the domain.

5. The dialog box includes two check boxes. You can specify the new computer account as a pre-Windows 2000 computer or as a backup domain controller (in cases when you are still running Windows NT Server on some of your server computers). After making your selection and providing the computer name, click OK. The new computer name appears in the Details pane of the snap-in.

Managing a Computer Account

After you have created the account, the Active Directory Users and Computers snap-in provides you with the capability to manage the computer. For example, you can disable the account if you think there is a security issue or some other issue related to the computer. Right-click the computer name in the Details pane and select Disable Account.

You can also move the account from one domain to another; right-click the computer account and then select Move. The Move dialog box opens. You can use it to expand the node for a particular domain that appears in the domain tree. When you're finished, click OK to relocate the computer account to that domain.

> If you want to delete a computer account, right-click the account in the Details pane and select Delete from the shortcut menu. Click Yes when prompted to delete the object.

You can also manage the client computer by opening its Computer Management snap-in from the Active Directory Users and Computers snap-in (this is true for Windows XP and Windows 2000 clients). You can then add or remove local user accounts and even manage partitions and drives on the client computer. Right-click the computer account and select Manage from the shortcut menu. The Computer Management snap-in for the computer opens (see Figure 10.3).

FIGURE 10.3

You can manage the client computer using the Computer Management snap-in.

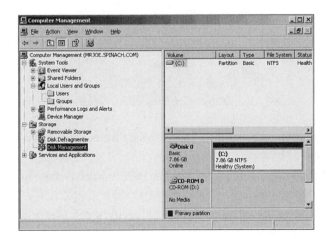

> For more information about using the Computer Management snap-in, see Hour 6, "Managing Hard Drives and Volumes."

Viewing Computer Account Properties

You can also view the properties for the computer associated with the Active Directory computer account. You can view the operating system that the computer is running (including service packs installed) and set other features related to the computer, such as whether the computer should be trusted for delegation (delegation is discussed in Hour 9, "Creating Active Directory Groups, Organizational Units, and Sites").

To open the Properties dialog box for a computer listed in the Active Directory, right-click the account and select Properties. The Properties dialog box for the computer opens. This dialog box contains seven tabs:

- **General**—This tab provides the computer name, the DNS name, and the role of the computer.

- **Operating System**—This tab (see Figure 10.4) shows the operating system running on the computer and the service packs that have been installed.

FIGURE 10.4

You can view and set the properties of a client computer in the domain.

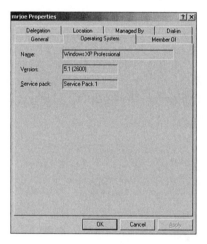

- **Location**—This enables you to specify the building or the floor where the computer is located.

- **Delegation**—On this tab, you can specify whether the computer should be trusted for delegation.

- **Managed By**—This tab is used to specify which user or group has the management rights to the computer.

- **Dial-In**—You can specify whether the computer can be used to dial in and remotely connect to remote access servers in your domain. Remote access and dial-in accounts are discussed in Hour 18, "Using Routing and Remote Access."

- **Member Of**—This tab shows the group that the computer belongs to. The default is Domain Computers. This tab also shows the domain container where the computer resides.

When you have finished viewing (or changing) the properties for a computer account, click OK to close the dialog box. You are returned to the Active Directory Computer and Users snap-in.

You can also access additional tabs related to a computer account's Properties dialog box by selecting the Advanced Features command under the View menu. After you enable Advanced Features (a check mark appears next to the command on the View menu), you also have access to the Object tab, which provides the canonical name of the object, and the Security tab. The Security tab enables you to set the different permission levels for users and groups in relation to the management of the computer account.

10

Adding and Configuring XP Clients

Although you can add computer accounts to the Active Directory using the Active Directory Users and Computers snap-in, you will still have to configure the client operating system so that the computer logs on to the domain when a user provides a logon name and password. You may also have to configure network protocols when you configure the client computer (adding network protocols to client configurations is discussed later in the hour).

And while the Active Directory Users and Computers snap-in provides an environment in which you can quickly add a number of computer accounts, you can also add the computer account for a Windows XP computer directly from the client workstation (as long as you have the administrative rights).

To configure an XP domain client (a computer running Windows XP Professional XP Home does not support domain membership) from the client computer, follow these steps:

1. Select Start. Then right-click My Computer and select Properties. The System Properties box for the XP computer appears. Select the Computer Name tab on the Properties dialog box.

2. To make the computer a member of the domain, select the Change button on the Computer Name tab. The Computer Name Changes dialog box appears (see Figure 10.5).

3. Click the Member of Domain option button and then type the name of the domain in the Name box. Click OK. A Computer Name Changes dialog box appears (yes, this is a second dialog box with the same name, as shown in Figure 10.6) asking you for a username and a password. The user must have administrative privileges to add the computer to the domain. This privilege is afforded to any user account that is a member of the Domain Administrator group.

FIGURE **10.5**

Specify the domain in the Computer Name Changes dialog box.

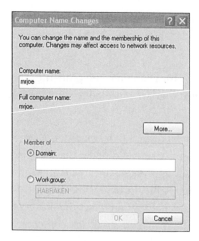

FIGURE **10.6**

Provide a user account with permission to join the domain.

4. Enter the username and password, and then click OK. It might take a moment, but a dialog box opens welcoming you to the domain. The computer is now configured to log on to the domain. A computer account is added to the Active Directory automatically because you provided an account with administrative privileges for joining the computer to the domain. The computer will need to reboot to complete the process.

5. You will now need to add domain user accounts to the local computer so that these users can log on to the domain from it. Open the Control Panel (select Start, Control Panel). In the Control Panel (see Figure 10.7), select the User Accounts link. The User Accounts applet opens.

6. Click the Add button in User Accounts. The Add New User dialog box appears (see Figure 10.8).

7. Enter the account name for the user and the domain that the user is a member of. Then click Next. On the next screen, assign the user account the rights to the local computer using the Standard User, Restricted User, or Other option button. Click Finish to add the account to the local computer. You can repeat the process as necessary, depending on the number of users who will use the client computer to log on to the domain.

FIGURE 10.7

Open the User Accounts applet from the Control Panel.

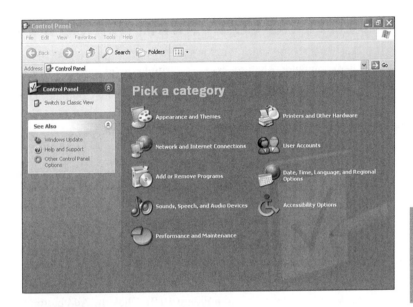

FIGURE 10.8

Enter the username and the domain.

10

Another option exists for adding XP Professional computers to the domain and adding a domain user account to the computer: using the Network Identification Wizard. This wizard is accessed on the Computer Name tab of the Systems Properties dialog box. Click the Network ID button to start the wizard; it walks you through the steps of adding the computer to the domain and then adding a domain user account. In my opinion, however, the wizard makes a very short process (the process already discussed in this section) longer than necessary.

Adding and Configuring Windows 2000 Clients

You can also configure Windows 2000 Professional computers as domain clients on the client computer. The process is very similar to adding an XP client to a domain.

1. On the computer desktop, right-click the My Computer icon and then select Properties. The Properties dialog box opens. Select the Network Identification tab.

2. On the Network Identification tab, select the Properties button. The Identification Changes dialog box appears.

3. Click the Member of Domain option button and then enter the name of the domain that the computer will be a member of. Then click OK. The computer must be rebooted for the process to be completed. As with Windows XP, a computer account is added to the Active Directory automatically.

As with Windows XP, you will want to add domain user accounts to the local computer. Select Start, point at Settings, and then select Control Panel. In the Windows 2000 Control Panel, double-click the Users and Passwords applet icon. The Users and Passwords applet opens (see Figure 10.9). Click the Add button to add domain user accounts to the computer as needed.

FIGURE 10.9

Add domain users to the Windows 2000 computer.

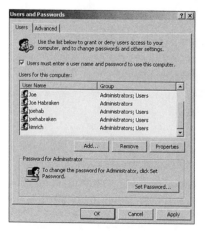

Configuring 9x/ME Clients

We have already discussed the fact that Windows 9x/ME client computers are not added to the domain. Instead, they are configured so that a user (or users) can log on to the domain.

1. On a computer running Windows 9x, right-click Network Neighborhood on the Windows desktop. Then click Properties (on a Windows ME computer, this is the My Network Places icon). The Network dialog box appears.

2. Click the Configuration tab if it is not currently the active tab. Click the Client for Microsoft Networks icon. Then click Properties. The Client for Microsoft Networks Properties dialog box appears.

3. Click the Log On to Windows NT Domain check box and then type the name of the domain in the Windows NT Domain box (see Figure 10.10). Also make sure that the Quick logon option button is selected. This allows the user to log on to the network without all the network drives that have been created on the computer being verified (allowing for a faster logon). The network drives are verified when they are accessed by the user.

FIGURE 10.10

Configure a Windows 9x computer for domain logon.

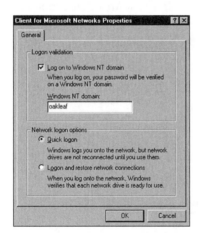

10

4. After you've entered the domain information, you can click OK to close the Properties dialog box. You are returned to the Network dialog box. Click OK to close it. When you are asked to restart the system, click Yes.

When the system restarts, the user logon is set up to log the computer on to the domain you specified. The users on that computer just need to supply a valid username and password for the computer to be logged on to the domain (users will also have to supply a password and confirm it for the Windows OS).

Windows 9x and ME do not provide the local security provided by other Microsoft client operating systems, such as Windows 2000 and Windows XP. This has always been problematic for network administrators because pretty much anyone can gain access to local files on a Windows 9x computer by clicking Cancel during the user logon process (when the computer is booted). If you have the hardware to run the more advanced client operating systems such as Windows 2000 or XP, you will be better off in the long run.

Configuring Client Computer Network Protocols

You can choose to run a single network protocol or multiple network protocols on your client computers. Each protocol that you do use must be correctly configured on the computer (a very basic factoid that we all learn related to network protocols is that multiple network protocols can be bound to a single network card). All the various flavors of Windows clients handle protocol configuration in a similar fashion. Network clients, protocols, and services are installed using a Properties dialog box for network connection. Figure 10.11 shows the Windows XP Local Area Connection Properties dialog box.

FIGURE 10.11

The Windows XP Local Area Connection Properties dialog box.

The process for adding network clients and protocols to Windows ME, Windows 2000, and Windows XP is very similar. Windows 9x is a slightly different story. Let's take a look at adding protocols to an XP computer and then adding protocols to a Windows 9x computer.

Adding Network Protocols on an XP Computer

To add a protocol to a Windows XP client, open the Control Panel (select Start, Control Panel) on the XP computer and then select Network and Internet Connections. In the Network and Internet Connections window, select the Network Connections icon.

To open the Properties dialog box for the Local Area Connection (as shown in Figure 10.11), right-click the Local Area Connection icon and select Properties from the shortcut menu. To install a new protocol on the computer, click the Install button. The Select Network Component Type dialog box opens. Select Protocol in the component install list (see Figure 10.12). Then click Add.

FIGURE 10.12

Select Protocol in the component dialog box.

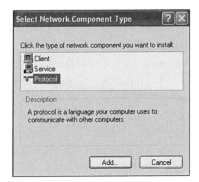

The Select Network Protocol dialog box opens. Select the protocol that you want to install, and then click OK. You are returned to the Local Area Connection Properties dialog box. To configure a protocol (such as TCP/IP), select the protocol and then click the Properties button. More information on configuring network protocols such as TCP/IP and NWlink (IPX/SPX) is discussed in Hour 7.

Adding Network Protocols on a Windows 9*x* Computer

Adding network protocols to a Windows 9*x* computer is similar to adding protocols to any of the other flavors of Windows. It is just a matter of locating the appropriate Properties dialog box. Follow these steps:

1. Right-click the Network Neighborhood icon on the Windows desktop and then select Properties. The Network dialog box appears. Protocols are configured on a Windows 9*x* computer using the Configuration tab of the Properties dialog box.

2. To add a protocol, click the Add button. The Select Network Component Type dialog box appears. Select Protocol and then click Add.

3. A list of available protocol manufacturers appears in the Select Network Protocol dialog box. If you are adding TCP/IP, IPX/SPX, or another standard network protocol, click the Microsoft icon. A list of available protocols appears in the Network Protocols pane of the dialog box.

4. Select the protocol that you want to add. After selecting the protocol, click the OK button. The protocol is added to the protocol list, and you are returned to the Configuration tab of the Network dialog box. When you close the Network dialog box (by clicking OK), you might be required to provide the Windows 9*x* CD-ROM. After the new protocol is added, you might also be asked to reboot your system.

Configuring the specifics of network protocols, such as NWlink and TCP/IP, for both network servers and clients is discussed in Hour 7.

Using Remote Installation Services

An alternative to installing client operating systems individually on desktop computers is to use the Windows Server 2003 Remote Installation Services (RIS). RIS enables you to outfit clients with a boot ROM chip to automatically connect to the RIS server (the boot ROM must support the PXE, Pre-Boot Execution, standard). Or, you can create a boot disk for clients that you want to set up that are not outfitted with the boot ROM chip (the network interface cards in these computers must be compatible with the Remote Installation Service, as discussed later in the hour). The boot ROM chip or the boot disk brings the client computer up on the network; you can then install the operating system from a shared folder (or shared CD-ROM drive on the server).

RIS can also be used to configure multiple servers with the Windows Server 2003 network operating system. This can be useful when you are rolling out a large network with a number of new servers.

To use RIS to deploy client operating systems (or the Windows Server 2003 OS to multiple servers), you must configure a RIS server on the network. Let's take a look at installing and then configuring RIS.

Installing the Remote Installation Service

You can install RIS on a domain member server or a domain controller. You cannot install RIS on a multihomed server (a server with more than one network card).

It is important for any domain server that will provide RIS to have enough dedicated hard drive space to hold the client images that you store on the RIS server. To install RIS on a Windows Server 2003, follow these steps:

1. Open the Add or Remove Programs applet in the Control Panel (click Start, Control Panel, Add or Remove Programs).

2. In the Add or Remove Programs window, select Add/Remove Windows Components. The Windows Components Wizard opens.

3. Scroll down through the list of components and select Remote Installation Services. Click Next to continue.

4. When the wizard has completed installing the service, click Finish.

You will need to reboot the system to successfully add RIS. You can then configure RIS, as discussed in the next section.

Configuring RIS

After RIS is installed on the server, you must set up the service. This is accomplished using the Remote Installation Services Setup Wizard. For the service to work correctly, you must have both a DNS server and a DHCP server available on the network.

1. To start the wizard, select Start, Administrative Tools, Remote Installation Services Setup. To bypass the initial wizard screen, click Next.

2. On the next screen (see Figure 10.13), you must specify the path that will hold the installation files for the client or server operating system. The volume must be an NTFS drive.

FIGURE 10.13

Specify the path for the client operating system files.

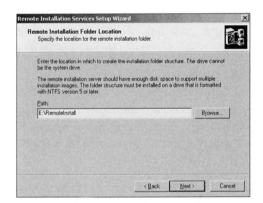

3. Click Next to continue. On the next screen, you can configure the RIS server to begin to immediately respond to clients requesting the service (or you can wait until you complete the initial setup of the service using the wizard). A check box is also provided that enables you to configure the RIS server to not respond to unknown clients on the network. After you make your selection, click Next to continue.

4. The next screen prompts you to provide the path to the CD-ROM that holds the Windows installation files that are to be used by the RIS server. Then click Next to continue.

5. Type in the name of the folder that will be created on the RIS server to hold the installation files that will be provided from the CD-ROM drive you specified in the previous step. For example, if you were configuring a folder to install Windows XP to client computers, you might want to call the folder windowsxp. After you provide the folder name, click Next to continue.

6. On the next screen (see Figure 10.14), you are asked to provide a friendly description for the installation files. You can also include help text. After you provide the information, click Next to continue.

*Provide a friendly
description and help
text for the installation
files.*

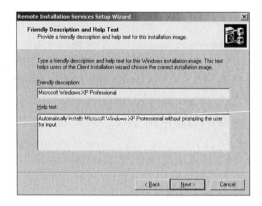

7. A summary screen appears, letting you know the image folder that will be created
    on the RIS server, the Windows version that will be installed using this folder, and
    the hardware platform. Click Finish to complete the process.

The files will be copied from the CD-ROM to the RIS folder that you specified during
setup. Client installation screens also are updated by the procedure (what you see on the
client when you use the RIS server), and the DHCP service on the network is authorized
(for use with RIS, each client logging on to the network using the RIS boot disk must be
assigned an IP address).

When you install the client (or server image) on the RIS server, an unattended answer
file is created so that when the installation process is begun on a client computer, no
interaction will be required by the user (or you). This means that when the computer
boots to the network with the PXE network card or the floppy disk that you create, the
installation should proceed automatically. There is even a way that you can configure the
RIS server so that it automatically provides the client computer with no interaction
required on the client computer. This is discussed in the next section.

The RIS server can also deploy Windows clients using system images (rather
than operating system files copied from an installation CD). An image of a
computer includes the operating system and the applications installed on
the computer. You can create images using the riprep.exe utility that is
installed in the \RemoteInstall\Admin\I386 folder created on the drive that
you designate for use by the Remote Installation Services.

Selecting the Client Computer Naming Conventions

You can also specify how you want the client computers to be named when the remote installation of the operating system takes place. Other settings that you can control related to the client installation include the location in the Active Directory where the client computer account will be created. Follow these steps:

1. Open the Active Directory Users and Computers snap-in (Start, Administrative Tools, Active Directory Users and Computers).

2. Locate the RIS server in the snap-in tree (if it's a member server, it will be in the Computers folder—if it is a domain controller, it will be in the Domain Controllers snap-in).

3. Right-click the server and then select Properties. The Properties dialog box for the server opens.

4. Click the Remote Install tab of the server's Properties dialog box.

5. Click the Advanced Settings button near the bottom of the tab.

6. On the Remote Installation Services Properties dialog box (see Figure 10.15), make sure the New Clients tab is selected. By default, the client computer names are generated using the username (truncated to seven characters) followed by a number (sequential numbers are used).

FIGURE 10.15

Select the client computer name scheme.

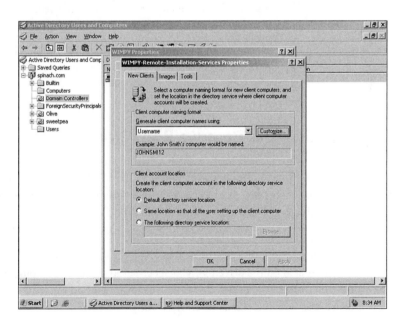

7. To change how the computer names are generated, click the Generate client computer names using drop-down box and select a naming scheme. If you want to create a custom naming scheme, click the Customize button. The Computer Account Generation dialog box opens.

8. Use the various variables shown in the dialog box to create the format for your client names (for example, %First specifies that the user's first name should be used in the computer name). After you select the codes to be used for the computer names, click OK.

9. To have the computer account created in the same location as the user account, select the Same Location option button.

10. To specify another location, select the Following Directory Service Location option button and then use the Browse button to specify the Active Directory container.

11. After you make your selections, click OK.

The fact that a naming strategy is defined on the RIS server means that client computers are automatically assigned their domain account during the installation of their OS. This again negates the need for user interaction during the remote installation process.

> You can also prestage client computer accounts in the Active Directory. Create the client computer account in the Active Directory Users and Computers snap-in. Make sure that you specify that the computer account is a managed computer account. You must also specify the Globally Unique Identifier for the machine (GUID): It is found on a label either outside or inside the computer case. Prestaging computer accounts should allow RIS installations to proceed more smoothly.

Creating the Remote Boot Floppy

The RIS server is ready to go as soon as you complete its setup and allow client computers to contact it (one of the choices provided by the RIS Wizard discussed in the previous section). Client computers boot to the RIS server over the network either because they are outfitted with a boot ROM chip (these boot ROMS provide a Pre-Boot eXecution Environment, or PXE) or because you boot them to the network and the RIS server by using a boot disk.

To create the boot disk, use Windows Explorer to locate the \RemoteInstall\Admin\I386 folder created on the drive that you specified to serve as the volume for the RIS server. In the I386 folder is a utility: rbfg.exe. This utility is used to create the boot disk that will be used to boot the clients to the network and the RIS server.

In Windows Explorer, double-click the rbfg.exe file. The Microsoft Windows Remote Boot Disk Generator opens (see Figure 10.16).

FIGURE 10.16

Use the disk generator to create your boot disk.

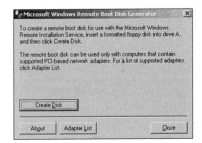

The boot disk works only with certain "standard" network interface cards. To see if your client network card is supported, click the Adapter List for a list of supported NICs (you can also consult the Microsoft Windows Server 2003 Web page for information on supported NICs). Click OK to return to the utility.

To create the boot disk, place a formatted floppy disk in the server's floppy drive and then click Create Disk. The disk then is created. If you want to create additional disks, click Yes when you are prompted. Having multiple disks enables you to bring a number of RIS clients online at the same time.

Installing a Client Operating System

Installing the client operating system from the RIS server is really just a matter of turning on the client computers that you want to configure (in some cases, you have to work with the BIOS settings on the computer to make it boot to the PXE ROM chip or the boot disk). Computers with the PXE ROM chip automatically contact the RIS server (they are assigned an IP address by the DHCP server). For client computers without the ROM chip, boot the computer using the boot floppy discussed in the previous section.

In either case, after booting the system to the network, the client should contact the RIS server. After the user logs in, the installation of the client software (or the server software, if you are installing Windows Server 2003) should proceed automatically (because of the answer file). The client operating system is installed with no interaction required of the user.

Adding Images to the RIS Server

RIS supplies an excellent platform for installing both client and server images to networked computers, and you can add additional images to your RIS server. This is accomplished through the Active Directory Users and Computers snap-in. Follow these steps:

1. Open the Active Directory Users and Computers snap-in (Start, Administrative Tools, Active Directory Users and Computers).

2. Locate the RIS server in the snap-in tree (if it's a member server, it will be in the Computers folder—if it's a domain controller, it will be in the Domain Controllers snap-in).

3. Right-click the server and then select Properties. The Properties dialog box for the server opens.

4. Click the Remote Install tab of the server's Properties dialog box.

5. Click the Advanced Settings button near the bottom of the tab.

6. Select the Images tab on the Remote Installation Services Properties dialog box. To add a CD-ROM image, click the Add button. The Add window opens.

7. Select the Add a New Installation Image option button and then click Next. The Add Image Wizard opens. Follow the prompts (it is the same set of steps as when adding the initial image, discussed earlier in the hour) to specify the location of the source files and the destination folder for the image.

You can add any number of images to your RIS server. This enables you to install any number of client operating systems remotely as well as add Windows Server 2003 images for new domain controllers or member servers.

Adding Member Servers to the Domain

Adding member servers to a domain is very similar to adding Windows XP and 2000 clients. You can add the server to the domain from the server itself. Follow these steps:

1. Open the Systems Properties dialog box for the member server (select Start, right-click My Computer, and then select Properties from the shortcut menu). On the Systems Properties dialog box, select the Computer Name tab.

2. To add the member server to the domain, select the Change button. The Computer Name Changes dialog box opens.

3. Select the Member of domain option button and then type the name of the domain. Then click OK. A dialog box opens requesting a username and password for an account that has the administrative rights to add computers to the domain. Provide the information and then click OK. The server then is added to the domain (see Figure 10.17).

Adding the Windows member server to the domain in this way automatically adds the server's computer account to the Active Directory. Member servers that have been added to the domain appear in the Computers node of the Active Directory Users and Computers snap-in (as opposed to domain controllers, which are listed in the Domain Controllers node of a particular domain).

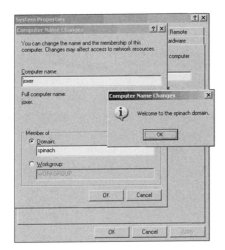

FIGURE 10.17

Add a member server to the domain.

10

Creating a Workgroup

In terms of Microsoft networking, the alternative to the domain is the workgroup. The workgroup is a collection of computers (in many cases, a peer-to-peer network that does not include a server) that share resources such as files and a printer. The workgroup certainly isn't a true alternative to the domain. When you have a very limited number of clients, you can use the workgroup model for networking the computers. However, adding a computer running Windows Server 2003 to this type of small network might be an expense that is difficult to justify.

When you install Windows Server 2003 on a computer, it is (by default) assigned to a workgroup called WORKGROUP. So, creating a workgroup and adding the server to the workgroup is really just a matter of configuring the clients and the server with the appropriate workgroup name.

The steps provided for adding a computer to a domain also apply (in part) to adding a peer computer or a server to a workgroup. Again, the process varies slightly among the Windows operating systems but is somewhat consistent. For example, to add a Windows XP computer or a Windows Server 2003 computer (which is similar to adding a computer running Windows 2000, ME, or 9x) to a workgroup, open the computer's Systems Properties dialog box and then select the Computer Name tab (this is the Network Identification tab on a Windows 2000 computer).

On the Computer Name tab, click the Change button (on Windows 2000 computers, click Properties). In the dialog box that appears, select the Workgroup option button (if necessary) and then type the name of the workgroup. Then click OK. The computer is welcomed to the workgroup that you specified.

Computers in workgroups (including servers) can share files, printers, and other resources. A computer running Windows Server 2003 can provide a workgroup a number of specialized services, such as Internet Connection, remote access/VPN, and basic firewall protection.

Client operating systems such as Windows XP and Windows ME actually provide a Network Setup Wizard. This wizard can be used to create and configure the small network workgroup. The Windows XP Network Setup Wizard actually enables you to create a setup disk that can be used to add legacy versions of Windows (9x or 2000) to the workgroup.

Summary

The Active Directory Users and Computers snap-in can be used to add Windows NT, 2000, or XP client computer accounts to the domain. Computer accounts are not required for Windows 9x/ME computers. Client computers running Windows NT, 2000, or XP can also be added to the Active Directory from the client workstation. This is accomplished using the Systems Properties dialog box. A username and password with administrative rights are required to add the client computer account to the domain.

You must configure client computers with the appropriate network protocols so that they can "talk" with other computers in the domain. Clients can run multiple network protocols, if required.

An option for installing Windows client operating systems is Windows Server 2003 Remote Installation Services (RIS). A RIS server provides a copy of the client operating system. Client computers can be booted to the network and the RIS server using a boot ROM chip or a boot disk. RIS servers can provide a number of different operating systems for remote installation over the network.

Windows Server 2003 member servers are added to the domain using the Computer Name tab on the computer's Systems Properties dialog box. Workgroups typically provide a peer-to-peer environment for sharing files and other resources such as printers. Client computers can easily be added to a workgroup (in the same manner that they are added to a domain).

Q&A

Q How can client computer accounts be added to the Active Directory?

A Client computer accounts can be added using the Active Directory Users and Computers snap-in. Client computer accounts can also be created via the client computer by joining the domain. This requires a user account that has administrative privileges, such as members of the Domain Administrator or Enterprise Administrator groups.

Q How are Windows 2000 and Windows XP accounts managed in contrast to Windows 9x client computer accounts?

A Windows 2000 and Windows XP clients require a computer account in the Active Directory. This account is managed using the Active Directory Users and Computers snap-in. Windows 9x clients do not require a domain computer account; they connect to the domain because their users posses domain user accounts.

Q What Windows Server 2003 service can be used to remotely install client and server operating systems on domain computers?

A The Remote Installation Service (RIS) can be used to install a Windows client or server image to a domain computer.

Q How does the remote computer boot to the network and then communicate with the RIS server?

A The remote computer must have either a network card that contains a PXE-compliant boot ROM or a network card that is compatible with the boot disk that can be generated on the RIS server.

10

HOUR 11

Understanding Group Policy and User Profiles

Two methods of controlling the user environment provided to your network clients are group policies and user profiles. In this hour, we take a look at how to use Group Policy to control the user environment and enable features such as user logon auditing. We also look at Group Policy in terms of the bigger picture of controlling domain policies related to security settings and their inheritance by downstream objects (such as Organizational Units). In addition, we look at user profiles and how they can control the Windows desktop and other user settings.

In this hour, the following topics are covered:

- Understanding Group Policy
- Installing and using the Group Policy Management Console
- Creating and linking Group Policies
- Editing Group Policies
- Enabling the Auditing policy
- Understanding Group Policy inheritance
- Working with user profiles

Understanding Group Policy

Group Policy provides a framework for controlling the user or computer environment in any Windows server container, including domains, sites, and Organizational Units (OUs). Group policies can also exist at the local computer level.

Group Policy objects actually dictate the rules or settings that determine how Group Policy affects users and computers in the target container (or on the local computer). For example, a Group Policy object (GPO) can determine the applications available to users in a particular domain or OU (creating OUs is discussed in Hour 9, "Creating Active Directory Groups, Organizational Units, and Sites"). To affect a container such as a domain or site with a particular GPO, the GPO is linked to the container.

GPOs can contain two types of settings: computer configuration settings and user configuration settings. Group Policy is managed using two different tools: The Group Policy Management snap-in, which is a new tool provided by Windows Server 2003, and the Group Policy Object Editor. We look at both these tools in this hour.

Installing the Group Policy Management Console

The new Group Policy Management snap-in makes it easy for you to view the Group Policies linked to objects in the Active Directory tree. However, because this snap-in is new, it takes some getting used to. It is certainly not a complete solution for Group Policy management because Group Policy must still be edited using the Group Policy Object Editor, which was available in Windows 2000 Server.

As of this writing, Microsoft has stated that the Group Policy Management Console will be available as a download for those who purchase Microsoft Windows Server 2003. The tool can be downloaded as an .msi package (a Windows installer package) and can be installed on your server by double-clicking the download in Windows Explorer. Or, you can use the Windows Run utility to install the software.

After you run the Windows installer package, you are guided through the installation process by the Microsoft Group Policy Management Console Setup Wizard. During the process, you are asked to agree to a license agreement.

After the Group Policy Management Console is installed, Group Policy Management is added to the Administrative Task menu. To start this newly added snap-in, select Start, Administrative Tasks, Group Policy Management.

The Group Policy Management snap-in opens in the Windows MMC. Figure 11.1 shows the Group Policy Management snap-in.

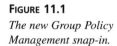

FIGURE 11.1

The new Group Policy Management snap-in.

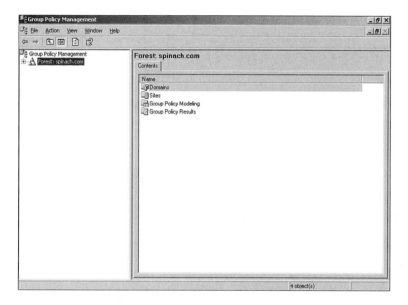

To view the domains in the current forest, expand the Forest node and then expand the Domains node. Although Group Policy can be applied to both sites and domains, our discussion this hour centers on domain Group Policies and the Group Policies of containers within a domain, such as an Organizational Unit.

> After you install the Group Policy Management Console, you disable the Group Policy tab that is found on the Properties dialog box of Active Directory objects such as domains and Organizational Units. This tab was commonly used in Windows 2000 to block inheritance and view the policies linked to the object. These functions are now handled by the Group Policy Management Console.

Creating Group Policies

You will find in the Group Policy Management snap-in that certain Group Policy objects (GPOs) exist by default. For example, on a domain controller, the snap-in shows that a default domain policy and default domain controllers policy exist. These policies can be edited and can include settings that enable you to control Registry-based settings, security options, and software installation and maintenance options. We look at editing GPOs in the next section. For example, to activate certain types of auditing on a domain controller, you must edit certain GPOs related to auditing events.

Before editing existing GPOs, it makes sense to create a new GPO and link it to a partic-
ular Active Directory container object. This also enables you to edit the settings for the
GPO. For practice, you might want to create a new OU using the Active Directory
Computers and Users snap-in, and then link a new GPO to it (using the Group Policy
Management snap-in, as discussed in a moment). You can then edit the settings for the
new GPO. You can later delete the OU and its GPO without affecting any of the default
Group Policies in force for your domain (creating OUs is discussed in Hour 9).

> The Group Policy Management snap-in also makes it easy to back up and
> restore individual GPOs. Right-click a GPO and select Back Up. You are asked
> to provide a location and description for the GPO backup. You then click
> Backup. You can also restore backups of a GPO; right-click the policy and
> select Restore from Backup.

Two different options exist for creating new GPOs in the Group Policy Management
snap-in. You can create a new GPO and simultaneously link it to an Active Directory
object such as a domain or an OU. Or, you can create a new GPO in the Group Policy
Objects folder and then link it to a container. The latter method provides you with the
capability to "play" with the settings of the GPO before you actually link it to a particular Active Directory object.

Let's look at creating the new GPO and link, and then look at creating a GPO in the
Group Policy Objects folder.

To create a new GPO and a link simultaneously, follow these steps:

1. Open the Group Policy Management Console (Start Administrative Tools, Group
   Policy Management).

2. Expand the various nodes in the snap-in tree until you see the container object that
   you want to link the new Group Policy to.

3. Right-click the object (such as an OU) and select Create and Link a GPO Here.
   The New GPO dialog box appears (see Figure 11.2).

FIGURE 11.2

*Supply a name for the
new GPO.*

4. Enter a name for the GPO and then click OK.

FIGURE 11.5

Software Settings can be configured in the Computer Configuration and User Configuration areas of a GPO.

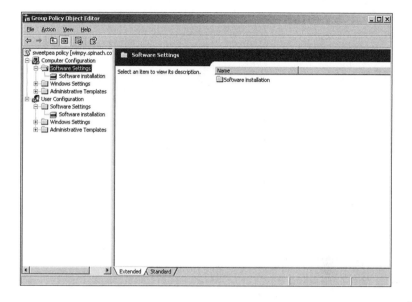

- **Windows Settings**—Windows Settings (for both the Computer Configuration and User Configuration settings) contains the security settings that you select and also holds any scripts that you choose to run. Because scripts are beyond the scope of this hour's discussion, we concentrate on security settings. Many of the important security settings are actually located in Windows Settings under the Computer Configuration node. These include account policies (which include Password, Account, and Kerberos, policies as shown in Figure 11.6), and local policies that include the Audit policy and User Right Assignments. We look at how you enable the Audit policy in the next section.

In the User Configuration area, Windows Settings also includes policies not found in the Computer Configuration area, such as maintenance settings related to Internet Explorer.

- **Administrative Templates**—Administrative Templates are found in both the Computer and User configurations. These templates enable you to control the settings for Windows components such as the Task Scheduler, Windows Messenger, and Windows Update. Settings related to the Control Panel can also be controlled using Administrative Templates, as can settings related to Network Connections and System Settings. We look at how you configure Administrative Templates later in this hour. Figure 11.7 shows the Administrative Templates found under the Computer Configuration node.

FIGURE 11.6

Settings for security policies and local policies are located in the Windows Settings folder of the Computer Configuration node.

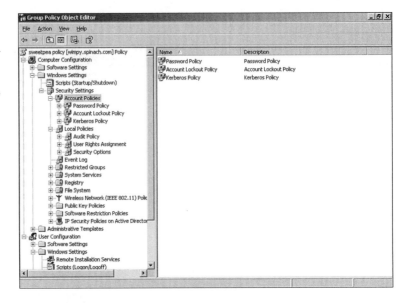

FIGURE 11.7

Administrative Templates enable you to control Windows components and system and network settings.

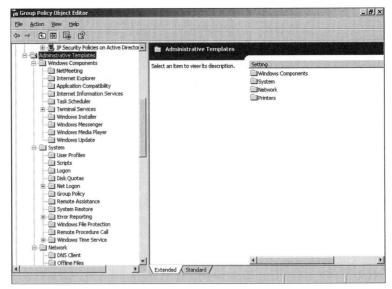

How you design and implement your Group Policy strategy depends on whether you decide to approach policies from the Computer Configuration or User Configuration settings. A particular GPO does not have to contain settings for both sections.

To make a long story short, editing a GPO is really a matter of locating individual policies and Administrative Templates that you want to use, and then enabling and configuring them. For example, let's say that you want some help in adding new workstations to the domain (this typically requires membership in a group that has administrative privileges). You can actually specify certain users who could help you add the new workstations by enabling and configuring the Add Workstations to Domain policy, which is found in the Local Policies node under the User Rights Assignment node (as shown in Figure 11.8) .

FIGURE 11.8

You can configure policies related to user rights, such as adding computers.

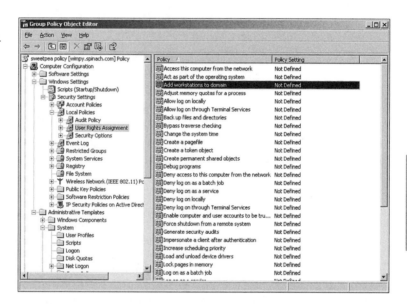

11

Policies that have not enabled or configured are labeled Not Defined in the Details pane. To enable and configure a particular policy, follow these steps:

1. In the Details pane, double-click the policy that you want to enable and configure (in this case, the Add workstation to domain policy). The Properties dialog box for the policy opens.

2. In the case of the Add workstations to domain policy, click the Define these policy settings check box and use the Add User or Group button to add users or groups to the policy. These users and groups now have the capability to add workstations to the domain (see Figure 11.9).

3. After you configure the policy (in some cases, you must actually click an Enable check box, but this varies from policy to policy), click the OK button.

FIGURE 11.9

Individual policies must be configured for them to take effect.

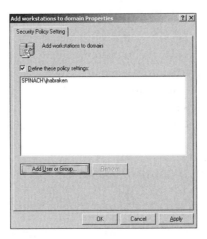

The policy is now enabled and so will affect the computers (or users) in the container (such as the domain) to which the GPO containing the enabled policy is linked. Obviously, to fully configure a GPO, you will want to enable and configure a number of the policies that reside in the GPO.

Obviously, a lot of the individual policies and Administrative Templates found in a GPO can relate to servers on the network and also to computers and users running client operating systems such as Windows XP and Windows 2000 Professional. Typically, you are trying to control client environments on the network (more so than what's happening with your servers, which are already controlled by password protection and access restraints), so as you peruse the basics of a GPO, you should be thinking in terms of how you can fashion the overall environment that users will experience as they work in the domain.

Enabling the Auditing Policy

For an individual policy to take effect in a GPO, you must enable and configure that policy (as we discussed at the end of the last section). In Hour 2, "Windows Server 2003 Security Overview," we looked at how you enable the strong password policy and the Kerberos authentication policy.

The policies that you enable in a GPO and how you apply that GPO to a domain or other Active Directory container depend on your overall plan for controlling the network environment for your users and computers. Some networks require very tight control using

Group Policy, while others do not require the same intensity (and amount of work for the network administrator) in relation to the Group Policy configuration.

Whether or not you totally buy into the controls provided by Group Policy, a useful capability for any network administrator is the capability to audit events on your domain controllers, such as successful or unsuccessful logons. So, it makes sense to take a look at how you enable the audit policy in a GPO (this also allows you to walk through the process of configuring another policy in a GPO—the more you enable and configure, the more it makes sense).

Let's say that you want to enable certain aspects of the Audit policy at the domain level. You would follow these steps:

1. Open the Group Policy Management snap-in (Start, Administrative Tools, Group Policy Management).

2. In the snap-in tree, locate the GPO that you want to edit (such as the default domain policy or a GPO that you've created to practice with).

3. Right-click the GPO and select Edit from the shortcut menu. The Group Policy Object Editor opens, with the GPO that you selected open in the snap-in.

4. Expand the Computer Configuration node and the Windows Settings node. Expand the Security Settings node and then the Local Policies node. The various local policies should appear in the Details pane, as shown in Figure 11.10.

11

FIGURE 11.10

Local security settings include policies for auditing object access and account logon events.

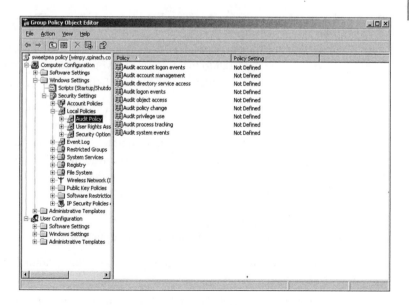

5. To enable and configure an audit policy such as the Audit Account Logon events policy, double-click the policy in the Details pane. The Properties dialog box for the policy opens.

6. In the case of the Audit account logon events policy (see Figure 11.11), click the Define these policy settings check box. To audit both successful and failed logon attempts, select both the Success and Failure check boxes.

FIGURE 11.11

You can enable poli-cies that allow logon events to be logged.

7. To close the Properties dialog box, click OK.

Now account logon events (such as a failed logon) will be logged in the security log of the Event Viewer. You can enable and configure other Audit policies as needed.

Configuring an Administrative Template

Although Administrative Templates are a component of a GPO, they have a slightly different look when compared to the policies that you enable and configure using the GPO Editor (such as the Audit policy, which you configured in the previous section).

As previously mentioned, Administrative Templates enable you to control processes, including Windows Server 2003 components and other system settings such as logon and logoff functions. For example, you might want to configure an Administrative Template related to the Windows Automatic Update feature so that when an update is installed, there is no autorestart. This would enable you to restart a server at a more appropriate time (such as in the evening or during the weekend) rather than disrupting network services with an autorestart.

To enable and configure an Administrative Template, follow these steps:

1. Open the Group Policy Management snap-in (Start, Administrative Tools, Group Policy Management).

2. In the snap-in tree, locate the GPO that you want to edit (such as the default domain policy or a GPO that you've created to practice with).

3. Right-click the GPO and select Edit from the shortcut menu. The Group Policy Object Editor opens, with the GPO you selected open in the snap-in.

4. Expand the Computer Configuration node, And then the Windows Settings node. Then Expand the Administrative Templates and the Windows Components nodes.

5. Under the Windows Components node, select the Windows Update folder. The individual template settings appear in the Details pane (see Figure 11.12).

FIGURE 11.12

Administrative Templates can be configured to control software and system settings.

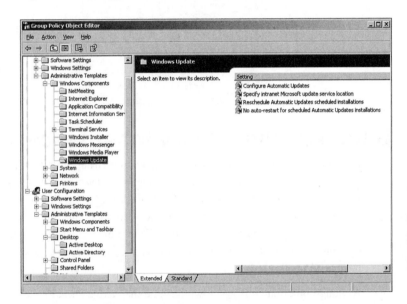

6. Double-click a template setting, such as No auto-restart for scheduled Automatic Updates installations. The Properties dialog box for that setting opens.

7. To enable the template setting, select Enable on the Setting tab of the Properties dialog box (see Figure 11.13). In most cases, an Explain tab is available for the setting, which provides a description of what the template setting actually does when enabled. Consult this information if needed.

8. After enabling the template setting, click OK.

The state of the template setting now changes from Not Configured to Enabled. You can enable Administrative Templates under the Computer Configuration and User Configuration nodes as required for your GPO.

Under the User Configuration node, there are Administrative Templates for configuring settings related to the user's desktop, such as the Active Desktop and the Start menu and taskbar.

FIGURE 11.13

Enable template set-
tings in the GPO
Editor.

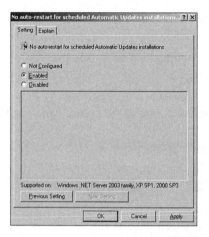

Understanding Policy Inheritance

An important aspect of understanding and using Group Policy is having a good grasp of policy inheritance. Enabled Group Policies flow down through the Active Directory tree from top to bottom. This means that domain-level Group Policies are inherited by OUs (and other Active Directory objects, such as domain controllers) that reside within the domain. A particular computer in an OU could then inherit GPO settings from the domain and the OU in which it resides. That computer might also have local policies that have been configured.

Although inheritance flows down through the Active Directory tree, the sequence in which Group Policy is actually processed by a computer is exactly the opposite. By default the local GPO is applied first, followed by site GPOs, then domain GPOs, and finally OU GPOs.

To view GPOs linked to an object such as an OU or a computer, select the object in the Group Policy Management tree. In the Details pane, click the Group Policy Inheritance tab (see Figure 11.14). Figure 11.14 shows the GPO inheritance for an OU named sweet-pea. The sweetpea policy is a policy created and linked specifically for the sweetpea OU. Notice that the OU also inherits the default domain policy.

> To view just the GPOs that are directly linked to an object, select the Linked Group Policy Objects tab.

FIGURE 11.14

The Group Policy Inheritance tab shows both directly linked and inherited GPOs for the object.

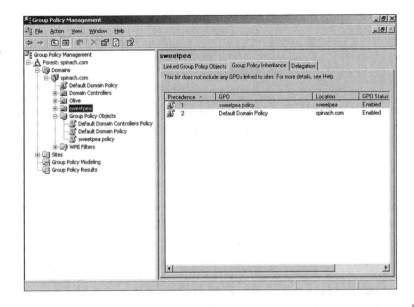

You can control which GPOs are inherited by a particular object. You can also have GPOs from higher in the Active Directory tree actually override local policies. Let's take a look at blocking inheritance and then enforcing a GPO to override local policies.

> The Delegation tab of an Active Directory object's Group Policy link enables you to change the permissions related to linking GPOs to that particular object. By default, the Administrators, Domain Admins, and Enterprise Admins groups have the link GPO permission for Active Directory objects such as sites, domains, and OUs.

Blocking Inheritance

You block the inheritance of policies from GPOs assigned farther up the Active Directory tree using the Group Policy Management snap-in. For example, you can block a domain GPO from affecting local policies or from affecting policies that you specifically assigned (linked) to an OU that you have populated with users and computers (in the Active Directory).

In the Group Policy Management snap-in, locate the container for which you want to block inheritance of the Group Policy provided by upstream Active Directory containers. For example, if you want to block domain policies from affecting an OU, right-click the OU in the Group Policy Management tree. A shortcut menu appears. Select Block Inheritance on the shortcut menu.

When you view the Group Policy Inheritance for the object, you will find that upstream GPOs have been removed from the Group Policy Inheritance tab. If you want to "unblock" the inheritance at any time, right-click the object (such as an OU) and select Block Inheritance to remove the check mark.

Enforcing a Group Policy Object

In some cases, you might want a particular GPO link to override any local Group Policy settings on an object. For example, you might want the domain Group Policy to override any settings made locally on a server (in the local Group Policy). You can do this by enforcing the GPO link for the Domain Group Policy.

In the Group Policy Management tree, right-click the GPO that you want to enforce. Select Enforced on the shortcut menu. If you want to no longer enforce a GPO, right-click the policy and select Enforced to remove the check mark.

Viewing GPO Details in the GPO Management Snap-In

Before ending our discussion of Group Policy, we should take a look at some of the other abilities that the new Group Policy Management snap-in provides. You can quickly view the scope (the objects that are linked to the GPO) and the details of the GPO (such as who owns the GPO, when it was created, and its current status). You can also view the enabled settings for the GP and view the current delegation of the GPO.

To view all of the GPOs in the current forest, expand the Group Policy Objects folder. Select any of the GPOs listed to view the policy details.

The information provided in the Details pane of the Group Policy Management snap-in for a selected GPO is divided into four tabs:

- **Scope**—This tab shows the sites, domains, and OUs that are linked to the GPO. This tab also shows the group users and computers that the TGPO is applied to.
- **Details**—This tab tells you the domain in which the GPO resides, the owner of the GPO, and when the GPO was created. It also supplies the date when the policy was last modified. The GPO Status drop-down list on the tab enables you to enable or disable the GPO, or disable only computer or user settings in the GPO.
- **Settings**—This tab (see Figure 11.15) shows you the different policies that have been enabled in Computer Configurations and User Configurations. Select a heading such as Security Settings, and expand the heading to see the actual policies that have been set. To view all the enabled settings, click show all at the top right

of the tab. This tab provides a listing of only enabled settings, whereas the Group Policy Object Editor (discussed earlier in the hour) shows you all the polices available in the GPO.

- **Delegation**—This tab shows the allowed permissions for the GPO. You can add or remove groups from this tab as required.

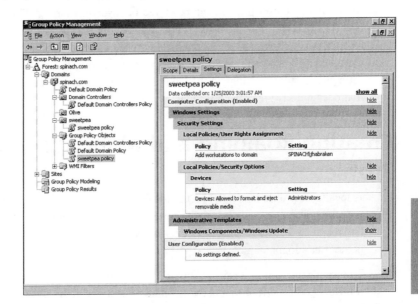

A final note on Group Policy: Group Policy is designed to provide consistency and security on the network. You should definitely create a number of GPOs and develop a clear understanding of how individual policies and Administrative Templates affect the user and computer configurations. It would be very wise to set up a small test network and deploy Group Policy so that you can see how the different GPOs at different levels in the Active Directory tree actually interact. Group Policy is not something that should be used without a very clear understanding of how it really works.

Understanding User Profiles

Although it is not as complex as Group Policy, there is another way to control and maintain the desktop settings for your domain users: You can create user profiles. This enables you to control the desktop environment for each user, even if multiple users work on the same network client computer.

User profiles control settings for Windows Explorer, My Documents, user-mapped network drives, and Internet Explorer Favorites. Other profile settings include screen colors and fonts, user-defined configurations for applications, network printer connections, and user settings in the Control Panel.

User profiles can be stored locally on a client computer or can be stored on a network server. Because user profiles can be stored on a server running Windows Server 2003, the user profile can follow the user around the network and be in force whenever that user logs on to a computer in the domain. This type of user profile is called a roaming profile. the user profile. When you do not want users to modify the desktop or other user-related settings (including settings in the Control Panel), you can create a mandatory user profile that does not save the changes made by the user.

Creating Roaming and Mandatory User Profiles

A local user profile is created on the local computer the first time a user logs on to that computer. The local user profile is stored on the client computer's hard drive in the C:\Documents and Settings\username folder (where C: is the system drive and username is the user's logon name).

To provide a roaming profile or a mandatory profile, the administrator must create the profile and then save it to a network share on a server running Windows Server 2003 (the server can also be running Windows NT 4.0 or Windows 2000 Server if you are running the domain in mixed mode or Windows 2000 native mode). It is a good practice to store the roaming or mandatory profiles on a member server rather than the domain controller. When the user logs on to a domain client computer, the roaming or mandatory profile is loaded on the client from the network share.

To create a roaming profile for domain users, follow these steps:

1. Create a shared folder on a domain server that will hold the roaming profiles for your users. For example, you might create a shared folder named \profile to store the user profiles (creating network shares is discussed in Hour 12, "Working with Network Shares and the Distributed File System"). You must make sure that the folder is configured with the appropriate permission so that the Everyone group has Full Control of the share.

2. On a domain controller, open the Active Directory Users and Computers snap-in (select Start, Administrative Tools) and then select the Users folder in the snap-in tree.

3. In the Details pane, select all the users that you want to configure for a roaming profile.

4. Right-click any user in the selected list and select Properties from the shortcut menu.

5. Select the Profile tab of the Properties dialog box.

6. Select the Profile path check box (see Figure 11.16).

FIGURE 11.16

Specify the share that will hold the roaming user profile.

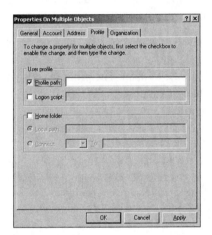

7. Enter the share name in the Profile Path text box using the Universal Naming Convention (UNC) name for the share (the UNC format is \\server name\share name), followed by the user's logon name. Because you have selected multiple users, use the variable %username%; this will automatically be replaced with the user account name when the path is established (this creates a separate folder for each user).

8. Click OK to close the Properties dialog box.

The next time a user (that is, a user who was included in the selected list that you configured for a roaming profile) logs off the local computer, that user's profile will be copied to the network share. Then when the user logs on to any computer on the network, the roaming profile will be loaded from the server to the local computer.

In some cases, you might want to standardize all the desktops in the domain. This can be done using a standard roaming profile for all users. To create a standard roaming profile for all users. Follow these steps:

1. Create a user account in the Active Directory Users and Computer snap-in that will serve as the template for the standard roaming (or mandatory) user profile file.

2. On a client computer (running Windows 2000 Professional or Windows XP, which depends on the client operating system or systems you are using on the network),

configure the desktop, Control Panel, and other user settings as you want them to be saved in the standard user profile.

3. Copy the file ntuser.dat from the local computer to the server share (the file is in the \Documents and Settings\user name\ folder on the local computer).

4. Configure your users' Properties in the Active Directory Users and Computers snap-in so that the path that identifies the folder where you placed the profile file is entered in the Profile path text box.

To make a standard roaming profile mandatory, use Windows Explorer to rename the standard profile that you created. Open the share that holds the standard profile and then change the file's extension from .dat to .man. The profile is now read-only (because of the .man extension), so any changes that users make to their desktops (or other settings) will not be saved to the profile file.

You can use the User Profiles tab on the System Properties dialog box on a Windows 2000 or XP Professional client computer to locate the local profile file. You can use this tab to copy the profile to a location on the network and then use the profile as the basis for a roaming or mandatory profile.

Summary

In this hour, you learned how to install the new Group Policy Management snap-in for Windows Server 2003. You also learned how to view the GPOs for an Active Directory forest and how to view the properties and settings of an individual GPO.

This hour also discussed the creation of new GPOs, the linking of GPOS to Active Directory containers, and the editing of GPO policies in the Group Policy Object Editor. You also learned how to enable and configure individual policies and Administrative Templates using the GPO Editor.

In addition, you learned how to use user profiles to control desktop and other Windows settings. Roaming profiles, which enable users to access their desktop settings from any network client, and the use of mandatory profiles were also discussed.

Q&A

Q What does the use of Group Policy provide you as a network administrator?

A Group Policy provides a method of controlling user and computer configuration settings for Active Directory containers such as sites, domains, and OUs. GPOs are linked to a particular container, and then individual policies and Administrative Templates are enabled to control the environment for the users or computers within that particular container.

Q What tools are involved in managing and deploying Group Policy?

A Group Policy GPOs and their settings, links, and other information such as permissions can be viewed in the Group Policy Management snap-in.

Q How do you deal with Group Policy inheritance issues?

A GPOs are inherited down through the Active Directory tree by default. You can block the inheritance of settings from upline GPOs (for a particular container such as an OU or a local computer) by selecting Block Inheritance for that particular object. If you want to enforce a higher-level GPO so that it overrides directly linked GPOs, you can use the Enforce command on the inherited (or upline) GPO.

Q How can you standardize all users' desktop settings so that they cannot make changes to the desktop and Control Panel settings?

A You can configure mandatory roaming profiles for your users. This enables you to provide a standard desktop to users, no matter what computer they log on to. By renaming the standard ntuser.dat file to ntuser.man, changes cannot be made to the file even when users change desktop settings on a particular network client.

11

HOUR 12

Working with Network Shares and the Distributed File System

Two of the most compelling reasons for networking computers are to share data files and to share printers. Early computer networks and the network operating systems that they used were designed around these needs. In this hour, we take a look at strategies for sharing files on a server running Windows Server 2003.

In this hour, the following topics are covered:

- Configuring a Windows Server 2003 file server
- Adding shares to the file server
- Using the File Server Management snap-in
- Working with the Volume Shadow Copy Service
- Understanding the Distributed File System

Configuring a File Server

A file server provides a repository for files that must be accessed by the users on your network. Not only do file servers provide data access to users, but they also often serve as a place where users can save files in either a home directory or a directory that can also be accessed by other users (home directories are discussed in Hour 11, "Group Policy and User Profiles").

You can configure a domain controller or a domain member server as a file server.

Whether you need a dedicated file server on the network depends on the amount of data that must be accessed and the number of users accessing this data. On a larger network, a dedicated file server that takes advantage of a RAID 5 configuration would provide fast and dependable access for your users (RAID 5 and configuring server drives are discussed in Hour 6, "Managing Hard Drives and Volumes").

> Before configuring a server as a file server, configure the drives and volumes that will be used to hold the shared folders. NTFS is your best bet as the drive file format on your file server. See Hour 6 for information on configuring drives and volumes (and using RAID). Hour 13, "Share and NTFS Permissions," discusses how to convert a FAT volume to NTFS.

The most straightforward way to assign the file server role to a server running Windows Server 2003 is to use the Configure Your Server Wizard.

1. Start the Configure Your Server Wizard either from the Start menu (select Start, Administrative Tools, Configure Your Server Wizard) or by selecting the Add or Remove Role link from the Manage Your Server window.

2. After bypassing the initial screens of the Configure Your Server Wizard, select File Server on the Server Role screen (see Figure 12.1). Then select Next to continue.

File Server Disk Quotas

On the next screen (see Figure 12.2), you are given the option of setting default disk quotas for your file server. Windows Server 2003 enables you to control and track shared volume usage on a per-volume and per-user basis. The wizard enables you to set a default disk quota for all users accessing shares on the volume. When a user saves a file on a file server volume, the disk space used for the file is charged to the user.

FIGURE 12.1

Select the File Server role.

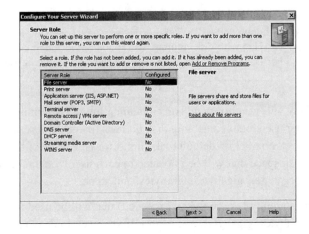

You can also fine-tune disk quotas on a per-user basis. Setting quotas by user and fine-tuning disk quotas are discussed in Hour 13. To take advantage of disk quotas, the volume must be formatted as NTFS.

FIGURE 12.2

You can set default disk quotas for the file server.

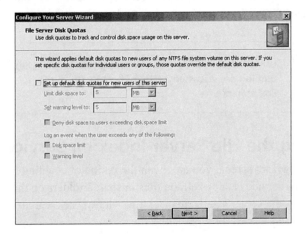

12

Other disk quota settings include a warning level setting where you can specify a space usage threshold. When this threshold is reached by a user, an event is logged in the system log, which can be viewed in the Event Viewer. You can also configure the default disk quotas so that users who exceed their space limit are denied any additional disk space. This event can also be logged to the system log.

Windows Server 2003 also provides a new command-line tool, fsutil, for working with disk volumes. Its capabilities include manipulating disk quotas. For example, fsutil quota is used to create and edit user disk quotas.

You definitely will want to spend some planning time to determine an appropriate disk space for your users before enabling disk quotas. To enable disk quotas using the wizard, select the check box Set up default disk quotas for new users of this server. Then set the amount of disk space that will be allocated to each user by default; you can set this amount in megabytes, gigabytes, terabytes, and so on.

Also set the amount of space (when exceeded) that will be used to determine the warning level (in megabytes, gigabytes, and so on). If you want to deny users extra space when they exceed their limit, select the check box Deny disk space to users exceeding disk space limit.

To log events associated with disk quotas, select either the check box Disk space limit or the check box Warning level (or select both). After setting the disk quota amount and the warning level (and selecting other options), click Next to continue.

Using the Event Viewer and viewing events in the log files such as the system log are discussed in Hour 20, "Monitoring Server and Network Performance."

Enabling the File Server Indexing Service

On the next wizard screen, you are given the option of enabling the File Server Indexing Service. This service catalogs all the files in shared folders on the drive. Although this service slows the server's performance, it provides faster searches and keyword queries when your users search for a particular file.

By default, the File Server Indexing Service is disabled. To enable the service, select the option Yes, Turn the Indexing Service On. After making your selection, click Next to continue.

The next screen provides a summary of your selections (such as setting disk quotas and enabling the Indexing Service). Click Next to continue. The Share a Folder Wizard starts.

Creating New Shares on the Server

You can use the Share a Folder Wizard to create a share on your file server. A *share* is simply a drive or folder that you share for access by your users.

To create a share using the Share a Folder Wizard (which starts automatically as you work with the Configure Your Server Wizard), click Next to bypass the initial wizard screen.

The next screen asks you to supply the path to the folder or drive that will serve as the new share. You can type the path in the Folder Path box (see Figure 12.3), or you can use the Browse button to locate the folder or drive on the computer. The Browse dialog box also provides you with the option of creating a new folder on a drive and then specifying it for the new share.

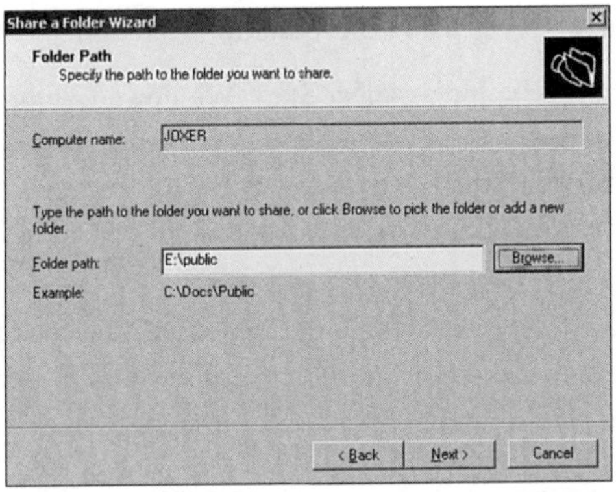

FIGURE 12.3

Specify the path of the folder for the share.

After specifying the path for the new share, click the Next button. On the next wizard screen, you are asked to provide a share name for the new share. You are also given the option of typing a description for the share.

A setting is also available related to the offline availability of files and programs on the share. By default, users can specify that items on the share be available offline, meaning that the files will be placed on the client computer for access if the file server is not available. In most cases, you will want to disable this setting so that sensitive material is not stored offline and is kept secure on the server (moving the data to the client computer also creates additional load on the network).

To change this setting, select the Change button on the wizard screen. The Offline Settings dialog box opens. To disable offline sharing, select the option Files or Shares from the Share Will Not Be Available Offline. Then click OK.

12

You are returned to the Share a Folder Wizard. Click Next to continue. The next wizard
screen relates to the permissions of the folder. Different permissions level can be
assigned to your users in relation to the share and the items that it holds. You will create
shares in detail in Hour 13. By default, the new share permission is set to All Users Have
Read-Only Access.

You will want to populate the share and be able to manipulate the files as the administra-
tor, so it makes sense at this point to change the default permission to Administrators
Have Full Access; Other Users Have Read-Only Access. Select this option and then click
Finish. This creates the new share. Click Close to close the wizard's summary screen.
The Configure Your Server Wizard appears, letting you know that this server is now a file
server. Click the Finish button.

Creating Shares Using Windows Explorer

You can also create new shares using the Windows Explorer.

1. Open the Windows Explorer (select Start, Windows Explorer), and select the drive
   in the Explorer tree that will contain the new share. You can use an existing folder
   or a new folder for the share. To create a new folder, open the File menu, point at
   new, and then select Folder. The new folder appears in the Details pane. Type a
   name for the new folder.

2. To share the new folder, right-click the folder and select Sharing and Security.
   The Properties dialog box for the folder opens with the Sharing tab selected (see
   Figure 12.4).

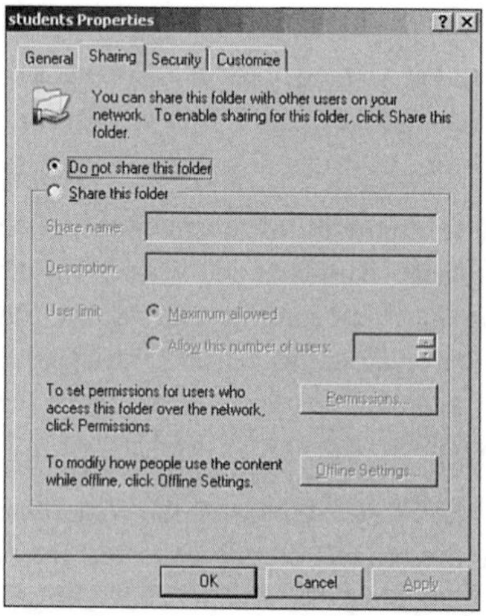

FIGURE 12.4

Share the folder.

3. Select the Share this folder option button. Then type a share name for the folder. You can also provide a description for the share. You can set user limits for the share, or you can go with the default. Permissions can also be set for the share (discussed in the next hour).

4. If you want to change the Offline settings for the folder (by default, it allows offline access), click the Offline Settings button and select the appropriate settings. (You can choose to turn off the offline access, as discussed in the previous section.) Offline access is useful in situations when a mobile computer such as a laptop is periodically disconnected from the network.

5. When you have named the share and set the other options, click the OK button. In Windows Explorer, the Share icon (the hand) is now present on the folder that serves as the new share.

Creating Hidden Shares

Administrators can set up shares that remote users cannot view using Windows Explorer or My Computer. When you create the share using the Windows Explorer (or the Share Wizard), follow the share name with a $ (dollar sign).

This makes the share an administrative or *hidden share*. Users will not be able to see this share when they browse the network for shares (although they can map a drive to this share). Only the administrator can see these shares. This means that you can store programs or other data on remote servers without worrying about them inadvertently being accessed by network users browsing the network.

Understanding Administrative Shares

Depending on the roles that you have configured for a server running Windows Server 2003, a number of administrative shares will be created automatically. These administrative shares serve as special resources related to specific server features. You do not access these special shares as a user would access a share providing files; instead, these administrative shares are accessed by server processes and services.

Whereas some of these administrative shares are configured as hidden shares, others are not. It is important that these special shares not be deleted, moved, or renamed—doing so affects the server's functionality. Some of these special administrative shares are listed here:

12

- **ADMIN$**—This hidden share is used during remote administration of a computer. It serves as the path to system root.
- **NETLOGON**—This share is installed on domain controllers and helps facilitate user logon.
- **SYSVOL**—This share serves as a domain controller resource and is important to domain client computer functionality.
- **PRINT$**—This share is used when you remotely administer a network printer.

Remember that these administrative shares are necessary for server functionality. They should not be tampered with.

Managing the File Server

You can use the File Server Management snap-in to view the shares on your file server (including administrative shares), a list of the users currently connected to the file server, and the actual files that are being accessed by users. This snap-in also makes it easy for you to quickly add a share using the Share Wizard and to back up the file server.

To open the File Server Management snap-in, select the Start button, point at Administrative Tools, and then select File Server Management. The snap-in opens in the MMC, as shown in Figure 12.5.

FIGURE 12.5

The File Server Management snap-in.

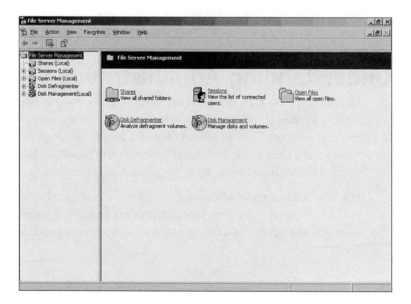

To view the local shares on the file server, select the Shares (local) node in the snap-in tree. The public and administrative shares appear in the Details pane. You can quickly view the Properties dialog box for a particular share by double-clicking the Share icon in the Details pane. If you want to open a particular share and work with the folder in the Windows Explorer, right-click the share and select Open.

You can also use the File Server Management snap-in to view the current sessions (meaning a list of the users connected to resources on the server) and view the files that are currently being accessed (and by which user or users). Select the Sessions (Local) node to view the current user connections in the Details pane.

When the Sessions (Local) node is selected, you can send a message to connected users; simply select the users in the Details pane and then click the Send Console Message link. The Send Console Message appears (see Figure 12.6). Type your message in the Message box.

FIGURE 12.6

You can send console messages to users connected to file server shares.

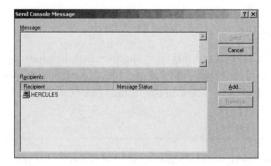

If you want to add other computers on the network that you want to receive the message, use the Add button. When you are ready to send the message, click Send.

You can also close sessions for particular users or close all the active sessions to file server resources. This is particularly useful if you need to make changes to the shares or their contents, and you want to disconnect users who have not logged off the domain and closed their connections to file server shares.

To view the files that are being accessed by domain users, select the Open Files (Local) node in the tree. The files being accessed by users appear in the snap-in Details pane (see Figure 12.7).

12

FIGURE 12.7

You can view the folders and files currently being accessed.

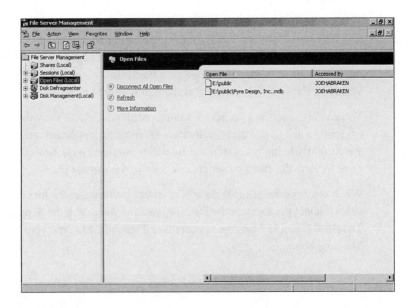

You can disconnect particular users from the files that they have open or choose to close all the currently accessed files on the server. Select a particular user or users, and then use the appropriate command link in the Details pane (when you have the Open Files [Local] node selected).

 The File Server Management snap-in also provides you quick access to the Backup Wizard, the Disk Defragmenter, and the Disk Management tool for the local file server. Disk Management, the Disk Defragmenter, and backups are discussed in Hour 6.

Publishing a Share to the Active Directory

You can publish a share (or shares) to the Active Directory. Publishing a share to the Active Directory makes the share an Active Directory object. This means that users can search for the share as they would any other object included in the Active Directory catalog. Publishing the share also allows it to be replicated to other domain servers in the domain as part of the Global Catalog.

 You must be a member of the Domain Administrators or the Enterprise Administrators groups to publish a share to the Active Directory.

To publish a share to the Active Directory, follow these steps:

1. In the File Server Management snap-in, select the Shares node. Then right-click the share you want to publish (all shares appear in the Details pane). Select Properties from the shortcut menu. The Properties dialog box for the share opens.

2. Select the Publish tab on the Properties dialog box (see Figure 12.8).

FIGURE 12.8

You can publish a share to the Active Directory.

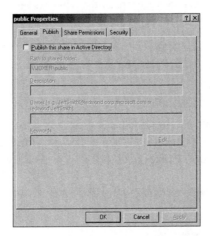

3. Select the check box Publish this share to Active Directory. Supply a description, ownership, and keywords for the share (all of these will aid in searches conducted to find the share). After entering the information, select OK. You are returned to the File Server Management snap-in.

12

 You can also publish folders to the Active Directory using the Active Directory Users and Computers snap-in. This enables you to place the folder in a particular container in the Active Directory. Right-click the container that will hold the published share; then select New, Shared Folder. Supply the name and the path for the share, and then click OK.

Using the Volume Shadow Copy Service

The Volume Shadow Copy Service is a new feature supplied by Windows Server 2003 that creates different point-in-time versions of files in a share. It is part of the new backup infrastructure provided by Windows Server 2003, and it enables users to recover a particular version of a file from the file server. This feature allows users to recover overwritten or inadvertently deleted shared files.

You can enable Volume Shadow copy on a file server share using the File Server Management snap-in. Client computers must also be configured (client computers running Windows XP or later) so that they can take advantage of the Shadow Copy Service.

> Do not use the Shadow Copy Service on servers that you have configured for dual boot with previous versions of the Windows Server software or other operating systems. Shadow Copy version files can become corrupted when you boot to the non–Windows Server 2003 and unusable when you reboot to Windows Server 2003.

Enabling a Share for Shadow Copy

The File Server Management snap-in provides easy access to the Shadow Copy Service. In the snap-in tree, select the Shares node. Then click the Configure Shadow Copies link in the Details pane. The Shadow Copies dialog box opens (see Figure 12.9).

FIGURE 12.9

Enable the Shadow Copy Service.

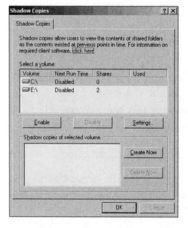

> You can also enable the Shadow Copy Service from the Computer Management snap-in. Right-click the Shared Folders node in the snap-in tree. Point at All Tasks on the shortcut menu, and then select Configure Shadow Copies. You then follow the same steps to enable the service as discussed in this section.

In the dialog box, select the volume you want to enable for Shadow Copy. Then click the Enable button. The Enable Shadow Copies dialog box opens asking if you want to enable shadow copies. Click Yes.

To change the settings for Shadow Copy, such as the schedule and the amount of space allotted for shadow copies on the file server, select the Settings button. The Settings dialog box opens. To set the maximum size available for shadow copies, use the Use Limit Spinner Box. The default is 856MB (be advised that you need a minimum of 100MB free space to create a shadow copy). Be advised that there is an upper limit of 64 shadow copies per volume. This means that you will want to create a schedule that retains an appropriately long enough history of the files without reaching the upper limit.

To set the schedule for the Shadow Copy server, select the Schedule button. The Schedule dialog box opens (see Figure 12.10) .

FIGURE 12.10

Use the Schedule dialog box to set the timing of the shadow copies.

12

The default schedules shadow copy files twice a day (during the work week, Monday through Friday) at 7 a.m. and 12 p.m. If you want to increase the number of scheduled shadow copies (Microsoft recommends that you do not increase the number beyond one shadow copy per hour), select New and then create a new scheduled shadow copy event. (It is best to select Weekly, specify the days in the week, and then specify a certain time, which is how the sample schedule has been configured.)

When you have finished setting the schedule, click the OK button. Then click OK again to close the Settings dialog box. You are returned to the Shadow Copies dialog box.

If you want to create Shadow copies of the selected volume, immediately select the Create Now button. A date and time listing appears in the Shadow Copies of Selected Volume box. Click OK to close the dialog box and return to the File Server Management snap-in.

The Shadow Copy Client Software

Client computers that will access and take advantage of a file server share enabled for Volume Shadow Copy require the installation of the client software for Shadow Copies of Shared Folders. This software is installed using the twclient.msi package. It is found in the windows\system32\clients\twclient\x86 folder on a computer running Windows Server 2003.

You can move the twclient.msi installer to a public share and allow users to install the client on their own computer (all they have to do is double-click the installer package and follow the prompts). You should also make users aware of the schedule that you have designed for the Shadow Copy Service and how they access previous versions of shared files (which is discussed in the next section).

At the time this book was written, only the twclient installation package was available for clients running Windows XP.

Accessing Volume Shadow Copy Files

Shadow Copy versions of files that have been copied according to your copy schedule can be accessed from enabled client computers on the network or other servers running Windows Server 2003.

To access a previous version of a current file, open Windows Explorer and locate the file in the network share (using My Network Places if a drive has not been mapped to the share).

Right-click the file and then select Properties. The Properties dialog box opens for the file. An additional tab, named Previous Versions, appears on the Properties dialog box. Select this tab (see Figure 12.11).

Previous versions of the file (as recorded by Shadow Copy) appear in the File Versions box. Users have two options related to a shadow copy of a file: They can restore the previous version, or they can copy the previous version to a new location.

Selecting Restore on the Previous Versions tab rolls back the file's status to the previous version copy that a user has selected. The Copy command allows a user to copy the previous version to any folder on the local computer or another network share.

As the administrator, you might have to set some policies related to the Shadow Copy feature. For example, a user could use the Restore command, but this might restore the file to a previous state that is not necessarily useful to the user or users who have changed the file recently. You might want to instruct users to copy previous versions of files to their local computers if they need information in a file that has been edited since the last Shadow Copy.

FIGURE 12.11

Previous versions of a file are listed.

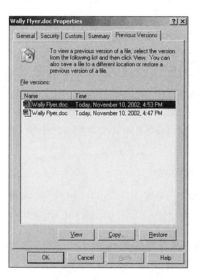

Understanding the Distributed File System

Another possibility for sharing resources on the network is to use the *Distributed File System* (DFS). DFS provides a hierarchical tree structure that enables users to access resources anywhere in the domain. The actual location of the resource, such as a volume or a folder, is transparent to the users. This allows resources to be spread across file servers and also supports the creation of identical shared folders that supply the same resources to the users and also provide fault tolerance for the resource or resources themselves.

The best thing about DFS is that users do not need to know the name of the server that is providing the shared resources (as a user does when trying to map a drive to a shared resource). Network administrators also benefit from the use of DFS because, if a file server fails, the DFS tree can be made to point to a redundant set of the shares on another server. This action is transparent to the users, who still can access the share or shares as if they were still available at the original location.

DFS enables you to use the shares that you have created and the various share and NTFS permissions that you have set for shares and files. DFS is really just supplying an overall structure for how users see and access the shares.

12

To take advantage of DFS, a client computer must contain the DFS client. Windows 2000 and later have the DFS client. Windows 98 and Windows NT 4.0 require a DFS client add-on (which can be downloaded from Microsoft.com) .

Configuring the Distributed File System

To take advantage of DFS, a DFS root must be installed. The DFS root supplies the main DFS container. Then child links can be added to the DFS root that point at other shares on the network. Users will see the DFS hierarchical tree when they want to map a network drive or access network shares.

To create a DFS root, follow these steps:

1. Open the Distributed File System snap-in (select Start, Administrative Tools, Distributed File System). Figure 12.12 shows the Distributed File System snap-in.

FIGURE 12.12

The Distributed File System snap-in.

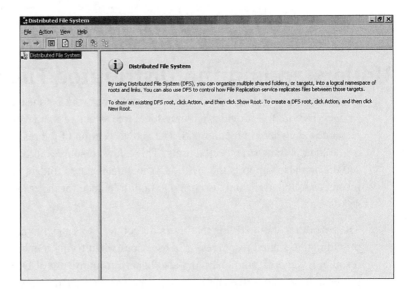

2. Right-click the Distributed File System node in the snap-in tree, and select New Root from the shortcut menu. Click Next to bypass the New Root Wizard's initial screen.

3. On the next screen, you can select Domain Root or Standalone Root. Domain roots replicate automatically and store the DFS configuration in the Active Directory. Standalone roots are appropriate when the server is part of a workgroup.

Domain Root is the default selection. Click Next to continue.

4. On the next screen, you must specify the domain that will host the root (see Figure 12.13). The domain can be the domain that the file server is a member of, or you can select any trusting domain in the network's domain tree.

FIGURE 12.13

Specify the host domain for the DFS root.

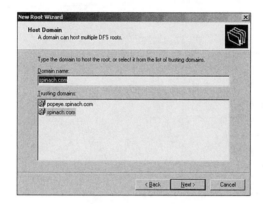

After you specify the host domain, click Next.

5. On the next screen, you are asked to specify the host server for the root. You can type the name of the server or use the Browse button to locate the server. After specifying the server (which can be the server you are currently working on), click Next.

6. On the next wizard screen, you are asked to supply a unique name for the DFS root. The root name can be the same as a shared folder on this server. For example, you could have a share named public and use this as the name for the DFS root. The Root Name screen (the current wizard screen) needs to have a name for the root and also have you associate it with an existing share on the server. So, the root name and the share to be used can be the same.

   After you specify the root name (and specify the share that the name will point to), click Next. A summary screen appears for the wizard; click Finish.

The DFS root appears in the Distributed File System snap-in (see Figure 12.14). The root share now serves as the main container (the root of the DFS hierarchy) for all other shares that are added as links to this particular DFS tree. Even when the shares in the DFS tree are on different file servers or are held on different file server volumes on the same file server, all the shares will appear to originate (be contained within) the root share.

12

FIGURE 12.14

The DFS root supplies the root container for the DFS tree.

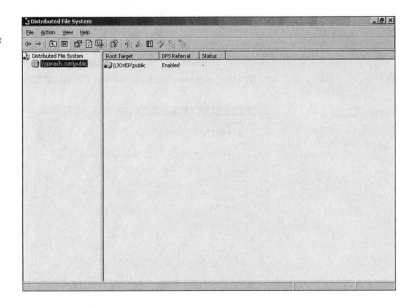

A domain can actually host multiple DFS roots. This means that you have a great deal of flexibility in creating DFS trees and organizing shares within these different hierarchical DFS containers.

Adding DFS Links

After the DFS root has been created, DFS links, also known as child links, can be added to the DFS tree. A link can be any share anywhere on the network.

To add a DFS link to the root, right-click New Link on the shortcut menu. The New Link dialog box opens (see Figure 12.15).

Type a new name for the link in the Link Name box. To specify the share that the link will point to, type the UNC name for the share (\\server name\share name), or use the Browse button to locate the share on the network. After you enter the path to the share, click the OK button. The link is added to the DFS root as a branch (see Figure 12.16). You can repeat this process as needed to add additional links to the DFS root.

FIGURE 12.15

Add links to the DFS root that point to shares on the network.

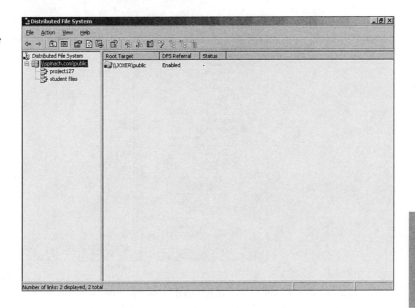

FIGURE 12.16

Links are added to the DFS root.

You can check the status of any root or link in the DFS hierarchy. In the Distributed File System snap-in, right-click the root or link in the snap-in tree and then select Check Status from the shortcut menu. If the link (or root) is online, an Agree checkmark appears next to the icon in the tree. You will also note that the target's status is designated as Online in the snap-in Details pane.

Accessing Shares in the DFS Tree

When the DFS tree (or trees) have been established for the domain, it becomes quite easy for users to access network shares using Windows Explorer or any of their software applications. When a user browses the network for shares, they will see the DFS root (or roots) as the share folder that holds the other shares on the network.

Users are not aware of these actual locations of these folders, and they do not have to browse by computer to find network resources. The DFS tree provides access to all the shares. Figure 12.17 shows a DFS root named public and the links that it contains. Note that the DFS root appears as a typical share to the user when browsing the network using Windows Explorer. The shares contained within the public DFS root are actually shares on other servers on the network and have been added to public as DFS links.

FIGURE 12.17

The DFS tree appears as typical shares when browsed by users.

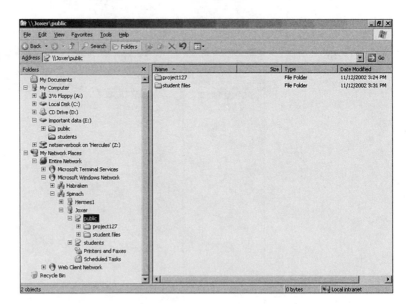

A user can quickly map a drive to any of the shares found in the DFS tree. All the user has to do is select a particular share (a share that he has permissions to access), select the Windows Explorer Tools menu, and then select Map Network Drive. The share will be mapped to the next available drive letter on the user's computer.

As with a number of other Windows Server 2003 utilities and tools, you can work with the Distributed File System from the command line. The dfscmd command can be used to create DFS roots and links. The Windows Server 2003 Help System provides a easy reference to New command-line tools and their uses.

Summary

In this hour, you learned how to configure and manage a file server.

Files are made available to users in a share. Shares can be created on a file server using the Share Wizard or using Windows Explorer.

File servers can be managed using the File Server Management snap-in. You can view the current shares on the server and also view user connections and a list of opened files. To make shares accessible throughout the domain and domain tree, you publish a share (or shares) to the Active Directory. This makes the share information part of the Global Catalog.

The Volume Shadow Copy Service creates point-in-time versions of files in a network share. Users can then recover previous versions of a file.

The Distributed File System provides a hierarchical, logical structure for arranging network shares. A DFS root provides the base container for the DFS tree, and other shares on the network are added as links.

Q&A

Q What is the fastest way to bring a file server online in the domain, including the configuration of disk quotas and the enabling of the File Server Indexing Service?

A Using the Configure Your Server Wizard, you can quickly add a file server role to a member server or domain controller and configure options such as disk quotas and the File Server Indexing Service.

Q What are two methods for adding shares to a file server?

A You can use the Share a Folder Wizard or Windows Explorer to share folders or volumes on a file server.

Q How can you create a hidden share on a server?

A Create the share and follow the share name with the $ (dollar sign) symbol. Only someone with administrative rights will be able to browse for the share on the network.

Q What can you do to make it easier for users on the network to locate a share?

A Publishing a share to the Active Directory places the share in the Global Catalog as an Active Directory Object. This makes it easier for users to locate the share on the network.

12

Q What feature can provide different point-in-time versions of files shared on a file server?

A The Volume Shadow Copy Service can be used to create point-in-time backups of files in a network share. This allows users to recover overwritten or deleted files by accessing an earlier version of the file.

Q What does the Distributed File System offer in terms of providing shares to users on the network?

A The Distributed File System provides a hierarchical tree structure that makes it easy for users to access resources no matter where the files are stored on the network. The DFS root provides the root of the DFS tree and allows users to view shares on the network as if they were stored in one location rather than on multiple file servers on the network.

HOUR 13

Understanding Share and NTFS Permissions

In Hour 12, "Working with Network Shares and the Distributed File System," we looked at configuring a file server and sharing drives and folders on the network. In this hour, we take a look at how you secure network shares. First, we examine share permissions. Then we cover the additional security from using NTFS permissions on your file server volumes. In this hour, the following topics are covered:

- Working with share permissions
- Understanding NTFS permissions
- Upgrading a drive to NTFS
- Using NTFS folder and file permissions
- Using file encryption
- Mixing share and NTFS permissions
- Fine-tuning disk quotas

Understanding Share Permissions

When you share a volume or folder on the network, the default share permission
assigned to the newly created share is Read Only for the Everyone group (all users on
the network belong to the Everyone group). A *share permission* is the access level that
you give to a particular user or group of users in relation to a particular share on your file
server (or other server on the network). Setting the share permission for a folder or volume also sets the share permission level for the files contained in the share.

> Although Read Only was the default permission for a share created with the
> Create a Share Wizard, the wizard supplied you with the capability to
> change the level of access for administrators and users during the share-cre-
> ation process. See Hour 12 for more information about the Create a Share
> Wizard and creating a new share.

You can view the current share permissions for a folder or volume using the File Server
Management snap-in. To open the snap-in select Start, Administrative Tools and then
select File Server Management. To view the permissions for a share, follow these steps:

1. Select the Shares (local) node in the snap-in tree.

2. To view the share permissions for a particular share, right-click the share in the
   Details pane and then select Properties.

3. Click the Share Permissions tab on the Properties dialog box (see Figure 13.1).

FIGURE 13.1

*The Share Permissions
tab shows the permis-
sions set for the share.*

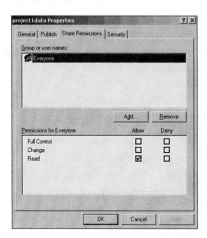

Share permissions can be set at three different levels: Full Control, Change, and Read. A description of each share permission level follows:

- **Full Control**—This permission level enables the user to modify file permissions and perform all the tasks permitted by the Change and Read permission levels. This access level gives a user the same access that an administrator would have to the share, meaning that a user with full control could change the permissions on the folder.

- **Change**—This permission level enables the user to create folders in the share and add new files. Users can change data in the files and add new data to the files contained in the shared folder.

- **Read**—This permission level enables the user to display folders and files in the share, open the files in the share (in read-only mode), and run program files that are contained in the share.

You have the option of either allowing each permission level (using the Allow check box) or denying a particular permission (using the Deny check box). Typically, you assign a permission level, such as a change to a user or group, by selecting the Allow check box to the right of the permission (in this case, Change).

The Deny setting is used to fine-tune permission levels. Typically, you will want to assign share access levels by domain groups (it makes sense to create groups for users and then assign share permissions to the groups). The Deny permission always overrides any granted permissions for the object.

You might run into a case, however, in which most of the users in a group need a higher permission level, such as the Full Control permission for a share. But you might not want to assign that level of access to a few other users in the group (they could destroy important files in the share).

Here's what you do: You assign the Full Control permission to the group using the Allow check box. You then add the users from the group who do not need this level of access, and you change their Full Control permission from Allow to Deny. Denying the permission level at the user level overrides the higher level of permission that you provided to the group.

13

In some cases, you might want to assign a group or user the No Access permission level. This permission level allows a connection to the shared folder (the folder can be seen on the network), but access to the folder and its contents are denied. To assign No Access, clear all the Allow check boxes for a particular group or user.

This permission level is useful when fine-tuning individual user access in a group that has been assigned an access permission level. For example, you might want the Accounting group to see the database, with the exception of the support people in the group, such as administrative assistants. You can allow the group access but use the No Access permission for the users whom you don't want to see this highly sensitive data.

Hopefully, you see that you need to plan the level of permissions that you will supply to your domain groups (and individual users, if necessary) for the shares on the network. You should analyze what users will be doing with the files in each share and plan access levels accordingly.

> You can also view (and edit) the Share permissions for a share via the Windows Explorer. Locate the share using Windows Explorer, and then right-click the share and Sharing and Security. The Properties dialog box for the share opens with the Sharing tab selected. Click the Permissions button to view the share's current permissions.

Assigning Share Permissions

Share permissions are assigned on the Share Permissions tab of the share's Properties dialog box. As already mentioned, you can add groups or users to the Group or User Names list in the dialog box and then assign the appropriate permission level.

Before you can assign share permissions, you will need to add the group or user to the Group or User Names list. Let's take a look at how you add a group or user to the list.

Adding a Group or User

Adding a group or user to the Group or User Names list on the Share Permissions tab is very straightforward. Follow these steps:

1. Select the Add button. The Select Users, Computers, or Groups dialog box appears (see Figure 13.2).

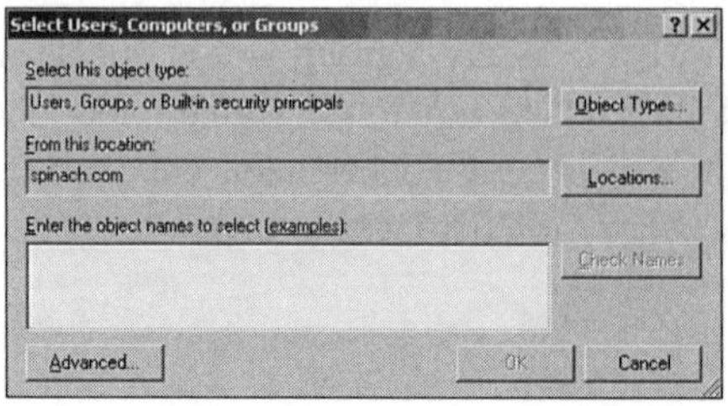

FIGURE 13.2

Use the Select Users, Computers, or Groups dialog box to specify groups or users to be added.

2. By default, the domain in which the server resides appears as the location in the dialog box. If you want to change the location (the domain) where the group or user resides, click the Location button. A domain tree enables you to select the domain to serve as the location. Click OK to return to the Users, Computers, or Groups dialog box.

3. The group or user (or groups and users) that you will add to the Share Permission list are entered in the Enter the object names to select box. Type the name of the first group or user. You can add multiple names to the box by separating the entries with a semicolon.

4. After adding the group names or usernames to the box, you can check the accuracy of your entries by clicking the Check Names button. If any of your entries are not found, the Name Not Found dialog box opens (see Figure 13.3).

FIGURE 13.3

The Name Not Found dialog box enables you to correct entries not found in the selected domain.

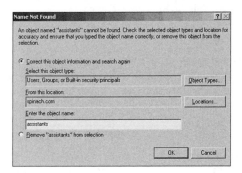

5. (Optional) You can change the entry (if you typed it incorrectly) or change the location to look for the entry. If you decide not to include the entry (for inclusion in the permission list), select the Remove option button. Then click OK. You are returned to the Select Users, Computers, or Groups dialog box.

6. To add the groups or users to the permission list, click the OK button. You are returned to the Share Permissions tab.

Assigning the Share Permission

To assign permissions to the group or user that you have added to the permission list, select the group or user. By default, the newly added group or user already is assigned the Read permission.

Select the permission level using the appropriate Allow check box that you want to provide for the group or user. Repeat this for other added groups or users as necessary. When you have completed assigning share permissions, click the OK button. This closes the Properties dialog box for the share.

13

When you assign permissions to groups and users, remember that the permissions are cumulative. A particular user will pick up permissions from both the groups that the user belongs to and any permissions applied specifically to the user.

Understanding NTFS Permissions

The NT File System, or NTFS, is a file system developed for the Windows NT environment (the NT stood for "New Technology"). It is now considered the standard file system for servers running Windows network operating systems such as Windows Server 2003. Folders and files on NTFS volumes can also be assigned NTFS permissions. This differs from Share permissions, which can be applied only to drives and folders. NTFS permissions can secure a folder or file on the local computer (these permissions actually affect local users on the computer) and also can secure the object in respect to users who access the folder or file over the network.

> Each file and folder on an NTFS volume has an Access Control List. This list is used to determine the access level of a user or a group to the file or folder. The Access Control List entry for a group or a user is based on the NTFS permissions set for that group or user (in relation to the file or the folder).

Standard NTFS permissions exist for both folders and files. The NTFS folder permissions are listed in Table 13.1.

TABLE 13.1   NTFS Folder Permissions

Folder Permission	Access Level
Full Control	Enables the user or group to change permissions; delete the folder, subfolders, and files; take ownership of the folder; and permit all other permission levels (Read, Write, List Folder Contents, and so on)
Modify	Enables the user or group to modify the folder, such as delete subfolders and files and permissions related to all other lower-level permissions (Read and Execute, List Folder Contents, Write, and Read)
Read and Execute	Enables the user or group to navigate the folder contents (subfolders and files) and execute contained executables and actions related to the List Folder Contents, Read, and Write permissions
List Folder Contents	Enables the user or group to view the contents of the folder, such as subfolders and files in the folders

Folder Permission	Access Level
Write	Enables the user or group to create new contents in the folder, such as subfolders and files; change the folder attributes; and view the folder ownership and permissions information for the folder
Read	Enables the user or group to view the files and subfolders in the folder and to view other information related to the folder, such as ownership, permissions, and file attributes

Setting NTFS Permissions for a folder requires two major steps. First, you add groups or users that you want to create permissions for. Then you assign the user or group the permissions. Remember that, by default, the Everyone group is assigned Full Control to any resource on a NTFS volume (whether it has been shared or not).

NTFS file permissions enable you to control access down to the file level (NTFS file permissions actually override NTFS folder permissions, which we discuss in a moment). Table 13.2 provides a list of standard NTFS file permissions.

TABLE 13.2 NTFS File Permissions

File Permission	Access Level
Full Control	Enables the user or group to change permissions, take ownership of the file, and exercise all other actions permitted by the other file permission levels
Modify	Enables the user or group to modify and delete the file, and provide permissions related to all other lower-level permissions (Read and Execute, and Write)
Read and Execute	Enables the user or group to navigate the folder contents (subfolders and files), execute contained executables, and list folder contents and Read and Write permissions
Write	Enables the user or group to create new contents in the folder, such as subfolders and files; change the folder attributes; and view the folder ownership and permissions information for the folder
Read	Enables the user or group to view the files and subfolders in the folder and to view other information related to the folder, such as ownership, permissions, and file attributes.

13

As with share permissions, NTFS permissions are set by selecting either Allow or Deny next to a particular permission. Figure 13.4 shows the different NTFS permissions for a file and the accompanying Allow or Deny check boxes.

NTFS permissions for a file are set using the Allow and Deny check boxes.

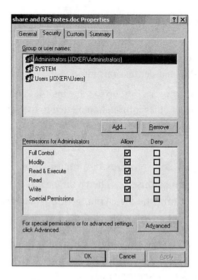

NTFS permissions might seem to be as straightforward as share permissions, but they are more complex because they can be assigned to files; therefore, a file can have different NTFS permissions than its parent folder. NTFS permissions can also become confusing because they can be assigned to both groups and users. Thus, a user might have NTFS permissions for a folder or a file that have been individually assigned, and NTFS permissions that have been assigned to a group that the user belongs to. These are important points to keep in mind when working with NTFS permissions:

- NTFS permissions are cumulative. A user's final NTFS permission is a combination of the NTFS permissions assigned to groups that the user is a member of and NTFS permissions assigned directly to the user.

- NTFS file permissions override NTFS folder permissions. Even if a user has the NTFS permission of Full Control for a folder, that user will be able to read a file in that folder only if the NTFS file permission for the user has been set to Read.

- If you use the Deny check box, you deny a user or group access to the folder or file. Using Deny effectively overrides any other cumulative NTFS permissions that a user might have for a folder or file.

- Permissions are inherited from parent folders. This means that subfolders and files contained in a parent folder will inherit the permissions that you set for the parent folder. However, you can choose to not allow permissions to be inherited from the parent if you want to set different permissions for the child subdirectory or file (we discuss turning off inheritance when we discuss setting NTFS permissions later in the hour).

Copying or moving files from one location to another can also be problematic when you are dealing with NTFS permissions. The final permissions depend on whether you are copying or moving, and whether you are copying or moving within or between NTFS partitions.

- When you copy a file within an NTFS volume (from folder to folder, it is treated as a new file and takes on the permissions of the parent folder), make sure that anyone who will copy a file on the volume has Write permissions for the destination folder. The user copying the file to the folder becomes the owner of the new folder.

- If you move a file from one folder to another on an NTFS volume, the file retains the original permissions assigned to that file (again, the user moving the file must have Write permissions for the destination folder, and Modify permission is necessary on the file that is being moved).

- When you move a file from one NTFS volume to another, the file takes on the permissions of the destination folder (again, Write permissions are necessary for the destination folder, and Modify permissions are necessary for the file being moved). The user moving the file becomes the owner of the file.

- When you copy or move NTFS folder or files to FAT partitions, all permissions are lost. FAT does not support NTFS permissions.

As you can see, you need to plan how you will use NTFS permissions to secure the various folders and files that you share on the network. Keeping track of your users' cumulative permissions can allow you to foresee problems that involve a user accessing a folder or file to a greater degree than you had intended as you assigned permissions. Using groups (instead of users) to assign NTFS permissions will probably make the entire process a little less confusing.

Upgrading a Drive to NTFS

Before we go any further in our discussion of NTFS permissions, we should take a quick look at how to upgrade a FAT-formatted drive to NTFS. You can't take advantage of NTFS permissions if your server partitions are not formatted with the NTFS file system. You can upgrade system partitions as well as other partitions on your server's hard drives. Upgrading a system partition requires that you reboot the computer.

When you convert a volume to NTFS using the convert command, the files and folder currently on the volume remain intact. When you convert to NTFS, you cannot convert the volume back to the previous file system.

13

To convert a volume, follow these steps:

1. Open a command prompt window. Click Start and then select Command Prompt.

2. At the command prompt, type **convert c:/fs:ntfs**, where c is the drive letter assigned to the volume (or partition).

3. Press Enter. The volume is converted to NTFS. If you are converting a system volume, you are notified that the conversion will take place the next time you restart the computer.

Assigning NTFS Permissions

NTFS permissions are assigned on the Security tab of a folder or file's Properties dialog box. If the Security tab is not available on a folder or file Properties dialog box, the volume is not formatted with NTFS. Let's look at assigning NTFS folder permissions and then setting NTFS file permissions.

Volumes can also be assigned NTFS permissions. This means that volume's NTFS permissions can be propagated to the folders and the files on that volume (there is an advanced setting to set the inheritance for the permissions).

Understanding NTFS Folder Permissions

You can assign NTFS permissions to folders on NTFS volumes. Files in the folder inherit their NTFS permissions from the folder. To assign NTFS permissions to a folder, follow these steps:

1. Open Windows Explorer to locate a folder. Right-click the folder and select Properties.

2. Select the Security tab on the Properties dialog box (see Figure 13.5).

3. To add a group or user (or groups and users) to the Group or user names list, click the Add button. The Select Users, Computers, or Groups dialog box opens.

4. Use the Location box to specify the domain that you want to access for the group or user to be added to the list.

5. Enter the group name or username (multiple entries can be made by separating each entry with a semicolon) in the Enter the object names to select box.

6. To check the validity of your entries, click the Check Names button.

7. After the names have been checked, click OK. You are returned to the Security tab.

FIGURE 13.5

NTFS permissions are assigned on the folder's Security tab.

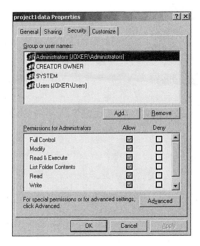

8. Select a group or user that you have added to the list, and set the permissions for the folder using the Allow (or Deny) check boxes for the NTFS folder permissions listed. By default, the group or user that you add to the list is given the Read and Execute, List Folder Contents, and Read permissions. Set the permissions for each group or user that you added to the list.

Remember that assigning NTFS permissions to a folder secures the folder both locally and as a share on the network. Make sure that you give local users the appropriate access to the folder if you are using NTFS permissions, and be sure that these users are not given the appropriate access level because of group membership in the domain.

Understanding NTFS File Permissions

Assigning NTFS permissions to groups or users for a file is similar to assigning NTFS permissions for a folder. Locate the file using Windows Explorer. Then right-click the file and select Properties from the shortcut menu.

On the Security tab of the file's Properties dialog box, use the Add button to add groups and users to the permission list (as you did for NTFS folder permissions). Then select each added group or user and assign the NTFS permissions for the file.

Negating NTFS Permission Inheritance

In some cases, you will not want a subfolder or file to inherit the NTFS permissions that have been set for the parent folder. On the Security tab of a file (or subfolder) Properties dialog box, click the Advanced button. The Advanced Security Settings for the file or subfolder open (see Figure 13.6).

13

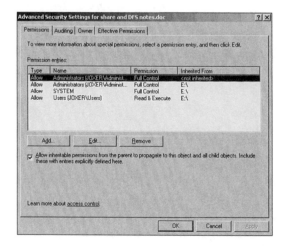

FIGURE 13.6

You can turn off permission inheritance.

To turn off the permission inheritance for the current object, click the Allow inheritable permissions to propagate from the parent check box to clear it. The file or subfolder will now no longer inherit permissions that have been set for a parent container.

Working with Special NTFS Permissions

The standard NTFS permissions discussed thus far are actually groupings of more specific NTFS permissions called special NTFS permissions. For example, the standard Read permission is actually made up of the special permissions: read data, read attributes, and read extended attributes.

You can use special NTFS permissions to fine-tune the access that you have supplied to a group or user using the standard NTFS permissions. To access the special NTFS permissions for a group or a user, open the Properties dialog box for a folder or a file.

Click the Advanced button to open the Advanced Security settings for the folder or file. Click a group or user listed in the Permission entries box, and then click Edit to view the Special NTFS permissions for that group or user (see Figure 13.7).

Special permissions that are "grayed out" are already active based on either the standard permissions set for that group or standard permissions that have been inherited from the parent container (either a volume or a folder). You can use the special permissions when you want to slightly upgrade (or downgrade) the NTFS permissions for a folder or file. Just select the special permission's check box to activate it. Table 13.3 provides a list of the special permissions.

FIGURE 13.7

You can view and set the special NTFS permissions for a group or user.

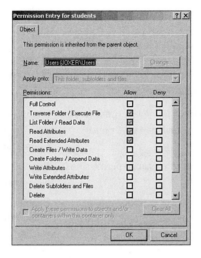

TABLE 13.3 NTFS Special File Permissions

Permission	Folder	File
Traverse Folder/ Execute File	Enables the user to move through the folders and files held in a folder	Enables the user to run executable files
List Folder/ Read Data	Enables the user to view the folder	Enables the user to read the files in the folder
Read Attributes	Enables the user to view folder attributes such as read only or hidden	Enables the user to view file attributes such as read only or hidden
Read Extended Attributes	Allows an application defined special attributes on a folder to be read	Allows an application defined special attributes on a file to be read
Create Files/ Write Data	Enables the user to create new files in the folder	Enables the user to write new data files and change existing files
Create Folders/ Append Data	Enables the user to create folders in the target folder	Enables the user to append data to be appended to a file, but the file cannot be overwritten or deleted
Write Attributes	Enables the user to change folder attributes	Enables the user to change file attributes
Write Extended Attributes	Enables the user to change special folder attributes (these are typically associated with a special application that allows extended attributes, such as SQL Server)	Enables the user to change special file attributes (these are typically associated with a special application that allows extended attributes, such as SQL server)

continues

13

TABLE 13.3   continued

Permission	Folder	File
Delete Subfolders and Files	Enables the user to delete subfolders in the target folder	Enables the user to delete files in the target folder
Delete	Enables the user to delete the folder	Enables the user to delete the file
Read Permissions	Enables the user to view permissions for the folder (such as Full Control and Read)	Enables the user to view permissions for the file (such as Full Control and Read)
Change Permissions	Enables the user to change permissions for the folder	Enables the user to change permissions for the file
Take Ownership	Enables the user or members of the group to take ownership of the folder and change permissions	Enables the user or member of the group to take ownership of the file and change permissions

As you can see from Table 13.3, there are a number of special permissions. As already stated, special permissions have been grouped into standard permissions to hopefully streamline the process of assigning NTFS permissions. It is a best practice to use standard permissions as much as possible and to use the special permissions only when absolutely necessary.

Taking Ownership of an NTFS File

By default, the creator of a folder or a file on NTFS volumes is the owner of that object. This enables that user to set the permissions related to that file or folder (or to delete the file and folder). Ownership of an NTFS file or folder is similar to having the Full Control permission.

Administrators (by virtue of the Administrator group) can take ownership of any file or folder (no matter what permissions have been assigned for that file or folder). Administrators can also grant ownership of files or folders to a group or user. In effect, this means that ownership of files or folders can be transferred from a group or user to another group or user.

Ownership can be given to a user or group by supplying the Full Control standard permission to that user or group. Ownership can also be given to the user or group using the Take Ownership special permission.

Using File Encryption

Another good reason why you should use NTFS volumes on your file servers is that files on an NTFS volume can be encrypted. The Encrypting File System (EFS) provides encryption using a system of public and private keys. The encryption/decryption process is transparent as files are accessed by network users.

You can encrypt a file or folder in this way:

1. Click Start and then Windows Explorer.
2. Right-click the file or folder that you want to encrypt, and then select Properties from the shortcut menu.
3. On the General tab of the file or folder's Properties dialog box, select the Advanced button. The Advanced Attributes dialog box opens (see Figure 13.8).

FIGURE 13.8
You can encrypt a file or folder.

4. To encrypt the file or folder, select the Encrypt contents to secure data check box. Then click OK to return to the Properties dialog box.

Obviously, encrypting a folder enables you to encrypt all the files in the folder. This means that you can quickly encrypt data files instead of encrypting the files one at a time.

Mixing Share and NTFS Permissions

Having two different sets of permissions—share and NTFS—to protect folders and files can lead to some confusion because these permissions will interact to determine a user or group's access to a particular object. Basically, the share permissions enable you to interact with the share (the folder), and the NTFS permissions determine what you can do with the files in that share (when both types of permissions have been used).

Because NTFS permissions and share permissions can both be assigned to a folder, the resulting access level that a user or group has is the most restrictive permission provided by the combined settings. For example, if the user's group membership gives Read permissions based on NTFS permissions, but another group membership provides Full Control based on share permissions, the user will have only read permissions. The most restrictive permission provides the final access level.

When planning how you will supply access to shares on the network, determine how you will use group membership to determine an individual user's access to a particular folder or file. A good rule of thumb is to assign only the minimum level of access that a user needs to get the job done in relation to a particular folder or file.

You might also want to use share permissions to control folder access, but then use NTFS permissions to drill down your security settings to the file level. However you determine to use these different permission possibilities, make sure that you create a written plan that provides guidelines for how permissions are assigned to the groups and users present on your network.

Fine-Tuning Disk Quotas

Before we leave the subject of shares, let's take another look at disk quotas. Disk quotas were discussed in Hour 12. Disk quotas for a file server could be set when the file server was created using the Configure Your Server Wizard. Setting disk quotas enables you to determine how much space your users can occupy on a file server volume.

Disk quotas can be fine-tuned and even set on a per-user basis. To set disk quotas for users, follow these steps:

1. Open Windows Explorer (Start, then Windows Explorer).

2. Right-click the volume (logical drive) that you want to work with, and then select Properties from the shortcut menu.

3. In the Properties dialog box, select the Quota tab. The default quota settings for all users (except administrators) are listed on this tab. If you want to configure alternative settings for a user, click the Quota Entries button. The Quota Entries dialog box for the volume opens (see Figure 13.9).

   By default, a built-in quota entry for administrators is present in the dialog box. This entry gives administrators no limit as far as their disk quota setting is concerned.

FIGURE 13.9

Custom settings can be configured for disk quotas.

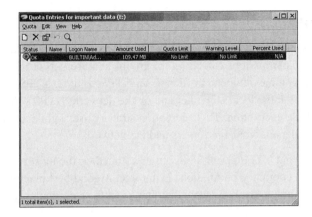

4. To create a new quota entry, select the Quota menu and then select New Quota Entry. The Select Users dialog box opens.

5. Enter the names of the users that you want to add to the Select Users dialog box (separate usernames with a semicolon). You can check your entries using the Check Names button.

6. When you have completed entering the usernames, click OK. The Add New Quota Entry dialog box appears for the user or users (see Figure 13.10).

FIGURE 13.10

Set custom disk quotas for a user or users.

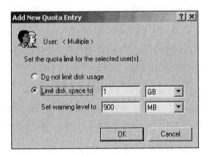

7. Set the disk space and the warning level for the disk quota. Then click OK. The new quota entry (or entries) appears in the Quota Entries dialog box. If you want to remove a particular entry, right-click the Entry, select Delete, and then click OK.

8. When you have completed entering quotas for specific users, you can close the Quota Entries dialog box and the Properties dialog box for the volume.

13

Summary

Share permissions enable you to control access to volume and folder shares on a file server. Share permissions can be set for groups and users. NTFS permissions can be assigned to volumes, folders, or files on an NTFS volume. NTFS permissions secure a folder or file on the local computer and on the network. NTFS volumes also provide folder and file encryption. This encryption strategy uses public and private keys to secure files and folders on your file servers and the network.

When share and NTFS permissions are used together, the most restrictive setting provided by the combined permissions is in force. A good best practice is to assign users only the minimum level of access that they need for a particular folder or file on the network.

Q&A

Q How can share permissions be used to secure a share in the domain?

A Share permissions for a share, such as a shared folder, can be assigned to both groups and users. Assigning different levels of access to a share, which typically means greatly limiting full control of the share, enables you to protect the data in a share from being overwritten or deleted.

Q How are share permissions assigned to groups and users?

A The Share Permissions tab of the share's Properties dialog box enables you to add users and groups and then assign them different permission levels for the share.

Q How do NTFS permissions differ from share permissions?

A NTFS permissions can be applied only to folders and files on a NTFS volume. NTFS permissions can be applied at the file level differing from Share permissions, which can be applied only at the share or folder levels (not the file level).

Q Can a FAT or FAT32 partition be converted to NTFS?

A Yes, the convert command can be used at the command prompt to convert any FAT or FAT32 partition to NTFS. The syntax for the convert command is convert c:/fs:ntfs, where c is the drive letter of the partition that you want to convert.

Q What security feature provided by NTFS volumes can be used to secure files both on the server and as they move across the network wire when they are accessed by users?

A Files on NTFS volumes can be encrypted using the Encrypting File System (EFS). This encryption system protects files transparently as they are accessed by domain users.

Q Can both share and NTFS permissions be applied to a folder?

A Yes, share and NTFS permissions can be assigned to a shared folder that resides on an NTFS volume. When these two permission systems are used together to secure an object such as a folder, the final permission level for a user or group is determined by the most restrictive permission provided by the combined share and NTFS permissions.

13

HOUR 14

Working with Network Printing

Another essential service that a network provides to users is the capability to print. Sharing printers was one of the "historical" reasons that personal computers were first networked. In this hour, we take a look at the Windows Server 2003 print services, including the configuration of a print server. We also look at managing the print environment in the domain.

In this hour, the following topics are covered:

- Working with local, remote, and direct-connect printers
- Configuring a print server
- Finding printers on the network
- Setting printer permissions
- Auditing printer access
- Managing print jobs

Networking Printing and Windows Server 2003

Windows Server 2003 has "wizardized" a number of the tasks related to configuring a print server for your domain. This makes it easy for you to configure a print server and manage your network print services.

Before we take a look at setting up a print server, we need to discuss some of the terminology used for working with domain print services. A *shared printer* is simply a printer that accepts print jobs from more than one computer. Printers on the network actually fall into two different categories, depending on where the printer is located in relation to your network server: local printer or remote printer.

A *local printer* is a printer that is directly attached to a server. The printer is only local, however, in relation to the server (that it is connected to). This server assumes the role of print server for the printer.

A *remote printer* is a printer attached to a computer other than your server. This can be pretty confusing because the computer that the printer is attached to considers the printer local. Whether a printer is local or remote depends on the computer on the network that you are actually referring to. You can configure a server running Windows Server 2003 to act as the print server for a printer that is attached to another computer on the network.

A third type of printer is used on networks: the *direct-connect printer*. This printer is outfitted with an internal or external direct connection hardware device (which acts as both a local print server and a network interface card for the printer). A direct-connect printer is connected to the network hub or other connectivity device using a twisted-pair cable (or the same networking media that you use to connect the computers on your network). A number of direct-connect laser printers are available, such as the Hewlett-Packard laserjets outfitted with an internal HP JetDirect device.

Direct-connect printers are much easier to deploy (physically) because they don't have to be directly connected to a computer. They can, however, be managed by a print server as if they were a local printer.

Establishing a print server on the network is really just a matter of connecting your printers (either locally, remotely, or directly) to the network so that the appropriate printer can be "identified" during the process of configuring a server for print services. Let's take a look at installing printers and then explore the steps for configuring a Windows print server.

Although you can share printers on the network that are connected to computers other than dedicated print servers, remember that the local computer hosting the printer will experience performance hits when queuing up print jobs and sending them to the printer. This is why dedicated print servers are used to handle the large number of print requests that are typically dealt with on a Windows domain.

Installing a Local Printer

Setting up a local printer is really just a matter of directly attaching the printer to the Windows Server 2003 using a parallel printer cable or some other type of attachment such as a USB cable. Because Windows Server 2003 embraces Plug and Play, most printers (unless you are dealing with a fairly old legacy printer) automatically are recognized and installed by the network operating system.

To add a plug-and-play printer to a server, follow these steps:

1. Power down the server: select Start, Shut Down, and then set the Planned Shutdown option as Hardware: Installation (Planned). Then click OK to shut down the server.

2. Connect the printer to the server (using a parallel or USB connection).

3. Power up the server and log on as administrator or with an account that has administrative privileges (this is necessary to configure the server as a print server). The plug-and-play printer is installed automatically.

4. To view the installed printer, select Start, Control Panel, Printers and Faxes. The Printers and Faxes window opens (see Figure 14.1). The printer appears as an installed (and the default) printer for the server.

When you are installing a non–plug-and-play printer, use the Add Printer Wizard (you can access it via the Control Panel's Printers and Faxes applet). This enables you to add a legacy printer locally or to add a printer that is connected locally using a serial connection.

14

FIGURE 14.1

Plug-and-play printers are installed automatically by the Windows network operating system.

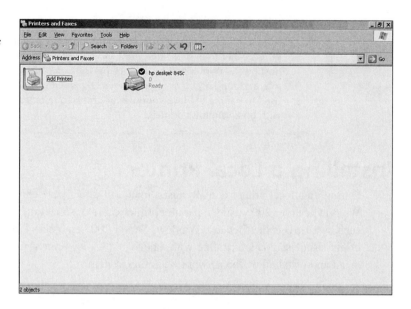

Installing Direct-Connect Printers

An alternative to attaching the printer directly to the server is to attach the printer directly to the network. To attach the printer directly to the network, the printer needs a network card that also provides the spooling and processing power to handle incoming print jobs (directly connected printers also typically have a lot more memory installed in them, to avoid print buffer overflow).

A number of manufacturers (such as Intel and Hewlett-Packard) make both internal and external print server devices that can be installed in (or on) a printer. These devices then connect directly to the network using the same network media (such as twisted-pair cable connected to a hub) that other devices and computers on the network use.

Because TCP/IP is the default network protocol for Windows Server 2003 (and is used on most networks today), printers using direct connect devices can be configured with an IP address (using the configuration software that ships with the device or the printer) or can receive an IP address from the domain's DHCP server. When a DHCP server is used on the network, you will find that as soon as the direct-connect printer is attached to the network and brought online, the DHCP server assigns an IP address. You can find this IP address using the DHCP snap-in; all you have to do is examine the new leases that have been supplied to devices on the network. (For more about DHCP, see Hour 16, "Dynamic Host Configuration Protocol.")

When you are not using TCP/IP on the network, you must install the management software that comes with direct-connect devices on the local server (the server that will function as the print server). You might also have to install another network protocol, such as DLC, on the server so that it can talk to the direct-connect device. When the server recognizes the direct-connect printer, you can establish the server as the print server for the printer by sharing the printer (which is discussed in this section) .

After you have established the IP address for the printer, you can connect the server to the printer by creating an IP port on the server. This is accomplished using the Add Printer Wizard; follow these steps:

1. Select Start, Control Panel, and then point at Printers and Faxes. Select Add Printer. The Add Printer Wizard opens.

2. Click Next to bypass the initial screen. On the next screen, make sure the Local Printer option button is selected (see Figure 14.2). Click the Automatically Detect and Install My Plug and Play Printer check box to deselect this option. Then click Next.

FIGURE 14.2

A direct-connect printer is installed as the local printer on your server.

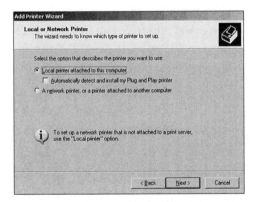

3. On the next screen, click the Create a New Port option button. Click the drop-down box and select Standard TCP/IP Port. Then click Next. The Add Standard TCP/IP Printer Port Wizard appears.

4. Click Next to bypass the initial screen. On the next screen of the Add Standard TCP/IP Port Wizard, type the IP address of the printer in the Printer Name or IP Address box (see Figure 14.3). A port name is created based on the IP address that you enter in the box.

14

FIGURE 14.3

Add a port for the net-work printer.

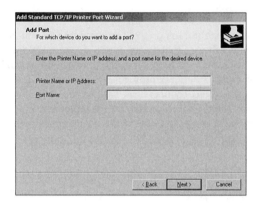

5. Click Next to continue. On the next screen, you are asked to specify the device port that the printer is attached to. This depends on the brand of direct-connect printer or external direct connect box you are using. Select the appropriate defini-tion for your printer and direct connect configuration using the drop-down list (in the case of external direct-connect boxes, this means the actual printer port on the print server box that the printer is connected to).

6. Click Next to continue. A summary screen is provided by the Add Standard TCP/IP Port Wizard. Click Finish.

7. You are returned to the Add Printer Wizard, which provides a list of printer manu-facturers and printers (see Figure 14.4). Select the manufacturer of the printer and then the appropriate printer. If you have a disk or CD that shipped with the printer and you want to use the driver on that medium, select the Have Disk button and then browse for the appropriate driver.

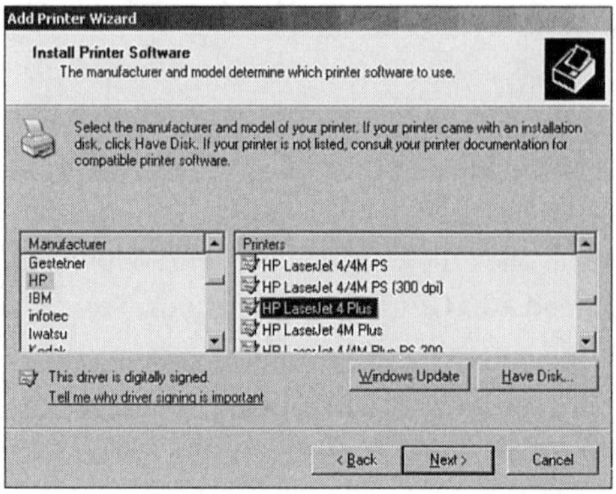

FIGURE 14.4

Specify the manufac-turer and printer.

8. After selecting the manufacturer and printer, click Next. On the next screen, supply the name that you want to use for the printer on the network (the entire friendly name for the printer cannot exceed 32 characters). You can go with the default name or type a new name in the Printer Name box. Click Next to continue.

9. On the next screen, you are given the option of sharing the printer. Newly installed printers are shared automatically when added to the server (this includes plug-and-play printers installed automatically). A default share name is supplied (see Figure 14.5). If you want to change the share name, type a new name. If you have computers on the network that will use NetBIOS for name resolution, do not use more than 15 characters for the share name.

FIGURE 14.5

Specify the share name for the printer.

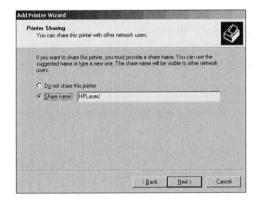

10. Click Next to continue. On the next screen, you can describe the location of the printer and other information related to the printer in the Comment box. Users can view this information when searching for printers on the network. Click Next to continue.

11. The next screen asks if you want to print a test page. Click Next to print the test page and continue. You are taken to the wizard's summary screen.

12. Click Finish. A message appears letting you know that the test page was sent to the printer. Click OK when the test page prints successfully.

The benefit of using direct-connect printers on the network is that they can be located on the network without needing to deploy a server to act as a print server in that same location. They also negate the need to overtax a server that might provide other network services because a server is not required to spool or process print jobs directed to the printer.

14

> When the test page does not print, click the Troubleshoot button in the Test Page message box. Windows Server 2003 walks you through a set of steps to help you get the printer operational.

Print Servers and the Configure Your Server Wizard

As soon as you have installed a local printer (or a direct-connect printer as a local printer, as discussed in the previous section), you have, in effect, created a print server. However, if you did not share a direct-connect printer (when using the Add Printer Wizard), or if you have turned off sharing on a plug-and-play printer or will configure your print server using a remote printer (a printer connected to another computer), you can use the Configure Your Server Wizard to make the server a print server.

> We discuss printer properties such as sharing and permissions later in the hour.

1. Start the Configure Your Server Wizard (select Start, Administrative Tools, Configure Your Server). Click Next to bypass the introductory screen.

2. You are asked to make sure all devices and peripherals are connected to the server. Click Next to continue.

3. On the Server Role screen, select Print Server and then click Next. On the next screen, you are provided with the option of selecting the print drivers that will be installed for client operating systems when a network client computer connects to your print server's printer.

   The default selection is for Windows 2000 and Windows XP clients. If you will use other clients such as Windows 98, select the All Windows Clients option button. Then click Next to continue.

4. On the next screen, you'll see a summary of the print options that you have chosen. New printers can be added with the Add Printer Wizard. If you chose to install drivers for network client computers other than Windows 2000 and Windows XP, the Add Printer Driver Wizard also is listed on the summary. It enables you to install the print drivers for your legacy clients (such as Windows 98; make sure that you have the print drivers on disk or available on the network). Click Next to continue.

FIGURE 14.6

Specify the client operating system drivers to be installed for the printer.

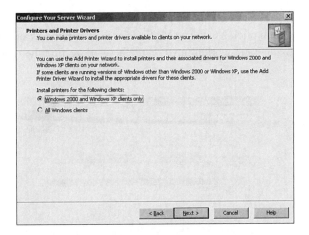

We continue with this sequence of steps in the next section, when the Add Printer Wizard is discussed. A benefit of using the Configure Your Server Wizard to actually create a print server (another role for your server running Windows Server 2003) is that it walks you through all the configuration possibilities for the print job, including the installation of the print drivers for client operating systems used in your domain.

The Add Printer Wizard

After you click Next on the Configure Your Server Wizard screen, the Add Printer Wizard appears. This wizard walks you through the steps of adding a local or remote printer to the server.

Click Next to bypass the initial Add Printer Wizard screen. On the next screen, you are asked to specify whether the new printer will be local or a network printer. As mentioned earlier in the hour, plug-and-play printers are installed automatically and do not require the Add Printer Wizard. In the case of direct-connect printers (which we discussed in this hour in the section "Installing Direct-Connect Printers"), you would choose the local option. Let's look at how you would select a printer that is connected to another computer on the network; follow these steps:

1. Select the Option A network printer or a printer attached to another computer, and then click Next.

2. On the next screen, you have the options of finding a printer in the Active Directory, typing in the name of a printer, browsing for a printer (the option we will look at), or specifying a URL for a remote printer (this is useful for satellite offices to connect to printers via the Internet at the home office; the print server for the Internet printer must support the Internet Printing Protocol).

14

To browse the network for a printer, select the Connect to This Printer option button and then click Next. The Browse for Printer window opens. You can browse all the domains (and workgroups) on the network to find the remote printer (see Figure 14.7).

FIGURE 14.7

Browse for the remote printer.

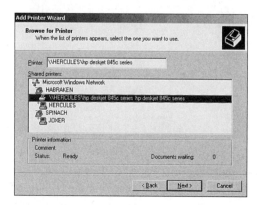

3. Select the remote printer in the Browse window and then click Next. The Add Printer Wizard supplies a summary screen.

4. If this is the only printer you are adding at this time, deselect the Restart This Wizard to Add Another Printer check box and then click Finish to close the wizard.

The Add Printer Driver Wizard

If you chose to add printer drivers for network clients other than Windows 2000 and Windows XP, the Add Printer Driver Wizard opens. This wizard walks you through the process of making the appropriate print drivers for your client operating systems available on the print server.

Click Next to bypass the introductory screen. Then follow these steps:

1. On the next screen, select the printer manufacturer and the printer that you want to install the print drivers for. If you have a disk or CD with a newer driver for the printer, select the Have Disk button and provide the path for the driver.

2. Click Next to continue. On the next screen (see Figure 14.8), you can select the processor types and operating systems that will use the printer.

   Selecting all the operating systems that will be used by network print clients makes the driver available to the client. Having printer drivers available for client computers on the print server allows clients connecting to a printer for the first time to

download the appropriate printer driver. This saves you a lot of time running
around and configuring client computers to work with a particular printer.

FIGURE 14.8

*Select the operating
systems that need
printer drivers.*

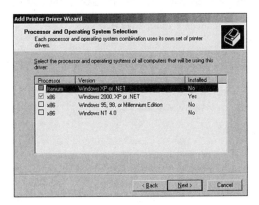

You must select at least one set of drivers other than the default installed Windows
2000 and Windows XP. After making your selection, click Next.

3. The summary screen for the Add Printer Driver Wizard appears. If you do not want
   to install any additional drivers, clear the Restart to Add Another Printer Driver
   option, and then click Finish to close the wizard.

4. Make sure that your Windows Server 2003 CD is in your CD-ROM drive. The
   Select Device window opens. Select the printer manufacturer and printer to add the
   drivers. (Yes, this is the second time this window has opened during the process.
   The first time was to install Windows 2000 and Windows XP drivers; this is to
   install additional client drivers.) Then click Next. The drivers are copied to the
   print server.

5. Click Finish to complete the process.

No matter how you have configured your print server (Plug and Play, Add Printer, or
Configure Your Server), after you have completed the appropriate steps (and shared the
printer), the new server role Print Server will appear in the Manage Your Server window
(see Figure 14.9). You can use this window to open the Printers and Faxes window or to
add other printers and print drivers.

14

FIGURE **14.9**

The Print Server role is added to the Manage Your Server window.

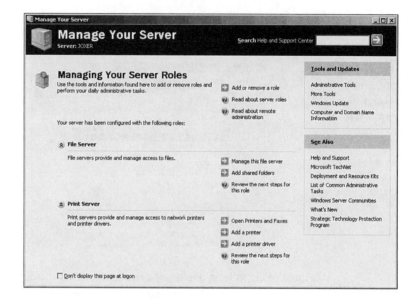

Finding Printers on the Network

When a printer is installed on a print server, it is shared by default. It is also automatically published to the Active Directory. When you open the printer's Properties dialog box (open the Printers and Faxes window via the Control Panel, right-click the Printer icon, and select Properties) and select the Sharing tab, you can view these properties (see Figure 14.10).

FIGURE **14.10**

Network users can easily find printers published to the Active Directory.

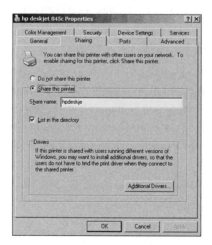

In some cases, you might want to share a printer but not use the Configure Your Server Wizard to add the print server role to a server. You also can deploy a few printers for network use that are connected to a network client such as a computer running Windows XP.

When a printer has not been previously shared, open the printer's Properties dialog box and select the Sharing tab. Select the Share This Printer option button and supply a share name for the printer (keep the share name to eight characters or fewer if you will have pre-Windows 95 clients on the network, such as DOS). To publish the printer to the Active Directory, select the List in the Directory checkbox (as mentioned earlier, you will not have to share the printer or publish it to the directory if the printer is installed on the print server).

When the printer is published to the Active Directory, it is important that you supply information such as the printer's location on the General tab of the printer's Properties dialog box. This will enable users to search for the printer based on location. They can also search based on the printer's capabilities, such as color printing or duplex printing.

Although the Search tool varies slightly among client operating systems, domain users can use Search to locate a printer and then connect to it. For example, a Windows XP client or a server running Windows Server 2003 that requires print services can use the Search Results dialog box to locate a printer. Follow these steps:

1. To begin the search, select Start, Search. The Search Results dialog box opens.

2. To specify a search for printers, select the Other Search Options link and then select Printers, Computers, People. Then select a printer on the network. The Find Printers dialog box opens (see Figure 14.11) .

FIGURE 14.11

Printers can be found using different search parameters.

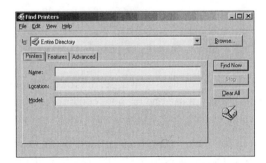

3. In the Find Printers dialog box, you have the option of searching for the printer in the entire Active Directory or in a particular domain. Other search parameters that can be used to find the printer are as follows:

14

- On the Printers tab, you can search by name (using the *Universal Naming Convention* [UNC] name of the printer), by location, or by the model of the printer.

> The Universal Naming Convention (UNC) is the system used to specify resources on a network. A printer with the share name of hplaser3 that is attached to a server named Hercules would be designated with the UNC name of \\hercules\ hplaser3. The two backslashes are always followed by the computer name, and a second backslash separates the computer name from the resource's share name.

- On the Features tab (see Figure 14.12), you can search by parameters such as a particular resolution, speed, or paper size; or whether the printer can staple, print in color, or print double-sided. Features are selected using a series of check boxes and drop-down lists.

FIGURE 14.12

Search for a printer by capabilities using the Features tab.

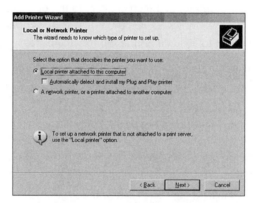

- The Advanced tab enables you to search for the printer using conditional statements. You can use one or more conditional statements to search for a printer using criteria such as the printer name and server name.

4. When the search parameters have been selected on the Advanced tab, click the Find Now button. The printers found by the search will appear in a list at the bottom of the Search window (see Figure 14.13).

Any user can quickly connect to the printer by right-clicking the Printer icon and selecting Connect from the shortcut menu. Because you have installed the required print drivers for the client operating systems in use in your domain, the client computer then can use the printer. The printer will appear in the client's Printers window after they connect.

FIGURE 14.13

Printers that meet your criteria will appear in the Search window.

Configuring Other Printer Properties

Printer properties are configured in the printer's Properties dialog box (as you saw with the Sharing tab earlier in the hour). Right-click the printer's icon in the Printers and Faxes window to view the properties for the printer.

The options available in the Properties dialog box are as follows:

- The General tab enables you to enter a location or comments relating to the printer and to print a test page to the printer. This tab also provides access to printing preferences (click the Printing Preferences button), which enables you to set parameters such as page layout and paper quality.

- The Ports tab enables you to set the port that is used by the printer when printing. Typically, the port is set during the installation of the printer. However, this tab does give you the option of changing the port or adding new ports, if necessary.

- The Sharing tab, as already discussed, enables you to share the printer, publish it to the Active Directory, and add printer drivers for network client operating systems.

- The Advanced tab enables you to control when the printer is available for printing and whether documents should be spooled when printed to the printer. This tab also provides you with the option of setting up a separator page for your users (see Figure 14.14). Advanced features vary from printer to printer, depending on the device's capabilities.

14

FIGURE 14.14

Spooling options and an optional separator page can be controlled for the printer.

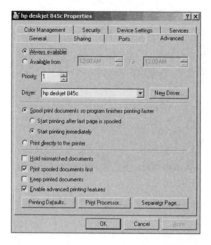

- The Device Settings tab enables you to set the paper types (including various paper and envelope sizes) that are available in the printer's paper bins. You can also change the type of form that is loaded into the manual feed bin for the printer (such as envelopes).

- The Security tab enables you to set print permissions for the various groups and users on your network. We discuss printer permissions in the next section.

Depending on the printer you have installed on the print server, other tabs might be available in the Properties dialog box. For example, a color printer might have a Color Management tab. Or, an inkjet printer might have a Services tab that enables you to align or clean the print cartridges.

After making changes on a particular tab in the Properties dialog box, you can immediately put the change into effect by clicking the Apply button. This means that you continue working in the Properties box. If you have completed all properties changes for a particular printer and no longer need that printer's Properties dialog box, click the OK button to close the dialog box.

Working with Printer Permissions

When a printer is shared on the network, different levels of default permissions are assigned to domain groups. For example, the Everyone group (which includes all users in the domain) is provided with the Print permission. Depending on your inclination toward printers and securities, you can remove the default permissions for the Everyone group and instead assign your users their basic access to printers by assigning the default permissions to the Authenticated Users group. This means that a user must be authenticated to the domain before acquiring print permissions.

The Print permission enables users (or members of a group assigned the permission) to print to the printer but does not provide them with the ability to manage the print queue (as discussed in the next section).

To view the default permissions for a printer, open the printer's Properties dialog box (right-click the printer in the Printers and Faxes window and select Properties). Then select the Security tab (see Figure 14.15).

FIGURE 14.15

Printer permissions are set on the Security tab.

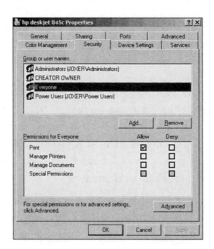

The default groups for printer permissions are Administrators, Creator Owner, Everyone, and Power Users. Administrators are assigned the Print, Manage Printer, and Manage Documents permission. The Creator Owner is assigned only the Manage Documents permission, by default. This means that users can manage documents that they create and send to the print server. They are not provided control over other users' print jobs.

The Power Users group is designed to be used to assign certain special users on the network the ability to manage the printer and its documents. Only responsible users should be included in the membership of the Power Users group.

Each permission provides a group or user with a different level of access to the printer. The Print permission enables a user to send documents to the printer. That's it—it provides no management permissions to the printer.

The Manage Printers permission provides a user with the capability to completely manage the printer. This permission level includes the capability to control job settings for

14

documents, such as pausing, resuming, or canceling print jobs. This permission level also allows the user to cancel documents in the print queue. This permission even provides the capability to delete the printer as a resource on the network.

The Manage Documents permission provides a subset of the Manage Printers permissions level privileges. A user with Manage Documents permission can control job settings for documents and can pause, resume, or cancel print jobs.

> As with share and NTFS permissions, printer permissions can be assigned to users and groups. For a discussion of share and NTFS permissions, see Hour 13, "Share and NTFS Permissions." For a discussion of group memberships, see Hour 9, "Active Directory Groups and Organizational Units."

Printer permissions are used ideally to determine who can print to a particular printer on the network (or who can manage the print jobs on that printer). Allowing the Everyone group access to all shared printers on the network can cause print traffic problems, particularly if many users print to the same printer. New groups that contain users who work on certain floors or in the same part of an office can be created so that users are compelled to print to a printer that is in their work area.

You might want to remove the Print permission from the Everyone group and create your own groups for printer access. You can then use the Add button to add Active Directory groups to the printer's Group list. The permissions for that particular group can then be sent. In most cases, you will want "typical" users to have only the Print permission.

Auditing Printer Access

You can also set up auditing for printer use (and management) via the Security tab of the printer's Properties dialog box. This enables you to track group (or specific user) access to printers.

1. Select the Advanced button on the Security tab. The Advanced Security Settings dialog box opens. Click the Auditing tab.

2. To add a group (or user) to the Auditing entries list, click the Add button. The Select User, Computer, or Group dialog box opens. Type the name of the group or the user. Then click OK. The Auditing Entry dialog box for the printer opens (see Figure 14.16).

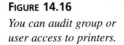

FIGURE **14.16**

You can audit group or user access to printers.

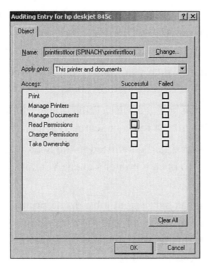

3. You can audit print access or events related to managing the printer or documents. Select either the Successful or Failed check boxes for the access event, and then click OK to close the Auditing Entry dialog box. You are returned to the Auditing tab. Add other users or groups as discussed for auditing, and then click OK to return to the printer's Properties dialog box. Click OK to close the dialog box.

Printer access events appear in the Event Viewer's security log. You can open the Event Viewer by selecting Start, Administrative Tools, Event Viewer.

Auditing and other security settings are part of the local computer or the domain's Group Policy settings. Group Policy is discussed in Hour 11, "Group Policy and User Profiles." The Event Viewer is discussed in Hour 20, "Monitoring Server and Network Performance."

Managing Print Jobs

You can view and control the print jobs that are currently in the print queue of a particular printer in the domain (or in the domain tree). You can locate the printer using the Search feature (then right-click the printer and select Open), or you can open the Printers and Faxes window and double-click the printer to view its queue window.

You can also search for a printer in the Active Directory Users and Computer snap-in. This provides you with access to any printers within the domain tree.

14

1. Make sure that you are logged in as an administrator (domain or enterprise administrator), and then open the Active Directory Users and Computers snap-in (Start, Administrative Tools, Active Directory Users and Computers).

2. Right-click the domain in which you want to search for the printer and select Find on the shortcut menu. The Find dialog box opens.

3. Click the Find drop-down box and select Printers. Use the Printers, Features, or Advanced tab to set the criteria for your search. Then click the Find Now button.

4. The printers meeting your criteria are listed in the Search results box at the bottom of the Find dialog box. To open a printer's queue window, right-click the printer's icon and select Open.

From the queue window, you can pause print jobs, delete print jobs, and change print job settings such as the priority of the print job and the user who should be notified when the print job is complete. The list that follows provides information on a number of the print options available in the Print Queue window:

- **Pause a Print Job**—To pause a print job, right-click the print job and select Pause from the shortcut menu.

- **Resume a Print Job**—Right-click the print job and select Resume from the shortcut menu.

- **Cancel a Print Job**—Right-click the print job and select Cancel from the shortcut menu. Or, select the print job and then select the Document menu and choose Cancel.

- **Cancel All Print Jobs**—To cancel all the print jobs currently in the queue, select the Printer menu and then select Cancel All Documents. You are asked if you want to cancel all the current print jobs. Click Yes to verify the cancellation.

- **Control Print Priority**—To change the priority of a particular print job or to change the user who will be notified when the print job is completed, right-click the print job and then select Properties from the shortcut menu. The Properties dialog box for the print job appears. To specify a new user for completion notification, type the user's name in the Notify box. After you have viewed or changed properties related to a particular print job, click the OK button to close the Properties box.

Summary

In this hour, you learned how to create a print server for local, remote, and direct-connect printers. Shared printers provide print services to users on the network.

When a printer is installed on a print server, installation options include the addition of client operating system print drivers. This allows network client computers to connect to the printer and use it for printing.

Printers published to the Active Directory can be found by any network client using the Search feature. Search parameters can include the location of the printer and features that the printer provides, such as color printing.

Printer properties are configured using the printer's Properties dialog box. Sharing and adding print drivers are controlled using the Sharing tab. The Security tab enables you to set permissions for the printer.

The Security tab also provides you with access to the auditing settings for the printer's access. User or group access to the printer can be audited. Audit events for object access, such as printers, is logged in the Event Viewer's security log.

Print jobs can be managed in the printer's queue window. Users with the appropriate permissions can pause or delete print jobs and control the print priority for queued jobs.

Q&A

Q How is a printer installed on a print server?

A Plug-and-play printers need only be connected to the server, which can then be booted to install the printer. Remote printers and direct-connect printers can be added to a server running Windows Server 2003 using either the Configure Your Server Wizard (to configure the print server role) or the Add Printer Wizard.

Q What is the benefit of direct-connect printers?

A This type of printer provides either an internal or external device that spools and processes print jobs at the printer.

Q What are some of the options that can be used in searching for a network printer?

A Because shared printers are published to the Active Directory, users can search for a printer by name (using the UNC name); search for the printer by the features it provides, such as color printing or automatic stapling; and search for the printer by creating conditional statements that contain different print criteria.

Q How are different access levels to print jobs and printer management determined?

A Printer permissions are set on a per-printer basis on each shared printer. Different permission levels include Print, Manage Printers, and Manage Documents.

14

HOUR 15

Understanding the Domain Name Service

As network operating systems have moved away from proprietary network protocols and have embraced the open TCP/IP protocol stack, the need for resolving names to IP addresses has arisen. In this hour, we look at the Domain Name Service provided by Windows Server 2003.

In this hour, the following topics are covered:

- How DNS works
- The hierarchical structure of the domain namespace
- How to install and configure DDNS on Window Server 2003
- How to create forward and reverse lookup zones
- How to manage DNS on a server running Windows Server 2003
- How to use the DNSMGMT snap-in

DNS Server Overview

The Domain Name Service (DNS) provides a hierarchical name-resolution strategy for resolving a Fully Qualified Domain Name (FQDN), hostnames, and other service-related names to IP addresses. DNS servers provide this resolution from a "friendly name" to logical address (the IP address) on TCP/IP networks such as the Internet. For example, when you type Microsoft.com into your Web browser address window, a DNS server somewhere on the Internet actually resolves the FQDN name (Microsoft.com) to the IP address of the Microsoft Web site.

So, in terms of TCP/IP networks and the Internet in particular, each organization deploys DNS servers that provide FQDN resolution to IP addresses. In effect, each large company, organization, or service provider manages the name-resolution duties for its own portion of the Internet. In fact, when a company registers a domain name with InterNIC, it must submit the IP addresses of two DNS servers that will handle the name-resolution duties for that domain. You can choose to run your own DNS implementation or outsource it to an ISP or other networking company that provides the service (for individuals who register a domain name, the DNS server addresses are typically provided by your service provider).

Servers maintained by InterNIC provide the mechanism for a local DNS server to resolve an FQDN to an IP address on a remote portion of the Internet. Because the InterNIC servers hold a database that provides a listing of all domain DNS servers and their IP addresses, the local DNS merely queries the InterNIC server for the IP address of the DNS server that services a particular domain (using the friendly name). When the local server receives the IP address of the remote DNS server, it can then query it directly for the resolution of the remote FQDN to an IP address.

With each network really responsible for the local mapping of friendly names to IP addresses using DNS servers, the DNS database is a distributed database. Each organization maintains its part of the overall DNS database.

An alternative to DNS is the hosts file. Hosts files are used as a system to resolve the friendly name to the IP address on TCP/IP networks when DNS is not employed (or was not employed—hosts files served as a precursor to DNS). A hosts file is an ASCII text file that contains two columns of information (and is stored in the %systemroot%\system32\etc\drivers folder). The computer's hostname is listed in the first column; the corresponding IP address is listed in the second column.

With Windows Server 2003 embracing the Active Directory as its directory services platform, DNS, FQDNs, and TCP/IP become an integral part of implementing and administering a Windows network. Because Windows Server 2003 is outfitted with the newer Dynamic DNS server standard (DDNS), the administrative chores related to maintaining the DNS database are greatly reduced (when compared to other DNS servers). The DDNS database is built dynamically by the server and the DNS clients.

The DNS Namespace

To understand how DNS or FQDN names are determined, you need to understand the domain namespace, which is an integral part of how Internet Web sites are named. The *domain namespace* is the actual scheme used to name domains that are at different levels in the DNS domain hierarchical tree. The domain namespace also provides for down-level names of individual computers and other devices on a network.

The first thing that we should define is what a domain is in relation to DNS. Each division on the DNS tree (which takes the form of an inverted tree) is considered a domain.

 DNS domains and Microsoft Active Directory domains are not directly the same thing and should not be confused (even though they are closely related and based upon different technologies). When you use the DNS naming structure on your network as the Active Directory domain structure, the two naming systems will appear to be the same.

At the base of the DNS tree is the root domain. The Internet's root domain is represented by a period (see Figure 15.1). Below the root domain are the top-level domains. The top-level domains consist of suffixes such as .com and .edu. Some of the top-level domain names available are listed here:

- **com**—Used by commercial organizations. For example, samspublishing.com is the domain name for SAMS Publishing.
- **edu**—Reserved for educational institutions. For example, une.edu is the domain of the University of New England.
- **org**—Used by noncommercial organizations and institutions. For example, gsusa.org is the domain name of the Girl Scouts of America.
- **gov**—Reserved by the United States for governmental entities. For example, senate.gov is the domain for the U.S. Senate.
- **net**—Used by companies involved in the Internet infrastructure, such as ISPs.

- **Country names**—For example, bs for the Bahamas and ga for Gabon. These are based upon the ISO-registered two-digit country codes.
- **biz**—A new top-level domain added recently to accommodate businesses.
- **info**—Another new top-level domain recently added that can be used for informational Web sites (or just about anybody looking for a domain name).

Below the top-level domains are the second-level domains; these secondary domains consist of company, institutional and private domains commonly used to access a site on the Web, such as samspublishing.com (SAMS Publishing's domain name) and une.edu (the domain name of the University of New England in Biddeford, Maine). Under the second-level domains are found subdomains. These subdomains are typically used to divide a larger secondary domain into geographical or functional units. For example, if I have a company that uses the secondary domain name of Habraken.com and my business is divided into two distinct divisions (consulting and sales), I could create the two subdomains consulting.Habraken.com and sales.Habraken.com (see Figure 15.1).

FIGURE 15.1

The domain name-space tree provides the naming conventions for domains and objects that reside in domains such as hosts.

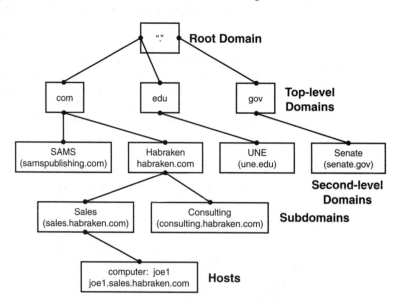

Second-level domains (and subdomains) also contain hosts, which are the computers and other devices that reside within the second-level domain or subdomain namespace. For example, if I have a computer named joe1 and it is in the sales.Habraken.com subdomain, it will be referred to as joe1.sales.Habraken.com using the DNS nomenclature.

How DNS Works

Now that we've looked at the DNS naming hierarchy, we should delve into how DNS resolves FQDNs to IP addresses, and vice versa. The DNS service consists of two different entities: the resolver and the server. The resolver is software built into a WinSock application, such as a Web browser that queries the server when a host's FQDN needs to be resolved to an IP address. The server component of DNS is handled by the DNS server, which, in this case, will be a server running Windows Server 2003 and the DDNS service.

When a client computer attempts to "resolve" a FQDN to an IP address, the resolver checks a local cache (if the resolver is set up to maintain a local cache) to see if the resolution information for going from FQDN to IP address is available. If the information is in the cache, the process is over when the FQDN is resolved to an IP address by the client computer itself.

> All Windows clients and servers maintain a DNS cache, which helps a DNS client quickly resolve a DNS query basically by itself. The cache is typically useful only when trying to resolve a friendly name to an IP address for a resource that is used often. All other queries go to the DNS server. You can view the DNS cache with the command-line utility ipconfig/displaydns.

If the information is not available in the cache, the resolver software obtains the IP address of the local DNS server using the settings found in the client computer's TCP/IP settings. Windows clients and servers on the network are configured with a preferred DNS server either statically or by a DHCP server (the types of TCP/IP settings that a DHCP server can provide are discussed in Hour 16, "Dynamic Host Configuration Protocol"). Figure 15.2 shows the TCP/IP properties of a Windows Server 2003 member server that specifies a preferred DNS server (and is also configured with a static IP address).

FIGURE 15.2

The preferred DNS server is listed in a client's TCP/IP properties.

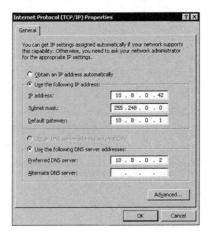

The client sends a request to the preferred DNS; if the FQDN to be resolved is for a host computer in the local DNS domain, the DNS server looks up the name in the DNS database and returns the appropriate IP address to the requesting computer. If the name is for a computer not on the local domain, two things can happen: The name can be resolved using the cache that is maintained by the local DNS server; the server will cache or remember host names that it has previously resolved. If the information is in this cache, the DNS server provides it to the requesting client.

When the information is not cached on the DNS server, your DNS server contacts the root server for the hostname's top-level domain (these IP addresses are built into the Windows Server 2003 DNS implementation) by querying it with the hostname. The root server uses the hostname to determine the IP address of the authoritative DNS server for the domain that the particular host belongs to. When your DNS server has the IP address of the other domain's DNS server, it can query that server, which then supplies the resolution information for moving from FQDN to IP address. The local DNS server can then pass this information on to the original requesting host.

Defining Your Domain Namespace

Before we look at installing DDNS on a Windows Server 2003, a few points should be made related to the domain names that you will assign to your DNS structure. When you create your DNS structure, keep in mind that you will also have a similar tree structure defined by your Active Directory domains, trees, and forests. How closely you will parallel the domain namespace and the Active Directory domain namespace is up to you. As you create your domain namespace, you should keep in mind some general rules:

- Keep your second-level domain names simple. The shorter and simpler a domain name is, the easier it is for users to remember. This is imperative for companies with a presence on the Internet and even for companies who are only deploying an intranet. Of course, your selection of domain name for a company on the Internet is affected by the domain names that are available.

- Use geographic location or company division information for subdomain names. Use a naming strategy for your subdomains that makes sense. Try to stick to particular criteria such as using department names for subdomain names—for example, accounting, sales, and so on. Remember that the subdomain name must be unique throughout the DNS namespace.

- Limit the number of domain levels, if possible. You don't need to divide your domain into subdomains just for the sake of creating divisions. Make sure that a greater division of the corporate domain makes sense instead of just creating a more complex administrative environment.

15

- Follow the standard rules for DNS names. A domain name can be up to 63 characters and can consist of alphanumeric or numeric characters. The hyphen is also considered a legal character. The entire FQDN, including the periods, can be up to 255 characters.

It probably makes sense to sit down with a piece of paper and map out how you want your DNS hierarchy to look on the network. Then when you configure your DNS server (or servers), you can use your DNS map as a guide.

Installing the Domain Name Service

With the Windows Server 2003 implementation of DNS, the Dynamic Domain Name Service (DDNS, which was originally implemented in the Windows 2000 Server product) provides for dynamic updates, which allows network clients using the DNS service to automatically update their client resource records in the DNS database. Microsoft's DDNS also allows for integration with the Active Directory, which means that the DNS database is replicated among all the domain controllers within the domain (domain controllers that also serve as DNS servers). DDNS is also integrated with the Windows Server 2003 implementation of DHCP; the DNS server can work with DHCP to synchronize mappings from hostname to IP address for the hosts on your network.

There is more than one way to install DNS on a Windows Server 2003. You can install DNS during the installation of Windows Server 2003 by selecting additional Networking Services options (for information on installing Windows Server 2003, see Hour 3, "Installing Windows Server 2003"). If you install Active Directory on your domain controller and a DNS server is not available on the network, DNS (and DHCP) will be installed during the Active Directory installation. Finally, you can add the DNS using the Configure Your Server Wizard (or the Add or Remove Software applet in the Control Panel).

> Before installing DNS on a server, you must configure the computer with a static IP address.

To install DNS using the Configure Your Server Wizard, follow these steps:

1. Start the wizard (Start, Administrative Tools, Configure Your Server Wizard). Click Next to bypass the initial wizard screen.
2. Connect all network media and server peripherals and then click Next again. The third wizard screen provides you with a list of server roles and services that can be installed (see Figure 15.3).

FIGURE 15.3

*Add DNS to the
server's roles.*

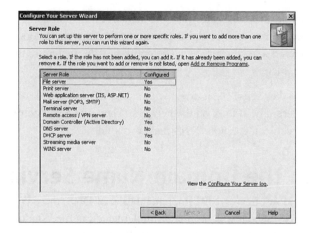

3. In the Server Role box, select DNS Server (it currently is marked No, meaning it is not installed). Then click Next to continue. A summary screen appears to let you know that DNS will be installed on the server.

4. Click Next to end the steps for the Configure Your Server Wizard. At this point, another wizard, the Configure a DNS Server Wizard, appears. The process of configuring a DNS server with this wizard is discussed in the next section. Click Next to continue.

Configuring the DNS Server

The next screen of the DNS wizard (see Figure 15.4) provides you with three DNS configuration possibilities:

- **Create a forward lookup zone**—This option enables you to create a forward lookup zone (zones are defined in a moment) so that your DNS server can resolve local DNS queries. You are also provided with the option of forwarding other queries to DNS servers farther up the DNS tree (such as your Internet service provider's DNS server). This option is recommended for small networks

- **Create forward and reverse lookup zones**—This option creates forward and reverse zones and sets up this DNS server to query DNS servers farther up the DNS tree. This option is recommended for large networks.

- **Configure root hints only**—This option, recommended for advanced users, configures the server only to forward queries up the DNS tree (by having root hints configured—root hints are also defined in a moment).

FIGURE 15.4

Select the configuration action for your DNS implementation.

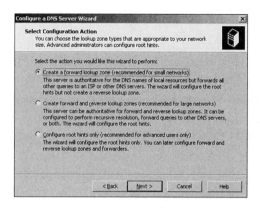

15

For the sake of further discussion, select the second option, Create forward and reverse lookup zones. You can take a look at forward and reverse lookup zones and root hints.

Select the Create forward and reverse lookup zones option button on the wizard screen. Then click Next. Creating the forward and reverse lookup zones is discussed in the next two sections.

Creating a Forward Lookup Zone

The next screen provides you with the option of creating a forward lookup zone (see Figure 15.5). A *forward lookup zone* allows for forward lookup queries, which enables a host to find the IP address using the hostname of a particular computer or device (it finds the address because the DNS answers the host computer's query). For DNS to work, at least one forward lookup zone is required.

FIGURE 15.5

Create a forward lookup zone for the DNS server.

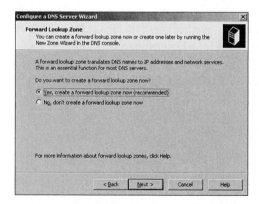

The default wizard selection is to create a new forward lookup zone. Click Next to continue.

You are provided with three options for creating different types of forward lookup zones:

- **Primary Zone**—A primary zone is the master copy of the DNS database. The primary zone is administered on the computer server where the zone was created. So, the server would be considered the authoritative DNS server for the zone.

- **Secondary Zone**—A secondary zone uses a database file that is a read-only replica of an existing zone. The DNS server configured with the standard secondary zone helps the primary DNS server handle the name resolution required for the network.

- **Stub Zone**—A stub zone contains only the records necessary to specify the authoritative DNS server (or servers) for a particular zone. The stub zone basically points at the servers that manage the primary zone.

Because (in theory) you are creating the first DNS server on the Windows Server 2003 network, select the Primary Zone option. Click Next to continue.

A check box on this DNS wizard screen also is selected by default to store the zone in the Active Directory. This means that the zone (along with the Active Directory) will be replicated to other domain controllers on the network that are also running DNS.

Zone Replication

The next screen (see Figure 15.6) provides options related to the replication of the DNS data for the new zone. It is important that DNS servers on the network replicate the DNS database (and the zone records) so that they share the same DNS records. The fact that each DNS server uses the same replicated database means that any of these DNS servers can field a query by a host for a hostname-to-IP-address resolution (or vice versa) .

FIGURE 15.6

Select replication options.

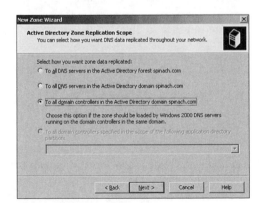

The options provided for how the DNS database should be replicated are listed here:

- **To all DNS servers in the Active Directory forest**—Using this option, all the DNS servers in the forest share and replicate their DNS databases. This means that all the DNS servers will have access to the same zones and records.

- **To all DNS servers in the Active Directory domain**—Using this option, all the domain DNS servers share their zones and records through replication.

- **To all domain controllers in the Active Directory domain**—This option is useful if you are running DNS on your domain controllers. The DNS database is stored as part of the Active Directory and is replicated (shared) among the domain controllers/DNS servers. Note that this is the default option and is considered the best practice for DNS deployment.

Select the option that you want to use (use the default option for sake of discussion) and then click Next.

Zone Names and Dynamic Updates

The next wizard screen requests a name for the new forward lookup zone (see Figure 15.7). The name of the zone is the same as the DNS domain name for the portion of your network that this DNS server is authoritative. For example, if your DNS domain for the network is spinach.com, the zone name would be spinach.com.

FIGURE 15.7

Enter a name for the new zone.

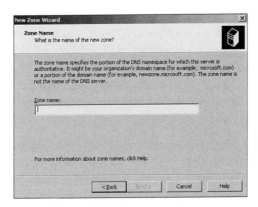

Enter the name of the zone (based on your DNS domain hierarchy). Then click Next to continue.

The next screen (Figure 15.8) provides a set of options related to the dynamic updates of your host computers as they register (and update) their records with the DNS server. The default option allows only secure updates. Other options include updates from any client (which could open some security holes in your network) and no dynamic updates (you would have to manually enter all the records for this zone).

FIGURE 15.8

Select the dynamic update options for the zone.

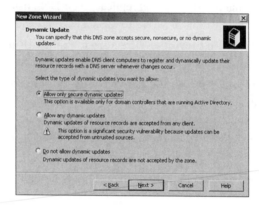

Select the dynamic update option for the new zone. The default option provides the greatest security, but it also requires that the DNS servers be running Active Directory (and thus serving as domain controllers). After selecting the update option, click Next to continue.

Creating a Reverse Lookup Zone

The next wizard screen asks if you want to create a *reverse lookup zone*. A reverse lookup zone allows for the resolution of IP addresses to hostnames, which is called a *reverse lookup query*. You don't have to configure a reverse lookup zone on your DNS server for it to work (as you did a forward lookup zone), but reverse lookup zones are useful. For example, if you want to enable Internet Information Server to record hostnames as well as IP addresses in its log file, you will need to configure your DNS server with a reverse lookup zone.

To go with the default (create a reverse lookup zone), click Next. As with the forward lookup zone, the next screen asks you to select the zone type: primary, secondary, or stub. Because this is the first reverse lookup zone on the authoritative DNS server, a primary reverse lookup zone is the appropriate choice (this is also the default). Click Next to continue.

The next screen asks you to select the type of replication for the new reverse lookup zone. Again, as for the forward lookup zone, you can have the zone data replicated to all the DNS servers in the forest, all the DNS servers in the domain, or all the DNS/domain controllers in the domain. The latter choice is the default (as it was for the forward lookup zone). It is also the best choice in environments in which DNS is running on your domain controllers. Click Next to continue.

Naming the Reverse Lookup Zone

On the next screen (see Figure 15.9), you are asked to provide your network ID. This is used to create the name for the reverse lookup zone. The network ID is the portion of an IP address that does not contain any references to host address. For example, in the Class C IP address 192.168.5.1, only the fourth octet contains host address information (the default Class C subnet mask of 255.255.255.0 basically tells you which octet is used for host addressing). This means that the 192.168.5 is the network ID and would be entered as the 192.168.5.

FIGURE 15.9

Enter the network ID to name the reverse lookup zone.

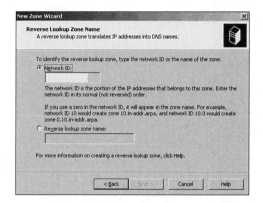

Enter your network ID. Then click Next to continue.

The next screen asks you to choose the type of dynamic updates (or no dynamic updates) that are to be used by the reverse lookup zone (this is the same screen that was configured for the dynamic update information related to the forward lookup zone). It is best to go with the default of secure dynamic updates. Click Next to continue.

Completing the DNS Configuration

The next wizard screen asks you to specify any forwarders that can be used by this DNS server. Forwarders are DNS servers that are used by the DNS server that you are currently configuring to resolve DNS queries that your DNS server cannot. Forwarders are typically DNS servers that function as the DNS conduit to the Internet. Any queries for information about hostnames and IP addresses outside your internal network would be forwarded to this DNS server (which, in many cases, might be the DNS server of your Internet service provider).

If you want to configure forwarders for the DNS server, select the Yes option and then provide the IP address (or IP addresses—the wizard allows you to specify two forwarders) of the DNS forwarder.

> If you are configuring the first DNS server on your network, you won't have the option of specifying forwarders. As your network grows, you can easily reconfigure any of your DNS servers to take advantage of forwarders.

After making your selection (either to specify forwarders or not, which is the default), click Next. The wizard searches for root hints based on the forwarder information that you provided and then completes the configuration of your DNS server. A summary screen appears. Click Finish to end the configuration process. You are now ready to manage the DNS server you have created.

Managing DNS

DNS is managed (and reconfigured, if necessary) using the DNSMGT Microsoft Management Console snap-in. To start the snap-in, select Start, Administrative Tools, DNS. The snap-in opens (see Figure 15.10).

FIGURE 15.10
The DNSMGT snap-in is used to manage and configure the DNS server.

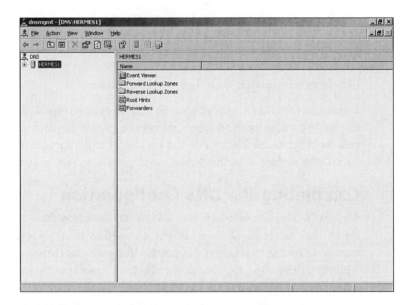

The DNSMGT snap-in enables you to view the records in your DNS zones and add zones to the DNS server. Because records are created dynamically, you can view the records in a particular zone (such as a forward lookup zone) by opening that zone in the snap-in.

15

Adding and deleting zones is easy in the DNSMGT snap-in. To add a zone, right-click either the Forward Lookup Zones node or the Reverse Lookup Zones node and select New Zone from the shortcut menu. The New Zone Wizard appears and walks you through the process of creating a zone in a series of steps very similar to those in the DNS Server Wizard. You can also delete zones: Right-click on the zone and select Delete. You must confirm the deletion. Remember, you must have one forward lookup zone for the DNS server to function correctly.

For example, to view the resource records in the forward lookup zone, expand the Forward Lookup Zones node and then select one of your forward lookup zones in the snap-in tree. The records contained in the zone appear in the snap-in pane (see Figure 15.11).

FIGURE 15.11

Zone records can be viewed in the details pane.

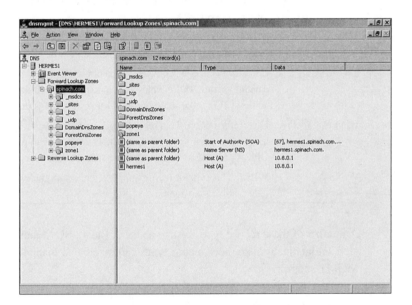

Actually a number of different resource record types are found in the DNS environment. One type of record is a host record, which is designated as an A record in the DNS environment. A records are found in forward lookup zones. The hermes1 host or A record is shown in the Details pane of Figure 15.11. You will also notice that other resource record types, such as Start of Authority (SOA) and Name Server (NS), appear in the DNS Details pane. A number of different types of DNS resource records exist; a summary of these types is provided in Table 15.1.

TABLE 15.1 DNS Resource Record Types

Record Type	DNS Snap-In Name and Description
SOA	Start of Authority. Identifies the name of the server that is authoritative for data within the domain and that is the first record in the zone database file. It is created automatically when you bring your primary name server online.
NS	Name Server. A record is created for each name server assigned to the domain.
A	Host. This record provides the mapping of hostname to IP address in a forward lookup zone.
PTR	Pointer. This type of record is the reverse of an A record and points to a host record. Found in the reverse lookup zone, the PTR record provides for mappings from IP address to hostname.
SRV	Service. This type of record shows which services are running on a particular host computer. For example, SRV records could identify the domain controllers on the network.
MX	Mail Exchanger. This record type identifies the mail servers on the network and details in what order the mail servers should be contacted.
CNAME	Canonical Name or Alias. This type of record is used to create an alias for an existing record. This enables you to point several different names at the same IP address. This is particularly useful for pointing at your Web server on the network.
HINFO	Host Information. This record type can be used as a sort of low-rent resource-tracking tool for your DNS server. This record can provide information on the CPU, operating system, and other software/hardware information.
WINS	WINS. This type of record supplies DNS with the capability to use WINS to help resolve a hostname.

A number of these record types—such as the A (host), SOA, and NS records—are created automatically. The other record types can be created manually within the DNS-MGMT snap-in.

Creating Resource Records

Although Dynamic DNS creates many of the resource records for the DNS database, you might want to create some resource records, such as a CNAME or a WINS record, manually. In some cases, you might also need to create host records for the DNS database (for clients that cannot work with DNS to dynamically create an A record).

To create a DNS resource record, follow these steps:

1. Expand a zone node (such as the forward lookup zones node) and then select a zone in the snap-in tree. The records currently in the zone appear in the Details pane.

2. Right-click the zone icon in the snap-in tree. A shortcut menu appears that contains choices such as New Host and New Alias. You can click any of these record types to start the process of creating a new resource record. For example, if you select New Host from the shortcut menu, the New Host dialog box appears (see Figure 15.12).

FIGURE 15.12

You can create resource records such as host records.

3. To create the new host record, supply the hostname for the computer and then supply the IP address of the computer (or other device, such as a printer). A check box is also included to create a PTR record for the host (the reverse lookup zone record). It makes sense to check this box and create both the host and PTR records simultaneously.

4. After supplying the appropriate information for the new record, click Add Host. The record is added to the selected zone.

You can view all the possible resource records that you can create; right-click a DNS zone in the snap-in tree and then select Other New Records from the shortcut menu. The Resource Record Type dialog box appears. Choose a resource record type from the list and then click the Create Record button to create the new resource record.

Configuring DNS Clients

We have been looking at DNS so far from the server side, but there are also DNS management duties related to clients on your network. You need to configure TCP/IP clients on the network to use the DNS service.

You will want to configure any clients on the network (which includes servers) that are set up with a static IP address to use a particular DNS server on the network to resolve hostnames. You can specify a preferred DNS server and a secondary DNS server for the client.

To configure a client for specific DNS servers, follow these steps:

1. Log on to the client computer or member server as an Administrator and open the Network and Dialup Connections window (on an XP client or Server 2003, select Start, Control Panel, Network Connection). Then right-click Local Area Connection and select Properties. This opens the Local Area Connection Properties dialog box.

2. Scroll down through the components list and click Internet Protocol (TCP/IP). Then click the Properties button.

3. The Internet Protocol (TCP/IP) properties box opens. Select the Use the following DNS server addresses option button. Then enter the preferred DNS server IP address and the alternate DNS server IP address (if one exists).

4. If you need to enter additional DNS server addresses, click the Advanced button and then select the DNS tab on the Advanced TCP/IP properties box. You can add other DNS servers on this tab. Enter the server addresses in the order that you want the host to query them.

5. Click OK to return to the TCP/IP properties box. Click OK to close the Local Area Connections dialog box. You can now close the various open windows and return to the desktop.

An alternative to manually entering information such as preferred DNS servers is to use DHCP in your domain. It can configure all the TCP/IP properties for your clients dynamically. See Hour 16 for more about DHCP.

Configuring a Caching-only Server

DNS servers cache information that they receive from queries that they have made to other DNS servers. You can configure a DNS server that operates as a *caching-only server*, meaning that it supplies information to hostname resolution queries based on the data that it has acquired in its cache.

Caching-only servers are very useful because they do not generate network traffic related to zone transfers; they are not authoritative for any zones. Caching-only servers are often used as a forwarder that sits outside a firewall and is used by a company's internal DNS server to resolve hostnames to IP addresses that reside outside the internal network, such as on the Internet.

To create a caching-only server, install DNS on a server running Windows Server 2003. When configuring DNS, do not create any zones on the server. A member server on your network is an ideal candidate for a caching-only server.

Monitoring and Troubleshooting the DNS Server Service

The DNSMGT snap-in not only lists dynamic updates resulting in host records for hosts on the network; the snap-in also provides you with a way to test the DNS server and monitor the results. Two different tests in the form of queries are available: a simple query and a recursive query.

- **Simple**—A simple query tests the mapping of host to IP address, so the simple query performed in the DNS snap-in uses the DNS client on the DNS server to query the name server. This is a test of the DNS server's capability to handle forward lookups.

- **Recursive**—A recursive query enables you to test the mapping of IP address to hostname, which is a test of the DNS server's reverse lookup capabilities. You must have a reverse lookup zone configured to run the recursive query.

To monitor and run these test queries, follow these steps:

1. Right-click the DNS name server in the DNSMGMT snap-in, and then select Properties from the shortcut menu that appears. The Properties dialog box opens for the DNS server.

2. Click the Monitoring tab to select it. Two check boxes are available on the tab (see Figure 15.13): a simple query against this DNS server and a recursive query to other DNS servers.

FIGURE 15.13

You can test the DNS server with queries.

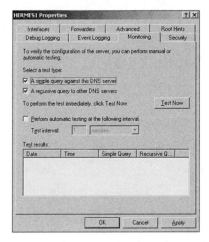

3. Click the appropriate check box to set up the test (you can select both check boxes). Then click the Test Now button. The test results appear in the Test results box of the Monitoring tab.

You can also monitor a DNS server over time using these query tests. Select the Perform automatic testing at the following interval check box and then use the Test interval.

If your server fails one of these tests when they are performed periodically (if you set up for automatic testing), the server is marked with an alert icon (a triangle with an exclamation point on it). This lets you know when you view the Server icon in the DNS-MGMT snap-in that there is a problem with the server.

Viewing DNS Events in the Event Viewer

You can view events related to your DNS server using the Event Viewer node provided in the DNSMGMT snap-in. The Event Viewer helps you to track a number of event logs related to the performance of your server, the network operating system, and the services installed on the server. For more about the Event Viewer and the type of information it provides in its log files (which operates in its own snap-in), see Hour 20, "Monitoring Server and Network Performance."

To view DNS log events, expand the Event Viewer node in the snap-in tree. Then select the DNS Events icon. The events logged in this file appear in the Details pane (see Figure 15.14).

FIGURE 15.14

You can view the events in the DNS log file.

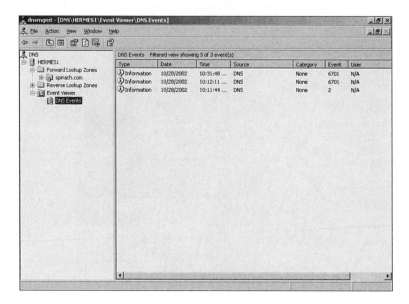

To view the properties of a particular event (the details of the event), right-click the event and select Properties. Additional information related to the logged event is provided. If your DNS service is running smoothly, you will typically see only information events in the log (as shown in Figure 15.14). If you see Warning or Error icons, you might have a DNS problem (see Hour 20 for more about the types of events logged by the Event Viewer).

Using Nslookup

Nslookup can be considered the primary troubleshooting tool for DNS. Nslookup is a command-line utility, and you can use it to view host records, do query testing of DNS servers, and perform other tasks related to DNS from the command line.

You can use the `nslookup` command to find information such as the IP address of a particular host on the network. The command takes the syntax `nslookup name1 name2`, where `name1` is the hostname for the host computer that you want to look up and `name2` is the name of the DNS server that you want to query. Running these queries with Nslookup allows you to see if the DNS server is dynamically recording the host records needed to resolve the queries.

Each time you run the `nslookup` command as described in the previous paragraph, you are returned to the command prompt. This is called the Nslookup noninteractive mode. If you want to run several Nslookup commands in succession, you can enter the Nslook interactive mode.

At the command line, type **nslookup** (with no additional parameters) and then press Enter. This command provides the default DNS server information and the IP address of the server (see Figure 15.15). This also places you in Nslookup interactive mode (notice that in Figure 15.15, the command prompt has been replaced by the Nslookup > prompt).

FIGURE 15.15

Nslookup provides a command-line DNS utility.

When you are in interactive mode, you do not have to type the `nslookup` command. So, the command syntax becomes `name1 name2`, where you supply the hostname (`name1`) to be resolved, followed by the DNS server (`name2`) you want to query.

When you want to exit Nslookup interactive mode, type **exit** at the Nslookup prompt (>) and then press Enter. You will be returned to the command prompt.

Nslookup can also be used to verify that a forward lookup zone is configured correctly. Let's look at the commands.

To test that a forward lookup zone is configured correctly, use the following steps to simulate a zone transfer:

1. At the command prompt (click Start and then select Command Prompt), type **nslookup** and press Enter. This places you in interactive mode.

2. Type the command `server ip address` (with the IP address of the DNS server that you want to test). Then press Enter.

3. Use the `set` command to set the query type to any type of record: `set querytype=any`. Then press Enter.

4. To simulate the zone transfer type, use the command `ls-d domain name`, where `domain name` is the name of the forward lookup zone. Then press Enter.

If the zone is configured correctly, you will see the results of the "fake" zone transfer in the command prompt window. Figure 15.16 shows the results of a successful (fake) zone transfer invoked using Nslookup interactive mode.

FIGURE 15.16

You can do fake zone transfers to check forward lookup zones.

```
Command Prompt - nslookup                                              _ | 8 | x
C:\Documents and Settings\Administrator>nslookup
Default Server:  hermes1.spinach.com
Address:  10.8.0.1

> server 10.8.0.1
Default Server:  hermes1.spinach.com
Address:  10.8.0.1

> set querytype=any
> ls -d spinach.com
[hermes1.spinach.com]
 spinach.com.                    SOA     hermes1.spinach.com hostmaster. (71 900 6
00 86400 3600)
 spinach.com.                    A       10.8.0.1
 spinach.com.                    NS      hermes1.spinach.com
 _msdcs                          NS      hermes1
 _gc._tcp.Default-First-Site._sites SRV    priority=0, weight=100, port=3268, he
rmes1.spinach.com
 _kerberos._tcp.Default-First-Site._sites SRV    priority=0, weight=100, port=88
, hermes1.spinach.com
 _ldap._tcp.Default-First-Site._sites SRV    priority=0, weight=100, port=389, h
ermes1.spinach.com
 _gc._tcp                        SRV     priority=0, weight=100, port=3268, hermes
1.spinach.com
 _kerberos._tcp                  SRV     priority=0, weight=100, port=88, hermes1.
spinach.com
 _kpasswd._tcp                   SRV     priority=0, weight=100, port=464, hermes1
.spinach.com
 _ldap._tcp                      SRV     priority=0, weight=100, port=389, hermes1
.spinach.com
 _kerberos._udp                  SRV     priority=0, weight=100, port=88, hermes1.
spinach.com
 _kpasswd._udp                   SRV     priority=0, weight=100, port=464, hermes1
.spinach.com
 DomainDnsZones                  A       10.8.0.1
 _ldap._tcp.Default-First-Site._sites.DomainDnsZones SRV    priority=0, weight=1
00, port=389, hermes1.spinach.com
 _ldap._tcp.DomainDnsZones       SRV     priority=0, weight=100, port=389, hermes1
.spinach.com
 ForestDnsZones                  A       10.8.0.1
 _ldap._tcp.Default-First-Site._sites.ForestDnsZones SRV    priority=0, weight=1
00, port=389, hermes1.spinach.com
 _ldap._tcp.ForestDnsZones       SRV     priority=0, weight=100, port=389, hermes1
.spinach.com
 hermes1                         A       10.8.0.1
 popeye                          A       10.8.0.42
```

15

Using the queries provided by the DNSMGMT snap-in, the Event Viewer DNS logs, and the nslookup command, can help you stay on top of your DNS implementation. Even when you know that you have configured the DNS service perfectly, you should periodically use these tools to check how successfully your DNS implementation is on your network.

Summary

In this hour, you looked at the Domain Name Service. DNS provides a hierarchical name-resolution system for resolving FQDNs (friendly) to IP addresses. Each organization typically deploys its own DNS server that handles the resolution duties of that domain.

The root of the DNS tree is represented by the . (dot). Top-level domains under the root are identified by suffixes such as com, edu, and biz. Computer hostnames consist of the name of the computer followed by the DNS domain name (the child domain preceding the parent domain).

The Windows Server 2003 implementation of DNS is the Dynamic Domain Name Service (DDNS). DDNS allows DNS clients to automatically update their client resource records in the DNS database. Because the database is automatically configured, you spend much less time creating resource records.

The Windows Server 2003 DNS service is installed using the Configure Your Server Wizard. For the DNS service to operate correctly, you must configure a forward lookup zone on the server. This allows for resolution from hostname to IP address. Reverse lookup zones are used to resolve IP addresses to hostnames. Reverse lookup zones are useful but are not required on your DNS server. DNS is managed in the DNSMGMT MMC snap-in. You can use the snap-in to view resource records in your zones, create new zones (and delete zones), and create new resource records. DNS clients are computers that have been configured to refer to a preferred DNS server when they need to resolve a hostname to an IP address (or vice versa). You can specify a preferred DNS server in the client's TCP/IP properties. Or, you can configure your DHCP server to provide DHCP clients with the IP address of a preferred DNS server.

Q&A

Q What is the purpose of deploying local DNS servers?

A A domain DNS server provides for the local mapping of fully qualified domain names to IP addresses. Because the DNS is a distributed database, the local DNS servers can provide record information to remote DNS servers to help resolve remote requests related to fully qualified domain names on your network.

Q What types of zones would you want to create on your DNS server so that both queries to resolve hostnames to IP addresses and queries to resolve IP addresses to hostnames are handled successfully?

A You would create both a forward zone and a reverse lookup zone on your Windows Server 2003 DNS server.

Q How do you specify the DNS servers that your local DNS server will contact when it cannot resolve a particular DNS query?

A During the DNS configuration, you specify any forwarders that are to be used by the local DNS server. The forwarders are the DNS servers that will handle queries that cannot be handled locally.

Q What tool enables you to manage your Windows Server 2003 DNS server?

A The DNSGMGT snap-in enables you to add or remove zones and to view the records in your DNS zones. You can also use the snap-in to create records such as a DNS resource record.

Q In terms of DNS, what is a caching-only server?

A A caching-only DNS server supplies information related to queries based on the data it contains in its DNS cache. Caching-only servers are often used as DNS forwards. Because they are not configured with any zones, they do not generate network traffic related to zone transfers.

HOUR **16**

Using the Dynamic Host Configuration Protocol

IP networks require that each device on the network (computer, printer, router, and so on) be assigned a unique IP address. Configuring static addresses on a large network can be both time-consuming and, in the case of poor or incomplete documentation, difficult to manage. Tracking and assigning unique IP addresses became the focus of the Internet Engineering Task Force and leading software developers; the result was the development of the Dynamic Host Configuration Protocol (DHCP). In this hour, we look at how to deploy DHCP on a server running Windows Server 2003.

In this hour, the following topics are covered:

- Understanding the Dynamic Host Configuration Protocol
- Installing DHCP
- Creating scopes and working with IP leases
- Working with DHCP and DNS integration

- Editing DHCP server settings
- Configuring DHCP clients
- Monitoring and managing DHCP

Understanding DHCP

The Dynamic Host Configuration Protocol (DHCP) enables you to dynamically assign IP addresses to your network computers and other devices. IP addresses are taken from a pool of addresses and are assigned to computers either permanently or for a fixed lease time. When you consider that you must configure every client computer on an IP network with such things as an IP address, a subnet mask, a default gateway address, and a DNS server address, you can see that there is an incredible margin for error.

DHCP provides a dynamic environment for assigning IP addresses to computers and devices on the network. It actually simplifies much of the drudgery that would be involved in manually assigning IP addresses.

DHCP evolved from a protocol called BOOTP, short for the Bootstrap Protocol, which was used to assign IP addresses to diskless workstations. BOOTP did not assign IP addresses dynamically, however; it pulled IP addresses from a static BOOTP file that was created by the network administrator.

A DHCP server (any Windows Server 2003 configured with the DHCP service) can supply an IP address, subnet mask, default gateway, DNS server address, and WINS server address to a DHCP client. A DHCP client is any computer or device on the network that is configured to acquire its IP address (and other TCP/IP settings) dynamically.

When a DHCP client boots up for the first time, it goes looking for an IP address. The client initializes TCP/IP (a stripped-down version) and broadcasts a DHCPDISCOVER message, which is a request for an IP lease that is sent to all DHCP servers (addressed to 255.255.255.255, meaning all nodes on the network). This broadcast message contains the hostname of the client (which, in most cases, is also the client's NetBIOS name) and the *MAC hardware address* of the client.

The MAC address is the hardware address burned into a ROM chip on a device such as a network interface card or a router interface by the device manufacturer.

In the next step, a DCHP server (or servers, if more than one is available) on the subnet responds with a DHCPOFFER message that includes an offered IP address, an accompanying subnet mask, and the length of the lease. The message also contains the IP address of the DHCP server, identifying the server. The DHCPOFFER message is also in the form of a broadcast because, at this point, the client does not have an IP address.

When the client receives the first DHCPOFFER message (it might receive multiple offers, but it goes with first appropriate offer that it receives), it then broadcasts a DHCPREQUEST message to all DHCP servers on the network, showing that it is accepting an offer. This broadcast message contains the IP address of the DHCP server whose offer the client accepted. Knowing which DHCP server was selected allows the other DHCP servers on the network to retract their offers and save their IP addresses for the next requesting client (yes, it does sound a little bit like a used car lot).

Finally, the DHCP server that supplied the accepted offer broadcasts an acknowledgement message to the client, a DHCPPACK message. This message contains a valid IP address lease and other TCP/IP configuration information. The client stores this information in its Windows Registry.

Installing the DHCP Service

DHCP can be installed using the Configure Your Server Wizard, or you can add the service to the server using the Add or Remove Programs utility in the Windows Control Panel. Before you install DHCP on a server, you must configure the server with a static IP address.

When you bring your first Windows Server 2003 domain controller online by installing Active Directory, the Active Directory Wizard gives you the option of installing DNS and DHCP if they are not already running on servers on the network. The instructions here are for installing a standalone DHCP server running Windows Server 2003 (the remainder of the hour provides you with useful configuration information whether DHCP was installed on the domain controller for you or by you on a separate DHCP server).

To add DHCP using the Configure Your Server Wizard, follow these steps:

1. Select Start, Administrative Tools, and then select the Configure Your Server Wizard. The Configure Your Server Wizard opens.

2. Click Next to bypass the initial wizard screen. On the next screen, the wizard provides a checklist of network connectivity hardware (such as network cards and modems) that you should have installed on the server. When you click Next, the wizard searches for network connections to your Windows server.

3. The next wizard screen provides a list of server roles. Services that you have added
   to your server are marked Yes. Services that you have not installed are marked No
   (see Figure 16.1).

FIGURE 16.1

*The wizard provides a
list of server roles.*

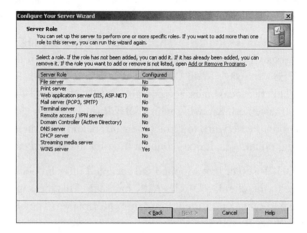

4. To add DHCP to your server's roles, select DHCP server in the Server Role list and
   then click Next. A wizard summary screen appears showing the server roles that
   you will add to the server (in this case, DHCP).

5. Click Next to continue. The DHCP service is added to your server, and the
   Configure Your Server Wizard automatically starts the New Scope Wizard (scopes
   are the subject of the next section).

If you prefer, you can install DHCP and other Windows Server 2003 services
and server roles using the Add or Remove Software utility in the Control
Panel. To install DHCP from the Add or Remove Software window, select the
Click Add/Remove Windows Components to open the Windows Component
Wizard. The Dynamic Host Configuration Protocol is one of the Networking
Services, so you select it by clicking Networking Services and selecting Details.

Configuring the DHCP Service with a Scope

The next step in configuring the DHCP server is to configure a scope of IP addresses.
The scope provides the range of IP addresses that the server can hand out to requesting
DHCP clients.

When you create the scope, the Scope Wizard walks you through the process of creating
the scope. This wizard can also assist you in configuring other parameters related to

DHCP, such as the exclusion range. The exclusion range is a subset of the IP addresses within the scope that you do not want to be offered to DHCP clients.

You want to exclude some of the IP addresses from the scope on computers that require static IP addresses (for example, your DHCP server requires a static IP address). Other devices on the network, such as routers and some printers (those directly connected to the network), also require static IP addresses, so the exclusion range that you specify might include a number of IP addresses (remember that this is supposed to be a range of addresses that are excluded, so pick a logical starting and stopping point in the address scope that is available).

Another parameter that you will want to configure for the scope is the length of time that the IP addresses will be leased to the clients. Although deciding on a particular lease time might seem low on the scale of importance when considering the other parameters that must be configured for DHCP, it is actually extremely important and affects how efficiently your IP address scope is used. It also has an impact on other issues, such as network security (we discuss lease time issues later in the hour).

In the previous section, the installation of DHCP using the Configure Your Server Wizard automatically opened the New Scope Wizard after the installation of the DHCP service. If you installed the DHCP service using the Add or Remove Programs utility, DHCP was installed, but the wizard was not automatically started.

DHCP is configured and managed using the Microsoft Management Console and the DHCP snap-in. The steps for configuring a new scope that follow provide a step to open the DHCP snap-in and start the New Scope Wizard. If you used the Configure Your Server Wizard to install DHCP, you can pick up the process at step 2.

1. Select Start, point at Administrative Tools, and then select DHCP. The DHCP snap-in opens; click the icon for DHCP to expand the node. Then right-click your server icon and Select New Scope on the shortcut menu that appears. The Create Scope Wizard appears.

2. Click Next to bypass the wizard's initial screen. On the next screen, enter a name and a description for the scope that you will create. Click Next to continue.

3. You are asked to provide the range of IP addresses that are available in the Scope (see Figure 16.2). Enter the scope range (the beginning and ending IP addresses in the range). Also enter the subnet mask for the network.

For basic information about IP addressing, subnet masks, and configuring the TCP/IP protocol stack, see Hour 7, "Working with Network Protocols."

16

FIGURE **16.2**

Provide the beginning and ending addresses for your IP scope.

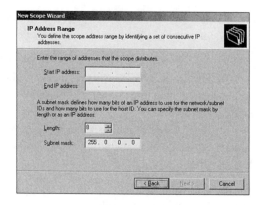

4. After you supply the scope and the subnet mask, click Next to continue. The next screen enables you to configure your exclusion range. Enter the start address and the end address for the range of IP addresses that will be excluded from the DCHP scope (excluded addresses are typically used on devices that need a fixed IP address). Then click the Add button to add the exclusion range (see Figure 16.3) .

You can add multiple exclusion ranges for a scope.

FIGURE **16.3**

Add the exclusion range or ranges for the scope.

As far as the scope and exclusion ranges go, your work is complete. Now we can move on to selecting the lease duration. Click Next to continue. Before you set the lease duration (keep your wizard on hold for a moment), let's discuss how you might arrive at the appropriate lease duration for your IP network.

Understanding DHCP Lease Issues

The duration that you set for your IP address leases can affect the efficiency of your network. If you have a number of computers, such as laptops, that are moved around on the network a great deal, shorter lease lengths will make it easier for these users to gain access to network resources if they connect on a different subnet (subnets are discussed in Hour 7).

You might even have fewer IP addresses than computers on the network. For example, you could have different shifts, on which the number of workers on the network is consistent, but different people during the day and night shifts are logged into different computers. Very short leases enable you to stretch an IP address pool among all the devices on the network because not all the devices need to be up and running at the same time.

If your network is fairly static in terms of the movement of devices and if bandwidth is an issue, longer leases lessen the number of DHCP broadcasts because computers do not have to renew their IP leases that frequently. Fewer broadcasts mean that less bandwidth is soaked up by the broadcast traffic.

You can set the lease duration on the Lease Duration screen of the New Scope Wizard (see Figure 16.4). After you set the lease duration, click Next (the default lease duration is eight hours).

FIGURE 16.4

Set the lease duration for your IP scope.

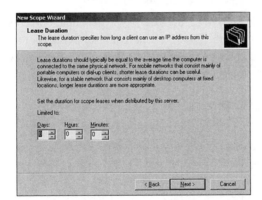

A DHCP client will actually request to renew its IP address lease halfway through the lease duration period that you set.

Setting Other DHCP Parameters

The next New Scope Wizard screen provides you with the capability of configuring other DHCP options, such as the *default gateway*, DNS server, and WINS server. Let's briefly discuss each of these options. We'll pause for a moment and discuss some of the other IP-related parameters that can be configured during your session with the Create a Scope Wizard:

- **Default gateway address**—The IP address of the router interface that the clients use as their default gateway
- **DNS server address**—The IP address of the default DNS server to be used (which can be the same server you are configuring DHCP on)
- **WINS server address**—The IP address of the WINS server to be used by the clients

You are not required to enter these parameters. However, allowing DHCP to configure all the IP settings for your DHCP clients means that you won't have to configure any of this information statically on the clients themselves.

To configure these parameters, follow these steps:

1. In the New Scope Wizard, make sure the option button Yes, I Want to Configure These Options Now is selected, and click Next.

2. On the next screen (see Figure 16.5), type the name of the default gateway (and other gateways that the DHCP clients can use) in the Gateway address box. Click Add to add the gateway to the list of gateways available (you can have multiple gateways). Click Next to continue.

FIGURE 16.5

Provide the default gateway for your DHCP clients.

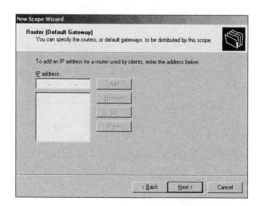

3. On this screen, you are asked to provide your domain name and any DNS servers that are being used on the network. Enter the IP address of the DNS server (or servers), and then click Add to add them to the list. Click Next to continue.

4. The next screen enables you to enter the IP address of any WINS servers on the network. Enter the IP address or addresses of this server and any others, and then click Add. When you have finished entering the WINS servers, click Next.

5. The next screen of the DHCP Scope Wizard asks if you want to activate the IP scope that you created using the wizard; make sure that the Yes option button is selected, and then click Next. This completes the scope-creation process. Click Finish.

Creating Superscopes

Before we leave the subject of scopes, we should discuss the superscope. When you create a scope on your DHCP server, it is assumed that the IP address range encompasses no more than one logical subnet (we discuss the basics of subnetting in Hour 7).

Now let's play devil's advocate and say that you need to implement more IP addresses than those available in one of the subnets that you have created; you need to create a scope that includes the addresses of more than one subnet. The easiest way to create a superscope is to create a new "regular" scope and include the IP addresses from more than one subnet. The Create a Scope Wizard recognizes that you have more than one subnet's worth of addresses in your IP address range and notifies you that you must create the scope as a superscope.

To create the superscope, follow these steps:

1. In the DHCP snap-in, right-click your DHCP server icon in the tree pane. select New Scope on the shortcut menu that appears.

2. The New Scope Wizard appears. Click Next to bypass the initial screen. On the IP Address Range screen, specify the start and end addresses of the IP scope (also supply the subnet mask). This scope should include IP addresses from more than one IP subnet, as shown in Figure 16.6.

FIGURE 16.6

Provide a range of IP addresses that encompass more than one logical subnet.

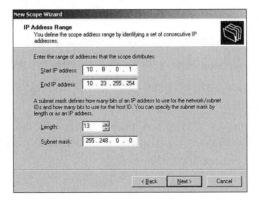

3. Click Next to go to the next screen, the Create Superscope screen. This screen tells you that you cannot create a single scope with the IP address range that you have specified (see Figure 16.7).

FIGURE 16.7

An IP address range of more than one subnet must be configured as a superscope.

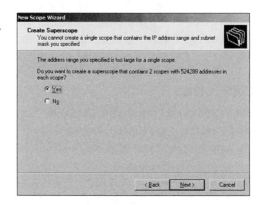

4. Click the Yes option button and then click Next.

5. On the next screen, set the lease duration for the superscope (as you would for any scope). Then click Next.

As was discussed in the section on creating a "regular" scope, the wizard now gives you the option of providing additional information, such as the default gateway, DNS server, and WINS server. You can click Next to continue and provide this information; you then complete the process as we discussed in this hour's section "Setting Other DHCP Parameters."

Creating Reservations

You might want to have certain devices on the network, such as network printers or other devices, to always receive the same IP address, although you still want the address assigned dynamically by the DHCP server. This is called a reservation.

To create a reservation (or reservations), follow these steps:

1. Double-click any scope in the Tree pane of the DHCP snap-in.

2. In the Details pane, right-click the Reservations icon and select New Reservation from the shortcut menu.

3. In the New Reservation dialog box, provide a name for the reservation, the MAC hardware address of the device that you want to reserve the IP address for, and the actual IP address. Then click OK.

To find the MAC hardware address for any computer running Windows NT, 2000, XP, or .NET, use the `ipconfig/all` command at the command line. For Windows 9x clients, use the command `winipcfg`. You can also use the `nbstat` command to find the MAC address of any computer on the network. Type `nbstat -a` followed by the IP address of the computer.

16

Activating a Scope

For a scope to be available to DHCP clients on the network, you must activate the scope. Right-click the Scope icon in the tree area of the DHCP snap-in, and select Activate for the shortcut menu. The scope is now activated (if Activate is not available on the shortcut menu and you see Deactivate, the scope is already active).

Authorizing the DCHP Server in Active Directory

All DHCP servers in your Windows Server 2003 domain must be authorized with the Active Directory for them to be valid DHCP servers on the network. This negates the possibility of a rogue DHCP server on the network (for example, someone testing a DHCP server that is unknowingly connected to the network) from assigning spurious IP addresses to your DHCP clients (which typically means that you get tons of support calls because everyone is having trouble getting at network resources).

When you open the DHCP snap-in (select Start, Administrative Tools, DHCP), you will find that the newly installed DHCP server (its icon) is marked with a red downward-pointing arrow, meaning that the server is not authorized. When you select the server icon, you will also find that the server status reads, "Authorize the DHCP Server" in the Details pane of the snap-in window (see Figure 16.8).

You authorize the server from the DHCP snap-in. Click the server icon to select it, and then select the Action menu and select Authorize. That's all it takes. To view this change to the configuration, select the Action menu and then select Refresh; your server is now marked with a green arrow, meaning that it has been authorized.

If the DHCP server is a member server of your domain, or if the domain controller is a child domain and you want to authorize it from another DHCP server on the network (for example, the domain controller for the domain, which is also running DHCP), open the DNS snap-in and click the DHCP icon in the snap-in window. Select the Action menu, and then select Manage Authorized Servers. The Manage Authorized Servers dialog box appears.

FIGURE **16.8**
DHCP servers must be registered with the Active Directory.

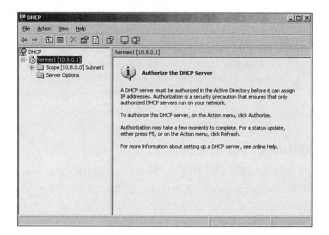

You authorize a DHCP server by adding it to the authorized list in the Manage Authorized Servers dialog box. Click the Authorize button. You are asked to provide the name or IP address of the DHCP server that you want to authorize (see Figure 16.9). Supply the hostname for the server, or provide the IP address.

FIGURE **16.9**
Provide the name or IP address of the DHCP server that you want to authorize.

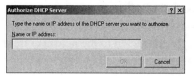

Click OK. You are advised that the server that you have designated will be added to the authorized list. If the IP address is listed correctly, click Yes. Then click Close on the Manage Authorized Servers dialog box to return to the DHCP Manager.

A DHCP server functioning in a workgroup self-authorizes when it determines that it is the only DHCP server on the network. This makes sense because a workgroup will not have a domain controller that can authorize the DHCP server.

Understanding DHCP and DNS Integration

Windows Server 2003 provides for the integration of DHCP with DNS (as did Windows 2000 Server). This integration simply means that if DHCP and DNS are both configured for dynamic updates, then whenever DCHP assigns an IP address to a requesting client, the client's hostname and IP address are also registered with the DNS database. To allow dynamic updates from DHCP to DNS, you must configure the DHCP server.

> You must also configure the DNS server for dynamic updates to integrate DHCP and DNS. This is discussed in Hour 15, "Understanding the Domain Name Service."

To configure DHCP for dynamic updates, follow these steps:

1. In the DHCP snap-in, right-click your DHCP server icon (the named server icon) and select Properties from the shortcut menu. The Properties dialog box appears.

2. Click the DNS tab on the Properties dialog box (see Figure 16.10). You are presented with several options related to DNS:

FIGURE 16.10

Options related to DHCP and DNS are found on the DNS tab.

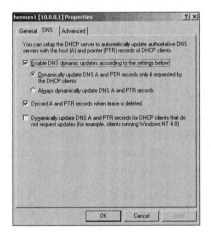

- **Enable DNS dynamic updates according to the settings below**—This check box is enabled by default; actual selections are made by selecting the options that follow in this list.

- **Dynamically update DNS A and PTR records only if requested by the DHCP clients**—This selection (the default) means that the DNS server will receive updated information only when the client requests an IP address from the DHCP server.

- **Always dynamically update DNS A and PTR records**—This option button allows for the updating of DNS records for any DHCP client that requests to renew its IP address.

- **Discard A and PTR records when lease is deleted**—This default option requires the DHCP server to send a message to the DNS server so that the records for the host are discarded when the IP address lease for the host expires.
- **Dynamically update DNS A and PTR records for DNS clients that do not request updates**—Enable this option to configure DHCP to send updates to the DNS server when an IP address lease is provided to a client computer that is running an operating system that does not support dynamic updates (operating systems earlier than Windows 2000 Professional, meaning the Windows 9*x* and Windows NT clients) .

5. After you make the appropriate selections (you might want to go with the defaults unless you are running pre–Windows 2000 clients), click the OK button. This returns you to the DHCP snap-in.

DNS record types such as A and PTR records are discussed in Hour 15.

Editing DHCP Server Options

You can edit data related to the DHCP server options such as the default gateway, DNS server, and WINS server settings. These options are edited (or entered for the first time, if you did not include them when configuring your scope) in the Server Option Properties dialog box.

Click to expand your DHCP server node in the snap-in tree. Then right-click the Server Options icon and select Configure Options. The Server Options dialog box appears.

Each option listed on the General tab (such as DNS Server or WINS Server) is designated by option number. For example, the router (the default gateway) is option number 003; the DNS server is 006, and the WINS server is 044.

So, for example, to set the router (or default gateway) for DHCP clients receiving this information from the DHCP server, you would click the 003 check box and then enter the IP address of the default gateway (router), as shown in Figure 16.11. The default DNS server and the WINS server can be configured in the same way (by selecting option numbers 006 or 044, respectively). After changing the configuration information, click the OK button to close the dialog box.

16

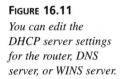

FIGURE 16.11

You can edit the DHCP server settings for the router, DNS server, or WINS server.

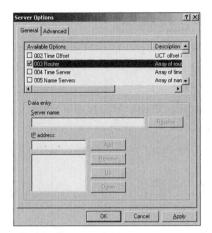

Configuring DHCP Clients

A DHCP client is any computer or device that is configured to receive its IP address dynamically from the DHCP server. All Windows clients and Windows servers that do not require a static IP address can be configured as a DHCP client (nearly all of them are configured as a DHCP client by default).

Figure 16.12 shows the Internet Protocol (TCP/IP) Properties dialog box for a server running Windows Server 2003 that has been configured as a DCHP client. Note that it is configured to get both its IP address and DNS server address automatically (both of which would be supplied by the DHCP server). All the Windows clients use a similar dialog box to configure their IP properties.

FIGURE 16.12

You can easily config-ure any computer run-ning Windows (all versions) to be a DHCP client.

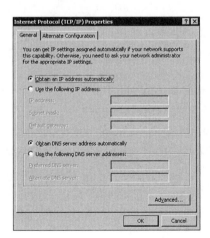

Monitoring DHCP Leases

Because the whole point of DHCP is to provide IP leases to DHCP clients, you will want to monitor the leases that the DHCP server provides. You can view current leases in the DHCP snap-in. Follow these steps:

1. In the DHCP snap-in, click the Expand (+) button to the left of the DHCP server icon. The Scope folder appears.

2. Expand the Scope folder (click the plus symbol next to it). This gives you access to the Address Leases icon.

3. Click the icon. All the current leases appear in the Details pane of the snap-in (Figure 16.13).

FIGURE 16.13

You can view the leases that have been assigned to your DHCP clients.

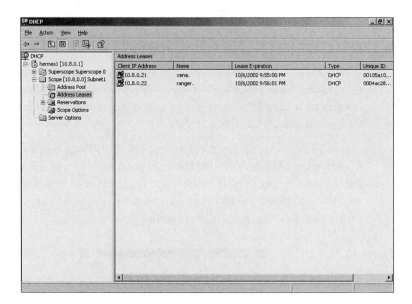

You can also add more servers to the snap-in. This enables you to monitor multiple DHCP servers from the same management console.

In the DHCP snap-in, click the DHCP icon in the tree. Then click the Action menu and select Manage Authorized Servers. The Manage Authorized Servers dialog box opens.

To add a server to the snap-in, click the server in the dialog box and then click OK. The computer is added to the DHCP snap-in. This enables you to monitor the server's IP address scope and current leases.

Loading the DCHP Database Backup

Another aspect of managing DHCP on the network is working with the backup of the DHCP database. By default, the database is automatically backed up every 60 minutes. If you find that clients are having trouble leasing addresses, the DHCP database could be corrupt.

To load the backup copy, do the following:

1. Right-click your DHCP server node in the Tree pane and select Restore from the shortcut menu. The Browse for Folder dialog box appears, enabling you to specify the folder that contains the DHCP backup (it typically points to the default backup folder, backup).

2. Click OK. You are notified that the server must be stopped and then restarted for the backup database to be loaded.

3. Click Yes. The backup database is loaded and the server is restarted.

Troubleshooting DHCP

Two commands that are very useful in troubleshooting DHCP connectivity are `ping` and `ipconfig`. Both are executed at the command line. `ping` enables you to check the connection between a client and a DHCP server, or a DHCP server and a client. For example, to `ping` a DHCP server with the IP address of 10.8.0.1, you would type **ping 10.8.0.1** in the command window. Figure 16.14 shows a successful `ping` of this address.

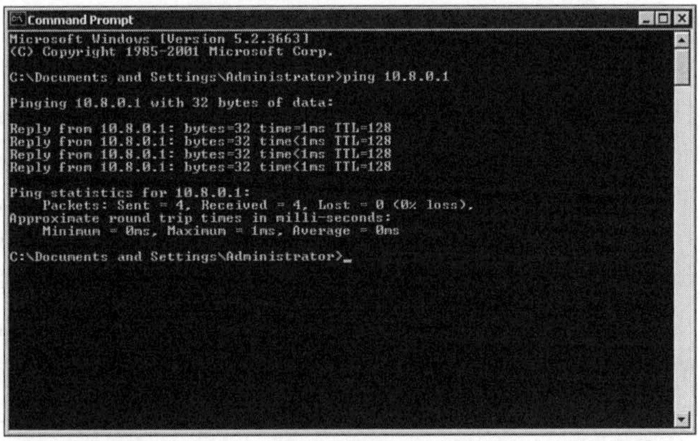

FIGURE 16.14

You can use ping to examine the connection between two computers.

`ipconfig` is useful on the client side. When executed at the command line, it tells you the IP configuration of the client (`ipconfig/all` provides more information). If you don't see an IP address and subnet mask (or a default gateway or DNS server) when you run this command, the client is not receiving the information from the DHCP server.

A problem that crops up with DHCP on routed networks is that the broadcast messages that are used to secure an IP lease for a client are not forwarded by routers from subnet to subnet. This can be remedied by configuring a DHCP Relay Agent, which is configured in the Routing and Remote Access Service. We discuss the DHCP Relay Agent configuration in Hour 18, "Using Routing and Remote Access."

Summary

In this hour, we looked at the Dynamic Host Configuration Protocol, which is used to dynamically assign IP addresses to DHCP clients on a Windows Server 2003 network. The DHCP server can provide the IP address, subnet mask, default gateway (router), DNS server, and WINS server to the DHCP clients.

The DHCP service can be installed using the Configure Your Server Wizard or the Add or Remove Programs utility in the Control Panel. DHCP servers are configured with a scope (or scopes), which contains a range of IP addresses that will be leased to the DHCP clients. Some IP addresses can be excluded from a scope; this is called an exclusion range. An important aspect of configuring a scope is determining the duration of the lease for the IP addresses that will be assigned to clients by the DHCP server. Windows Server 2003 requires that DHCP servers be authorized with the Active Directory. DCHP is configured, monitored, and managed in the Microsoft Management Console's DCHP snap-in.

Q&A

Q How is the range of IP addresses defined for a Windows Server 2003 DHCP server?

A The IP addresses supplied by the DHCP server are held in a scope. A scope that contains more than one subnet of IP addresses is called a superscope. IP addresses in a scope that you do not want to lease can be included in an exclusion range.

Q What TCP/IP configuration parameters can be provided to a DHCP client?

A The DHCP server can supply a DHCP client an IP address and subnet mask. It also can optionally include the default gateway address, the DNS server address, and the WINS server address to the client.

Q How can you configure the DHCP server so that it provides certain devices with the same IP address each time the address is renewed?

A You can create a reservation for the device (or create reservations for a number of devices). To create a reservation, you need to know the MAC hardware address of the device. You can use the ipconfig or nbstat command-line utilities to determine the MAC address for a network device such as a computer or printer.

Q To negate "rogue" DHCP servers from running with a domain, what is required for your DHCP server to function?

A The DHCP server must be authorized in the Active Directory before it can function in the domain

16

Hour **17**

Understanding WINS

In this hour, we take a look at the Windows Internet Naming Service (WINS) and issues related to use of the NetBIOS interface, NetBIOS services, NetBIOS names, and NetBIOS name-to-IP-address resolution.

In this hour, the following topics are covered:

- Understanding NetBIOS names
- Working with LMHOSTS files
- Understanding NetBIOS node types
- Installing a WINS server
- Configuring a WINS server
- Configuring WINS clients
- Using NBTSTAT

Understanding WINS and NetBIOS

The Network Basic Input/Output System (NetBIOS) was developed in 1983 and used by IBM as a way for computer applications to communicate over a network. NetBIOS is also firmly ingrained into all Microsoft operating systems that have come before the Windows 2000 series. Windows clients running Windows NT Professional or Windows 9*x* require NetBIOS on the network to identify computers and resources.

NetBIOS provides a way for identifying resources on a network (such as a printer, file server, and so on). All devices running on the network are assigned a unique 16-byte name that defines the particular computer or printer to the network (or a service on a computer—this means that a single computer may provide services identified by different NetBIOS names). NetBIOS names are typically assigned when you install a particular operating system on a computer. Down-level operating systems such as Windows 95/98 and Windows NT all request that a unique, 15-character NetBIOS name be entered for the computer during the installation process of the OS. When you install Windows 2000 on a computer, you are asked to provide the hostname for the computer; if that is less than 15 characters, it also becomes the NetBIOS name for the computer (otherwise, the hostname is truncated to a 15-character NetBIOS name).

In fact, NetBIOS names are 16 characters long. The last character is used by the operating system of the computer to specify the special functions of certain computers such as domain controllers and browsers.

Even though the default networking protocol for Windows Server 2003 is TCP/IP and the primary name-resolution strategy is DNS, an important issue related to NetBIOS names rears it head on your Windows Server 2003 domain. Down-level operating systems that still use NetBIOS for identifying other computers and resources on the network must have a way of resolving these NetBIOS names to IP addresses. This process is cleverly called NetBIOS name resolution. NetBIOS is also required in the networking environment for NetBIOS-dependant applications.

NetBIOS Broadcasts

When a computer seeks to resolve a NetBIOS name to an IP address, it sends a NetBIOS broadcast. Because the name-resolution request takes the form of a broadcast message, it is sent to all nodes on the local subnet (the subnet being a particular segment on a routed network).

For example, let's say a computer named Kirk wants to send data to a computer named Spock. Kirk broadcasts that it would like to send data to Spock but does not know Spock's IP address. When Spock hears this broadcast (as do all nodes on the subnet), Spock sends a response providing Kirk with the IP address. Kirk can now proceed with establishing a network session with Spock and transferring data as needed.

Two obvious problems plague the use of broadcasts for NetBIOS name resolution. First, the broadcast messages clog your network with broadcast traffic, which sucks up your bandwidth.

Another problem is that broadcast messages are not typically forwarded by routers on the network (unless the router has also been configured as a bridge). So, if a computer on one subnet uses a broadcast message to resolve a NetBIOS name for a computer that is on another subnet, the broadcast message is never forwarded to the intended target.

One strategy that has been worked out to cut down on the number of broadcast messages is as follows: Once a computer has discovered the IP addresses of other computers on the segment using broadcasts, these IP addresses are kept in a NetBIOS name cache on that computer. This cuts down on broadcasts in the case of "repeat" business with a particular computer or computers on the network.

You can view the NetBIOS name cache on a computer running Windows Server 2003 using the NBTSTAT command. We discuss this command-line tool later in the hour.

Working with LMHOSTS Files

Another alternative for NetBIOS name resolution is to use an LMHOSTS file. The LMHOSTS file is a text file that lists the IP addresses of computers on the network followed by their NetBIOS name. LMHOSTS files are static and must be updated by the network administrator (that means you). And although they provide the computer with a quick way to look up an IP address based on a NetBIOS name, you must place them on each computer on the network (and whenever you add computers to the network, you also have to update all the LMHOSTS files on all the computers).

Some network administrators still use LMHOSTS files to resolve NetBIOS names to IP addresses on their networks. On a server running Windows Server 2003, the LMHOSTS file is kept in the \WINNT\system32\drivers\etc folder. The basic structure of an LMHOSTS file is a two-column text file:

```
IP address  NetBIOS name
```

Windows 2003 actually provides a sample LMHOSTS file in the \WINNT\system32\ drivers\etc folder. You can open it using Windows Notepad or other text editor.

Included in the Windows 2003 LMHOSTS file are explicit directions for building your own LMHOSTS lists. Pay special attention to the fact that descriptive entries in the file are always followed by the number sign (#). All other entries are read as mapping records.

The major problem with LMHOSTS files is that they are a fairly labor-intensive way to manage NetBIOS name resolution. If LMHOSTS files have been used on the network in the past, however, they can be integrated into the WINS database on your WINS server. An Import LMHOSTS File command is available on the WINS snap-in Action menu. We discuss the WINS snap-in later in the hour.

17

Understanding NetBIOS Node Types

Before concentrating on the Windows Server 2003 WINS service and its installation and configuration, it is important that we discuss the different node types that can exist in the NetBIOS environment. A node type simply refers to the way that a computer on the network registers with a NetBIOS name server (such as WINS) and seeks to resolve NetBIOS names to IP addresses. There are four node types, as described in Table 17.1.

TABLE 17.1 Node Types

Node Type	Description
B	The client uses broadcast messages for name registration and name resolution.
P	The client uses unicast (directly to the server's IP address) messages to a NetBIOS name server for both name registration and NetBIOS name resolution.
H	A hybrid node type, these clients use unicast messages to the NetBIOS name server for registration and resolution. If they cannot find a NetBIOS name server (a WINS server), the client resorts to broadcast messages for registration and resolution.
M	Clients use broadcasts for name registration and broadcasts for name resolution. However, if the name cannot be resolved by broadcast, the client attempts to contact a NetBIOS name server.

Windows 2003 WINS clients (those configured for WINS, including computers running legacy operating systems such as Windows 9x), act as H nodes. They attempts to resolve names using the WINS sever first, and then they resort to broadcasts if a WINS server is not available. As a last resort, these clients consult their LMHOSTS file if one is available locally.

Deploying a WINS Server

The most foolproof method for dealing with NetBIOS naming issues is to deploy a WINS server (or servers) on your network. WINS provides the greatest amount of efficiency in terms of your network bandwidth. The series of steps that allows a WINS client to take advantage of the WINS server for NetBIOS name resolution is very straightforward:

1. When a WINS client computer boots up, it registers its NetBIOS name and IP address with the WINS server.

2. When a WINS client on the network wants to communicate with a network resource designated by a particular NetBIOS name, it communicates with the WINS server to handle the NetBIOS name resolution of its intended target, rather than sending out a broadcast to all nodes on the segment.

3. The WINS server finds the appropriate mapping of NetBIOS name to IP address in its database and returns the IP address to the WINS client.

4. If the WINS client cannot contact the primary WINS server, the client makes two more attempts to contact the primary WINS server. Then it attempts to contact the secondary WINS server if one has been designated in the TCP/IP properties for the client (or if the client is a DHCP client with multiple WINS servers configured).

5. If the secondary WINS server (or other WINS server, because the client attempts to contact WINS servers in the order that they are designated in the TCP/IP properties) can handle the request, no problem. However, if the client cannot contact any designated WINS server, the client resorts to a network broadcast. If a number of WINS servers are available on the network, the chances of the client having to resort to a broadcast message is slim.

The great thing about WINS is that the database compiled by the server is dynamic. The WINS clients actually register with the server, supplying the entries in the WINS database.

17

A WINS client is actually a network client running any Windows operating system that has the IP address of the primary WINS server configured as part of its TCP/IP properties. WINS client can also be set up when you use a DHCP server and configure the WINS server IP address with the other DHCP client information. (DHCP is discussed in Hour 16, "Dynamic Host Configuration Protocol.") We discuss WINS client configuration later in the chapter.

Installing and Configuring WINS

WINS can be installed on any computer that runs Windows Server 2003 (you might not want to overburden your domain controllers by placing WINS on them). Before you install the WINS component, make sure that the server is configured with static IP address and a default gateway (we discuss TCP/IP settings for a server in Hour 3, "Installing Windows Server 2003").

To install WINS, follow these steps:

1. WINS is installed using the Add or Remove Programs tool in the Windows Control Panel. Select Start, point at the Control Panel, and select Add or Remove Programs.

2. Click the Add/Remove Windows Components buttons in the Add or Remove Programs window. The Windows Component Wizard opens.

3. WINS is a subcomponent of the Networking Services components. Click the Networking Services heading and then click Details to open the component category.

4. In the Networking Services subcomponent box, click the WINS check box to select the WINS component (as shown in Figure 17.1). Then click OK. You are returned to the Component Wizard.

FIGURE 17.1

WINS is a component of Windows Networking Services.

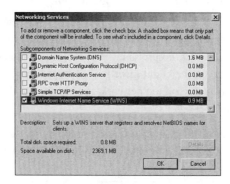

5. Click Next to continue. The WINS service is added to the server's configuration (you are prompted to provide the Windows Server 2003 CD-ROM). After all the files have been copied, click Finish when prompted.

After the WINS installation is complete, you can close the Add or Remove Programs window. The next time you click the Start button and point at All Programs, a word balloon appears letting you know that new programs have been installed on the server.

WINS Configuration Issues

After you add the WINS component to your Windows server installation, you can view the status of the service and configure various WINS features.

To start the WINS service, click Start, point at Administrative Tools, and then click the WINS icon on the menu. WINS is administered as a snap-in within the Management Console. Figure 17.2 shows the WINS snap-in.

The WINS snap-in enables you to configure replication partners (which are other WINS servers on the network) and manage WINS records. You can also manually add static mappings (NetBIOS-to-IP mappings) or delete records in the WINS database.

Settings related to the operation of the WINS server can also be configured in the WINS snap-in. Select the WINS Server icon (identified using the name you gave your server when you installed Windows) on the left side of the console window. Then right-click the Server icon and select Properties. The Properties dialog box for the server opens.

FIGURE 17.2

WINS is managed in the Management Console.

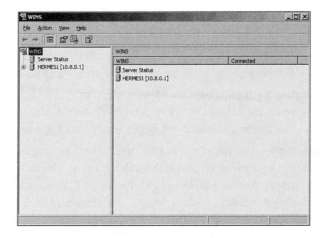

The WINS server's Properties dialog box has four tabs:

- **General**—On this tab, you can set the time interval for when to update the WINS statistics. The default is set at every 10 minutes. You can also specify the default path that you want to use for backing up the WINS server.

- **Intervals**—This tab (see Figure 17.3) is where you control the time interval for settings related to how records in the database are handled. Settings include Renew interval, Extinction interval, Extinction timeout, and Verification interval.

FIGURE 17.3

The Intervals tab is used to set renew, extinction, and verification intervals for the WINS server.

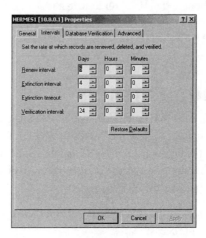

- Renew interval controls how often a WINS client renews its registration of its name. Increasing this interval lessens the performance load on a WINS server.

- Extinction interval specifies the time interval between when an entry is marked as Released and when it is marked as Extinct in the WINS database.

- Extinction timeout determines when a record that has been marked as extinct is actually removed (also known as scavenging) from the database.

- Verification interval specifies when the WINS server must verify the names in the database that it has received from other WINS servers during replication.

- **Database Verification**—This tab allows you to enable the WINS server to periodically verify its database with a remote WINS server. This setting basically allows you to check the consistency of WINS server on a large network.

- **Advanced**—This tab allows you to enable event logging of WINS events to the Windows system log (accessed through the Event Viewer, discussed in Hour 20, "Monitoring Server and Network Performance"). You can also change the setting for the Enable Burst Handling feature. This feature, which can be configured as low, medium, high, or a custom setting, sets the number of requests that the WINS server can handle at one time. The default setting is Medium.

Although you can configure many of these parameters using the WINS snap-in, Microsoft recommends that you attempt to run your WINS implementation using the default settings. This provides you with a performance baseline for WINS, which you can then fine-tune, if required.

> To determine whether the default WINS settings work best for your network, use the Performance Monitor (we look at the Performance Monitor briefly in this hour and in Hour 20) to take a look at parameters such as CPU usage and disk I/O. Upgrading server memory or using a RAID stripe set can often enhance performance of WINS better than changing WINS settings.

Adding Replication Partners

On large networks that require the WINS service, you will want to deploy more than one WINS server. These servers can then share the WINS database information as replication partners. This provides load balancing for the WINS database and also helps conserve bandwidth across slower WAN connections (a single WINS server would tie up bandwidth when communicating with NetBIOS clients).

Designating replication partners for your WINS server and then synchronizing the databases is a very straightforward process:

1. In the WINS snap-in, select the icon that represents your WINS server. Then right-click the Replication Partners subfolder in the Details pane. Point at New on the shortcut menu that appears, and select New Replication Partner.

2. The New Replication Partner dialog box opens (see Figure 17.4). Enter the name or IP address of the server that you want to add as a partner (you can also use the Browse button to locate the server on the network).

FIGURE 17.4

Replication partners can be added for your WINS server.

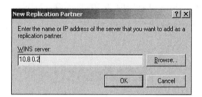

3. Click OK to designate the partner. Repeat the process as needed to add replication partners.

To view the replication partners, double-click the Replication Partners icon. A list of all added partners appears in the Details pane, as shown in Figure 17.5.

17

FIGURE 17.5

You can list the replication partners.

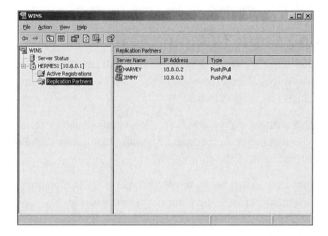

To start the replication between your WINS server and its partners on the network, right-click the Replication Partners icon and then point at All Tasks on the shortcut menu. Select Replicate Now. You are asked whether you want to replicate the WINS database. Click Yes to continue.

You are told that the replication request has been queued on the server. You can check to see when the replication actually takes place using the Windows Event Viewer (which, again, is discussed in Hour 20).

By default, a persistent connection is set up between WINS replication partners. This means that replication partners maintain an open line of communication between them on the network. This negates the need for setting up and closing a connection during replication, which can use up network bandwidth.

Managing the WINS Database

The WINS snap-in provides you with a monitoring tool that can be used to view the mappings that are dynamically placed in the WINS database by communication between WINS clients and the WINS server. In the WINS snap-in, double-click the Active Registrations folder. The current mappings in the database appear in the Details pane.

The WINS snap-in also provides you with the management tools that enable you to manipulate the WINS database and keep it healthy. You can use the WINS snap-in to add static records to the database, delete records, and even back up the WINS database.

Creating Static Mappings

You can add static WINS records to the WINS database. This is useful when you need to support non-WINS clients (computers running operating systems that you cannot configure to take advantage of WINS).

In the WINS snap-in, right-click Active Registrations and select New Static Mapping from the shortcut menu. In the Static Mapping dialog box (see Figure 17.6), provide the name and IP address of the computer.

Use the Type drop-down list to select the type of static mapping you are creating. Table 17.2 defines the different static mapping types available.

TABLE 17.2 Mapping Types

Mapping Type	Description
Unique	Used to associate a single IP address with a computer name.
Group	Used to include a computer that is already specified in a static mapping as part of a Windows workgroup.
Domain Name	Used to map a domain name to Windows NT domain controller IP addresses.
Internet Group	Used to group resources on the network under a group name. IP addresses are mapped to resource IP addresses in the static mapping.
Multihomed	Used to create a static mapping of multiple IP addresses (up to 25) to 1 NetBIOS name.

After specifying the static mapping type, click OK. the Mapping becomes part of the WINS database.

The NetBIOS name is 15 characters, but a 16th character in hexadecimal format indicates the resource type. For example, when the Unique type is used to create a static mapping, actually three records are added to the WINS database: [00h] WorkStation, 03hMessenger, and 20h File Server.

FIGURE 17.6

You can create static mappings in the WINS snap-in.

To view the active registrations for the WINS server, click the Action menu and then click Display Records. The Display Records dialog box opens, enabling you to filter the records by name and record types. Click OK in the dialog box to view all the records in the Details pane.

Deleting or Tombstoning Mappings

You can also delete or tombstone records from the WINS database. When you tombstone a record, it is removed from all replication partners the next time the databases are synchronized.

Right-click a particular record in the database (in the Details pane) and then select Delete (see Figure 17.7). If you want to delete the record just on this server, select the option Delete the record only from this server. If you want to remove the record from all WINS servers on the network, select Replicate deletion of the record to other servers (tombstone). After making your selection, click OK.

FIGURE 17.7

*You can delete or
tombstone records.*

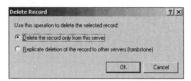

Backing Up and Restoring the WINS Database

Another aspect of managing the WINS is backing up the WINS database. Because the
WINS database is constantly changing as a result of the dynamic registration process
(WINS clients communicate with the server to set up their records), there can be file corruption. So, it makes sense to back up the WINS database periodically. Then if you are
experiencing difficulties with the WINS service, you can restore the database file.

The backup of the WINS server is automatic after you specify a location for the database. To configure the backup of the WINS database, follow these steps:

1. In the WINS snap-in, right-click the WINS Server icon and then select Properties
   from the shortcut menu that appears. The Properties dialog box appears (see
   Figure 17.8).

FIGURE 17.8

*Specify a location for
the WINS backup.*

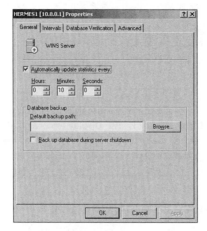

2. Specify a path for the backup (you can use the Browse button) in the Default
   backup path box.
3. If you want, you can select the option Back up database during server shutdown.
   This will back up the WINS database whenever you shut down the WINS server.
4. Click OK to close the Properties dialog box.

The WINS database is backed up by default every three hours. The WINS database, wins.mdb, is placed in a \wins_back\new folder that is created in the path that you specified for the backup.

> To manually back up the server, right-click your WINS Server icon and select Back Up Database. The Browse for Folder dialog box opens; use it to specify the folder for the backup. Then click to back up the WINS database.

Now that you have a backup of your WINS server, when you begin to have problems with the service and suspect database corruption, you can restore the WINS database. First you must stop the WINS service. Right-click your WINS Server icon in the snap-in tree, point at the All Tasks selection on the shortcut menu, and then select Stop. This stops the WINS service (the green icon turns red).

To restore the database, right-click your WINS Server icon and select Restore Database. The Browse for Folder dialog box appears. Specify the folder that holds the backup file; then click OK. The database file is restored and the WINS service restarts.

Configuring WINS Clients

Another aspect of WINS is configuring WINS clients so that they use the service for NetBIOS name-to-IP resolution.

Any Microsoft Windows client or server version (including the Windows 3x clients) can be configured as a WINS client. Even MS-DOS clients can be configured as WINS clients.

Although each client operating system is configured for WINS in a slightly different way, you are basically providing the client with the IP address of your WINS server so that it will use it as a mapping resource of NetBIOS name to IP address instead of sending broadcasts onto the network. In the case of the Windows 9x, 2000, and XP clients, a WINS tab is associated with the TCP/IP settings, enabling you to specify the IP addresses of available WINS servers.

Figure 17.9 shows the WINS tab of the Advanced TCP/IP settings for a Windows Server 2003. To add the IP addresses of WINS servers, click the Add button and then supply the IP address of the WINS server (repeat if several WINS servers reside on the network). The WINS tab on a Windows Server 2003 is very similar to the tab that you find on Windows XP, Windows 2000, and Windows 9x clients.

FIGURE 17.9

Both client computers and servers, such as this Windows server, can be configured as WINS clients.

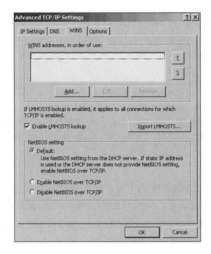

Remember that a WINS client is merely a computer that has been configured to take its NetBIOS name requests to the WINS server. DHCP clients can also be set up to use the WINS server; this is discussed in Hour 16.

> Computers running Windows Server 2003, Windows XP, and Windows 2000 do not require a reboot when you change the TCP/IP properties to set them up as WINS clients. Windows 9*x* and Windows NT clients do.

Avoiding WINS Problems

One way to avoid WINS-related problems (according to Microsoft) is to use the preconfigured WINS settings on a newly established WINS server. These settings should serve you well in most situations.

Microsoft also advises against using static WINS entries in the WINS database, although using static entries can protect you from conflicts related to the NetBIOS names of key servers on the network. You would not want an incorrectly configured client (as far as NetBIOS name goes) to come online on the network and register with the WINS database, negating the important resource server from using its configured name (which computers on the network use to get at resources on the server).

As far as an upper threshold goes for a WINS server, Microsoft says that one WINS server can accommodate around 10,000 WINS clients on a network. And if you are having problems with client connectivity, make sure that the client's TCP/IP properties have been configured so that the use of WINS servers has been enabled.

If you find that the "best practices" discussed in this hour still don't provide you with a smooth-running WINS deployment, you can monitor WINS performance and server performance using the Performance Monitor. Problems with the WINS service might also show up in the Event Viewer logs (both of these tools are discussed in Hour 20). Also remember that a backup of the WINS database can be very useful when you are having problems with a single WINS server implementation.

Using NBTSTAT

A useful command-line tool related to our discussion of NetBIOS and WINS is NBTSTAT. NBTSTAT can be used to determine whether the client's NetBIOS names are registered in the WINS database. It can also be used to release and renew a computer's NetBIOS names registered with the name server and to show the current NetBIOS sessions for a computer.

To use NBTSTAT, follow these steps:

1. Open a command prompt window (Start, Command Prompt).
2. To view the local computer's locally registered NetBIOS names, type **nbtstat –n**.
3. Press Enter.

The NetBIOS local name table for the computer appears. Note that in Figure 17.10, two tables of NetBIOS names are provided: a table for each IP address assigned to the server.

FIGURE 17.10

NBTSTAT can be used to view the local NetBIOS names.

As already mentioned, NBTSTAT provides a number of different command extensions that enable you to view NetBIOS information and even renew name registrations or purge the computer's NetBIOS cache. Some of the more useful forms of the NBTSTAT command are as follows:

- NBTSTAT -c—Shows the name-to-address mapping for other computers found in the NetBIOS name cache

- NBTSTAT -rr—Enables you to release the NetBIOS names of a computer registered with a WINS server and renew their registration

- NBTSTAT -s—Lists the current NetBIOS sessions (for the local computer and connected computers) and their status

Other switches also are available for NBTSTAT. You can view all of the different switches for the command; at the command line, type nbtstat/help and then press Enter.

Summary

In this hour, you learned how to install and configure the WINS service. NetBIOS is used by legacy Windows client operating systems such as Windows 9x to identify resources on the network. NetBIOS names must be resolved to IP addresses by these clients, which use broadcast messages for the resolution.

The Windows Internet Naming Service (WINS) provides an environment in which a dynamic database is built that resolves NetBIOS names to IP addresses. WINS clients can then query the database for name resolution to identify resources on the network. Larger networks might require more than one WINS server, and these servers can be set up as replication partners, allowing them to share WINS database records. A WINS client is any computer that has been configured to use the WINS server for resolution of NetBIOS names to IP addresses. Windows clients and servers must have their TCP/IP properties configured so that they point at the WINS server or servers on the network. This configuration makes them WINS clients.

Q&A

Q What are three strategies available for resolving NetBIOS names to IP addresses?

A Resolving NetBIOS names to IP addresses can be handled by NetBIOS broadcasts and the storage of mappings in a computer's local cache. LMHOSTS files can also be deployed on computers to provide a static database of mappings of names to IP addresses. A dynamic database of mappings of NetBIOS names to IP addresses can be created by deploying a WINS server in the domain.

Q What is required to implement WINS in a Windows domain?

A A server running WINS needs to be deployed in the domain. The client computers on the network must also be configured with the IP address of the WINS server. This makes them WINS clients. They then query the WINS server when they need to resolve a NetBIOS name to an IP address.

Q What is the best way to deploy WINS on a larger network that might use some WAN connections?

A It is a good practice to deploy more than one WINS server on the network. These WINS servers will function as replication partners and share their databases. This cuts down on clients using slow WAN connections to reach a single WINS server in a domain. The presence of multiple WINS servers allows client computers to connect to the closest WINS server for name-resolution queries.

Q What tool is used to add static records to the WINS database, delete records, and back up the WINS database?

A The WINS snap-in enables you to both monitor and manage the WINS database.

17

PART III

Advanced Networking

Hour

HOUR **18**

Using Routing and Remote Access

In this hour, the following topics are covered:

- Understanding RAS
- Installing RAS hardware
- Installing and configuring RAS
- Understanding authentication protocols
- Configuring remote access clients
- Monitoring and managing remote access
- Understanding RADIUS and Windows remote access
- Understanding route networks
- Enabling, configuring, and monitoring IP routing
- Using the DHCP Relay Agent

Microsoft has combined a number of connectivity services into the Routing and Remote Access Service (RRAS). RRAS can be used to configure a Windows Server 2003 as a router (the computer is configured with more than one network card), as a remote access server (RAS), and for the deployment of a virtual private network (VPN, discussed in Hour 21, "Working with Virtual Private Networking and IP Security").

In this hour, we look at the installation and configuration of remote access and the authentication protocols available when configuring RAS. We also look at how you can configure a Windows Server 2003 as an IP router. This discussion includes the configuration of routing protocols such as RIP and OSPF.

Understanding RAS

A server supplying the Remote Access Service (RAS) is a Windows Server 2003 that supplies a remote host with a connection to the network and provides the remote host with access to the same network resources that can be accessed by computers directly connected to the network. A domain controller or a member server can function as a RAS server for your domain.

RAS provides two basic strategies for connecting the remote host to your network: dial-up networking and virtual private networks (VPN). We concentrate on dial-up networking in this hour. VPN is discussed in Hour 21.

Dial-up access requires the installation of communications hardware such as an analog modem (or modems in a modem pool), an ISDN modem (an ISDN terminal adapter), or some other connectivity device on the computer. Basically, the end user will also use a modem to connect via a network such as the Plain Old Telephone System (POTS) to the RAS server (by dialing the modem connected to the RAS server).

Window's Remote Access Service actually has the option of using a technique called *tunneling* to provide a secure connection between the user and the RAS server. This means that packets from your network, which are encapsulated into a particular frame type by the network protocol that you are using, are moved across the public switched telephone network in a virtual tunnel that is hosted by a particular wide area networking protocol (which we discuss later in the hour).

Installing RAS Hardware

Before you configure the RAS server for dial-in, you should install any connectivity device, such as a modem, that will be the medium for the remote client's connection. Because most individual client connections are handled by dial-up using a modem, we stress the use of asynchronous modem connections in our discussion of RAS in this hour.

Plug-and-play modems are installed automatically when you attach the device to the server (or when you install the device internally) and then reboot the server. Or, you can use the Add Hardware Wizard to recognize the device when you attach it to the computer. The Add Hardware Wizard can also be used to install legacy devices.

To start the Add Hardware Wizard, select Start, point at the Control Panel, and then select Add Hardware. The Add Hardware Wizard opens. Click Next to bypass the initial wizard screen. The wizard searches for newly attached hardware. Figure 18.1 shows new modem hardware that was installed automatically by the Add Hardware Wizard.

FIGURE 18.1

Use the Add Hardware Wizard to install new hardware.

When the hardware is not found and installed automatically, the wizard walks you through a series of steps to help you install the hardware. First, you must acknowledge (to the wizard) that the hardware is connected and then click the Next button. The wizard provides a list of installed hardware devices. To add new hardware, click Add a New Hardware Device in the Hardware list and then click Next.

At this point, the wizard can search for and install the hardware automatically, or you can install the hardware from a list or a third-party disk. Because the hardware was not initially recognized by the wizard (when you first ran it), it probably won't locate it on a second scan; you will probably want to install the device from a list (or a third-party disk or CD). When the connectivity device, such as a modem, is installed on the computer, you can install the RAS service.

You might want to check the operation of the modem after installing it (whether it is plug-and-play or not). Select Start, Control Panel, System. On the System Properties dialog box, select the Hardware tab. Click the Device Manager to access a list of installed devices. Expand the Modems node in the Device Manager, and then double-click the installed modem to open its Properties dialog box. You can use the utilities on the Diagnostics tab of the Properties dialog box to test the functioning of the modem.

Installing and Configuring RAS

The Routing and Remote Access service is installed as part of the default Windows Server 2003 configuration. To set up RRAS, you can go directly to the Routing and Remote Access snap-in and run the RRAS Setup Wizard. Remember to log in as Administrator to complete this task.

1. Select the Start menu, point at Administrative Tools, and then click Routing and Remote Access. The RRAS snap-in opens.

2. Right-click your server icon in the RRAS snap-in tree, and select Configure and Enable Routing and Remote Access. The Routing and Remote Access Server Setup Wizard appears.

3. Click Next to bypass the opening screen. The next screen supplies a list of common configurations for the RRAS service (see Figure 18.2); you can install remote access via dialup and VPN, or you can install VPN and NAT and a number of other RRAS configuration possibilities. Because we are concentrating on remote access, select the Remote Access (dial-up or VPN) option button and then click Next.

FIGURE 18.2

Select the RRAS service that you want to install.

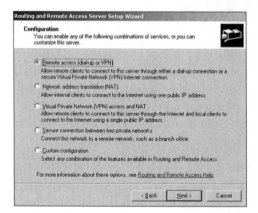

4. On the next screen, you can select either VPN or Dial-Up to add the remote access connection (or you can select both). In this case, click the Dial-Up check box and then click Next to continue.

5. On the next screen, you are asked to select the network connection that you want the remote clients to use for network addressing. Select Local Area Connection in the Network Interfaces box, and then click Next to continue.

6. On the next wizard screen, you are asked to choose how remote access clients will be assigned their IP addresses. You can choose Automatically, which uses the network DHCP server to assign addresses, or you can choose to have the addresses

assigned from a specified range. After making your selection, click Next. If you select to use a specified range, the next screen asks you to supply that range. Then click Next.

7. The next screen relates to how connection requests are authenticated. You can use the local Routing and Remote Access service to authenticate connection requests, or you can set up the RAS server to use a *RADIUS* (Remote Authentication Dial-In User Service) server for authentication. We discuss RADIUS later in the chapter; to get a feel for remote access, select the option No, Use Routing and Remote Access to Authenticate Connection Requests, and then click Next.

8. The wizard summary screen appears. To finish the remote access installation, click Finish. A message box appears letting you know that the DHCP Relay Agent must be configured so that DHCP messages are relayed from remote access clients. We discuss the DHCP Relay Agent later in the hour. Click OK to close the message box.

The Routing and Remote Access service starts on the server. You are returned to the Routing and Remote Access snap-in.

Configuring Modem Ports

When the RRAS service is started for the first time, it configures ports for any modems that are installed on the server. You must configure these modem ports to allow remote client connections.

To configure a modem port, follow these steps:

1. In the Routing and Remote Access snap-in, click the server icon in the tree to expand the node. Right-click the Ports icon and select Properties. The Ports Properties dialog box appears (see Figure 18.3).

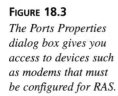

FIGURE 18.3

The Ports Properties dialog box gives you access to devices such as modems that must be configured for RAS.

2. Select the device (such as a modem) that you want to configure the port for, and click the Configure button. The Configure Device dialog box opens.

3. To configure the device for inbound connections, click the Remote access connections (inbound only) check box to select it. You must also supply a phone number if you are configuring a modem port, so enter the number in the appropriate box (see Figure 18.4). Then click OK.

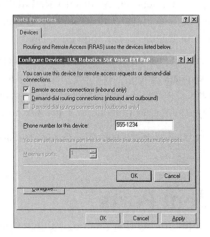

FIGURE 18.4
Configure the modem port for incoming calls and supply the phone number of the modem.

4. You are returned to the Ports Properties dialog box. Click OK to close it.

The modem is added to the Ports list (seen in the Details pane when you select the Ports node). After the modem port has been enabled, the remote access server is ready to accept incoming calls. Another aspect of configuring dial-in remote access is determining the authentication protocol (or protocols) used to authenticate remote users. We discuss authentication protocols in the next section.

Understanding Authentication Protocols

Windows Server 2003 supplies you with several protocol choices to authenticate remote users dialing into your RAS server. These protocols supply different "strengths" of authentication. You choose the protocol or protocols that you want to use for remote user authentication on the Security tab of your RAS server's Properties dialog box (which we look at after sorting out the different authentication protocols).

The authentication protocols available (in order of security strength) are the Extensible Authentication Protocol (EAP), Microsoft Encrypted Authentication Version 2 (MS-CHAP v2), Microsoft Encrypted Authentication (MS-CHAP), Encrypted authentication

(CHAP), Shiva Password Authentication Protocol (SPAP), Unencrypted password (PAP), and unauthenticated access (meaning that no protocol is used to control authentication). The sections that follow briefly describe each of these protocols.

> By default, EAP, MS-CHAP v2, and MS-CHAP are the selected authentication protocols for remote access.

Understanding the Extensible Authentication Protocol

The *Extensible Authentication Protocol* (EAP) was first introduced with the Windows 2000 Server operating system. EAP is actually an extension of the Point-to-Point Protocol and is designed to provide for the authentication of users through additional security devices. These additional security devices can take the form of a *smart card reader* attached to the computer that requires the user to place a smart card in the reader for authentication. EAP can also take advantage of authentication strategies such as one-time passwords and the use of certificates for authentication (using certificates is discussed in Hour 23, "Working with Certificate Services"). Because EAP is extensible (after all, it's part of the name), additional EAP authentication types will be added to the protocol.

Currently, EAP supports three EAP methods:

- **MD5-Challenge**—This EAP method is similar to CHAP, but it uses EAP messages when sending challenges and responses.
- **EAP-TLS**—This is a mutual authentication method, which means that both the client and the server prove their identities.
- **Smart card or other certificate**—This method requires a smart card reader or Certificate Authority to provide certificates for authentication. This method cannot be deployed on a standalone RAS server.

Understanding the Challenge Handshake Authentication Protocol

The *Challenge Handshake Authentication Protocol* (CHAP) is a more secure authentication scheme than PAP (which is discussed in a moment) because the username and password are not disclosed over the link as clear text. CHAP uses a three-way handshake scheme for authentication when the remote host requests a connection. The receiving server sends a challenge message that contains a random number and asks the dialing device to send its username and password. The host responds with an encrypted value that is unencrypted by the receiving device yielding the username and password. There are two Microsoft-proprietary versions of CHAP:

- **Microsoft Challenge Handshake Authentication Protocol (MS-CHAP)**—MS-CHAP is the Microsoft-proprietary version of CHAP and has been modified for the Windows environment. MS-CHAP uses a response packet specifically designed for computers running the Windows operating system.
- **Microsoft Challenge Handshake Authentication Protocol Version 2 (MS-CHAP v2)**—MS-CHAP v2 is a further modified version of CHAP that provides greater security than the premier version and provides for the use of separate cryptographic keys for sending and receiving data. Version 2 of MS-CHAP also supports mutual authentication. This means that both the remote host and the server must provide proof of their identities for the connection to be successful.

Understanding the Shiva Password Authentication Protocol

The *Shiva Password Authentication Protocol* (SPAP) is the authentication scheme for the Shiva proprietary connectivity software that supplies client and server operability. If you are using a Shiva client to connect to a Windows RAS server, the server can use SPAP to validate the user's connection. Be advised that data encryption cannot be used with SPAP. SPAP also provides Windows clients with the capability to connect to Shiva servers.

Understanding the Password Authentication Protocol

The *Password Authentication Protocol* (PAP) uses a username and password in clear-text format. When the remote host creates the connection to the server, it sends a username and password; these are authenticated by the RAS server. If the username and password are not accepted, the connection is terminated. This type of password protection is referred to as a two-way handshake. The problem with PAP is that the clear-text username and password are susceptible to snooping, so the username and password could actually be captured with some sort of protocol analyzer.

Understanding Unauthenticated Access

The final alternative offered for authenticating users to the RAS server is to have no authentication. When you enable unauthenticated access, you are no longer requiring a username and password of the remote host. You are also not requiring the host machine to be configured with the same authentication protocol that is configured on the RAS server.

Although unauthenticated access might be useful when end users have inappropriately configured remote hosts and you still want them to log on to the network, you are making it very easy for anyone with the phone number of the RAS server to attach to your network. Microsoft recommends "strong" authentication for securing your RAS environment. This means using authentication protocols such as EAP and the two flavors of CHAP.

Configuring Authentication

You can select the type of remote access authentication that you want to use on your RAS server. To configure the authentication protocol (or protocols) supported by the RAS server, follow these steps:

1. In the Routing and Remote Access snap-in, right-click the server icon in the tree and select Properties from the shortcut menu that appears. The Properties dialog box for the server appears as well.

2. Click the Security tab on the Properties dialog box. The Security tab lists the current Authentication provider. To view the authentication methods, click the Authentication Methods button. The Authentication Methods dialog box appears.

3. Check boxes enable you to specify the authentication methods that will be supported by the RAS server (see Figure 18.5). Check the appropriate boxes (EAP, MS-CHAP, and MS-CHAPv2 are selected by default).

FIGURE 18.5

Authentication methods are chosen using a series of check boxes.

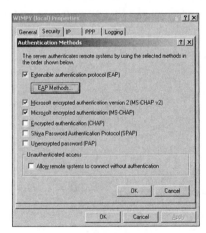

4. If you use EAP as a authentication method, you can select the EAP methods used. Click the EAP Methods button. The EAP Methods dialog box appears.

5. Select the EAP method. Then click OK to return to the Authentication Methods dialog box.

6. When you have completed selecting the authentication methods, click OK to close the Authentication Methods dialog box.

7. Click OK to close the server's Properties dialog box.

Your server is now configured with remote access authentication methods. For a client to attach to the server through a dial-in connection, it must support one of these authentication methods—that is, it must be configured for a particular authentication protocol or protocols.

Configuring Remote Access Clients

After the RAS server has been installed and configured, you must enable user accounts for remote access (or vice versa). You enable dial-in capabilities for your users in the Active Directory Users and Computers snap-in.

1. Open the Active Directory Users and Computers snap-in (Start, Administrative Tools, Active Directory Users and Computers).

2. Expand the domain node and then click the Users folder. The domain users and groups appear in the Details pane.

3. At this point, you can add new users and then enable the account for dial-in or enable existing accounts (adding new domain users is discussed in Hour 8, "Introducing Active Directory"). To enable an existing account for dial-in, double-click the user account. The account's Properties dialog box appears.

4. Click the Dial-in tab of the user's Properties dialog box (see Figure 18.6).

FIGURE 18.6

Authentication methods are chosen using a series of check boxes.

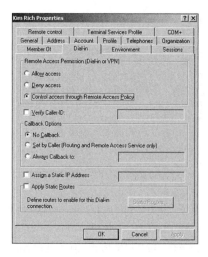

5. Select the Allow access option button to allow the account to use dial-in to connect to the network (or you can choose to control access through the Remote Access policies that you have set in the RRAS snap-in).

6. If you want to limit the user to a dial-in connection that is initiated from a particular phone number, click the Verify Caller ID check box and enter the user's phone number in the accompanying box.

7. If you want to add callback security to the connection, click the Set by Caller option button or the Always Callback to option button. With the Set by Caller option, the caller dials into the server and then provides a number that the server will use to call back the user and provide a connection to the network. With the Always Callback to option, you provide the phone number that the server always uses to call back the user and set up the network connection.

8. You also have an option of specifying a static IP address for the connection. Click the Assign a Static IP Address check box and then type an IP address in the accompanying box.

9. After making your selections on the Dial-in tab, click OK to close the Properties dialog box.

You can now configure other user accounts for dial-in. After you've installed your modem, enabled and configured the RAS server, and configured user accounts for dial-in access, you have completed the setup that is necessary on the server side of the RAS connection. You also need to configure remote workstations to dial into the RAS server using a modem or some other connectivity device. For example, on a Windows XP remote client workstation, you would use the New Connection Wizard to create a dial-up connection.

18

Monitoring and Managing Remote Access

The remote access features provided by Windows Server 2003 are managed and monitored using the RRAS snap-in. To open the snap-in, select Start, Administrative Tools, Routing and Remote Access (see Figure 18.7).

When remote users are connected to the RAS server, a number appears next to the Dial-In Clients node designating the number of clients connected. To view a list of the clients, click the Dial-In Client node. The list of clients appears in the Details pane.

You can also view the properties related to a particular remote client. Double-click the user in the Details pane to see a status box for the user.

FIGURE 18.7

The RRAS snap-in.

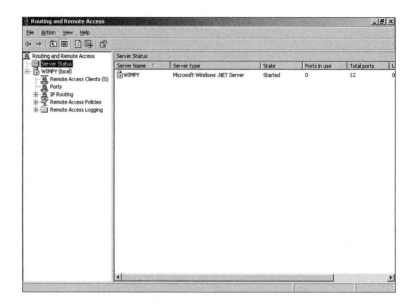

The status box provides the user's name, the duration of the connection, and other information related to the connection itself. If you want to disconnect the user, click Hang Up in the user's status box. When you have finished viewing the user's connection statistics, click Close.

Another aspect of managing your RAS server is troubleshooting connection issues. Some problems related to RAS connections can be resolved from the RRAS snap-in. If users are having problems connecting to the RAS server, check the status of the modem. The easiest way to do this is to select the Ports node and then double-click the modem in the Details pane. If the modem status box indicates that the modem is Listening, your problem is not related to the modem. However, make sure that the modem is connected to an active phone line (the status of individual ports can also be checked by double-clicking a particular port in the Details pane).

If a user still cannot connect, the Remote Access Service might have stopped. Click the Server Status node in the snap-in tree; in the Details pane, the RAS server name should appear. In the Status column, Started should appear.

If the status is Stopped, you need to start the service. Right-click the server icon in the snap-in tree and select Start.

> You can reset connections and get your RRAS server back online in two quick and dirty ways. The first is to turn off the modem (or the modems in a modem pool) and then turn the device back on. Another is to restart the RRAS server; right-click the server in the RRAS snap-in, point at All Tasks, and then select Restart.

Understanding RADIUS and Windows Remote Access

A RADIUS (Remote Authentication Dial-In User Service) server provides authentication of remote access users and also provides an accounting system for tracking access to your RAS server. RADIUS servers are typically used by Internet service providers to authenticate and track remote users. The Windows Server 2003 RRAS implementation can use RADIUS for authentication (as discussed in the "Installing and Configuring RAS" section earlier in this hour).

Installing the Internet Authentication Service

RADIUS comes in a number of different third-party software vendor flavors and runs on various network operating system platforms. You can use RADIUS authentication in your domain without buying additional RADIUS software; the Windows Server 2003 Internet Authentication Service (IAS) can be configured as a RADIUS server. This means that all RAS remote client requests for authentication in the domain will be forwarded from the RAS server to the server running IAS.

Windows Server 2003 IAS can be configured for a maximum of 50 RADIUS clients. The RADIUS clients are the various remote and network access servers that use the IAS server for user authentication.

To install and configure IAS, follow these steps:

1. Select Start, Control Panel, then Add or Remove Programs. In the Add or Remove Programs window, select the Add/Remove Windows Components button.

2. In the Windows Components Wizard, select the Networking Services component and then click Details.

3. In the Networking Services box, select Internet Authentication Service. Then click OK. Click Next to continue.

4. IAS is added to the server. Click Finish. You can close the Add or Remove Programs window.

18

> RADIUS embraces the same authentication protocols (such as EAP and CHAP) that can be set for the Windows authentication of remote clients. If you deploy IAS or have another RADIUS platform running on your network, select RADIUS as your authentication method when you use the Routing and Remote Access Server Setup Wizard to configure the RAS server. Then select your authentication protocols on the Security tab of the RAS server's Properties dialog box.

Configuring IAS Properties

To get IAS up and running as a RADIUS server, you must register the IAS server with the Active Directory (it reads the remote access properties of user accounts in the Active Directory). You can then create RADIUS clients.

To register the IAS server, open the Internet Authentication Service snap-in (Start, Administrative Tools, Internet Authentication Service—see Figure 18.8). Right-click the Internet Authentication Service (Local) node and select Register Server in Active Directory.

FIGURE 18.8

The IAS snap-in enables you to config-ure the Internet Authentication Service.

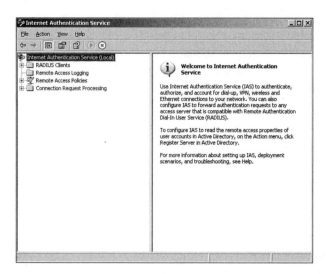

Another aspect of configuring IAS is determining what types of events are logged in the IAS log files. These settings are controlled in two different places: the IAS server Properties dialog box and the Remote Access Logging folder. The Properties dialog box enables you to set the type of events logged in the file; the Remote Access Logging folder enables you to set event types that are logged and to choose the type of logging file that is created by the IAS server.

To open the Internet Authentication Service Properties dialog box, click the Internet Authentication Service node in the snap-in tree and then select Properties. The Properties dialog box appears (see Figure 18.9).

FIGURE 18.9

You can choose to log rejected and successful authentication requests.

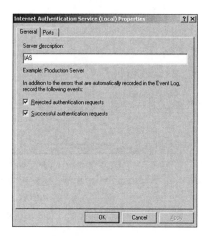

By default, both rejected and successful authentication requests are logged in the Remote Access logging file. You can clear either or both of these check boxes if you want to use settings other than the defaults. To close the IAS Properties dialog box, click OK (or Cancel).

As already mentioned, you can also set event logging parameters for the IAS log file via the Remote Access Logging folder. Click the folder in the snap-in tree. The two possible logging methods appear in the Details pane.

By default, the log file is stored in a local file. You also have the option of logging the information in a file that is saved as a database file on a SQL Server in your domain (you can configure the SQL Server file by opening the Properties dialog box for the SQL Server node and then clicking the Configure button).

Both the local file and the SQL Server can be configured in relation to the types of events that are logged in the file. For example, right-click the Local File icon and then select Properties. The types of events that can be logged are listed on the Settings tab of the dialog box (see Figure 18.10).

Figure **18.10**

Select the events to be logged in the log file.

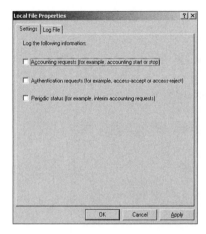

- **Accounting requests**—Accounting requests are sent by the access server (or servers) to the IAS server (and logged). Account On requests mean that the access server is ready to provide connections (to the network). Accounting Off requests tell you that the access server is going offline (or has already gone offline). Other accounting request events that are logged include the start of and the end of a user session.

- **Authentication requests**—This option logs authentication requests by RADIUS clients (access servers) on behalf of users attempting to connect to the RAS server. Events logged include requests that authentication accepts and rejects. These types of events are good ones to log because they enable you to see who is attempting to be authenticated (and connect) to your network via the RAS server.

- **Periodic status**—These events include events logged during user sessions and other accounting information recorded based on policies configured on the RAS server.

IAS errors are automatically recorded in the system event log. For more information about the Event Viewer and its log files, see Hour 20, "Monitoring Server and Network Performance."

By default, all the request logging types are disabled. To select the type of events to be logged, select the appropriate check boxes on the Settings tab.

In terms of the local log file, you can also specify a new location for the file (other than the default), determine the time frame when a new log file is created, and determine the format for the log file (IAS or Database Compatible). To view the local log file configuration settings, click the Log File tab on the Local File Properties dialog box (see Figure 18.11).

FIGURE 18.11

Select the settings for the local log file.

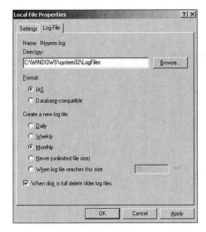

To set the time frame for the creation of a new log file, select the appropriate option button (Daily, Weekly, Monthly, and so on). You can also choose to have older files deleted when the disk is full (this option is on by default). After you make your selections on the Log File tab, click OK to close the dialog box.

Remote access policies can also be set for the IAS server. These policies are created by right-clicking the Remote Access Policy node and selecting New. Two policies are provided by default, and you might want to view their properties before you attempt to create your own policies. A good understanding of Windows Server 2003 Group Policy (discussed in Hour 11, "Understanding Group Policy and User Profiles") will provide you with the knowledge base required to create more advanced policies for specific services such as IAS.

Adding RADIUS Clients

RADIUS clients are the access servers (such as a server running the Windows Server 2003 Routing and Remote Access Service) that use IAS for authentication. A RADIUS client is built into the Windows implementation of RRAS. So, you only have to add the appropriate client or clients to your IAS implementation.

You can specify RADIUS clients using either the DNS name or an IP address (IAS limits you to 50 RADIUS clients). To add a RADIUS client to the IAS server, follow these steps:

1. Right-click the RADIUS Clients folder in the Internet Authentication Service snap-in tree. Then select New Radius Client from the shortcut menu. The New RADIUS Client dialog box opens (see Figure 18.12).

FIGURE 18.12

Adding the RADIUS client.

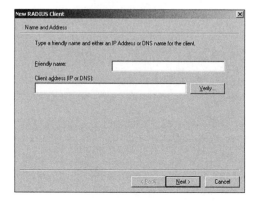

2. Enter a friendly name for the client (this name will appear in the snap-in when you list the DNS clients). You must also supply either the IP address or the DNS name of the RADIUS client. If you supply the DNS name, you can verify it by clicking the Verify button. The Verify Client dialog box appears.

3. Click Resolve and then select the IP address to use for the client. Then click OK to return to the New RADIUS Client dialog box.

4. After you supply the friendly name and then the DNS name or IP address of the client, click the Next button. On the next screen, you are asked to supply the client vendor that your RAS server is using if you are using remote access policies to control access. A number of different client-vendor possibilities are listed in the drop-down box. In the case of a Microsoft RRAS implementation, you would choose Microsoft as the client-vendor.

You also have the option of enabling the Message Authenticator attribute by clicking the Request Must Contain the Message Authenticator attribute. This encrypts the messages between the RADIUS server and the RADIUS client. You must also supply a shared secret password (22 characters consisting of letters or numbers). This password is entered and then verified; it is used as the key for the encrypted messages between IAS and the RRAS servers.

> The secret password that you configure for the RADIUS client must be the same as the secret password configured on the RRAS server when you enable RADIUS authentication. In the Add RADIUS Server box, the secret password is entered in the Secret text box.

5. When you have finished configuring the client, click Finish. You are returned to the IAS snap-in. The new RADIUS client appears in the Details pane of the snap-in.

You can add additional clients as needed. After you have configured the RADIUS client (and configured RADIUS authentication on the RRAS server), the IAS server handles authentication for remote access requests from remote clients.

Understanding Routed Networks

Another feature provided by the Windows Server 2003 RRAS is the capability to configure a multihomed server (a server with two or more network interface cards) as a router. Windows Server 2003 supports the routing of IPX, AppleTalk, and IP, but we look exclusively at IP routing (the most prevalent) in this hour.

A *router* is a device that enables you to connect separate local area networks (LANs). Routers keep local traffic on each local segment, and the separate segments communicate through the router, with each network segment connected to the router by an interface. In the case of a Windows Server 2003 router, the interfaces for the different segments or subnets are provided by the multiple network interface cards installed in the server.

> In many cases, routing is handled by a specialized hardware device from any number of vendors, such as Cisco and 3Com. Routers typically have network interfaces such as Ethernet or Token Ring and also have serial interfaces for connection to other media such as ISDN.

Connecting networks to other networks (typically LANs to LANs using LAN and WAN technologies) is called internetworking; an *internetwork* is a network of networks. Data traffic on the internetwork is controlled by a router. The router is responsible for determining the path for data (from source to destination) and then for routing the data packets to their destination (this is called packet switching). Path determination is handled by a routing protocol (or protocols) running on the router (or configured statically by the administrator). The routing protocol is used to build routing tables, which is, in essence, a routing map for the movement of data packets around the internetwork. Routing protocols such as RIP and OSPF are used as routing protocols for IP internetworks. These protocols are discussed later in the hour.

> Routers do not forward broadcast messages from one LAN to another on the internetwork. This means that a lot of bandwidth is conserved by keeping broadcasts local. However, the fact that broadcasts are not forwarded makes the assignment of IP addresses by DHCP servers problematic when there is not a DHCP server on each subnet (or segment). This problem is handled by the DHCP Relay Agent, which is discussed later in the hour.

Enabling IP Routing

To enable a Windows Server 2003 as a router, you add routing as one of the services provided by RRAS. Routing can be enabled on the server when you first configure RRAS or after the fact by changing the server's RRAS properties.

To enable the server as a router when first configuring RRAS, follow these steps:

1. Open the Routing and Remote Access snap-in (Start, Administrative Tools, Routing and Remote Access).

2. Right-click the server icon in the snap-in tree and select Configure and Enable Routing and Remote Access. The Routing and Remote Access Server Setup Wizard appears.

3. Click Next to bypass the initial screen. On the next screen (see Figure 18.13), select Custom configuration and then click Next.

FIGURE 18.13
Selecting the RRAS configuration.

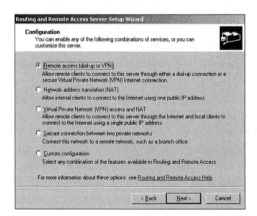

4. On the next screen, select the LAN Routing check box and then click Next. On the summary wizard screen, click Finish.

5. You are asked if you want to start the Routing and Remote Access Service. Click Yes.

To enable a server for routing that is already running RRAS (for dial-in, VPN, or other service), right-click the server's icon in the RRAS snap-in tree. Select Properties from the shortcut menu. The Properties dialog box for the server opens. On the General tab, select the Router check box. Then click OK to close the dialog box. The RRAS server must be restarted for the changes to take effect. Click Yes when prompted to restart the service.

Configuring IP Routing

When the router service is enabled on the server, you can configure it for routing IP. Routing can be handled in two different ways: dynamic routing and static routing.

Dynamic routing is handled by a routing protocol. As already mentioned, routing protocols build and maintain routing tables that determine the network topology for your internetwork. Dynamic routing is a good idea for large networks in which the network topology could change. The routing protocol can respond to changes in the LAN or WAN connections and can update the routing table appropriately.

Static routing is handled by the network administrator. Routes are actually entered on the router (in this case, the RRAS server) and are used to determine how packets are routed in the internetwork. Static routing is fine when the network topology is very constant and consistent. Any change in network connections requires the administer to re-enter the static routes. Let's take a look at entering static routes on the RRAS server; then we'll tackle dynamic routing and routing protocols.

Configuring Static Routing

Static routing is configured in the RRAS snap-in. A static route configuration consists of an interface selection (one of the network interfaces on the routing server), a destination address, a gateway, and a metric.

In terms of routing, the *gateway* is the address of the device that provides the connection between the networks that will embrace the static route that you are creating. The gateway basically functions as a forwarding agent as the packets move to their final destination.

A *metric* is the number of hops (from router to router) that are required to move the packets from source to destination. You want to create routes with the fewest number of hops (also known as the cost of the route) and, thus, the lowest metric.

To configure a static route, follow these steps:

1. Expand the RRAS server node in the Routing and Remote Access snap-in tree. Then expand the IP routing node.

2. Right-click the Static Routes node, and select New Static Route. The Static Route dialog box appears (see Figure 18.14).

FIGURE **18.14**

The Static Route dialog box.

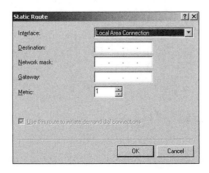

3. Use the Interface drop-down list to select the interface on the router (the RRAS server) that you will configure with the static route.

4. Enter the destination IP address in the Destination box.

5. Enter the network mask (the net mask that you computed when you subnetted your network—this is discussed in Hour 7, "Working with Network Protocols") for your network. If you want to make the route proprietary for packets with the destination address that you entered in the Destination box, use the mask of 255.255.2555.255. If you want to make the route available for any destination, enter the mask of 0.0.0.0.

The static route can be configured for multiple destinations. For example, you can configure the destination as 10.8.0.0 and the subnet mask as 255.248.0.0. This means that the route will work for any hosts in the 10.8.0.0 subnet.

6. In the Gateway box, enter the IP address of the forwarder for your network segment.

7. Enter the metric for the route using the Metric spin box. The metric will be the number of hops (routers) that the packets must travel through to reach the final destination.

8. Click OK to complete the creation of the static route.

Other static routes can be created as needed. You can edit any static route by right-clicking the route in the Details pane and then selecting Properties. Static routes can be deleted by right-clicking the route and then selecting Delete.

If the number of hops or other network topology changes in relation to your static routes, you must reconfigure the routes as needed. Because static routes are static (and require hands-on editing and management), the alternative of dynamic routing might be more to your liking.

> You can also create static routes at the command line using the route command. The routing table can be viewed using the route print command.

Configuring Dynamic Routing

To configure dynamic routing, you must add a routing protocol to the IP Routing node of your RRAS server. As already mentioned, routing protocols build routing tables, which are used to route data packets on the internetwork. In the case of IP routing, you can select between two routing protocols: RIP and OSPF.

- **RIP**—The Routing Information Protocol (RIP) is a distance-vector routing protocol that uses hop count as its metric. RIP sends out routing update messages every 30 seconds to neighboring routers. Because RIP is a distance-vector routing protocol, it requires routers to share complete copies of their routing tables with other routers. RIP has a limit of 15 hops and, thus, is not appropriate for very large Enterprise-size internetworks.

- **OSPF**—Open Shortest Path First (OSPF) is a link-state protocol (it was developed by the Internet Engineering Task Force as a replacement for RIP). As its name implies, OSPF computes the shortest path from source to destination when determining a route for data packets. Link-state protocols such as OSPF send updates to their routing tables to neighboring routers. This eats up less bandwidth than RIP broadcasts of entire routing tables.

To add a routing protocol to your RRAS server, follow these steps:

1. Expand the IP routing node in the snap-in tree.

2. Right-click the General node and select New Routing Protocol from the shortcut menu. The New Routing Protocol dialog box opens (see Figure 18.15).

3. Select either Open Shortest Path First (OSPF) or RIP Version 2 for Internet Protocol.

4. After selecting the protocol, click OK. The protocol is added to the IP routing node list.

18

FIGURE 18.15

Adding a routing protocol.

After you've added a routing protocol to the RRAS IP Routing configuration, you need to create an interface for the routing protocol. We discuss configuring RIP and OSPF interfaces in the two sections that follow.

Configuring RIP Interfaces

RIP interfaces are configured for a number of settings, including the protocol type used for outgoing packets and whether your router will accept routes from all its neighbors (other nearby routers). To configure an interface for RIP, follow these steps:

1. Right-click the RIP node (under the IP Routing node in the snap-in tree) and select New Interface.

2. In the New Interface for RIP dialog box, select the interface for the protocol.

3. Click OK. The RIP Properties dialog box for the interface that you selected appears (see Figure 18.16).

FIGURE 18.16

The RIP Properties dialog box for the interface.

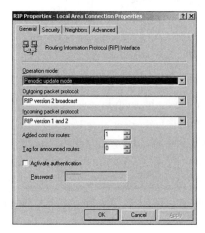

4. The Advanced tab handles configuration of the intervals related to sending routing table updates. The defaults provide the typical settings (which will suffice in most situations). If you want your router to broadcast route changes less frequently, you can increase the Hello interval (the Hello protocol is used for broadcasts between the routers).

5. When you have finished configuring the OSPF interface, click OK.

The new interface appears in the Details pane. You can add other OSPF interfaces as needed.

Monitoring IP Routing

Routing can be monitored in the RRAS snap-in. For example, to see a list of neighbor routers for either RIP or the OSPF protocol, click the Routing Protocol node and then select Show Neighbors. A Neighbors dialog box opens that lists the addresses of neighboring routers.

To view the status of the router interfaces and other information, such as the incoming and outgoing bytes from the interface, expand the IP Routing node and then click the General node (see Figure 18.19).

FIGURE 18.19

View the status of the router's interfaces.

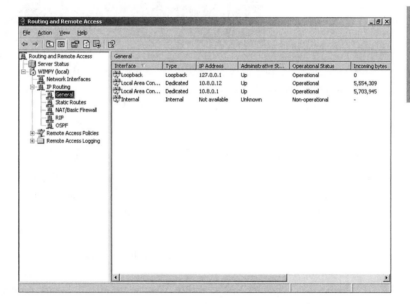

To view the routing table for the router, right-click one of the interfaces and select Show IP Routing Table from the shortcut menu. The routing table appears.

A useful command-line utility for monitoring IP routes is the tracert command. It provides you with the number of hops between a source and a destination IP address. To use tracert, open a command prompt window. Type **tracert** followed by the IP address of the destination. Figure 18.20 shows a tracert result that was four hops to the destination address.

tracert is actually a very good way to determine whether a router or route is down on your internetwork. If the number of hops changes dramatically over time to the same destination, there is a problem on the network.

Understanding the DHCP Relay Agent

Before we leave our discussion of remote access and routing, we should discuss issues related to running DHCP in environments where remote clients receive their IP addresses from a DHCP server and in routed environments that consist of two or more IP subnets. In both cases, the DHCP Relay Agent is required for DHCP to function correctly.

In the case of routed networks, the DHCP Relay Agent is configured so that it knows the location of a DHCP server or servers on other subnets of the network (that is, on the other side of the router). The Relay Agent takes the broadcast request from DHCP clients on the subnet (that both the client and the Relay Agent reside on) and relays a point-to-point communication to the DHCP server that there has been a request for an IP address lease (this type of communication is passed on by the router because it is not a broadcast message, but is directed to the specific IP address of the DHCP server).

As already mentioned, the DHCP Relay Agent is also necessary when you are providing remote access clients with IP addresses from a DHCP server. The DHCP Relay Agent relays IP address requests from remote clients to the DHCP server.

You cannot set up the DHCP Relay Agent on a server that is a DHCP server, nor can you install it on a server that is running Network Address Translation (Network Address Translation is discussed in Hour 22, "Using Internet Connection Sharing and Network Address Translation").

The DHCP Relay Agent is added and configured in much the same way that you added and configured routing protocols such as RIP and OSPF. To configure a server as a DHCP Relay Agent, follow these steps:

1. In the Routing and Remote Access snap-in, expand the Server node and then the IP Routing node.

2. Right-click the General node and select New Routing Protocol. The New Routing Protocol dialog box appears.

3. Select DHCP Relay Agent in the routing protocol list. Then click OK. DHCP Relay Agent appears as a subnode of the IP Routing node.

4. To add an interface (or interfaces) for the DHCP Relay Agent, right-click the DHCP Relay Agent node and select New Interface. The New Interface dialog box opens. Select the interface from the list and then click OK. The DHCP Relay Properties dialog box for the connection opens.

5. By default, the interface relays DHCP packets. You can change the hop count threshold or boot threshold for the interface. The hop count threshold is the number of Relay Agents that can relay the DHCP requests. The maximum hop count is 16. The boot threshold is the number of seconds that the Relay Agent waits before it forwards DHCP messages. In both cases, the defaults generally will suffice. Click OK to continue.

6. To complete the DHCP Relay Agent configuration, right-click the DHCP Relay Agent node and select Properties (see Figure 18.21).

18

FIGURE 18.21

Configure the Relay Agent with the IP addresses of the DHCP servers.

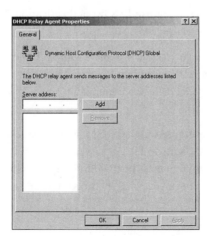

7. Add the IP addresses of the DHCP servers to which the DHCP Relay Agent will forward DHCP requests.

8. Click OK to close the dialog box.

The server will now act as a DHCP Relay Agent. Remember that is necessary to configure the DHCP Relay Agent when remote access clients are provide IP addressing by a DHCP server and when you have multiple subnets but do not have a DHCP server on each subnet.

Summary

Remote access servers can provide dial-in remote access using asynchronous modems and a number of other technologies provided by POTS.

Remote access is enabled on the Routing and Remote Access Service.

RAS ports must be configured for dial-in service. The modem or other connectivity device on the RAS server must be configured for incoming calls.

Remote users are authenticated to the RAS server using a number of different authentication protocols, such as EAP, MS-CHAP, and Shiva. The remote client must be configured with the same authentication protocol that is required by the RRAS server.

RAS servers can embrace Windows authentication or then can take advantage of RADIUS authentication, in which a dedicated RADIUS server provides authentication of remote users. The Windows Server 2003 Internet Authentication Service can be configured as a RADIUS server.

The IAS server must be registered in the Active Directory, and the IAS server is configured using the Internet Authentication Service snap-in.

RADIUS clients are RAS servers that use IAS for authentication. RADIUS clients are added via the Internet Authentication Service snap-in.

A server running Windows Server 2003 configured with multiple network cards can be configured as a network router. IP routing protocols such as RIP and OSPF can be added to the router to build routing tables. Or, the administrator can create static routes to move data packets on the internetwork.

The DHCP Relay Agent is configured in the RRAS snap-in to relay requests for IP addresses from remote access clients to DHCP servers on the network. The DHCP Relay Agent can also be used to relay requests for IP addressing on routed networks, where subnets on the network do not have access to their own DHCP server.

Q&A

Q What two types of authentication can be used with a RAS server?

A Authentication can be handled by the local Routing and Remote Access service or by a special RADIUS server. If RADIUS authentication is used, the RAS server becomes a client of the RADIUS server. The Internet Authentication Service installed on a Windows server can be used as a RADIUS server.

Q How are remote users authenticated when authentication is handled by the RAS server?

A A number of different authentication protocols are available to authenticate remote users to a dial-in RAS server. These protocols provide different strengths of authentication. The Extensible Authentication Protocol provides the strongest authentication and is followed by the MS-CHAP V2 and MS-CHAP protocols. The weakest form of authentication is to configure unauthenticated access, which means that no protocol is used to control authentication.

Q How are remote access clients configured in the domain?

A The Active Directory Users and Computers snap-in is used to configure user settings related to remote access.

Q How are remote access clients configured in the domain?

A The Active Directory Users and Computers snap-in is used to configure user settings related to remote access.

Q What is required to make a Windows server a router?

A The server must be configured with at least two network interface cards. The RRAS service must also be installed and configured on the server.

Q What type of routing can be configured on a Windows RRAS router?

A Both static and dynamic routing can be configured on a server running the RRAS service. Static routes can be configured using the RRAS snap-in. Dynamic routing can be enabled by configuring a routing protocol such as RIP or OSPF. The routing protocol builds the routing table for the router.

18

Hour **19**

Implementing Windows Terminal Services

The typical notion of a network desktop client on a Microsoft network is a computer configured with a Windows operating system and running application software (such as Microsoft Office) that is installed locally on the computer's hard disk. However, you might have users who need to connect to the network and use network resources with computers or other devices that do not supply the configuration needed for a typical network client. The Windows Terminal Services enables you to supply "nonstandard" network clients with Windows-based applications and an emulated Windows desktop environment.

In this hour, we look at the Windows Terminal Services. The hour discusses Terminal Services installation and configuration and the management of the server running Terminal Services. We also look at the configuration of Terminal Services clients.

In this hour, the following topics are covered:

- Installing and configuring Terminal Services
- Working with Terminal Services licensing
- Using the Terminal Services Manager
- Installing and configuring remote desktop clients
- Using remote server administration

Understanding Terminal Services

The concept of the network thin client has been around nearly as long as desktop computing. A *thin client* is software (although it is often used to refer to the computer itself) that allows a computer with a minimal hardware configuration to connect to an application server. The thin client computer, which normally would not be capable of running a full-blown copy of a particular desktop operating system or desktop applications, is "served" these items by the application server. In the Windows Server 2003 environment, Terminal Services provides the desktop OS and required applications to the network thin client.

Using Terminal Services to provide thin clients with a Windows desktop operating system and applications enables users to access network resources on older desktop computers or computers with minimal hardware configurations. All the application processing and data storage is handled by the server. In essence, the Terminal Server functions as an *application server,* providing applications that would not run as standalone software on the thin client. A server running Terminal Services is referred to as a Terminal Server.

Terminal Services clients can access the applications provided over any TCP/IP connection. This means that users can connect via your local area network or can use remote access strategies such as dial-in or VPN to connect to the Terminal Server.

> Terminal Services clients are not necessarily limited to computers running different versions of the Windows operating system. These clients can include computers running the Macintosh OS and UNIX. The Macintosh Terminal Services client can be downloaded from the Microsoft Web site (www.microsoft.com). Third-party software is available so that UNIX clients be configured as Terminal Services clients.

Another aspect of Windows Terminal Services is Remote Desktop for Administration. This tool enables an administrator to connect to any Windows Server 2003 remotely over an IP connection. This then enables you to manage such things as file and print sharing or other administrative tasks.

You do not have to configure the Terminal Services feature to take advantage of the Remote Desktop for administration feature. The two Terminal Services environments (the application server and the Remote Desktop) are actually mutually exclusive. The Remote Desktop for Administration feature is already installed on computers running Windows Server 2003. The feature is enabled on the Remote tab of the System Properties dialog box (which is discussed later in the hour).

Windows XP provides a similar feature to Remote Desktop for Administration called Remote Desktop. This feature allows a remote connection to a computer running the Windows XP desktop operating system.

Understanding Terminal Services Hardware Considerations

Before adding Terminal Services to the roles of a particular server, you need to make sure that the server has the necessary hardware to provide a number of concurrent connections to Terminal Services clients. Microsoft recommends that you do not configure a domain controller with the additional role of Terminal Server because providing Terminal Services places additional performance hits on the server's memory and processor.

At a minimum, a Terminal Server should be configured with a base RAM of 128MB and then 10MB for each Terminal Server user. This is considered a "light" user, who runs only one application at a time when connected to the server. When users will run three or more programs concurrently (from the Terminal Server), 21MB of RAM per user is suggested. So, the bottom line is that a Terminal Server should be configured with an almost excessive amount of memory. An ideal starting point is 256MB of RAM and then 32MB of RAM per user. This requires server memory near the gigabyte level when you have a large number of Terminal Server clients. However, you don't want memory to be a service bottleneck on this type of environment.

The Terminal Server should also be configured with ample space on the server's hard drives because they will supply not only the space for the applications, but also storage space for users. All drives used on a Terminal Server should be formatted using NTFS, which supplies the added security of NTFS permissions and encryption (for more about NTFS permissions, see Hour 13, "Share and NTFS Permissions").

Finally, you really want to create the Terminal Server environment on a clean slate. So, there should be no applications currently installed on the server. They should be installed after you add the Terminal Server role to the server.

19

Adding the Terminal Server Role

Terminal Services can be added to any domain member server that has the required hardware configuration (as discussed in the last section). You can add the Terminal Server role to a Windows Server 2003 using the Configure Your Server Wizard.

1. Start the wizard via the Manage Your Server window (select the Add or Remove Role links) or by selecting Start, Administrative Tools, and then Configure Your Server. The Configure Your Server Wizard appears.

2. Click Next to bypass the first wizard screen (if you started the Configure Your Server Wizard via the Start menu). The Preliminary Steps screen can also be bypassed by clicking Next. On the Server Role screen, select the Terminal Server role and then click Next.

3. A summary of your server role addition (Terminal Server) is provided. Click Next to continue.

4. A message appears that during the Terminal Server installation process the computer will be restarted. Click OK.

5. The Windows Component Wizard appears (briefly), and Terminal Services is added to the server. The server then restarts. Log on to the server as an administrator (or with an account that has administrative rights).

6. After you log on to the computer, you will find the summary screen of the Configure Your Server Wizard, which lets you know that the server is now a Terminal Server (the Help feature also opens, highlighting the steps to configure your Terminal Server). Click Finish to close the wizard.

Understanding Terminal Services Licensing

An important aspect of providing Terminal Services to clients is licensing. Each client that connects to the Terminal Server must have a license. These licenses are provided by a Terminal Server license server. A server other than the Terminal Server (the computer you just configured for the Terminal Server role) should be configured as a license server.

Terminal Services licenses are not the same as the licenses that are used to license your Windows Server 2003 network clients (Windows Server 2003 licensing is discussed in Hour 3, "Installing Windows Server 2003"). When a Terminal Services client requests a connection to the Terminal Server, it is provided a license by the license server. Each client connecting to the Terminal Server requires a client access license.

Terminal Servers that are not supported by a Terminal Server license server will not provide connections to clients beyond a 120-day evaluation period. So, you must configure a license server on the network (and purchase licenses) if you really plan to use Terminal Server as a network connectivity option.

Setting up a Terminal Server license server is really a two-step process. First you add the license server service to a server on the network and activate the service. Then you acquire client access licenses from Microsoft and install them on the License Server.

As far as placement of the Terminal Server license server goes, you can deploy a license server in each domain or in one that handles the entire enterprise, such as a domain tree (or forest). When a license server is used in each domain, the license server must also be a domain controller.

Installing the Terminal Server License Service

The Terminal Server Licensing service is added to a Windows Server 2003 using the Add or Remove Programs applet in the Control Panel.

1. Select Start, Control Panel, Add or Remove Programs.

2. In the Add or Remove Programs window, select Add/Remove Windows Components. Scroll down through the Windows component list and then select the Terminal Server Licensing option (see Figure 19.1). Click Next to continue.

FIGURE 19.1

Select Terminal Server Licensing.

19

3. On the next screen, you are provided with two options: your entire enterprise or your domain or workgroup. The entire enterprise option enables you to set the Terminal Server license server as the licensing agent for the entire enterprise

network (only one licensing server is required, no matter what the forest or tree structure is). Or, you can choose to deploy the licensing server just for the domain (or workgroup). Select the appropriate option and click Next to continue. The Licensing service is installed on the server.

4. Click Finish. You can then close the Add or Remove Programs window.

Activating the License Server

Before you can install licenses on the Terminal Server license server, you must activate the server. This is accomplished in the Terminal Server Licensing snap-in.

1. Open the Terminal Server Licensing snap-in: Select Start, Administrative Tools, Terminal Server Licensing. The Terminal Server Licensing snap-in opens and connects to the licensing sever (the local computer).

2. (Optional) If you receive a message that no Terminal Server licensing server is currently available in the enterprise or domain (depending on the selection that you made when you installed the Licensing service), click OK.

3. (Optional) To specify the local server as the license server that you will activate, click Action and then Connect. Type the name of the server on the connection box and then click OK. The server appears in the Details pane of the Snap-in.

4. When the server icon is available in the snap-in, you can then activate the server (this step picks up after either Step 1 or the optional Steps 2 and 3). To activate the license server, right-click the server icon and then select Activate Server.

5. The Terminal Server License Server Activation Wizard opens. Click Next to bypass the initial wizard screen.

6. You have three options for activating the License Server; select one of the following options: Automatically via the Internet, By Web Browser from Another Computer, or By Telephone.

   - The most direct and easiest method is the automatic connection (the default), which requires only that the server be connected to the Internet.

   - The Web browser method enables you to connect to the Microsoft Clearinghouse Web site from another computer that is connected to the Internet and that is outfitted with a Web browser. You supply the license server's product ID (which is provided onscreen by the wizard). The Web site then provides you with a license server ID, which you type on the appropriate wizard screen. This method requires that you jockey back and forth between your license server and the computer that is providing you with the Internet connection.

- The third method enables you to use the telephone. The wizard provides a toll-free number (you select your location, and the number is provided), and then you give the operator your product ID. The operator supplies you with a license server ID that enables you to activate the server.

7. After you select your activation method, follow the steps provided by the wizard. In the case of automatic activation, you must supply your name, company name, and location to complete the process.

Adding Licenses

When activation is complete, the Activation Wizard supplies a summary screen letting you know that the license server has been activated. It also provides you with the option of starting the Client Licensing Wizard for Terminal Server.

1. Click Next to continue past the summary screen (and start the Client Licensing Wizard), and then click Next again to bypass the initial Client Licensing Wizard screen.

2. On the next screen, you are asked to provide the licensing program that you are using to license your Terminal Server clients. These licenses can come in the form of prepurchased retail packages, educational licenses, or other types of licensing agreements from Microsoft or other vendors (see Figure 19.2). After you select your licensing mode, click Next.

FIGURE 19.2

Select your client licensing.

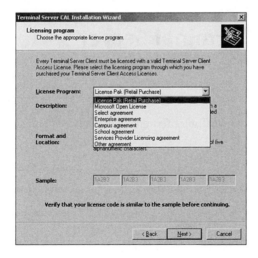

19

3. You are asked to provide your license or agreement number. After you supply the information, click Next.

4. On the next screen, you are asked to supply the product version for the license (Windows Server 2003 or Windows 2000 Server) and whether the licenses are per client or per connection. You also are asked to supply the number of licenses that you have purchased. After you supply this information, click Next to continue; then click Next again to complete the process.

You are returned to the Terminal Server Licensing snap-in (see Figure 19.3). You can add additional licenses at any time by right-clicking the licensing server icon and then selecting Install Licenses. The License Wizard will walk you through the process, as we have already discussed.

FIGURE 19.3

The Terminal Server Licensing snap-in.

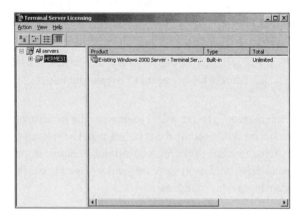

Configuring Terminal Server

After you have added Terminal Services to a server and configured a Terminal Server licensing server on the network, you can configure the Terminal Server. This is accomplished using the Terminal Services Configuration\Connections (TSCC) snap-in.

Select Start, Administrative Tools, Terminal Services Configuration. The TSCC snap-in opens (see Figure 19.4).

> You can also open the TSCC snap-in via the Manage Your Server window. Select the Open Terminal Services Configuration link in the Terminal Server area of the windows.

The TSCC snap-in enables you to configure the Terminal Services connection (or connections) that is used by remote desktop clients. The snap-in is also used to select the Server Settings for the Terminal Server. Let's look at connection configuration and then Server Settings.

FIGURE 19.4

The TSCC snap-in.

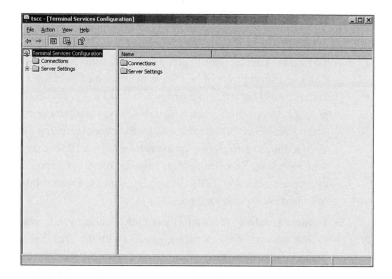

Configuring Connections

By default, a connection is created by the Remote Desktop/TCP protocol. This connection should be sufficient for all your remote connection users (although you can add additional connections if you feel that it is necessary). To view the default connection, click the Connections folder in the snap-in tree.

To manage the default connection (or any connection that you create), right-click the Connection icon in the Details pane of the snap-in and select Properties. The RDP-Tcp Properties dialog box opens (this is the Properties dialog box for the default connection—see Figure 19.5.

19

FIGURE 19.5

The connection's Properties dialog box.

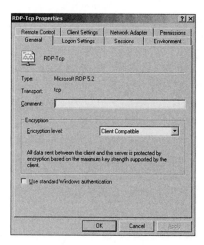

The Properties dialog box for a Terminal Server connection consists of a number of different tabs. These tabs are used to configure the connection as follows:

- **General**—This tab (see Figure 19.5) shows the connection type and the connection's transport protocol. You have the option of entering a comment related to the connection. This tab also enables you to set the encryption method used when data is sent between the Terminal Services server and the client. The Client Compatible setting uses encryption embraced by the client operating system used to make the connection. The High encryption setting uses a 128-bit key and is compatible only with Windows XP or computers running Windows Server 2003. An additional encryption selection, FIPS Complaint, uses the Federal Information Processing Standard encryption method.

- **Remote Control**—This tab (by default) enables you to control or observe a user's remote session. You control the session with the Terminal Service Manager (discussed later in the hour). This tab also provides the options of not allowing remote control of sessions or requiring the user's permission for the Administrator to view or control the session.

- **Logon Settings**—This tab provides a default setting of having all Terminal Server users connect using client-provided logon information. This means that the user would provide a domain username and password to log on (when using the Remote Desktop Connection client, discussed later in the hour). The other option provided (see Figure 19.6) is to set up the connection so that only one username and password is used by all clients. This enables all users to log on using the same name and password. This can become problematic when you want to track a specific user. This tab also enables you to require that users are always prompted for a password when logging on to the server.

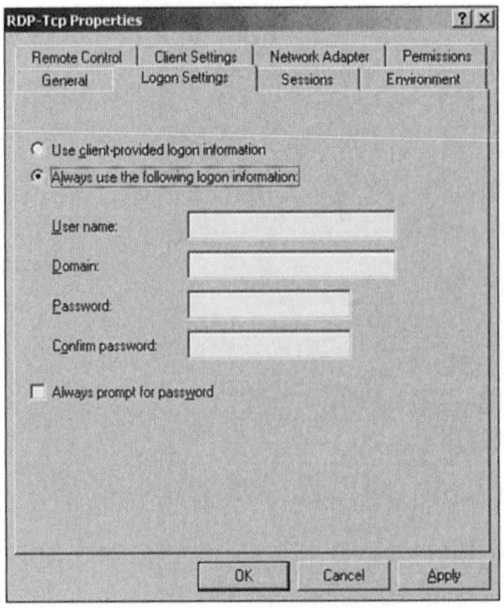

FIGURE 19.6

The connection's Logon Settings tab enables you to specify how users log on.

- **Client Settings**—This tab enables you to configure a number of connection settings, including the color depth used on the client monitor and the client's capability to create drive or printer mappings. By default, the Use Connection Settings from User Settings option is enabled (this means that the connection settings are taken from the client's Remote Desktop Connection client). You also have the capability of disabling a number of settings, including the user's ability to map drives, connect to printers, and map LPT or COM ports.

- **Sessions**—This tab enables you to override user settings, such as setting time limits for ending a disconnected session, setting a time limit for connection sessions, or setting an idle session time limit. If you select the Override User Settings options, the time limits are set using a series of drop-down boxes.

- **Network Adapter**—This tab enables you to select the network adapter (or adapters) that you want to bind to the Terminal Server transport protocol. You can choose to have all adapters configured with the protocol or specify a single adapter to be configured with the protocol. Selecting a single adapter is actually a way of selecting the network interface that will field the incoming connection from Remote Desktop clients. This tab also enables you to set the number of connections for the network adapter or adapters. The default is Unlimited Connections.

- **Environment**—This tab enables you to override settings assigned to a user by a user profile or the settings that have been configured on the user's Remote Desktop Connection client. You can also specify that a particular program will start when the users log on to the connection. This is particularly useful when you are using Terminal Services to provide access to an application such as Microsoft Word. Word could be started automatically when clients connect to the Terminal Server.

- **Permissions**—This tab is used to set the permission levels for groups or users that will access the Terminal Server (see Figure 19.7). The access levels are Full Control, User Access, Guest Access, and Special Permissions. Groups or users can be added to the group or user names using the Advanced button on the tab (just as groups or users are added to NTFS permissions, as discussed in Hour 13). A Remote Desktop Users group is added to the domain when the Terminal Server is added to the domain. This gives you the option of managing remote connection users by making them members of this group.

19

FIGURE **19.7**

The connection's Permissions tab enables you to set the level of access that groups and users have to the Terminal Server.

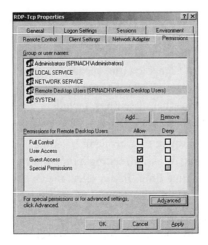

Server Settings

You can also configure the server settings for the Terminal Server using the TSCC snap-in. In the snap-in tree, select the Server Settings node. The different settings appear in the Details pane (see Figure 19.8).

FIGURE **19.8**

The Terminal Server settings.

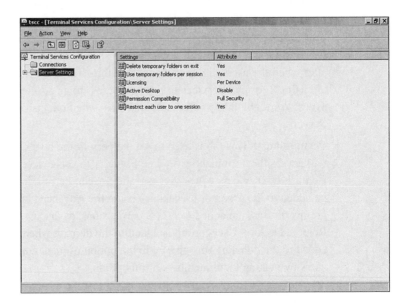

These settings basically provide the environment that Terminal Server clients will experience when connected. The settings also provide some housekeeping duties, such as cleaning up temporary folders created during Terminal Server sessions.

Many of these settings are Yes or No propositions; you are turning a particular server setting either on or off (or enabling or disabling the feature). To change the default for a setting, right-click the setting and select Yes, No, Enable, or Disable (depending on the setting). You can also set a setting or view properties related to the setting by selecting Properties from the shortcut menu. The Properties dialog box for the setting opens (the Permission Compatibility setting is shown in Figure 19.9). The Terminal Server settings available are listed here:

- **Delete Temporary Folders on Exit**—By default, temporary folders created during the Terminal Services session are deleted. If you want to save temporary folders created, you can disable this setting.

- **Use Temporary Folders Per Sessions**—By default, temporary folders are used during Terminal Services sessions. This setting can be disabled by accessing the setting's Properties dialog box.

- **Licensing**—As we already discussed, Terminal Server client licensing is either on a per-device or per-session basis. The licensing type listed is based on how you have configured the licensing server for the domain (or the enterprise).

- **Off for Terminal Server Sessions**—You can enable this feature if you want your users to have an "interactive" desktop during their sessions.

- **Permission Compatibility**—This is one of the most important settings related to Terminal Server sessions. The default is Full Security, which limits access to the server registry and system directories and negates the running of many legacy software applications that must access the OS kernel. If you need to allow users to run legacy software, and you don't mind operating in a slightly more unstable Terminal Server environment, you can reduce the security level to Relaxed Security.

- **Restrict Each User to One Session**—By default, each user is restricted to one session on the Terminal Server. This conserves your Terminal Server's resources because it doesn't have to deal with idle but still connected sessions resulting from a user who is computer "hopping." If you want to allow multiple sessions, you can disable this setting.

- **Session Directory**—These settings are related to the use of a session directory server in an environment that deploys multiple Terminal Servers. In the Session Directory settings, you specify the session directory server name (or IP address). A session directory server keeps a database of Terminal Services clients and makes sure that they connect to the appropriate Terminal Server on the network. Any server running Windows Server 2003 can act as a session directory server; all you have to do is enable the Terminal Services Session Directory service in the Services snap-in.

19

FIGURE 19.9

Each setting has a Properties dialog box.

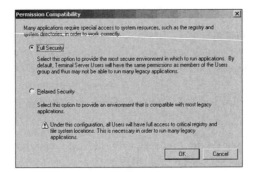

Using the Terminal Services Manager

The Terminal Services Manager enables you to view information related to your Terminal Servers, such as users' sessions. This MMC snap-in also provides you with the capability to end sessions, log off users, and send messages to users. To start the Terminal Services Manager, select Start, Administrative Tools, then Terminal Services Manager. When the snap-in opens, you might receive a message that remote control and connect will not be available if you are running the snap-in in a console session (meaning that you are using it to view the local server rather than to connect to a remote server). Figure 19.10 shows the Terminal Services Manager snap-in.

FIGURE 19.10

You can manage a connection using the Terminal Services Manager.

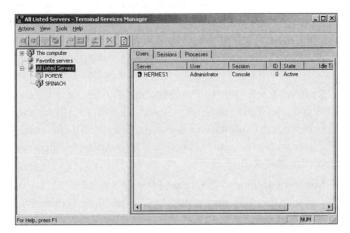

To view the sessions on the local server, click the This Computer node in the snap-in tree. Any sessions (including the console sessions) are listed in the Details pane.

If you want to connect to a remote Terminal Server, double-click the domain icon in the snap-in tree. A list of Terminal Servers in the domain are listed to connect to a particular server. Right-click the server icon and select Connect (or double-click the icon). The connections for that server appear in the Details pane (see Figure 19.11).

FIGURE 19.11

Current connections for a server appear in the Details pane.

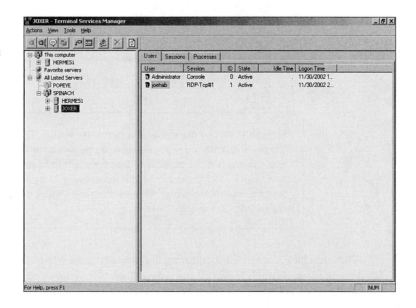

As already mentioned, you can disconnect sessions, log off users, and send messages to users. Each of these tasks is quickly accomplished in the Details pane.

For example, to disconnect a particular session, right-click the sessions and select Disconnect. Then click OK when the Disconnect message box appears.

You can also control user connections. For example, if you want to log off a particular user, right-click a user session and select Logoff. Click OK when the Logoff message box appears. Logging off a user actually closes down the applications and other services that were being used by that particular user.

The Terminal Services Manager also makes it easy for you to quickly communicate with attached users. You can actually send messages to a user (or send a message to multiple connected users) on the network. Right-click on the user (or selected users) and then select Send Message on the shortcut menu. The Send Message window opens (see Figure 19.12) .

Type your message and then click OK. The message appears on the user's remote desktop connection window.

19

FIGURE 19.12

*You can send messages
to users.*

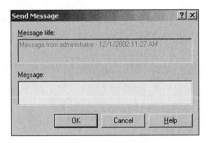

> You can also view the status of a particular session. This enables you to view
> the bytes and frames sent and received between the client and the server,
> and also to view the number of bad frames that have passed between the
> two (many bad frames can be the indication of a problem). To view the sta-
> tus of a session, right-click the session in the Details pane and then select
> Status from the shortcut menu.

When you have completed monitoring and managing the Terminal Servers in your
domain, you can quickly end all the connections. Select the Actions menu and then select
Disconnect from All Servers. You can then close the snap-in.

Installing and Configuring the Remote Desktop Client

To connect a client to the Terminal Server, the client computer needs to have the Remote
Desktop Connection client installed on it. You can install the client on any of the
Windows family of desktop operating systems (computers running Windows Server 2003
and Windows XP already have the client installed).

You can install the client over the network to any connected computer by sharing the
C:\WINDOWS\System32\clients\tsclient folder. The Setup executable to install the
Remote Desktop client is found in the System32 folder (which is a subfolder of the
tsclient folder—see Figure 19.13).

Another option is to download the client from www.microsoft.com/windows.netserver/
technologies/terminalservice/. This download, the msrdpcli.exe file, installs the client
on Windows 9*x*, ME, NT, and 2000.

After the Remote Desktop Connection client is installed on a computer on the network, a
connection can be made to a Terminal Server on the network. Settings for the connection
can include the Terminal Server that the client will use for the connection, the resolution
of the screen provided by the Terminal Server (to the client), and the selection of an

application to automatically start when the client connects to the server. Figure 19.14 shows the Remote Desktop Connection client on a computer running Windows XP.

FIGURE 19.13

The Remote Desktop client setup executable can be used to install the client.

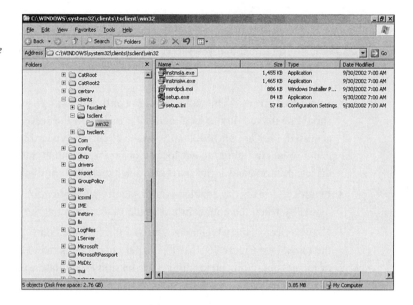

FIGURE 19.14

The Remote Desktop client enables a user to connect to the Terminal Server.

19

The Remote Desktop Connection client consists of five tabs:

- **General**—This tab (shown in Figure 19.14) enables you to specify the name (or IP address) of the Terminal Server. It also provides a text box for the username, password, and domain that the client will be logging on to. The connection settings can be saved using the Save As button.

- **Display**—This tab enables you to set the display resolution and colors that will be provided by the Terminal Server. Colors can range from 256 to True Color.

> The screen colors and resolution achieved by the client depend on the threshold that you set when you configured the Terminal Server settings.

- **Local Resources**—This tab is used to configure settings such as whether sounds should be played on the local computer or left on the server (when they are accessed, they are played locally on the client). Keyboard hotkeys such as Alt+Tab can also be configured to act locally or on the Terminal Server. Connections to disk drives, printers, and serial ports can also be enabled or disabled on this tab.

- **Programs**—This tab enables you to specify an application (and path) to start automatically when the connection is made to the Terminal Server.

- **Experience**—This tab enables you to configure the connection "experience" for the client (see Figure 19.15). The experience relates mainly to the apparent speed of the session. You can configure the session to emulate a modem, broadband, or LAN connection.

FIGURE 19.15

The Experience tab enables you to set the connection speed that the user will experience.

When the Remote Desktop Connection client is configured for the Terminal Server client, the client can connect to the server. This is just a matter of clicking the Connect button on the General tab (and supplying the username and password). Figure 19.16 shows a connection to a Terminal Server (Hermes1). Note that Microsoft Word is started automatically when the client connects to the Terminal Server.

FIGURE 19.16

A connection to a Terminal Server.

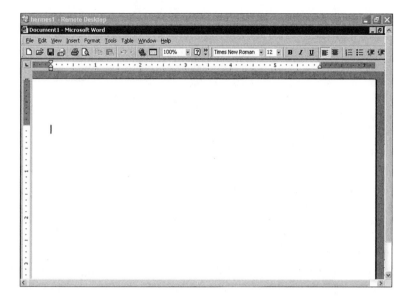

When the user closes the connection, the software will actually continue to "run." This enables a user to pick up right where he left off when he reconnects to the Terminal Server.

Using Remote Administration

Another aspect of Terminal Services is the Remote Administration tool. This enables you to manage any server on your network that allows remote connections. You can manage your servers from any server or client workstation that provides a remote connection. You also need to be able to log on to the server with an Administrator's account or other account that provides administrative privileges.

1. To allow remote administration on a server, open the System Properties dialog box (click Start, right-click My Computer, and then select Properties). Select the Remote tab of the dialog box (see Figure 19.17).

2. Click the All Users to Connect Remotely to Your Computer check box (this option will already be checked if you have configured the server for Terminal Services).

3. Click OK to close the dialog box.

Remote administration is really no different than the process by which a client attaches to a Terminal Server, although remote administration means that you (the administrator) will be using the connection to configure and monitor the server that you attach to. You can connect to a server that allows remote connections either from another server or from a client computer on the network—any computer that you have configured with the Remote Desktop Connection client.

19

FIGURE **19.17**

*Remote Desktop must
be selected on the
Remote tab.*

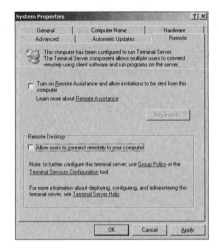

FIGURE **19.17**

*Remote Desktop must
be selected on the
Remote tab.*

Figure 19.18 shows a remote connection to a Windows Server 2003. Notice that the
remote connection (because of the rights assigned to the user who logged on to the server
remotely) allows the user to administer server functions such as file-server settings.

FIGURE **19.18**

*A remote connection
to a Windows Server
2003.*

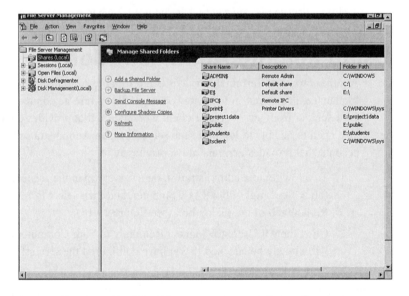

Remote connections enable you to not only administer servers, but also monitor them at
any location. Make sure that the account you use to remotely connect has administrative
privileges for the remote server.

Summary

A Terminal Server provides a desktop environment and applications to thin clients. Windows Server 2003 Terminal Server can provide remote connections to clients running Windows, the Macintosh operating system, and other non-Windows operating systems.

Windows Server 2003 Terminal Services provides the Terminal Server functionality that allows a server to function as an application server. Another feature, Remote Desktop for Administration, is categorized with Terminal Server but is an exclusive feature that enables you to connect remotely to your network servers.

Q&A

Q What Windows Server 2003 service can be used to accommodate thin clients with a Windows desktop environment and user applications?

A Windows Terminal Services is used to provide thin clients with minimal hardware configurations with a desktop and application environment that keeps application processing and data storage on the Terminal Server.

Q Running Terminal Services on a Windows domain also requires what type of server to handle the licensing of Terminal Services clients?

A A Terminal Server license server holds the clients licenses for the Terminal Services clients that connect to your domain Terminal Servers. Each client requires a client access license. These licenses are recorded on the Terminal Server License server using the Client Licensing Wizard.

Q What tool is used to configure a Terminal Server?

A The Terminal Services Configuration/Connections (TSCC) snap-in is used to configure both connection settings and Terminal Server settings. You can configure connection settings such as the encryption method used and the logon settings for the connection. Server settings include the type of licensing used for Terminal Services (per device or per session) and other settings, such as the use of temporary folders during sessions and the permission compatibility for client sessions.

Q What Windows Server 2003 snap-in enables you to view and manage connections and even log off users connected to the Terminal Server?

A The Terminal Services Manager enables you to view connections to the Terminal Server and view user sessions. You can manage connections and sessions and even send messages to connected users using the Terminal Services Manager. The snap-in can also be used to monitor remote Terminal Servers on the network.

19

Q What software is required on a thin client computer to connect to a Terminal Server?

A The thin client must have a Remote Desktop client installed. The client software can be downloaded from Microsoft; versions exist for Windows 9*x*, ME, NT, 2000, and XP. The Remote Desktop client software is configured to connect to a particular Terminal Server in the domain. The client can also be configured for desktop colors and the connection type experienced by the user

PART IV

Performance Monitoring, Security, and Web Services

Hour

HOUR **20**

Monitoring Server and Network Performance

An important aspect of administering a Windows Server 2003 network is keeping tabs on the performance of the servers on your network and monitoring network traffic. Windows Server 2003 provides you with the capability of monitoring server performance using the System Monitor. Not only can hardware parameters such as memory and processor usage be monitored, but specific services such as WINS also can be monitored using this tool.

Another tool, the Event Viewer, provides you with the capability of monitoring a number of different log files that can be used to identify problems and troubleshoot server and network issues. Windows Server 2003 even provides you with the capability of monitoring network traffic using Network Monitor. We look at all three of these tools in this hour.

In this hour, the following topics are covered:

- Using the Performance Console
- Working with the System Monitor

- Creating performance logs and alerts
- Using the Event Viewer
- Using the Network Monitor

Using the Performance Console

The *Performance Console* provides access to the System Monitor snap-in (used for real-time monitoring of server function) and the Performance Logs and Alerts node that enables you to create reports using log files created by the System Monitor. The Performance snap-in also provides you with the capability of creating alerts that are activated when the monitored hardware (such as a drive, processor, or memory) reaches a usage level that you have defined as a threshold (these alerts can then be viewed in the Event Viewer, which is discussed later in this hour).

To open the Performance Console, click the Start button, point at Administrative Tools, and then select Performance. The Performance Console opens (see Figure 20.1).

FIGURE 20.1

The Performance Console provides access to server-monitoring tools.

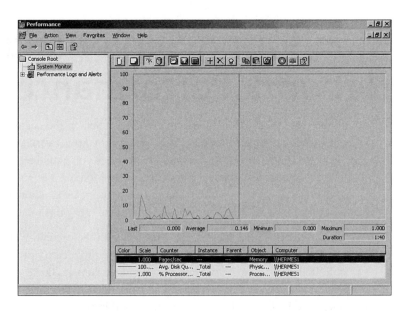

The default view in the console is the System Monitor's graph. In the next section, we take a look at the System Monitor snap-in.

Exploring the System Monitor

The Windows Server 2003 System Monitor enables you to measure the performance of your Windows server (you can also monitor other computers on the network). System Monitor looks at such hardware performance parameters as processor utilization, drive performance, and memory usage. Each item (such as the processor) that can be analyzed using the System Monitor is referred to as an *object*.

A performance data item that can be measured for a particular object is called a *counter*. For example, the processor (an object) has a number of counters that you can view, including the % Processor Time and the Interrupts/Sec counters.

Using counters to analyze the various performance aspects of a particular hardware component (an object) enables you to determine whether a piece of hardware on a server (such as the processor or hard drive) has become a bottleneck in terms of server performance.

The System Monitor can display the data as a graph, a histogram (a horizontal or vertical bar graph format), or a report. You can set and view counter logs, create reports using log files, and create alerts that are activated when the monitored hardware (such as a drive, a processor, or memory) reaches a usage level that you have defined as a threshold. We discuss how you create performance alerts later in the hour.

You set the performance counters that are viewed in the System Monitor Details pane. You select a particular object and then add the counters related to that object that you want to monitor. In the next section, we take a look at adding object counters.

Adding Objects to the Monitor

Objects can be added to the System Monitor using the Add button (+) on the Monitor toolbar. Click the Add button; the Add Counters dialog box appears (see Figure 20.2).

> You can also open the Add Counters dialog box by right-clicking the graph or the legend at the bottom of the graph and selecting Add Counters from the shortcut menu.

20

The Add Counters dialog box enables you to select where the counters are located (on the local computer or other computer on the network) and which performance object you want to add a counter for. Each performance object, such as Processor, has a number of performance counters. Each of these counters measures the object's performance using different parameters.

FIGURE 20.2

The Add Counters dialog box is used to add counters to the System Monitor.

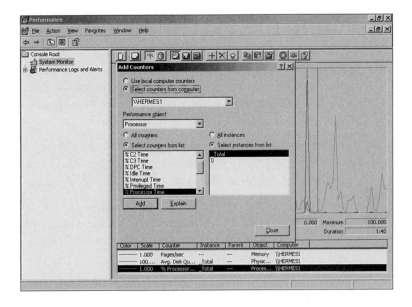

 By default, three counters appear in the System Monitor Details pane: Pages/Sec (monitoring virtual memory or paging usage), Av. Disk Queue Length (monitoring disk usage), and % Processor Time (monitoring the processor).

A number of different options are available in the Add Counters dialog box (almost too many). For clarity, some of these options are listed and defined in Table 20.1.

TABLE 20.1 Add Counters Dialog Box Options

Use Local Computer Counters	Provides a list of counters for the local computer.
Select Counters from Computer	A drop-down box is used to select the computer to be monitored.
All Counters	All counters for the object will be selected.
Performance Object	A drop-down list for selecting the object.
Select Counters from List	Provides a list of counters for the current object.
All Instances	Selects all instances of a particular object, such as viewing aggregate drive performance rather than a particular drive.

When you are ready to add a particular counter, select the counter and then click the Add button. If you want to view an explanation of a particular counter, click the counter and then click the Explain button. You can add any number of counters; however, remember that in Graph view, a large number of counters gives rise to a very busy (and confusing) graph.

When you have finished adding the appropriate counters, click the Close button. When you close the Add Counters dialog box, you are returned to the System Monitor. Your new counters appear on the graph.

Each counter that you add to the graph is assigned a different graph color. This enables you to monitor multiple counters on the graph.

Remote performance monitoring is nothing more than selecting performance objects and counters that are on a remote server on the network. Selecting the computer to be monitored is handled in the Add Counters dialog box.

Although the graph provides a visual look at your counters, you can view statistics for a particular counter by selecting the counter name in the legend at the bottom of the graph. The last instance measured (Instance), an average, a minimum, a maximum, and the duration (monitoring time) are provided directly below the graph for the selected counter.

You can highlight a particular counter by selecting the counter in the legend and then clicking the Highlight button on the toolbar. This turns the graph lines white so that they are easily viewed. Click the Highlight button a second time to turn off highlighting.

You can also delete counters from the graph. Select the counter in the legend area and then click the Delete button on the Graph toolbar. If you want to remove all the counters on the Graph, click the New Counter Set button on the toolbar.

20

To clear the current activity on the chart in the Details pane (but not remove the current counters), click the Clear Display button on the toolbar.

Adding counters is a simple process, but understanding what the various counters mean is another story. We'll look at some of the counters that you might want to use in the System Monitor and how the values that they provide give you insight into the performance of a particular object (coming up later in this hour).

To clear the graph (all those colored lines) but keep the current counters and allow them to continue to accumulate data, click the Clear Display button on the toolbar.

Viewing Performance Data

The default view for the System Monitor is Graph view. It provides real-time data using a line graph plotted to an x-axis of time and a y-axis that relates to the particular counter that you are using (such as %use, where the chart would plot from 0 to 100%). Two other views are available: Histogram view and Report view.

Using the Histogram View

Histogram view provides a bar-graph view of each counter that you add to the chart. To switch to Histogram view, click the View Histogram button on the toolbar.

This view is useful for comparing different objects and their overall affect on computer performance. Figure 20.3 shows a histogram displaying the default System Monitor counters.

FIGURE 20.3

The histogram is useful for comparing overall performance effects.

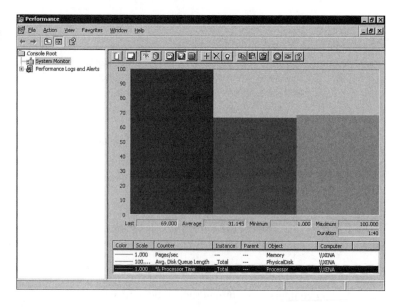

Using the Report View

Report view enables you to see the various counter statistics (in real time) as a text report that lists each counter. To switch to Report view, click the View Report button on the toolbar. The chart and Histogram view give you a visual look at your performance counters, but Report view provides actual running statistics (see Figure 20.4).

FIGURE 20.4

Report view provides running statistics for the counters.

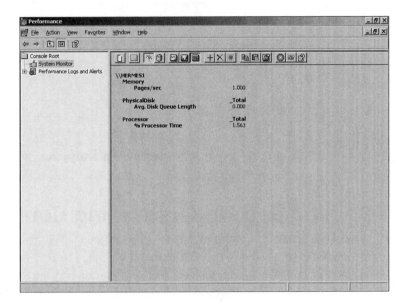

Changing Counter Attributes

You can customize the look of a chart or histogram in the System Monitor by changing the colors associated with a particular counter or counters. A number of settings related to the System Monitor are found in the System Monitor Properties dialog box.

Right-click anywhere on your graph or histogram, and then select Properties from the shortcut menu. The System Monitor Properties dialog box appears, as shown in Figure 20.5.

The Data tab enables you to add or remove counters from the System Monitor and change the graph and histogram color, line width, line style, and scale used. After changing any of these parameters, click OK to close the dialog box.

20

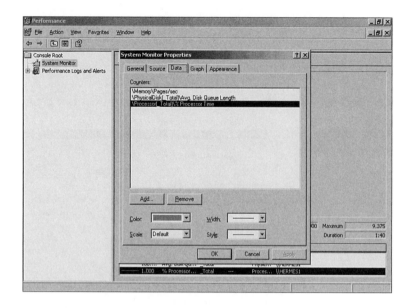

FIGURE 20.5
*You can change
counter attributes
using the System
Monitor Properties
dialog box.*

Selecting and Understanding Counters

Selecting counters that will actually tell you something about the performance of your servers and help you understand what they are telling you is an extremely important aspect of using the System Monitor. As already mentioned, the System Monitor provides counters for hardware objects such as hard drives and processors, and includes counters for services that you have installed such as DNS and WINS. Counters are also available to track protocol performance such as IP4 and NWlink.

Because hardware can often be a limiting factor in server performance, let's look at some of the counters that you will want to watch as you assess the performance of a server's processor, hard drives, and memory.

Useful Processor Counters

A potential bottleneck on a server is the processor. That is why high-end servers support multiple processors. The bottleneck arises because the processor can't keep up with all the system calls that it gets from different software processes running on the server.

Counters that can help you track processor performance are listed here:

- **%Processor Time**—This counter (found under the Processor object) is a measure of the time that the processor is executing a nonidle thread. If it is consistently around 75–80%, you might need to upgrade the processor on the server (or add another processor if the motherboard allows for dual processing).

- **Interrupts/sec**—If this counter (found under the Processor object) increases beyond 3,500 (it's the average number of interrupt calls that the processor is receiving from hardware devices, such as a network card or modem) and the %Processor Time counter does not, your problem might not be your processor, but a device that is sending spurious interrupts to the processor (such as a bad network card or SCSI card). This can be caused by the device itself or by the driver you are using for the device.

> Make sure you are using the most up-to-date drivers for hardware devices on a server. This can negate issues with interrupt overload.

- **Processor Queue Length**—This counter, found under the System object, measures the number of threads waiting to be processed. If it reaches a value of 10 or more, the processor might be a bottleneck. This means that you can go to a faster processor or upgrade to a multiprocessor motherboard on the server.

Useful Disk Counters

Another hardware device that can be a potential bottleneck on a server is the computer's physical drives. Not only is the space available important, but the drive's read/write speed is also an issue. Counters that you might want to monitor related to disk performance are listed here (the object type precedes the counter name):

- **Logical Disk, %Disk Time**—This counter (found under the Logical Disk object) shows the percentage of elapsed time that the drive is busy with read/write functions. If the counter consistently reads around 90%, the drive is having problems. You can defragment the drive, replace the drive, or configure a volume stripe to replace the drive (stripe sets are faster than a single disk).

- **Disk Reads/sec, or Disk Writes/sec**—These counters are found under the PhysicalDisk object. Check the manufacturer's specifications for the drive. If the I/O operations shown by this counter are lower than the specifications, the drive is having problems. Defragmenting might help remedy the problem.

- **%Free Space**—This counter, found under the Logical Disk object, indicates free space on a volume. If this counter goes below 20%, you need to increase the volume size or put a larger drive in the system.

- **Current Disk Queue Length**—The counter under the Logical Disk object measures the number of outstanding or queued requests for the volume at a particular moment in time (when the measurement is taken). If the average value is more than 2, disk waits are slowing down access to the volume. You can install a faster drive or consider using a stripe set or using a volume on another server.

20

Useful Memory Counters

Another key resource on network servers is memory (RAM). More memory (above the
Windows Server 2003 suggested memory specification of 256MB) is always better.
Remember that when a Windows server uses its entire RAM, it resorts to the paging file
on the hard drive (we use to call this virtual memory); this means that data dropped to
the paging file must be reloaded into RAM to be used. To track memory issues, use these
counters:

> All the counters presented in the Memory list are found under the Memory
> object.

- **Available Bytes**—This counter is a measure of the physical memory available to
  running processes. If it consistently falls to less than 4MB, you need more memory
  on the server.

- **Pages/Sec**—This counter measures the number of times the computer must rely on
  the paging file (dumping items in RAM to the hard drive temporarily). This event
  is known as a *page fault*. If this counter consistently reads at 20 on the System
  Monitor, you should add more RAM. Excessive page faults can cause system-wide
  delays in terms of server access.

- **Committed Bytes**—This counter shows the amount of RAM being used and the
  amount of space that will be needed for the paging file if the data had to be moved
  to the disk. You should see a value on this counter that is less than the RAM
  installed on the server. If the value is more than the RAM, you are using the paging
  file too often; add more memory.

Creating Performance Logs

A *performance log* is data that is collected or logged related to a selected counter or
counters. Performance logs enable you to monitor local or remote computer resources
and then save that information in the log file. The log can then be viewed using the
Performance Monitor (just as you view real-time data), or the log can be imported into
spreadsheet software such as Microsoft Excel. Log files can be set up to collect the data
in comma- or tab-delimited files (making them easy to import).

Two types of performance logs exist: counter logs and trace logs. A *counter log* collects
the data set from the counter or counters that you select when you configure the log
(similar to selecting counters in the System Monitor and viewing their real-time activity).

When you "play back" a counter log, it appears in the System Monitor the same as real-time counter data (as a graph, histogram, or report). Counter logs can include any number of counters from any number of performance objects. Counter logs monitor data at set intervals.

A *trace log* does not collect data using counters; instead, it tracks data continuously monitoring a particular process as dictated by a *trace provider*. A trace provider (a set of code) is built into the Windows Server 2003 kernel and enables you to log certain processes such as a Windows kernel trace and Active Directory: Kerberos functions. Some software vendors provide their own trace providers, which enable you to monitor additional processes related to their software. Trace logs monitor data continuously.

Creating a Counter Log

You will use a counter log to collect data related to hardware and service processes on your server. Next we look at how you configure a counter log (trace logs are configured in an almost identical manner, but you will typically use them to a lesser degree).

 Windows Server 2003 provides a ready-made counter log named System Overview. It includes counters to measure memory, disk, and processor performance. You can "play" with this counter log file to get a feel for the type of counters you might want to include in your own log files.

To create a counter log, perform the following steps:

1. In the Performance Monitor window, click the Performance Logs and Alerts icon.
2. In the Details pane, right-click the Counter Logs icon and select New Log Settings on the shortcut menu. The New Log Settings box appears.
3. Type a name for your new counter and then click OK. The Log dialog box appears labeled with the name that you entered in the New Log Settings dialog box (see Figure 20.6).
4. A default log name appears in the current log filename box. If you want to change the filename, type your preference.
5. To add counters, click the Add button on the General tab of the dialog box. The Add Counters dialog box appears, as shown in Figure 20.7.

20

FIGURE 20.6

The Log dialog box is used to select the counters for your counter log.

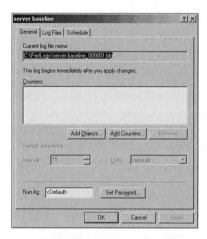

FIGURE 20.7

Select the objects and counters that you want to include in the log file.

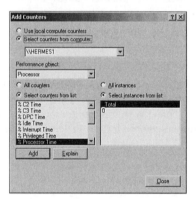

6. You can select objects such as the processor or memory using the Performance Object drop-down list. After you've selected a particular object, use the Counter list to select a counter and then click to add the counter to the log. Repeat the process until all counters have been selected for the log file.

7. Click Close. You are turned to the General tab of the Log Properties dialog box. The counters that you selected appear in a list on the General tab.

8. On the General tab, you can also set the interval used for data sampling and the unit of time used for the interval. The default is 15 seconds. The unit types available are seconds, minutes, hours, and days. After you select a unit (such as minutes), use the Interval box to determine how often (such as every 20 minutes).

9. Another aspect of creating a counter log is to specify the file type used for the log file. Click the Log Files tab of the dialog box.

10. Use the Log File Type drop-down box to select a file type (the default is Binary File). You can save the log files in several different formats, including text files (comma- or tab-delimited), which can easily be opened in other software packages (such as Excel or Word) and SQL database format.

11. If you want to end the log file's name with a date, select the End Files Name With drop-down list and select a date format. By default, log files also are numbered sequentially starting with 1 (see Figure 20.8).

FIGURE 20.8

Select the file type for the log file and choose a date format for the filename.

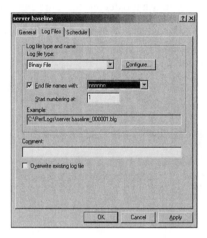

12. Almost finished: There's one more set of parameters to set for the log. Click the Schedule tab on the log's Properties dialog box. Set a time and date to start the log (see Figure 20.9) in the Start log area. Also set a time interval (such as three days) or a specific time and date to stop the log's recording process.

FIGURE 20.9

Set the start and stop parameters for your log file.

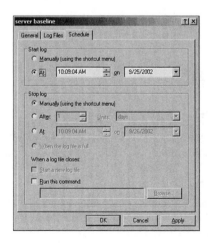

20

You can also choose to start and stop the log recording manually using the appropriate Manually option button on the Schedule tab. You would then start and stop the log file using its shortcut menu.

13. After you have set all the various parameters for the log file (using the different tabs on the dialog box), click OK. A message appears that the folder designated for the log file must be created (if you use the default filename and path settings). Click Yes.

The new counter log that you created can be accessed by double-clicking the Counter Logs icon in the Details pane of the Performance Monitor console. Figure 20.10 shows a server baseline counter log that has been created. When a log is not accumulating data, it is red. When it becomes active (either because of the start time you selected or because you started it manually), it is green.

FIGURE 20.10

Your log files are listed in the Details pane.

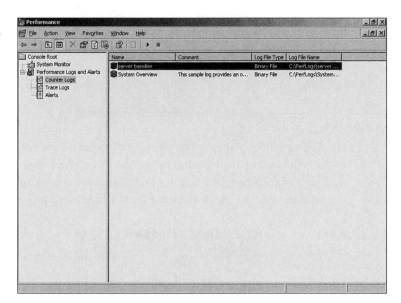

Viewing a Counter Log

After you have recorded a log file, you can "play it back" using the System Monitor. If you saved the log file as text delimited, you can open it in an application such as Excel.

Windows Server 2003 supports log files in excess of 1GB, so you can record counter data for longer periods of time than in previous versions of the Windows server products.

To actually "read" a log file, you use the System Monitor. However, you must add the counters that you used in the counter log to the System Monitor to actually see the data points. You can add these counters before or after loading the log file (it might be easier to add the counters after loading the log file because only the objects and counters that you used for the counter log are available). Without the appropriate counter loaded, you cannot see any of the log file's data.

1. To open the counter log file, click the View Log Data button on the System Monitor's toolbar. The System Monitor Properties dialog box opens with the Source tab selected, as shown in Figure 20.11.

FIGURE 20.11

Use the Source tab to specify the log you want to view.

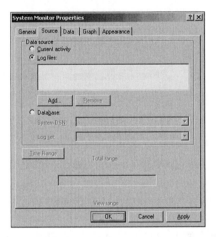

2. Select the Log files option button and then click the Add button. The Select Log file dialog box opens (the default path is the perflogs folder). Select the counter log file that you want to load, and then click the OK button.

3. If you want to select a particular time range in the log to view, click the Time Range button. A slider bar appears on the Source tab. Drag the slider bar to bracket the time range that you want to view.

4. When you have completed your selections, click the Close button. You are returned to the System Monitor; you can view the data in any of the views available. Figure 20.12 shows a short log file of a server that is having some major performance problems.

20

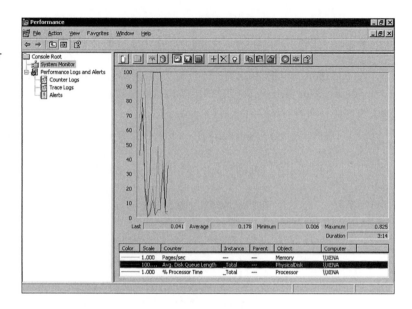

FIGURE 20.12
Performance logs enable you to log your server's performance over a period of time.

Creating Performance Alerts

Another useful tool that the Performance Monitor console provides is the performance alert. A *performance alert* actually notifies you when a predefined threshold has been reached on a particular counter. Alerts can let you know when a volume's space is becoming dangerously full or when a server's memory is being taxed beyond a certain limit (for example, you could set up an alert using the pages/sec counter).

Performance alerts are configured in a similar fashion to counter logs. Performance alerts do not log information, so they can't be "played back" in the System Monitor. Alerts can be used, however, to trigger the recording of an event in a particular counter log file. Alerts can also be configured to send a network message to a particular computer on the network when a threshold has been reached or to send an alert to the Event Viewer's application log (we discuss the Event Viewer in this next section of this hour).

To create a performance alert, follow these steps:

1. Double-click the Performance Logs and Alerts icon in the Performance Monitor console. Right-click the Alerts icon (in the Details pane) and select New Alert Settings.

2. The New Alert Settings dialog box appears. Type a name for the alert and then click OK. The Properties dialog box for the new alert appears, as shown in Figure 20.13.

FIGURE 20.13

Set the properties for your new alert.

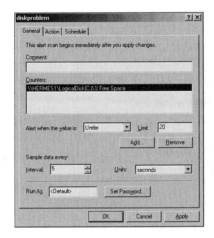

3. Select the Add button to choose the objects and their counters that will be used by the alert. For example, to be alerted when a specified amount of free space remains on a volume, you would add the LogicalDisk object's % Free Space counter to the dialog box.

4. After you've specified the counters for the alert, you are returned to the Properties dialog box. You can now set the thresholds for the counters contained in the alert. Select a counter and then use the Alert when the value is drop-down box to select either Over or Under as the deciding factor for the threshold amount that you set. Then type the threshold amount in the value box.

5. To set the data-sampling interval, select a unit of time and an interval.

6. To set what the alert should do when your configured threshold is reached, click the Action tab on the dialog box.

7. By default, the alert sends an event that is logged in the Event Viewer's application log. If you would rather (or also) have a network message sent by the alert, click the Send a Network Message To check box and then type a computer name in the box provided.

8. A check box is also provided on the Action tab to have a particular performance log started when the alert threshold is reached. A check box to start a particular program when the alert threshold is reached, is also provided (for example, when you have poor seek time on a disk, you might want to start the Disk Defragmenter). Figure 20.14 shows the Action tab.

9. A Schedule tab is also provided on the alert's Properties dialog box. You can select to have the alert start its counters on a particular time and date, and run for a particular duration (just as you do for performance logs). Or, you can choose to start and stop the alert manually.

10. After setting the appropriate parameters for your alert, click OK.

20

FIGURE 20.14

Select the actions that you want the alert to take.

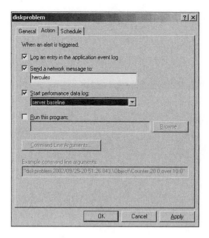

As already discussed, the alert can be started automatically (at a certain time and date), or you can start the alert manually. To view the alert, expand the Performance Logs and Alerts node and then click the Alert node. Alerts that you have created appear in the Details pane.

To start an alert, right-click the alert and select Start. When the alert reaches the threshold that you set, you will perform the action or actions you specified on the Action tab of the Properties dialog box. For example, if you specified that an alert should be sent to the applications log of the Event Viewer, an event will appear. Figure 20.15 shows the properties of an event triggered by an alert (we discuss Event Viewer events in the next section) .

FIGURE 20.15

Alerts can send events to the Event Viewer's application log.

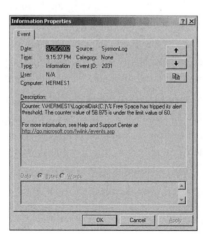

Working with the Event Viewer

A huge number of things are happening at any one time on a server: Users are logging in and accessing files, drives are spinning away, and processors are trying to make sense of it all. Each of these instances is considered an event. Being able to monitor these events and use them to interpret the health of your servers is an important aspect of administering a Windows Server 2003 network.

As its name suggests, the Event Viewer is used to view events. Although it is more of a passive tool (it doesn't supply you with the configuration possibilities provided by the Performance Monitor console), it does give you access to a great deal of information. It accumulates events in a number of log files: Event Viewer can help you monitor hardware, application, service and security issues.

By default, three logs are provided in the Event Viewer to track events:

- **Application log**—This log records events about the various applications running on the system. The developer typically presets these events in the software. The application log also records alerts configured in the System Monitor.

- **Security log**—This log records events related to the audit policies that you configure in Group Policy (Group Policy is discussed in Hour 11, "Understanding Group Policy and User Profiles"), such as the auditing of file access or the logon of a particular user or group of users.

- **System Log**—This log provides log entries based on a number of Windows Server 2003 presets. This includes information on things such as driver failures and services that fail to load. Anything to do with services or system resources can show up in this log.

 Additional event logs appear in the Event Viewer when you have installed additional services on your Windows Server 2003. For example, DNS events are recorded in the DNS Server log. Domain controllers have two additional logs: the Directory Service and File Replication.

A system of icons is used to classify the type of event that has been recorded in a particular event log. In the system log and the application log, you will find the following event categories (each represented by a different icon in the Event Viewer) :

- **The Information icon**—Denotes the logging of successful system events and other processes

- **The Warning icon**—Shows a noncritical error on the system

- **The Error icon**—Indicates the failure of a major function (such as a driver failure)

20

Figure 20.16 shows Information, Warning, and Error icons in the system log.

FIGURE 20.16

*Icons are used to iden-
tify the type of event
recorded in a log file.*

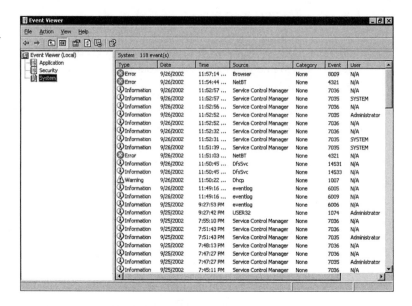

Two additional icons are found in the security log:

- **The Success Audit icon**—Shows that a security access event was successful (such as the access of a certain folder or file on the network)

- **The Failure Audit icon**—Shows that an audited security event failed (such as the failure of a user logon) .

Running the Event Viewer

To open the Event Viewer, select Start, point at Administrative Tools, and then select Event Viewer (you can also run the Event Viewer from the Run dialog box using the command eventvwr). The Event Viewer Window appears, as shown in Figure 20.17.

The Event Viewer runs as a Management console snap-in and so contains a tree pane on the left and a details area on the right. The Application, Security, and System log icons appear in the snap-in tree along with any other event logs that have been included because of services that you have installed on your server (for example, Figure 20.17 shows a DNS Server log that is included because DNS has been installed on this server).

FIGURE 20.17

The Event Monitor enables you to view events recorded in the various log files.

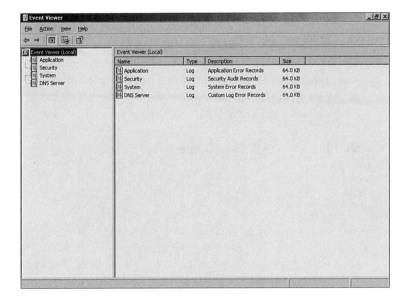

Viewing Log Events

To view one of the logs in the Event Monitor, select the log's icon in the tree pane. The events recorded by the particular log file appear in the Details pane. For example, if you click the application log, any events related to system processes are recorded.

For example in Figure 20.18, two Error icons and an Information icon appear in the application log.

FIGURE 20.18

Recorded events appear in each of the Event Viewer logs.

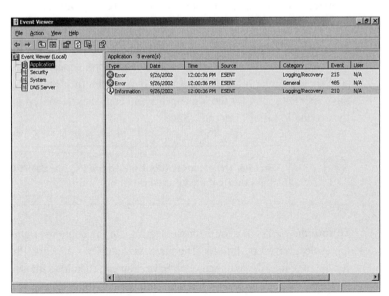

20

Notice that each event is labeled with the same date and time, so it appears that these three events are probably related.

To view the details or properties of a particular event in a log, double click on and event's icon. The Information Properties dialog box for the event opens. Figure 20.19 shows the properties of an Information icon that detailed an event related to the backup of the WINS database on the server (WINS is discussed in Hour 17, "Understanding WINS").

FIGURE 20.19

You can view the Properties of a logged event.

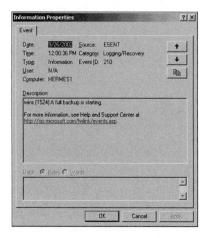

Clearing and Saving Log Events

Over time, a number of events build up in the various log files. You can clear the events from a particular log and (if you want) save the log events to a file for later inspection or reference.

In the Event Viewer snap-in, right-click any of the log icons in the tree pane. Select Clear All Events from the shortcut menu. A message box appears asking you if you want to save the particular log before clearing. If you want to save the log file, click Yes. The Save As dialog box for the log appears and enables you to designate a filename and path to save the log file. Then click Save.

> To clear the events without saving the log file, select Clear All Events on the log's shortcut menu; then click No.

To save the events in a log without clearing the log contents, right-click a log icon and then select Save Log File As. The Save As dialog box appears. Provide a name and a path for the new log file, and then click Save. You can then load the saved event log file into the Event Viewer for later reference (right-click a log icon and select Open Log File).

Using the Event Viewer on a regular basis will help you keep your server and your network up and running. Becoming familiar with the different types of events that are logged will help you get a handle on potential server problems before they become a major meltdown.

Using the Network Monitor

Another Windows Server 2003 administrative tool is *Network Monitor*. This tool enables you to view what is actually taking place on the network and to see how your network protocols are running. Network Monitor can capture data frames (data packets) on the network that it both sends and receives. Network Monitor can look at data traveling on your local area network and also over remote access connections (remote access is discussed in Hour 18, "Using Routing and Remote Access").

One thing that you should be aware of is that Network Monitor that is included with Windows Server 2003 does not have all the capabilities of the full-blown Network Monitor that is supplied with the Microsoft Systems Management Server (the version that ships with .NET Server is actually called Network Monitor 2.1 Light). The Windows Server 2003 Network Monitor allows you to capture only frames that are sent to or from your Server. The SMS version allows you to also capture data on remote computers on the network. Now, having said that, you will find that the Windows Server 2003 Network Monitor can still provide you with a great deal of useful information related to network traffic.

Installing the Network Monitor

Network Monitor is installed using the Add or Remove Programs utility in the Windows Control Panel:

1. Click the Start button, point at the Control Panel, and then click Add/Remove Programs. The Add/Remove Programs window opens. Click the Add/Remove Windows Components icon in the left pane of the Add/Remove Programs window. The Windows Component Wizard appears.

2. In the Windows Component Wizard, select Management and Monitoring Tools and then click Details. In the Management and Monitoring Tools list (see Figure 20.20), click the Network Monitor Tools check box.

3. After selecting Network Monitor tools, click OK. Then click Next on the Windows Component Wizard screen. Network Monitor will be installed.

4. Click Finish to close the wizard. You can also close the Add or Remove Programs window.

20

FIGURE 20.20

Select Network Monitor Tools to install Network Monitor.

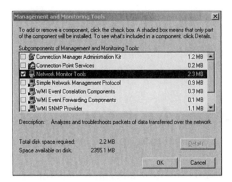

When you install Network Monitor on your server, the Network Monitor driver is installed in the Local Area Connection Properties box (along with your network clients and protocols). This enables Network Monitor to capture data frames using the network interface card.

Collecting Data with Network Monitor

After you have installed Network Monitor, you can begin to collect data. To use the Network Monitor, follow these steps:

1. Click the Start button, point at Administrative Tools, and then click Network Monitor. The Network Monitor window opens.

   The first time you open Network Monitor, the Select a network dialog box opens (see Figure 20.21). It asks you to select the network to monitor. This can be your local area network or a VPN or remote-access dial-up connection.

FIGURE 20.21

Select the network connection to be monitored by Network Monitor.

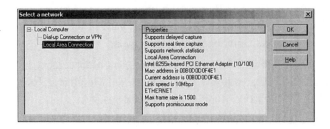

2. Click the Local Computer node in the left pane of the dialog box. Then select the network connection that you want to monitor. Click OK to close the dialog box. You are now in the Network Monitor windows, which will not contain any data until you capture it. The captured network data will be displayed as a graph and as statistics.

You can access the Select a network dialog box at any time in Network Monitor by selecting the Capture menu and then choosing Networks.

3. To start capturing data in Network Monitor, select Capture and then select Start. Network Monitor begins to acquire data, as shown in Figure 20.22.

FIGURE 20.22

Select the network connection to be monitored by Network Monitor.

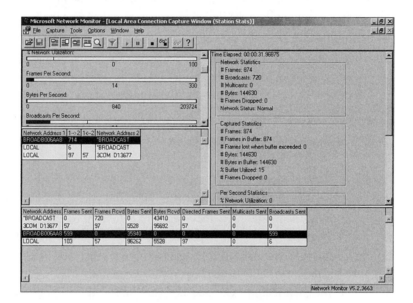

As data is captured by Network Monitor (using your network card), the various areas of the Monitor window provide you with different capture information and statistics. The Graph pane provides horizontal bar charts that show network activity as you capture your packets:

- **% Network Utilization**—Shows the percentage of available network resources that the current capture uses

- **Frames Per Second**—Shows the number of frames that are transmitted on the network per second

- **Bytes Per Second**—Shows the number of bytes transmitted on the network per second

- **Broadcasts Per Second**—Shows the number of messages transmitted to all devices on the network per second

- **Multicasts Per Second**—shows the number of multicasts that the network transmits every second

20

The Session Statistics pane provides information on each session captured, with a *session* being a communication between two computers (your server and another computer) or devices on the network. The first column in this pane provides the hardware address (the MAC address of the device's network interface card) of the device that is sending the packets.

The second column provides the number of frames (packets) sent to the receiving device from the sending device during the communication. The third column shows the number of frames sent back to the initiating device. And the last column in the Session Statistics pane provides the hardware address of the receiving device participating in the session.

The Station Statistics pane appears below the Session Statistics pane in the Network Monitor window. It provides statistics related to your computer's activity on the network. A number of different columns of information appear in this pane as follows:

- **Network Address**—Provides the network address that frames were captured from.
- **Frames Sent**—Provides the number of frames that were sent from the network address appearing in column 1.
- **Frames Rcvd**—Shows the number of frames received (by the local computer) from the device hardware address appearing in the first column.
- **Bytes Sent**—Displays the number of bytes sent by the device, whose hardware address is listed in the Network Address column (the first column in the pane).
- **Bytes Rcvd**—Displays the number of bytes that were received from the network address listed in the Network Address column.
- **Directed Frames Sent**—Shows the number of nonbroadcast and nonmulticast frames that were sent over the network by the device (whose hardware address is listed in the first column of the record).
- **Multicasts Sent**—Shows the number of times the address listed in the Network Address column has sent frames to a subset of computers on the network (a *multicast* is a broadcast message to certain computers on the network).
- **Broadcasts Sent**—Shows the number of times the address listed in the Network Address column has sent broadcast messages to all computers on the network (a *broadcast* message is a message sent to all the devices on the network by a particular computer).

The Total Statistics pane (which appears on the right side of the Network Monitor window) provides an overview of network activity. It gives you information, such as the number of frames sent (the total sent during the capture session), the number of broadcasts, and the total number of bytes transmitted.

To stop a capture, select the Capture menu and then select Stop. If you want to save the statistics from the capture session, click the File Save As button on the Network Monitor toolbar. The Save As dialog box opens; provide a location and filename for the capture data. You can then open this data set in Network Monitor if you want to look at the data later.

Filtering Data

You can create filters for Network Monitor that enable you to capture on certain types of frames. These filters can be used to capture frames from selected network protocols or to capture frames from a particular computer on the network.

To create a filter, follow these steps:

1. Select Capture, Filter. The Capture Filter dialog box opens (see Figure 20.23).

FIGURE 20.23

You can filter the data frames captured by Network Monitor.

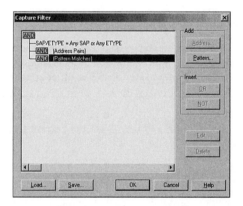

2. Double-click the SAP/ETYPE= designator in the Capture filter dialog box. The Capture Filter's SAPS and ETYPES dialog box opens. This dialog box provides a list of all the protocols that have been enabled for capture.

3. To disable a particular protocol (meaning to cut down on the type of frames that will be collected when you use the filter), select a protocol in the list and click the Disable button. Disabled protocols are listed in the bottom pane of the dialog box.

4. When you have completed disabling protocols to filter the data frames collected, click the OK button. You are returned to the Capture filter dialog box.

5. To preclude certain computers on the network from the capture, double-click the AND (address pairs) designator in the dialog box. The Address Expression dialog box opens.

20

6. The Station 2 pane is a list of computers and other devices that had frames captured the first time you ran Network Monitor. To exclude a particular device, click the device in the Station 2 pane and then click the Exclude option button. When you have completed your exclusions, click the OK button.

> Don't exclude items in the Station 1 pane. These refer to your server that is running Network Monitor.

7. To save the filter, click the Save button. The Save Capture Filter dialog box appears. Provide a name for the filter and click Save.

8. After you have set up the filter (you don't have to save it to run it on a one-time basis), click OK.

> The Capture Filter dialog box is also used to load capture filters that you have saved. You click the Load button in the dialog box and then choose a filter in the Load Capture Filter dialog box that appears.

Now you can run Network Monitor, and it will use the current filter to determine which frames your server should capture.

Viewing Capture Data

The Network Monitor window provides more than enough data collection and statistics areas. You can list all the frames captured in one list. Select the Capture menu and then select Display Capture Data. The Data Capture window opens (see Figure 20.24).

Using the Capture window makes it easier for you to identify which devices were involved during a session. This window also provides you with data on the protocol that generated the frame.

To view the details related to a particular captured frame, double-click the capture in the Capture window. An overlay window appears at the bottom of the Capture window, providing the frame in hexadecimal format with the frame type and other details related to the frame listed above.

To view the details of another captured frame, double-click that frame in the Capture list. When you have completed viewing the Capture list, click the window's Close button to return to the Network Monitor window.

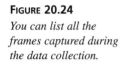

FIGURE 20.24

You can list all the frames captured during the data collection.

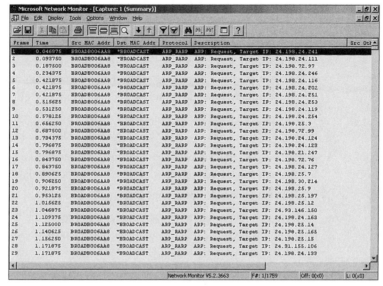

Because you can save and then open different capture sessions in Network Monitor, it makes sense to create a baseline capture session when the network is first up and running. This enables you to compare future capture session data with your baseline and to identify problems related to network traffic.

Summary

The System Monitor provides you with the capability of monitoring server hardware and services. You can choose any number of performance objects and counters using System Monitor as you track system performance.

Performance logs, counter logs, and trace logs enable you to log server performance data. You can then view the logs in System Monitor. Performance alerts enable you to select objects and counters, and specify a threshold for a particular hardware or service counter. When this threshold is reached, the alert registers an event in the Windows Event Viewer's application log. The Event Viewer enables you to view events that have been logged in the system, application, and security logs or other logs that apply to specific services that you have installed on the Windows Server 2003.

Network Monitor is used to capture frames on the network. Information related to captured frames can then be viewed in the monitor window. Capture filters can also be created that enable you to select which types of frames you want to capture and the computers that you want to capture frames from.

20

Q&A

Q How does the System Monitor provide performance data?

A You must set object counters in the System Monitor to view performance data. After a counter such as a processor or a memory counter has been added to the System Monitor, the data can be viewed as a graph, as a histogram, or in a report format.

Q How can counter data from the System Monitor be saved for later viewing?

A A performance log can be created using any counters. The data is then saved in the log file and can be loaded into the System Monitor for later viewing.

Q What is the purpose of performance alerts?

A Performance alerts can be used to trigger an event in the Event Viewer's application log. The alert event is tied to a specific performance threshold, such as available disk space.

Q What type of log events can be viewed in the Event Viewer?

A The Event Viewer maintains an application log, a security log, and a system log. These log files contain events related to system and application processes on the server. Additional logs might also be available on the server, depending on the services that you have installed on the server. Events found in the log files are identified by icons, including the Information icon, the Warning icon, and the Error icon.

Q How can data frames sent or received by the local computer running Windows Server 2003 be captured?

A The Network Monitor provided by the Windows Server 2003 operating system enables you to capture data frames sent and received by the server. This enables you to view a number of statistics related to the computer's network communications, including the frames transmitted, the network address of sending computers, and the number of frames received by the local computer.

HOUR 21

Working with Virtual Private Networking and IP Security

As you learned in Hour 18, "Using Routing and Remote Access," Windows Server 2003 provides you with the capability to configure a remote access server that allows dial-in clients to access network resources. Dial-in accounts, however, require a modem on the client side and a modem (or modems) on the server side.

With many Internet users now taking advantage of high-speed connection services (such as DSL and broadband), another remote access strategy, the virtual private network (VPN), is gaining popularity. In this hour, we look at VPNs and a strategy for securing IP traffic called IP Security (typically shortened to IPSec).

In this hour, the following topics are covered:

- Understanding virtual private networks
- Creating a VPN server

- Configuring VPN clients
- Managing VPN
- Working with the IP Security protocol
- Managing and monitoring IPSec

Understanding Virtual Private Networks (VPNs)

An alternative to remote access via dial-in (which is discussed in Hour 18) is the virtual private network. Because most computer users either already have some type of connection to the Internet from any number of Internet service providers both at home and on the road (and often have a connection speed faster than a dial-up modem), you can take advantage of this in how you provide remote access to your remote clients.

A *virtual private network* (VPN) is a secure and private way for a remote user connected to the Internet to connect to your private corporate network. In effect, you are creating a private communication line over an otherwise public communication system. VPN is also useful in that users on business trips, for example, can use local phone connections to an ISP instead of using long-distance connections with a RAS dial-in server.

VPN uses a tunneling protocol that provides the secure connection over the Internet between the client and the VPN server. You can take advantage of VPNs for remote client connections and for connecting different Windows Server 2003 network sites into one seamless network.

The VPN Tunneling Protocols

VPN uses tunneling protocols to provide the secure "tunnel" through an unsecured, public network such as the Internet. In effect, a point-to-point connection is made between the client and the VPN server. Windows Server 2003 provides two tunneling protocols for VPN:

- **Point-to-Point Tunneling Protocol (PPTP)**—PPTP is an extension of PPP (the Point-to-Point Protocol used for many dial-up Internet connections). This tunneling protocol encapsulates network data packets (such as IP or IPX) in encrypted PPP data packets. PPTP requires IP communication between the client and the server. Authentication protocols such as CHAP, MS-CHAP, and EAP are used to provide security to the connection (these protocols are defined in Hour 18). PPTP uses Microsoft Point-to-Point Encryption (MPPE) for data encryption.

- **Layer 2 Tunneling Protocol (L2TP)**—L2TP is an industry-standard tunneling protocol that can also be used to create VPN connections over the Internet. L2TP does not require IP communication between the client and the server, as PPTP does. This means that L2TP can be used with other media than the Internet, such as X.25, Frame Relay, and Asynchronous Transfer Mode (ATM). Connections made using L2TP can be secured using IP Security Protocol (IPSec), discussed later in this hour.

Both PPTP and L2TP are automatically installed on computers running Windows 2000, Windows XP, and Windows Server 2003, which makes it easy to configure both clients and servers as VPN clients. VPN servers are configured in the Windows Server 2003 environment using the Routing and Remote Access Service.

Creating a VPN Server

A VPN server is created and configured using the Windows Server 2003 Routing and Remote Access Service (RRAS). The RRAS Setup Wizard walks you through the steps of enabling RRAS for VPN. To be configured as a VPN server, the server needs to contain two network cards. This makes it a multihomed computer (a fancy name for a computer with two or more network cards), which could also be configured as a router or as an Internet Connection Server (both of which are discussed in this book).

One network card provides the IP address that the VPN clients will use to connect to the VPN server (which can be a NIC that is configured with a public IP address for connection to the Internet); the other network card is the VPN server's connection to the local area network.

A VPN server can be created when Routing and Remote Access is first configured on a server. Follow these steps:

1. Select Start, Administrative Tools, click Routing and Remote Access. The RRAS snap-in opens.

2. Right-click your server icon in the RRAS snap-in tree, and select Configure and Enable Routing and Remote Access. The Routing and Remote Access Server Setup Wizard appears. Click Next to bypass the opening screen.

3. The next screen supplies a list of common configurations for the RRAS service; you can install remote access via dialup and VPN, and you can install VPN and NAT and a number of other RRAS configuration possibilities. Because you are going to configure only VPN (the other services are covered separately in the appropriate hour), select Custom Configuration and then click Next to continue.

21

4. The next screen provides a list of each of the RRAS configuration possibilities, as shown in Figure 21.1 (as single entities rather than the grouped options provided by the previous wizard screen). Click the VPN access check box and then click Next to continue.

FIGURE **21.1**

Select the VPN Access option to configure the server for VPN.

5. The next screen provides a summary screen of your RRAS configuration selections (in this case, VPN). Click Finish.

6. If this is the first time that you have configured the RRAS service, a message appears asking you if you want to start the service. Click Yes.

Understanding Virtual Private Network Ports

When you configure the RRAS service for VPN (as you did using the preceding steps), ports are created that remote clients use to connect to the VPN server (or that the VPN server uses to connect to another server using an outbound connection). A *port* is a channel that provides a single point-to-point connection. Two types of ports are created: WAN Miniport (PPTP) and WAN Miniport (L2TP). By default, 128 of each of these port types are created.

PPTP and L2TP are the two tunneling protocols used by VPN. So, 128 ports are created for each of the tunneling protocols.

You can view the ports created by the RRAS configuration for VPN; expand the local server node and then click the Ports icon in the RRAS snap-in tree. The VPN ports appear in the Details pane (see Figure 21.2).

FIGURE 21.2

Ports are created for the VPN connection.

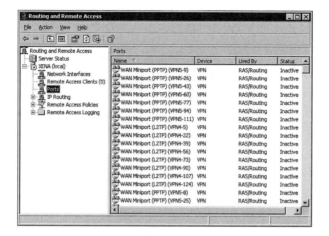

For the VPN ports to work, you must provide the IP addressthat remote users will use for the VPN connection. You can also change the number of VPN ports that are available on the RRAS server (you might find the default of 128 for each tunneling protocol inadequate if you have a large number of potential VPN connections). Right-click the Ports node and select Properties. The Ports Properties dialog box appears (see Figure 21.3).

FIGURE 21.3

You can configure VPN ports.

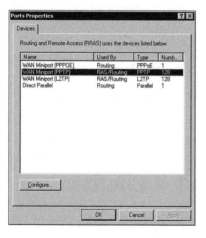

Select either WAN Miniport (PPTP) or WAN Miniport (L2TP) in the Properties dialog box, and then click the Configure button. The Configure Device dialog box for the WAN Miniport type that you selected (either PPTP or L2TP) opens.

By default, the ports are configured for inbound connections and demand-dial routing (both inbound and outbound). You can change the number of ports available using the Maximum Ports check box (see Figure 21.4). The maximum number of ports that you can configure is 1,000.

21

FIGURE **21.4**

Provide the IP address for the connection and specify the number of VPN ports.

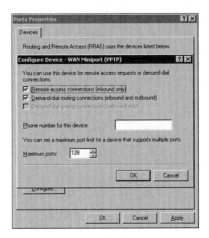

The Configure Device dialog box asks for the phone number to the device. This can be confusing because you are configuring a VPN port that provides its connection via an IP address. To configure the ports, type in the IP address of the VPN server that provides the public connection for the VPN clients. Make sure that you provide this IP address for both the PPTP and L2TP ports.

After completing the configuration of a particular port type (such as PPTP), click OK. You can now configure the other port types as needed. When you have completed the VPN port configurations, click OK to close the Ports Properties dialog box.

Obviously, the number of ports that you decide to provide for incoming connections should depend on the amount of bandwidth that you have available on your server's Internet connection. If the server is using a T1 line or other high-speed service and has a great deal of bandwidth available, you can increase the number of calls—that is, you can provide a fairly large number of VPN ports for client connections.

Configuring the VPN Client

Configuring a VPN client is actually a two-step process. First, you must enable the user's domain account for VPN access (creating domain user accounts is discussed in Hour 8, "Introducing Active Directory").

Second, you must configure the client computer for a remote connection. When the client computer attempts to connect via the VPN connection, the user's domain account is used to validate the remote access session. Let's look at enabling the user account for VPN access in the Active Directory Users and Computers snap-in; then we'll look at configuring a client computer to take advantage of a remote connection.

Enabling the Domain Account for VPN Access

The users who will connect to the domain via the VPN must have their user accounts configured for VPN access. User account configuration settings are configured in the user's Properties dialog box (although multiple accounts can be configured en masse for VPN access). Follow these steps:

1. Open the Active Directory Users and Computers snap-in (Start, Administrative Tools, Active Directory Users and Computers). Expand the Domain node and then select the Users folder in the snap-in tree.

2. Right-click the user you want to enable for remote access, and then click Properties on the shortcut menu that appears. The user's Properties dialog box appears.

3. Click the Dial-in tab of the user's Properties dialog box (see Figure 21.5). To allow access via dial-in or VPN, select the Allow access option button.

FIGURE 21.5

Enable the user account for remote access.

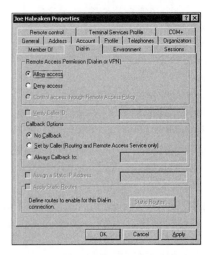

4. Click OK to close the Properties dialog box and return to the Active Directory Users and Computers snap-in.

Creating a Client Connection

The next step is to create a client connection on the remote computer. You can configure Windows 9x/ME, Windows 2000, Windows XP, and Windows Server 2003 for remote connection.

21

For a computer running Windows XP or Windows Server 2003, follow these steps:

1. Open the Control Panel and then open the Network Connections window. Double-click the New Connection Wizard. Click Next to bypass the wizard's initial screen.

2. On the next screen (see Figure 21.6), select Connect to the network at my workplace. This option sets up the VPN connection.

FIGURE 21.6

Select the Connect to the network at my workplace option.

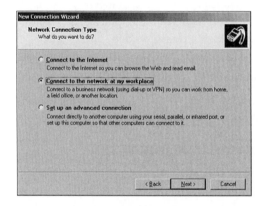

3. Click Next to continue. On the next screen, you are asked to specify the type of connection that will be used: dial-up or VPN. Select the Virtual Private Network connection option and then click Next to continue.

4. On the next screen, you are asked to provide a name for the connection. Type your company name or another descriptive name for the VPN connection. Click Next to continue.

5. On the next screen (see Figure 21.7), type the hostname or the IP address of the VPN server. After specifying the hostname or IP address, click Next.

FIGURE 21.7

Provide the public IP address of the VPN server.

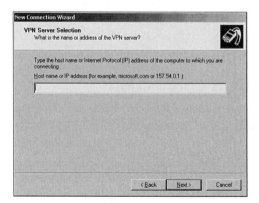

6. You are asked to specify whether this connection is for anyone who logs onto this computer or for your use only. As far as security goes, specifying the dial-in account for you only is the best practice. The connection will be available only when you are logged on to the system. Make sure that the My Use Only option button is selected, and then click Next.

7. A summary screen appears for the new connection. Click Finish. The connection box for the new VPN connection appears (see Figure 21.8). You must type the username and the password for the connection in the Connection box.

FIGURE 21.8

The remote client must provide the domain username and the appropriate password.

8. To connect, click the Connect button. The connection is made from the remote client to the VPN server. A remote connection icon appears in the system tray of the client computer when the connection has been made.

> To connect to subsequent VPN sessions, open the Network Connection window and then double-click your virtual private network connection icon.

After the connection has been made, remote users can access any resources on the network that they could if they were directly connected to the local area network. Figure 21.9 shows a remote client using Microsoft Word that is connecting to shared folders in a domain where access has been provided by the VPN connection.

21

FIGURE **21.9**

The remote client can use resources on the network through the VPN connection as if it was connected directly to the LAN.

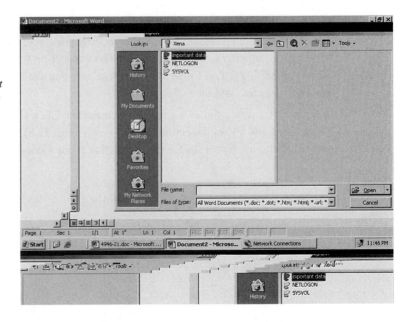

Managing VPN

You can manage (and troubleshoot) the VPN connection using the RRAS snap-in. For example, the number of remote access connections is displayed on the Remote Access Clients node in the snap-in tree. If you want to view individual users, click this node. The currently connected users then are listed in the Details pane (see Figure 21.10).

FIGURE **21.10**

You can view a list of the currently connected remote users.

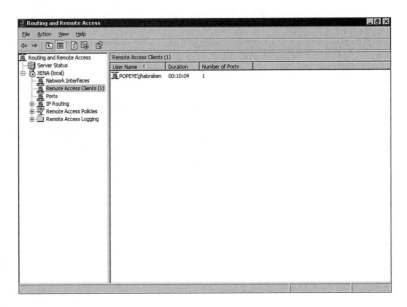

You can also view the properties associated with a particular user; double-click the user in the Details pane. The Status box that appears provides the user's name, the duration of the connection, and other information related to the connection itself.

Not only can you view details related to an individual user connection, but you also can view the status of the VPN ports provided by the server. In the snap-in tree, click the Ports node. The current ports available on the VPN server appear in the Details pane. Figure 21.11 shows an active port connection on a VPN server.

FIGURE 21.11

Click the Ports node to view the status of the server's VPN ports.

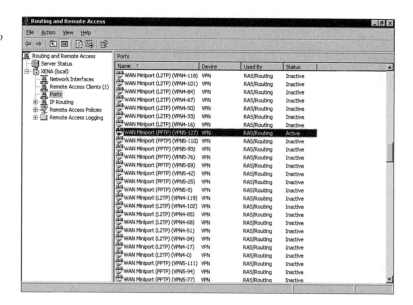

To view a particular port's status, double-click the port in the Details pane. A status box opens for the port. This status box is very similar to the status box for your remote users; it shows the connection time and other parameters related to the current connection. You can close the connection (basically cutting off the remote user) by clicking the Disconnect button.

We have been discussing the management of a local VPN server using the RRAS snap-in, but you can also use it to manage a number of remote VPN servers in the domain. This gives you an overall picture of RAS connections in the domain.

To add other servers to the RRAS snap-in, right-click the Routing and Remote Access icon in the snap-in tree and select Add Server. The Add Server dialog box appears. You can specify the addition of a particular server or add all Routing and Remote Access servers in the domain by providing the domain name.

21

The Add Server dialog box also provides for the browsing of the Active Directory, to enable you to find a particular remote access server and add it to the snap-in. After the server has been added to the snap-in, you can view its status and view the current connections to the server.

> You can also view information related to remote client connections to your RAS or VPN server in the Event Viewer. Information related to VPN and RAS connections is found in the system log. For more information about the Event Viewer, see Hour 20, "Monitoring Server and Network Performance."

Understanding IPSec

The *IP Security Protocol* (IPSec) is a suite of cryptography-based protection services and security protocols that can be used to secure internal networks that use remote access connections (such as VPN). IPSec secures the data even if the routers and other devices involved in moving the data from sender to receiver do not support IPSec. IPSec can be used to secure the movement of data on LANs, WANs, and remote access connections.

IPSec uses strong cryptography and provides protection for network data because it protects the data while en route and can even be used to protect private network data that is transmitted across public network environments such as the Internet. The biggest plus related to IPSec is that it can be used to protect data inside the network and eliminate snooping and hacking by employees, contractors, or attackers that have actually gained access to the network.

IP packets are encrypted on a packet-by-packet basic. IPSec also makes use of authentication keys such as certificates (discussed in Hour 23, "Working with Certificate Services") as a way of establishing a trust between the sending and receiving computers.

Using IPSec Policies

IPSec is implemented on the network using IPSec policies. An *IPSec policy* is a set of filters and filter actions that are used to determine how IP packets will be treated by a particular computer or group of computers. Because IPSec policies are integrated with the Windows Server 2003 Group Policy, IPSec policies can be assigned to individual computers, Organizational Units, and domains. This makes it easy for you to design (and lowers the management overhead of) a domain- or enterprise-level plan for IPSec deployment.

You can create IPSec policies on a local machine and store them in the computer's local registry. Or, you can assign IPSec policy in Active Directory for Organizational Units or entire domains. When using Group Policy and the Active Directory to assign IPSec policy, you should keep in mind the following:

- IPSec policies assigned to a domain policy override any local IPSec policies that you have assigned to individual computers on the domain.

- IPSec policies assigned at the organizational unit level override domain-level IPSec policy.

- If organizational units contain other organizational units, the IPSec policies assigned to the lowest level of organizational unit in the grouping override any higher-level policies set in the organizational unit hierarchy.

To sum this up, the closer the IPSec policy is to the actual computers in the Active Directory tree hierarchy (say, for instance, the Organizational Unit level rather than the domain level), the more likely it is that these policies will take effect. However, remember that any policies assigned to individual computers (assigned locally on that computer) will be overridden if an IPSec policy has been assigned to the computer via the Active Directory because of its domain or Organizational Unit membership.

Understanding IPSec Components and Processes

Before taking a look at how IPSec policies are configured, it is important to have a feel for how the various IPSec components (along with IPSec policies) actually drive the protective schemes used by IPSec. When you install Windows Server 2003, all the components necessary to implement IPSec are installed.

These IPSec components are as follows:

- **Policy Agent**—The *Policy Agent* retrieves the IPSec policy from the Active Directory or uses the local Registry IPSec policy (if no policy exists in the Active Directory or the computer is not attached to a domain).

- **Internet Key Exchange (IKE)**—IKE provides the mechanism for establishing a *security association* (SA) between the sending and receiving computers. An SA is an agreement on how to exchange and protect the data packets that will move from the sender to the receiver. IKE generates and manages the authentication keys that will be used for the SA.

- **IPSec driver**—The *IPSec driver* uses the filters contained in the IPSec policy to watch for outgoing IP packets that will need to be secured and any inbound IP packets that will need to be verified and then decrypted.

Now that we have identified the three major components of IPSec, let's look at the part these components play in protecting the data as a secure session is set up with another computer. As already mentioned, the IPSec policy for a particular computer can reside locally in the Registry or be held in the Active Directory.

21

Let's look at the sending computer first. A computer that is not part of a domain will retrieve the local IPSec policy from its Registry. However, because we have been discussing domain networking and domain membership throughout this book, we concentrate more closely on a sending computer that is part of a domain. The domain must be configured with an active IPSec policy or policies.

On the domain member computer, the Policy Agent loads the policy from the Windows Active Directory. Because IPSec policies can be defined that allow the policy to be renewed at a defined interval, the domain member computer can retrieve the latest version of IPSec policy at various preset intervals.

After the Policy Agent retrieves the IPSec policy, it sends the active IPSec policy information to the IPSec driver. The IPSec driver uses the filter list provided by the IPSec policy to determine which outgoing packets must be secured.

When packets are identified that must be secured (based on the filter list), the driver notifies the IKE to arrange a security association between the sending and receiving computers. The SA contains the session key and also supplies a security parameters index (*SPI*), which uniquely identifies the SA. This is important when a client machine is connecting to a file server that might be negotiating multiple SAs (with multiple file server clients).

After negotiations of the SA have been completed between the two computers, the IPSec driver inserts the SPI from the SA into the IPSec header. It then signs and encrypts the packets if encryption is called for, and sends the packets to the IP layer, where they are sent off to the receiving device.

On the receiving computer, the IPSec driver receives the session's key, the SA, and the SPI from the IKE. It looks up the SA in its local database based on the destination address and the SPI. It then checks the signature on the packets and decrypts them if they are encrypted. The encrypted data is then passed on to the TCP/IP driver, which takes care of getting the packets to the appropriate destination application.

So, to make a long story short, after communication is established between the IPSec drivers on the sending and receiving computers (by virtue of the SA), packets are encrypted and decrypted as needed. Packets to be encrypted (and then decrypted on the receiving end) are defined in the IPSec policy.

Creating an IPSec Snap-In

IPSec can be configured and managed using an IPSec snap-in in the Microsoft Management Console. However, a default IPSec MMC snap-in is not available on the

Administrative Tools menu list (as is DNS, DHCP, and so on). To create an IPSec snap-in perform the following steps:

1. Select Start, Run. In the Run box, type **mmc** and then click OK. A blank MMC window (that is, one that does not contain a snap-in) opens on your desktop.

2. In the console, select File, Add/Remove Snap-In. The Add/Remove Snap-In dialog box opens. This dialog box is used to add snap-ins to the console's root (which is what you want to do with the IPSec snap-in).

3. In the Add/Remove Snap-In dialog box, click the Add button. The Add Standalone Snap-In dialog box opens (see Figure 21.12).

FIGURE 21.12

Add snap-ins to the MMC console.

4. In the dialog box, locate and select the IP Security Policy Management snap-in. Then click Add. The Select Computer or Domain dialog box opens.

5. The Select Computer or Domain dialog box enables you to select the computer or domain that this snap-in will manage. If you are creating this snap-in on a member server or other server where you want to set the local IPSec properties, select the Local Computer option button. If you are creating this snap-in on a domain controller and want to manage the IPSec policies for the domain, select the Active Directory domain of which this computer is a member option (there is also an option to create the snap-in for a domain other than the default). Click Finish.

6. You are returned to the Add Standalone snap-in dialog box. At this point, you can add additional snap-ins to the console or click Close.

21

You also might want to add the IP Security Monitor to this console. This enables you to access both the IP Security Policy Management snap-in and the IP Security Monitor snap-in in one console. We discuss the IP Security Monitor later in this hour.

7. When you click Close, you are returned to the Add/Remove Snap-In dialog box, which supplies a list of the snap-ins that you will add to the console. Click OK to close the dialog box. You are returned to the MMC, which now contains the snap-ins that you selected.

8. To save the console, select File, Save. In the Save As dialog box, supply the console with a name, such as IPSec. Then click Save.

Figure 21.13 shows an MMC that contains the IP Security Policy Management snap-in and the IP Security Monitor snap-in. When you have the snap-in, you can configure the local machine (or the domain, depending on your selections when you created the snap-in) for IPSec.

FIGURE 21.13

Create an IPSec snap-in.

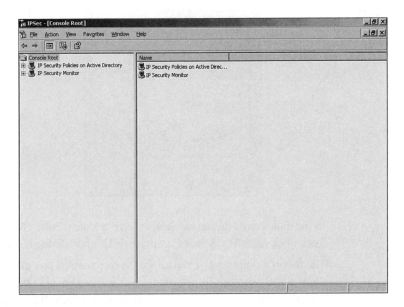

You can create a shortcut for the new MMC on the Administrative Tools menu. Click Start and then right-click the Administrative Tools folder and select Open. In the Administrative Tools window, Select File, New, Shortcut. In the Create shortcut dialog box, use the Browse button to locate your IPSec snap-in. It will be found in the path c:\Documents and Settings\Administrator\Start Menu\Programs\Administrative Tools. After you locate the MMC file using browse click OK. Then click Next and then Finish.

Working with IPSec Policies

As already mentioned in the hour, IPSec security is based on IPSec policies. By default, you are provided with three IPSec policies for the domain (there are also three default policies when you are working with IPSec on a local computer):

- **Server (Request Security)**—This policy can be assigned to computers that need to have secure communications, such as important file servers or other network servers. Computers assigned this policy accept unsecured communications but still attempt to secure traffic by requesting security from the sender of the data. This policy allows the entire communication to be unsecured if the other computer is not IPSec-enabled.

- **Client (Respond Only)**—This is available for computers on an intranet that do not need to secure communications with other computers on the intranet most of the time, but they might be involved in a communication (such as one initiated by a computer from outside the domain) that needs to be secured. This policy sets up the computers in the domain to use IPSec only in response to computers that request a secure communication. The policy contains a default response rule, which enables negotiation with computers requesting IPSec. Only the protocol and port traffic requested by the computer (the computer outside the domain) are used for the secure communication.

- **Secure Server (Require Security)**—This policy is used for computers that definitely require secured transmissions. All outbound communications from computers assigned this policy are secured. Microsoft states, however, that this policy must be customized for your particular network needs and is not an "out-of-the-box" solution for IPSec security.

Editing IPSec Policies

A complete understanding of IPSec and how it works with the different protocols in the TCP/IP stack (such as ICMP and UDP) is certainly beyond the scope of this book. However, a good way to get an overall feel for creating and implementing IPSec policies is to edit one of the existing policies provided by Windows Server 2003. Be advised that the policies are not actually in force until you enable them in Group Policy (we discuss enabling IPSec policies later in the hour. For an overview of Group Policy, see Hour 11, "Understanding Group Policy and User Profiles").

You can edit an existing IPSec policy using the snap-in. To view the default policies (in the Details pane), select the IP Security Policy node in the snap-in tree. Right-click one of the existing policies, such as the Secure Server (Require Security) policy. Select Properties from the shortcut menu. The Properties dialog box for the policy opens (see Figure 21.14).

21

FIGURE 21.14

You can view the Properties dialog box of an existing policy.

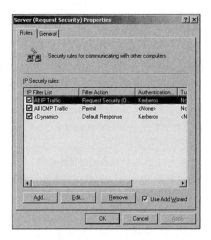

The Properties dialog box consists of two tabs: the General tab and the Rules tab. The General tab shows the name of the policy and a description of the policy (which can be edited on this tab), and the setting for how often computers assigned the policy check for changes to the policy.

The Rules tab (see Figure 21.14) enables you to add, edit, and delete rules. To edit one of the rules (such as the All IP Traffic rule, shown in Figure 21.14), select the rule and then click Edit. The Edit Rule Properties dialog box appears.

This dialog box contains five tabs:

- **IP Filter List**—This tab is where you specify the filters that the rule will use to identify IP traffic that it should act upon. You can add filters to the list or edit filters as needed. All the filters available to IPSec policies are listed on the tab.

- **Filter Action**—This tab lists the filter actions that are available to the rule and those that are being used by the rule.

- **Authentication Methods**—This tab lists the authentication methods used by the rule. Kerberos is set as the default. Additional authentication methods such as certificates can be added by clicking the Add button.

- **Tunnel Setting**—This tab is used to specify the IP address of a computer that will be provided a tunnel for remote access to the computer that embraces the IPSec policy being edited.

- **Connection Type**—This tab provides for the selection of the type of network connections that will be allowed by the rule you are currently editing. Three choices are available: All Network Connections, Local Area Network (LAN), and Remote Access.

You can edit any of the information on the tabs of this dialog box (Figure 21.15 shows the Edit Rule Properties dialog box). After you have edited a particular rule, click OK to return to the Rules tab of the policy's Properties dialog box. After you create a new IPSec policy, you must set the various properties for any rules that you create in the new policy.

FIGURE 21.15

Rules can be customized using the Edit Rule Properties dialog box.

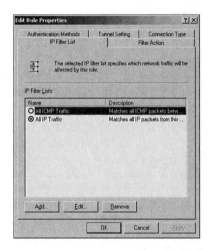

 You can also create your own IPSec policies from scratch. Right-click the Details pane that shows the existing policies. Then select Create IP Security Policy from the shortcut menu. The IP Security Policy Wizard opens and walks you through the steps of creating your new policy. Specifying the rules for the new policy is accomplished in the policy's Properties dialog box (as already discussed in this section) .

Enabling IPSec Policies

After you configure a IPSec policy and its rules in the IPSec snap-in, you will want to enable the policy (or policies) on the local computer or your domain. IPSec policies are enabled in Group Policy. To enable IPSec policies that apply to the entire domain, select Start, Administrative Tools, Domain Security Policy. The Default Domain Security Policy snap-in opens.

Expand the Default Domain Policy node and then expand the Windows Settings node, followed by the Security Settings node. In the Security Settings node list, select IP Security Policies. The default IPSec polces appear in the Details pane, as shown in Figure 21.16 (this list will vary if you added new policies or deleted any of the default policies).

21

FIGURE 21.16

You can view the
existing IPSec poli-
cies in the Group
Policy snap-in.

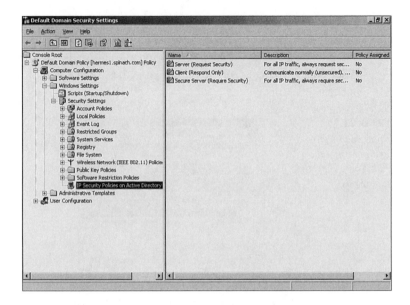

To assign one (or more) of the policies to the domain (or local computer, if you are working with the local computer's Group Policy settings), right-click the policy and select Assign from the shortcut menu. The IPSec policy then is assigned as part of the Group Policy for the domain (or local computer).

IPSec policies that you assign to the Group Policy are flagged by Yes in the Policy Assigned column of the Details pane. When you have completed assigning IPSec policies to the Group Policy, you can close the Group Policy snap-in.

> IPSec is definitely an advanced Windows Server 2003 security feature. Because IPSec policies must be enabled in Group Policy, you can feel free to experiment with IPSec policy and rule creation in the IPSec snap-in. None of the policies or their rules actually affect IP traffic on the network until you enable the policies in Group Policy. IPSec is one of those Windows Server 2003 features that you might want to experiment with for a while before implementing it on the network.

Monitoring IPSec

You can monitor IP Security using the IPSec monitor. You can use the monitor to view active security associations on a local or remote computer (you must have administrative rights to view the IPSec monitor for other computers in the domain).

The easiest way to access the IPSec monitor is to create a MMC snap-in for the program (discussed earlier in the hour). When you have the new snap-in open, expand the IP Security Monitor node and then expand the node for the local computer. To view the statistics related to the active policy, click the Active Policy folder. The active policy (or policies) description and other information related to the policy appear in the Details pane (see Figure 21.17).

FIGURE 21.17

You can view the IPSec stats in the IPSec Monitor.

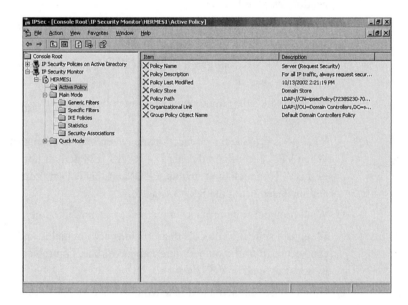

Summary

Virtual private networking allows remote clients to connect to your network using public networks such as the Internet. VPNs use the tunneling protocols PPTP and L2TP to provide a secure connection over public networks. To configure a server as a VPN server, the computer must be outfitted with two or more network cards. The VPN service is configured using the RRAS snap-in.

IPSec provides security for IP traffic on internal and remote network connections. IPSec encrypts IP packets and uses authentication keys to establish a trust between the sending and receiving computers.

IPSec is controlled on a Windows Server 2003 network through IPSec policies. After IPSec policies (such as the existing IPSec policies) have been edited or new policies have been created with the appropriate rules, these policies must be enabled in Group Policy.

21

Q&A

Q How does VPN provide a secure connection between sending and receiving computers over a public network such as the Internet?

A VPN uses tunneling protocols such as the Point-to-Point Tunneling Protocol (PPTP) and the Layer 2 Tunneling Protocol (L2TP) that create a secure VPN connection over the Internet.

Q How is VPN configured on a server running Windows Server 2003?

A VPN is one of the services supplied by the Routing and Remote Access Service (RRAS). VPN is configured as part of RRAS and is monitored and managed via the RRAS snap-in.

Q What provides the single point-to-point connection between a remote client and a VPN server?

A VPN ports provide the connections between remote clients and the VPN server. When VPN is configured as part of RRAS, 128 default ports are created for each of the VPN tunneling protocols, PPTP and L2TP. Port properties can be accessed and managed using the RRAS snap-in.

Q What protocol suite provides a method to secure both internal and VPN IP traffic?

A IPSec is a suite of protocols that provides cryptographic and security protocols that can secure IP traffic on both internal network and on remote connections provided by services such as VPN.

Q How is IPSec implemented in a Windows Server 2003 domain?

A IPSec is implemented in the domain (or a multidomain enterprise network) using IPSec policies. These policies use filters to determine how specific IP packets (based on a filtering mechanism) are protected when in transit between the sending and receiving computers.

Hour **22**

Using Internet Connection Sharing and Network Address Translation

So far, we have looked at a number of the features provided by the Routing and Remote Access Service (RRAS), including dial-in access, routing, and virtual private networks. In this hour, we look at another RRAS feature provided by Windows Server 2003: Network Address Translation (NAT). NAT provides a method for connecting a group of computers to a single Internet connection.

We also consider a simple alternative to NAT: the Internet Connection Sharing feature provided by Windows Server 2003. It can be considered NAT "Light" (ICS provides the same type of service that NAT does, but not the configuration possibilities). We begin our discussion of shared Internet connections and public and private IP addressing with the Internet Connection Sharing (ICS) feature.

In this hour, the following topics are covered:

- Understanding Internet Connection Sharing
- Working with private and public IP addressing

- Installing and Configuring ICS
- Using the Internet Connection Firewall
- Working with Network Address Translation
- Installing and configuring Network Address Translation

Understanding Internet Connection Sharing (ICS)

Internet Connection Sharing (ICS) is an easy-to-use (and easy-to-configure) feature that enables a number of computers in a home or small office setting to share a single Internet connection. ICS has actually been around since the second edition of Windows 98 and is also available in the most recent versions of the Windows client operating system, Windows XP.

ICS is certainly not an option for large or even medium-size networks. A large number of computers sharing the bandwidth provided by a single Internet connection would make each of the individual connections painfully slow. Microsoft actually created ICS as part of its Small Office/Home Office (SOHO) initiative. It is designed for connecting workgroups, not domains, to the Internet. To implement ICS on a computer running Windows Server 2003, the computer must be outfitted with two or more network interface cards (which is referred to as a multihomed computer).

Understanding Public Versus Private Addressing

Before we look at how to configure the ICS feature, we need to look at how ICS handles the internal (the small office) and external IP addressing. To do its job, ICS actually takes advantage of two different types of IP addresses: public addresses and private addresses.

A *public IP address* is an address assigned to you by your Internet service provider (ISP). This is the address that provides your computer with access to the Internet. Typically, ISPs (including providers of DSL and broadband) provide a home user or small business user with either one static IP address or a dynamically assigned IP address (from the ISP's DHCP server, although in some cases multiple public IP addresses are available). ICS can take advantage of one public IP address.

IP addressing is discussed in Hour 7, "Working with Network Protocols." For information on how DHCP works, see Hour 16, "Using the Dynamic Host Configuration Protocol."

Private addressing is used to assign IP addresses to the computers on the internal network. So, a *private address* is an IP address that is assigned to a computer so that it can take advantage of the TCP/IP protocol. However, the address holds no significance for the computer on a public network. The private IP addressing simply allows the computers on the internal network to talk to each other using TCP/IP (we talk more about public versus private addressing later in the hour when we discuss Network Address Translation).

Windows Server 2003 embraces a feature called *Automatic Private IP Addressing*. When a computer on a network that is configured as a DHCP client and cannot communicate with the DHCP server, this feature automatically assigns an address to a computer's NIC using a range of IP addresses from 169.254.0.1 to 169.254.255.254, with the subnet mask of 255.255.0.0.

> The Internet Assigned Number Authority (IANA) has actually reserved the IP range of 169.254.0.1 to 169.254.255.254 for private addressing. Therefore, these addresses won't conflict with any IP addresses on the Internet (more about reserved IP ranges later in the hour) .

So, where does the automatic addressing come from? Well, ICS actually has a DHCP Allocator built in. So, when you configure ICS, the private addressing on the network is handled by the DHCP Allocator (a low-rent version of DHCP). The DHCP Allocator cannot be configured in the same way as a full-blown DHCP server, but it does make sure that no two computers in the workgroup will end up with the same IP address.

So, because the computers have all automatically assigned themselves addresses from a specific range of IP addresses (actually, addresses that all fall into one network range), the computers use these addresses to communicate. They communicate with the ICS-enabled computer on that computer's internal network interface card. The external network interface card supplies the public IP address and connects all the computers in the workgroup to the Internet.

Working with ICS Connection Possibilities

Before we take a look at how to configure the ICS feature, let's take a look at some of the types of Internet connections that this service can take advantage of in a home or small office environment. ICS is well suited for the following connection types:

- **Asynchronous modem connection**—This type of modem is used over a regular analog voice-grade telephone line to connect with an ISP via a dial-up account. Millions of people use this type of device to connect to the Internet. This type of modem can supply only a 56K (actually, 57,600 bits per second [bps]) transfer rate.

> Regular phone lines typically cannot provide a modem connection speed greater than 53K. This is due to two different issues: line noise and static, and the FCC. Noise and static on an analog phone line can impair the connection speed of a modem. Also, in some areas of the country, the FCC actually limits the connection speed possible to 53K because of restrictions on the power that can be transmitted on a phone circuit.

- **Digital Subscriber Line**—*Digital Subscriber Line (DSL)* offers voice and data communication over most regular phone lines, with speeds of up to 7Mbps (in research situations, connections of 50Mbps have been realized). The great thing about DSL in the small office or home networking environment is that the data and voice communication can take place simultaneously over the very same phone line. DSL shares the line with the analog voice signal by using a different frequency for the digital data (that is sent and received using the line). This means that you can make a phone call while sending data over the line. DSL is available from most of the Baby Bells across the United States.

- **Cable broadband**—An alternative to phone-line connections is the *cable broadband* connection. This type of connection is provided by television cable providers such as AOL-Time Warner. A cable modem box is supplied by the broadband provider and is connected to the television cable connection in the home or office. Data is moved on different frequencies (or *channels*, if you prefer). Upstream and downstream data typically require separate frequencies. The broadband or cable modem can be directly connected to a computer using the Internet Connection Sharing feature (many broadband providers provide multiple IP addresses, however, enabling you to connect the cable modem to a hub rather than a single computer).

> Satellite television providers such as DirectTV also provide Internet connection services. If your local telephone carrier does not provide DSL and you can't get cable TV in your area, faster (than a modem) connections are available from the various "dish" television providers.

Because the connection bandwidth is shared by the computers in a workgroup using ICS, the speed of the connection becomes very important. A slow analog modem connection provides only an extremely slow connection when shared by a number of computers. If you will use ICS in your home or a small office, a faster connection such as DSL or broadband is probably in order.

To use ICS, directly connect the computer that will run ICS to the Internet connection. Then connect the computer's second network interface to a hub that includes connections to the other computers in the workgroup.

22

Configuring a Windows Server 2003 as part of a workgroup is discussed in Hour 3, "Installing Windows Server 2003." Setting up a workgroup that includes client computers is discussed in Hour 10, "Adding Client Computers and Member Servers to the Domain."

Configuring ICS

Setting up Windows Server 2003 to share an Internet connection is very straightforward. You set up the network connection that is assigned the public IP address so that it is connected to the ISP.

If you have Routing and Remote Access configured on your Windows Server 2003, you will not be able to add the Internet Connection Sharing feature or the Internet Connection Firewall to the server's configuration.

To configure ICS, follow these steps:

1. Select Start, Control Panel, and then open Network Connections (see Figure 22.1).

FIGURE 22.1

Open the Network Connections window.

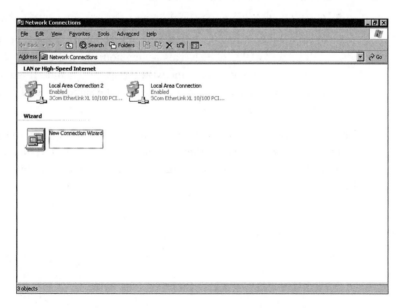

2. Right-click the network connection (it can be a dial-up, LAN or high-speed Internet connection) that will be configured for the public IP address (it can be a network card with a fixed IP address or it can be configured as a DHCP client or a modem) and that will provide the connection to the Internet. Select Properties from the shortcut menu.

3. The Properties dialog box opens. Select the Advanced tab on the connection's Properties dialog box (see Figure 22.2).

FIGURE 22.2

Select the Advanced tab on the Properties dialog box.

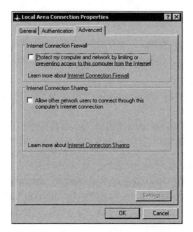

4. On the Advanced tab, select Allow other network users to connect through this computer's internet connection.

5. Click OK to close the dialog box.

6. A message box may open, letting you know that the LAN connection for the server will be set to 192.168.0.1. This is an automatic address and should remind you to set up all the computers in the workgroup for dynamic IP address configuration so that they also are assigned an address in the same range of private addresses. Click OK to close the message box.

This computer now allows computers in the same workgroup to share the Internet connection. Another feature that you might find useful in terms of protecting your Internet connection and the computers in the network is the Internet Connection Firewall.

Understanding the Internet Connection Firewall

22

The Internet Connection Firewall enables you to protect the computers within your workgroup and negates outside access to the computer that is running the ICS feature. A *firewall* is designed to sit between your network and the Internet, to protect the internal network from outside attack.

The Internet Connection Firewall is a software firewall; more complex firewalls that can filter incoming and outgoing Internet traffic are often a combination of hardware and software. The Internet Connection Firewall is designed to examine all the incoming data on the public portion of your Internet connection. It does not provide you with the capability to block certain types of activity from within your workgroup.

The Internet Connection Firewall builds a table based on the addresses contained in data packets that have been sent by the computers in your workgroup or the computer connected to the ICS. It then examines both the sending and receiving addresses of all the data packets that attempt to enter the network through the public connection. If the inbound traffic matches an entry in the firewall table showing that the incoming data is the product of a request from a computer on the workgroup side of the firewall, the data is allowed to enter the workgroup.

The Windows Server 2003 Internet Connection Firewall is a stateful firewall. It examines the entire content of packets (many firewalls examine only the headers) and determines more information related to the packet than just the source and destination addresses. A stateful firewall also closes off ports on the computer until there is a request to use these ports. This negates port scanning as a possible method of gaining entry to the computer and workgroup by a hacker. It's a pretty decent firewall when you consider that you get it for free as part of the network operating system.

Like the ICS feature, the Internet Connection Firewall is designed to be used with small workgroups. And although the Internet Connection Firewall does not allow you to configure most of the settings related to how the firewall filters traffic (pretty much in the same vein as the limited configuration possibilities for the ICS feature), it does provide you with the capability to allow certain types of unsolicited Internet traffic to reach your workgroup.

For example, if you want to run a Web server within the workgroup or set up an FTP site so that Internet users can download files from your workgroup, you can configure the Internet Connection Firewall to allow connections from the public network to these Internet services.

Configuring the Internet Connection Firewall

The Internet Connection Firewall is easy to configure and requires little more than a click on the appropriate check box on the Advanced tab of the Properties dialog box of the network connection that provides the external conduit to the Internet.

Open the Properties dialog box for the LAN or other connection that is hosting the Internet connection.

Select Protect my computer and network by limiting or preventing access to this computer from the Internet (this assumes that you have already enabled ICS on this computer). After you select the check box, the firewall is enabled.

You can allow external traffic (that would normally be disallowed by the firewall) if you are running services such as a Web server or an FTP server, or if you want to allow a computer outside your network to be capable of using the remote desktop feature (this basically means it takes control of your computer, which might not be that great of an idea even in a workgroup that is using Windows Server 2003 as a member server).

To configure the services that will be allowed for an external connection to the ICS firewall, click the Settings button on the connection's Advanced tab (of the Properties dialog box). The Advanced Settings dialog box opens (see Figure 22.3).

FIGURE 22.3

Select the services that will be allowed external connections.

Select the appropriate check boxes in this dialog box. For example, if you are going to run a Web server on one of the workgroup computers (such as IIS on a Windows Server 2003), select the Web Server (HTTP) check box. When you have finished selecting the services, click OK.

You are returned to the connection's Properties dialog box. Click OK to close the Properties dialog box. The connection that has been configured for ICS and the Internet Connection Firewall will be marked as shown in Figure 22.4. The local area connection is marked with a hand symbol signifying ICS and a lock signifying that the Internet Connection Firewall has been turned on.

FIGURE 22.4

Your connection will be marked as shared and firewalled.

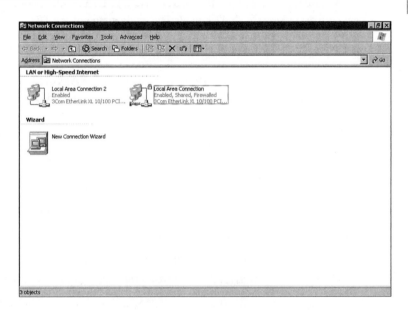

 The Internet Connection Firewall can also be used to protect any computer directly connected to the Internet (without enabling the ICS feature). It basically becomes a personal firewall on that computer. While this feature is available on computers running Windows Server 2003, you might find it more useful on computers that you use at home that run such client operating systems as Windows XP.

Understanding Network Address Translation

Network Address Translation (NAT) enables you to hide a group of computers (such as a network) behind one IP address. In the good old days of computing, which weren't that good and certainly weren't that long ago, this was known as IP masquerading. Basically, your network sits behind the NAT server, meaning that you need only one "legal" IP address for the server running the NAT software. The IP addressing scheme that you use on the computer network behind the NAT server is really up to you (although ranges of IP addresses are reserved for this purpose, which we discuss in a moment).

As we've already discussed, the ICS feature enables you to quickly share a single Internet connection with a number of computers in a workgroup. Although NAT provides the same basic function as ICS (sharing a single connection and public IP address), it also provides greater flexibility and a number of different configuration possibilities.

We've already said that the ICS feature uses the DHCP Allocator to configure the internal network addresses. NAT can also take advantage of the DHCP Allocator, or you can configure your internal network addresses from ranges that have been set aside just for this purpose.

When the Internet Assigned Numbers Authority (IANA) developed the IP addressing for each IP address class (A, B, and C), it designated a range in each class to serve as private addresses. So, a private address (as mentioned earlier in the hour) is an IP address taken from one of the private ranges designated by IANA.

These addresses are meant to be used, as their name suggests, on private networks. They are not to be used as legitimate IP addresses for connecting to the Internet. These private addresses provide a means of assigning unique IP addresses to an internal network that then uses Network Address Translation to actually connect to the public Internet.

There are Class A, B, and C private ranges:

- Class A: 10.0.0.0 to 10.255.255.255, with a subnet mask of 255.0.0.0
- Class B: 172.16.0.0 to 172.31.255.255, with a subnet mask of 255.255.0.0
- Class C: 192.168.0.0 to 192.168.255.255, with a subnet mask of 255.255.255.0

The great thing about using NAT is that you can use as many IP addresses as required internally. For example, you can treat your internal network as if it is a Class A or a Class B network, which provides a huge number of addresses. Remember, NAT requires only one "official" IP address for the NAT server that sits between your network and your ISP.

Configuring NAT on the Server

NAT is configured using the RRAS snap-in. You can configure NAT when you first enable the RRAS feature on a Windows Server 2003, or you can add the NAT protocol to an existing RRAS server (RRAS is also discussed in Hour 18, "Using Routing and Remote Access" and Hour 21, "Working with Virtual Private Networking and IP Security"). Let's take a look at how to install NAT when you enable RRAS and then how to add NAT to an existing RRAS server.

Adding NAT When Enabling RRAS

Adding NAT to the configuration when you enable RRAS on a Windows Server 2003 is very straightforward. Be advised, however, that you should make sure that ICS is not enabled on the server before proceeding with the addition of NAT. If ICS is installed on the server, you will receive an error message when installing NAT.

To install NAT, follow these steps:

1. Open the RRAS snap-in (Start, Administrative Tools, Routing and Remote Access).

2. Right-click the Server (Local) node in the snap-in tree and select Configure and Enable Routing and Remote Access on the shortcut menu. The Routing and Remote Access Server Setup Wizard appears. Click Next to bypass the opening screen.

3. The next screen supplies a list of common configurations for the RRAS service (see Figure 22.5); options are provided to install NAT alone or to install NAT and VPN together. For sake of discussion of NAT configuration, select Network address translation and then click Next (VPN is discussed in Hour 21).

FIGURE 22.5

Select NAT to be installed on the RRAS server.

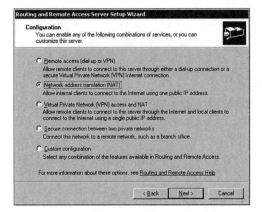

 If you want to install a different combination of RRAS services than those provided by the wizard options, select the Custom configuration option. You can then select any and all RRAS services to be installed when you enable RRAS.

4. On the next wizard screen, you are provided a list of your current LAN network interfaces. You can specify one of the local area connections as the NAT connection to the public network. You also have the option to configure a new dial-on-demand connection, if you will use a modem to connect the NAT server to the public network (you are walked through the dial-up connection creation process by a wizard). Select the LAN interface that will supply the public connection (and be configured with the public IP address).

5. This wizard screen also provides you with the option of enabling the Basic Firewall feature, as shown in Figure 22.6 (this option is selected by default). This provides you with the same type of firewall protection that we discussed for the Internet Connection Firewall. After you select the LAN interface (and allow the firewall to be enabled), click Next.

FIGURE 22.6

Select the LAN interface and the firewall option.

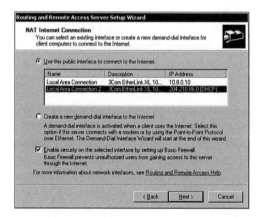

6. A summary screen appears telling you that NAT and the basic firewall (if you selected it to be enabled) will be enabled on the LAN interface that you selected (RRAS is also enabled). Click Finish to complete the process.

You are returned to the Routing and Remote Access snap-in. The NAT/Basic Firewall icon is found in the IP Routing node in the snap-in tree.

If you are having trouble with your network connections after installing NAT, open the Network Connections window. Double-click any of the connections and then select the Support tab on the connection's dialog box. Click the Repair button on the tab to attempt to repair the connection (and request an IP address from the DHCP Allocator).

Adding NAT to an Existing RRAS Server

You can also add NAT to an RRAS server that has already been enabled. The steps provided here assume that you have not previously installed NAT, as discussed in the previous sections.

Follow these steps:

1. Open the Routing and Remote Access snap-in (Start, Administrative Tools, Routing and Remote Access). In the snap-in tree, expand the Server (Local) node and then expand the IP Routing node (see Figure 22.7).

FIGURE 22.7

Expand the IP Routing node.

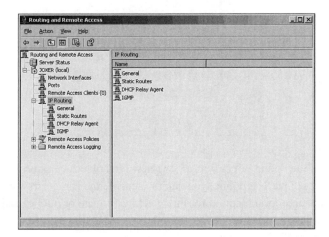

2. Right-click the General node (in the snap-in tree) and select New Routing Protocol from the shortcut menu. The New Routing Protocol dialog box opens.

3. Select NAT/Basic Firewall in the New Routing Protocol dialog box. Then click OK.

NAT/Basic Firewall is added to the IP Routing node's list of folders (providing the same results that you would have gotten had you added NAT when the RRAS service was first enabled).

Adding NAT Interfaces

When you add NAT to an enabled RRAS server, you also need to add the NAT interfaces that will be used for the public and private connections (these are configured for you when you enable NAT and the RRAS service together, as discussed earlier in the hour). To add a NAT interface, right-click the NAT/Basic Firewall icon in the snap-in tree and select New Interface. The New Interface for Network Address Translation dialog box opens.

This dialog box shows the current network connections (LAN) available on your computer. Select one of the LAN connections and then click OK. The Network Address Translation Properties–Network Connection dialog box opens (see Figure 22.8).

FIGURE 22.8

Configure the new NAT interface.

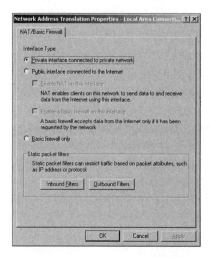

You have the option of configuring the new NAT interface as private or public. If you opt to make the interface public, you can also enable the Basic Firewall on the interface. Select the appropriate option for the interface (private or public) and then click OK. The new interface appears in the Details pane of the Routing and Remote Access snap-in (when the NAT/Basic Firewall folder is selected).

Repeat the process to add another interface. Remember, for NAT to work, you need one private interface to connect to the other workgroup computers and the public interface that connects to the Internet.

Configuring NAT

You can set the properties for NAT, such as the events that are logged related to NAT (which you can view in the Event Viewer, covered in Hour 20, "Monitoring Server and Network Performance") and the range of IP addresses that are assigned to the NAT clients in the workgroup. To open the NAT Properties dialog box, right-click the NAT/Basic Firewall folder (or NAT, if the firewall was not installed) in the Routing and Remote Access snap-in; then select Properties from the shortcut menu.

The NAT Properties dialog box has four tabs:

- **General**—Enables you to select the type of events that are logged in the Event Viewer's log files. You can choose to have errors only logged or to have errors and warnings logged. You also have the option of disabling event logging.

- **Translation**—Used to set the duration of TCP and UDP mappings. These protocols provide the transport mechanism for the TCP/IP protocol. It is best to go with the defaults on this tab.

- **Address Assignment**—allows you to enable the DHCP Allocator (see Figure 22.9). You can also use the Exclude button to specify IP addresses that should not be used from the private range of addresses in the 192.169.0.0 network.

- **Name Resolution**—Allows you to enable DNS resolution for the NAT clients.

FIGURE 22.9

You can enable the DHCP Allocator and create an exclusion range.

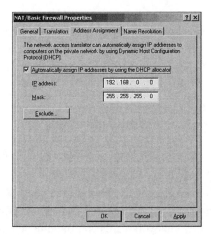

When you have finished changing the NAT Properties, click OK to close the Properties dialog box. You are returned to the Routing and Remote Access snap-in.

When NAT is installed and configured on the RRAS server, computers on the internal network can use private addressing to communicate. NAT provides the connection point between the private network and the external, public network (the Internet) .

If you have configured the NAT interfaces correctly, the NAT server should operate without errors. If computers on the network have trouble communicating with the Internet or computers outside the network have trouble communicating with computers on the private network, use the Event Viewer to check NAT-related log files. These should provide some insight into configuration errors that might have occurred when NAT was implemented on the server.

Summary

The Internet Connection Sharing feature enables you to share a single Internet connection with a workgroup of computers. This feature requires two network cards to be installed in the server. One LAN connection is configured as the public connection; the other LAN connection is configured as the private connection. Only one public IP address is needed.

ICS can be used with modem connections, DSL, and cable modems. You can protect the computer providing the Internet connection from outside attacks with the Internet Connection Firewall.

Network Address Translation is similar to the ICS feature, but it provides more configuration flexibility. NAT enables you to share a single public IP address with a number of computers.

NAT can be installed when you enable the RRAS service using the Routing and Remote Access snap-in. Installing NAT in this way also creates the NAT interfaces that will be used for the public and private connections. A Basic Firewall can also be installed when you install NAT.

Q&A

Q In a small workgroup networking situation, how can you share a single Internet connection with all the computers in the workgroup?

A The Internet Connection Service (ICS) provides a method of connecting multiple computers in a workgroup to a single Internet connection. ICS requires a computer configured with at least two network cards and running an operating system that supports ICS, such as Windows Server 2003.

Q What types of Internet connections can ICS use?

A ICS is compatible with asynchronous modem connections, DSL connections, cable modem connections, as well as other connection types typically used in home or small office settings.

Q How can the risk of an outside attack be minimized when using ICS?

A ICS includes the Internet Connection Firewall, a software firewall that can be used to protect the internal network from outside attack.

Q How does Network Address Translation work?

A Network Address Translation (NAT) allows an internal network using private IP addressing to connect to a public network such as the Internet using one valid IP address. The NAT server (a server running RRAS with NAT installed) serves as the connection point between the private and public interfaces.

Q Does NAT also provide firewall protection?

A When NAT is installed on the RRAS server, the basic firewall feature is also installed. It provides a software firewall that protects the internal network from outside attacks.

22

Hour **23**

Working with Certificate Services

As we discussed briefly in Hour 21, "Working with Virtual Private Networking and IP Security," there is a need for a high level of security related to data exchange between private and public networks. The public key infrastructure embraced by Windows Server 2003 provides a method of authenticating users involved in data transactions. One aspect of creating an environment in which the identity of users involved in transactions is known is to use the digital certificate. In this hour, we look at how you install and use Windows Server 2003 Certificate Services.

In this hour, the following topics are covered:

- Understanding Certificate Services
- Creating a Certificate Authority
- Configuring a CA using the Certificate Authority snap-in
- Using the Certificates snap-in to request and manage user and local computer certificates

Understanding Certificate Services

Certificates play an important role in the public key infrastructure that Microsoft has developed to protect network data. A *certificate* (also known as a digital certificate) is used to identify an entity on the network. The holder of a certificate (we discuss how the certificate is obtained in a moment) is trusted by the network.

The public key infrastructure actually uses both secret keys and public keys when data is exchanged. The secret key provides the security for the exchange and is often generated just for the session when the data moves from sender to receiver. The secret key (which is encrypted) is shared between the users in the data exchange session; each user is identified by a public key.

A certificate, then, is used to identify a public key user. Certificates are provided by a Certificate Authority, which is basically a trusted third party that authenticates a user's public key with a certificate (somewhat like a certificate of authenticity that you receive for expensive jewelry or an antique). A number of public Certificate Authorities, such as Verisign, provide digital certificates. If a user who wants to send data is identified by a certificate, the receiver of the data will have no problem accepting the data because it is from a "trusted and certified" user. A number of applications can use certificates for secure data exchange such as Microsoft Outlook and Microsoft Internet Explorer.

Although a number of Certificate Authorities can be used to purchase certificates, you might want to take advantage of certificates as another level of security on your Windows Server 2003 domain (or enterprise network). A server running Windows Server 2003 can be configured for Certificate Services. The server can then act as your own internal Certificate Authority.

Adding the Certificate Services

Microsoft's Certificate Services enables you to issue, renew, and revoke digital certificates. Certificate Services is added to Windows Server 2003 via the Add or Remove Programs applet in the Windows Control Panel.

1. Open the Add or Remove Programs window (select Start, Control Panel, Add or Remove Programs). In the window, select the Add/Remove Windows Components icon. The Windows Components Wizard opens.

2. In the Components list, select Certificate Services (see Figure 23.1). A message appears stating that after Certificate Services is installed on the server, you cannot change the machine name or the domain membership. This is because the machine name becomes bound to the Certificate Authority (CA) information that is stored in the Active Directory. Click Yes to continue.

FIGURE 23.1

Add Certificate Services to the server.

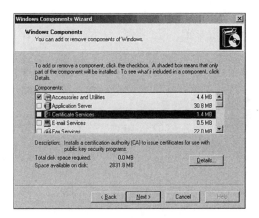

23

3. To add the service, click Next.

4. On the next screen, you must specify the type of Certificate Authority that you want to set up. The types of Certificate Authorities are as follows:

- **Enterprise root CA**—This CA becomes the root certificate server for your network. Active Directory is required to create an enterprise root because the CA will serve your entire domain tree.

- **Enterprise subordinate CA**—If you already have an enterprise root CA established, you can create subordinate CAs. A subordinate CA is actually verified by a certificate from the enterprise root CA.

- **Standalone root CA**—You can create a root CA for your network hierarchy that does not require Active Directory.

- **Standalone subordinate CA**—You can create a subordinate CA to a standalone root CA (when you are not using Active Directory on the network) .

You can also specify custom settings, such as the cryptographic strategy used to generate private and public key pairs. Select the Use Custom Settings to Generate the Key Pair and CA Certificate check box before clicking Next. Choices include the Microsoft Strong Cryptographic Provider (the default) and other providers, such as the Schlumberger Cryptographic Service Provider. Without a fairly good understanding of how key pairs are generated and how key length and algorithms are used in key generation, you should probably go with the default.

5. Select the CA type (the appropriate option button) and then click Next to continue. On the next screen, you are asked to provide CA identifying information (see Figure 23.2).

FIGURE 23.2

Provide a common name for the CA.

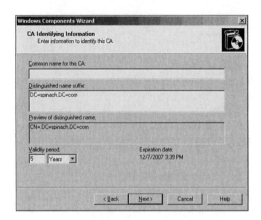

6. The identifying information includes a common name for the CA (for example, you could call an enterprise CA simply Enterprise CA). You can also set the validity period for the CA using the Validity Period spin boxes. After supplying the appropriate information, click Next to continue.

7. On the next screen, you are asked to specify the path for the certificate database and the certificate database log. Default paths are provided. You also have the option of storing the information in a shared folder on the network. After making your selections (or going with the defaults), click Next.

8. The Certificate Services files are copied to the server. You might get a message that the Certificate Services Web Enrollment Support will not be available until the Internet Information Services is installed on the server. Click OK to clear this information box.

9. When the summary screen for the Windows Component Wizard appears, click Finish to complete the installation process.

After you have installed Certificate Services on a server running Windows Server 2003, you will find that the Certification Authority snap-in is added to the server's administrative tools. We discuss this snap-in in the next section.

Configuring a Certificate Authority

The CA is configured and managed using the Certification Authority snap-in. To open the Certification Authority snap-in, select Start, Administrative Tools, Certification Authority. Figure 23.3 shows the Certification Authority snap-in.

FIGURE 23.3

*The Certification
Authority snap-in.*

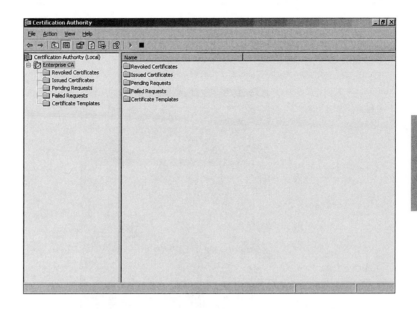

The Certification Authority snap-in provides you with access to the certificate server's properties and enables you to view certificates that have been revoked or issued, certificates that are pending, and certificate requests that have failed. These different certificate nodes in the snap-in can be used to view actual certificates and manage certificates (such as revoking certificates, as discussed later in the hour).

The snap-in also enables you to list and view the default certificate templates that are provided. These certificate templates include Domain Controller, Computer, and User certificate templates. Certificates can be assigned to users, computers, and even computer services.

Certificate Services is an advanced Windows Server 2003 feature that is used in conjunction with Group Policy and other Windows security features such as IPSec to secure the domain. Manipulating certificate templates is beyond the scope of this book. However, to get your feet wet working with certificate templates, open the Certificate Templates snap-in by selecting Start, Run. Type **certtmpl.msc** in the Run box and then press Enter. You can copy any of the existing templates and change the properties of the copies as you require. You can delete any of these copies after you are finished experimenting with them.

To view (and edit, if necessary) the properties for your certificate server, right-click the CA icon in the tree of the snap-in and select Properties from the shortcut menu. The CA Properties dialog box opens (see Figure 23.4).

FIGURE 23.4

The CA Properties dialog box.

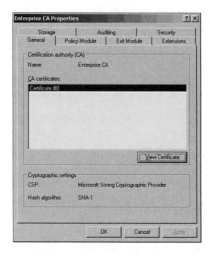

The Properties dialog box consists of seven tabs:

- **General**—this tab (see Figure 23.4) is provided mainly for information. It lists the name and the cryptographic settings for the CA. These settings cannot be changed. The tab also shows the CA's certificate, which grants it the ability to assign certificates within the domain. To view the details of the CA certificate, click the View Certificate button. Figure 23.5 shows the CA certificate for an enterprise root CA. To close the certificate, click OK.

FIGURE 23.5

You can view the CA certificate details.

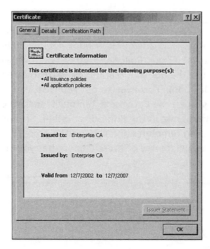

- **Storage**—Shows the paths that you selected for the CA to keep its certificate database and request log. These settings cannot be changed.

- **Policy Module**—Shows the current policy that is used to determine how the CA handles certificate requests. The default policy module is the Windows default. Unless you have access to a third-party module (or write your own), the default (Windows) will be the only possibility when you click the Select button. If you want to adjust the properties of the default policy module, select the Properties buttons. Two option buttons are provided related to request handling. You can set certificate requests to Pending, so that the administrator must issue the certificate, or you can choose to follow the default certificate template for the type of certificate being requested. If no template exists, the certificate is issued automatically. This is the default (and best practice) setting.

- **Auditing**—Enables you to select the types of CA events that you want to audit. Audited events appear in the security log of the Event Viewer (enabling auditing in Group Policy is discussed in Hour 11, "Understanding Group Policy and User Profiles"). You can audit any backup or restore of the CA database, changes made to the CA configuration, and other events related to various CA activities (see Figure 23.6) .

FIGURE 23.6

You can audit CA events.

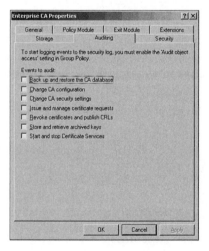

- **Exit Module**—Shows the current exit module selected for the CA. A Windows default Exit module is available (set as the default); unless you have access to additional custom Exit modules, it will be the only possibility.

- **Security**—Enables you to set the permissions for the certificates generated by the CA (see Figure 23.7). The permissions include Read, Issue and Manage Certificates, Manage CA, and Request Certificates. By default, all authenticated users can request certificates. You can add or remove groups or users from the list using the Add or Remove buttons. Permission settings for the CA and its certificates are similar to the permissions that can be applied to any number of services and resources in the Windows domain.

FIGURE 23.7

Permissions can be set for CA objects.

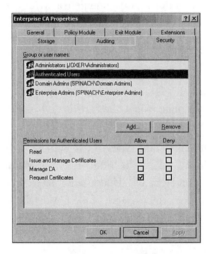

• **Extensions**—Enables you to configure where the certification-revocation list (CRL) is published on the CA (the path, which can be a URL). You can also configure the path for the Authority Information Access Points (AIAs), which specify the location where users can get the CA's certificate. Default paths are set for both of these parameters (and, in most cases, the defaults are probably what you will want to go with) .

When you have completed viewing and editing the configuration settings for the CA, click OK. You are returned to the Certification Authority snap-in.

Requesting Certificates

Any user in the domain can request a certificate. Certificates can be granted to a user or another object in the domain, such as a computer. Although certificates are often added to a computer when certain software is installed, domain users can request certificates directly from the enterprise or another CA.

Utilities for requesting certificates are available to Windows domain clients; Windows 2000, Windows XP, and Windows Server 2003 computers use the Certificates snap-in to manage and request certificates on the local computer (for the domain user).

To create an MMC snap-in for certificates (either in Windows XP or in Windows Server 2003), follow these steps:

1. Select Start, Run. In the Run dialog box, type **mmc**. Then click OK. A blank MMC console opens. To add the Certificates snap-in, select File, Add/Remove Snap-in.

2. In the Add/Remove Snap-In dialog box, select the Add button.

3. In the Add Standalone Snap-In dialog box that opens, select the Certificates snap-in. Then click the Add button. A Certificates snap-in box opens with option buttons that dictate which certificates the snap-in will manage.

4. Select either My User Account (the default), Service Account, or Computer Account to select the certificate type that the snap-in will manage. Then click Finish.

5. Click Close to close the Add Standalone Snap-in dialog box, and click OK to close the Add/Remove Snap-In dialog box.

The Certificates (local user) snap-in appears (see Figure 23.8) to manage the certificates on a local computer. This snap-in also enables you to request a new certificate for the local user (yourself) or the local computer. As with any snap-in created using the MMC command, you can save the snap-in. The snap-in in Figure 23.8 was saved as certmgr.

FIGURE 23.8

Certificates are managed locally using the Certificates snap-in.

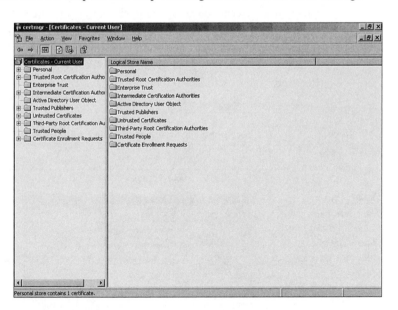

You can view personal certificates assigned to the current user. Expand the Personal node and then click the Certificates folder to view the certificates in the Details pane. To view certificates related to trusted root CAs, select the Trusted Root Certification Authorities node and then select the Certificates folder that it contains. Certificates for trusted CAs are displayed in the Details pane.

> Use the File menu and the Save command to save the MMC containing the Certificates snap-in. This enables you to quickly open the Certificates snap-in from any MMC session (using the File, Open command).

The Certificates snap-in is also used to request certificates from the CA (which is more germane to our discussion of a user requesting a certificate).

1. In the snap-in tree, expand the Certificates–Current User node so that you can see the Personal node in the tree.

2. Right-click the Personal node and then point at All Tasks on the shortcut menu that appears.

3. Select Request New Certificate.

4. The Certificate Request Wizard opens. Click Next to bypass the initial screen.

5. On the next screen, you are asked to select the type of certificate you want to request (see Figure 23.9). You can request an Administrator certificate (if you are logged on as an Administrator) or a User certificate. Other certificate types are related to the Encrypting File System (EFS) (they are the Basic EFS and EFS Recovery Agent certificates) .

> The Encrypting File System is discussed in Hour 13, "Understanding Share and NTFS Permissions."

FIGURE 23.9

The Certificate Request Wizard provides a list of certificates that you can request.

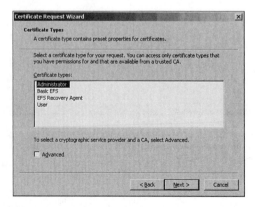

6. Select the type of certificate you wish to request and then click Next to continue. On the next screen you are asked to type a friendly name and an optional description for the certificate. After doing so, click Next. A summary screen will appear for the new certificate including information on the type of certificate and the friendly name for the certificate. Click Finish.

7. A message appears letting you know that that certificate request was successful. Click OK to close the message box. Certificates added to the snap-in will appear in the Certificates folder of the Personal node.

23

> The types of certificates available to a user depend on the certificate templates that are active on the CA (through the Active Directory and Group Policy for the domain). The certificates available are also related to the services running on a server; for example, when Internet Information Server is available, certificates related to this Web service can be requested. The use of certificates can also be tied to security and hardware devices such as smart card devices on computers. The interaction of certificates and other domain security measures, and all the ins and outs of Group Policy, are certainly beyond the scope of this book. For a primer of Windows Server 2003 security issues, check out Hour 2, "Windows Server 2003 Security Overview."

Managing the CA

If your users (and you, the administrator) can request certificates from your CA and receive them successfully, this means that your CA has been configured correctly and is up and running. The CA and its certificates are managed using the Certification Authority snap-in (open the snap-in by selecting Start, Administrative Tools, Certification Authority).

You can view certificates that the CA has issued by expanding the CA node (in this case, an enterprise CA) and then selecting the Issued Certificates folder (see Figure 23.10).

You also can view pending requests and failed requests for certificates by selecting the appropriate folder in the snap-in tree. That brings us to revoked certificates. Revoked certificates are issued certificates that you revoke for a particular reason. For example, the key of the certificate might have been compromised, or the CA itself might have been compromised (meaning that you are going to revoke a lot of bad certificates). In some cases, you might also want to put a hold on a certificate by temporarily revoking it. This type of revocation can be reversed later so that the certificate can again be used by the assignee.

FIGURE 23.10

*You can view issued
certificates.*

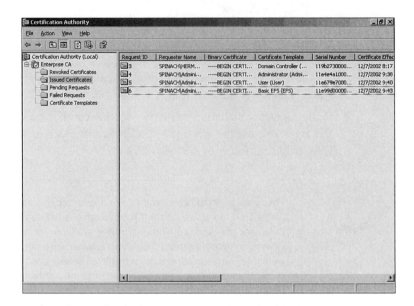

To revoke a particular certificate, follow these steps:

1. Right-click the certificate in the Issue Certificates folder (the certificate is selected in the Details pane).

2. On the shortcut menu, point at All Tasks and then Revoke Certificate. The Certificate Revocation dialog box opens.

3. To select a reason for revoking the certificate, click the Reason code drop-down box and select a listed reason. If you plan to take the revocation off the certificate at a later time, you must select the Certificate Hold reason code.

4. After selecting the reason code, click Yes to revoke the certificate.

Revoked certificates can be viewed by selecting the Revoked Certificates folder in the snap-in tree (see Figure 23.11). The revocation date and other specifics related to the revoked certificates are displayed in the Details pane.

You can unrevoke certificates that have been placed on hold. Certificate Hold then appears in the Revocation Reason column of the Details pane for these certificates. To unrevoke a certificate, right-click the certificate, point at All Tasks, and then select Unrevoke Certificate. The certificate is removed from the Revoked Certificates folder and placed in the Issued Certificates folder. When you have completed working with the Certification Authority snap-in, you can close it by clicking its Close button in the upper right corner.

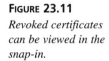

FIGURE 23.11
Revoked certificates can be viewed in the snap-in.

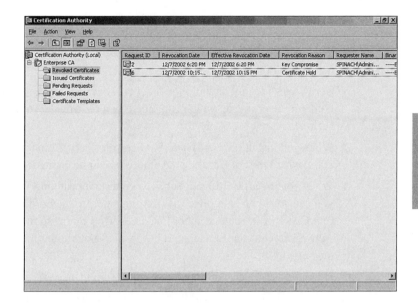

Summary

Certificate Services provides a method of identifying public key holders with digital certificates. A number of public Certificate Authorities are available that can provide digital certificates for network services and security signing of software applications. You can also configure a Certificate Authority (CA) for your domain or enterprise network using a server running Windows Server 2003.

The server is made a CA by adding Certificate Services to the server's configuration using the Add or Remove Programs applet.

After Certificates Services has been added to the server, you can fine-tune the settings for the certificate server using the Certification Authority snap-in. When a CA is up and running on the network, users can request certificates. Clients such as Windows XP (and Windows Server 2003) use the Certificates snap-in to manage and request certificates for the local computer (and local users). Certificate requests are handled by the Certificate Request Wizard. This wizard enables you to select the type of certificate that is being requested and specify a friendly name for the certificate. When the certificate is received, it is added to the local computer certificates store.

Q&A

Q What purpose do certificates play in the public key infrastructure used to protect network data?

A Certificates identify an entity on a network, such as a user or a computer. The holder of a certificate, which is granted by a Certificate Authority, is trusted by the network.

Q When you install the Certificate Services on a server running Windows Server 2003, what types of Certificate Authorities can be created?

A When you install Certificate Services on a server running Windows Server 2003, you can create an enterprise root CA, an enterprise subordinate CA, a standalone root CA, or a standalone subordinate CA. An Enterprise root CA requires the Active Directory; a standalone root CA does not require the Active Directory on the network.

Q How is a Certificate Authority configured and managed?

A The Certificate Authority is configured and managed using the Certification Authority snap-in. It can be used to set properties for the Certificate Authority and to view and manage issued, revoked, and pending certificates.

Q How can network users request and manage certificates on their local computer?

A Users can create a Certificates snap-in for the Microsoft Management Console. This snap-in can be used to view both user and local computer certificates. Requests for certificates from a Certificate Authority can also be made using the Certificates snap-in.

Hour 24

Using Internet Information Service 6.0

Communication and marketing strategies for most of today's businesses and institutions include the use of the World Wide Web. In many cases, businesses use the Web because they feel compelled to have a corporate presence on the Web.

In this hour, we take a look at the Internet Information Service, IIS 6.0. This latest version of IIS has been improved and enhanced to provide a stable and secure platform for delivering Web content. We also look at adding the FTP service to an IIS server.

In this hour, the following topics are covered:

- Reviewing new IIS 6.0 features
- Installing Internet Information Service 6.0
- Configuring the Web server and Web sites
- Creating a new Web site
- Using the Remote Administration Web tool
- Backing up the Web server metabase
- Adding and configuring an FTP site

Examining New IIS 6.0 Features

New features and enhancements added to this latest version of the IIS software (6.0) revolve mainly around security and scalability. This means that many of the enhancements are designed to provide a more stable Web server platform as additional security strategies operate behind the scenes.

Some of the new IIS 6.0 features include these:

- **New request-processing architecture**—The new architecture for IIS 6.0 provides a two-component system (as opposed to IIS 5's one-process design) that keeps core Web server code and user processes separate (these processes are now called worker processes). Part of this updated architecture is a new kernel-mode driver, HTTP.SYS, which listens for and queues requests to the server. This new driver keeps user code separate from the IIS internal code. This increases server throughput and negates the possibility that worker processes will affect server performance.

- **Security enhancements**—By default, IIS is not installed when Windows Server 2003 is installed on a computer. In fact, IIS implementations that have been accidentally installed on Windows servers (such as Windows 2000) will be removed when the server is upgraded to Windows Server 2003. When IIS is installed as part of the application server role, it is installed in a locked-down state in which only static content is served. The administrator must configure additional functionality. Other security features include the capability to negate users from installing IIS on network computers using group policy and the capability to write protect content on the Web server so that hackers cannot deface the site.

 IIS has historically been one of the most hacked Microsoft products. IIS 6.0 has been developed to provide a more secure Web platform than previous versions of the software.

- **Application server role**—Another change in the IIS implementation relates to the Application Server role that can be added to a server running Windows Server 2003. IIS is now grouped under the Application Server role with other services such as XML Web services, COM+, and ASP.NET.

- **Remote Administration**—Another new feature of note is the IIS Remote Administration tool. This enables you to administer the application server running IIS across the Internet or an intranet from a remote Web browser.

In a nutshell, IIS 6.0 provides a more scalable and secure environment than its predecessors. This means that a single IIS application server can provide the home for a number of Web sites. This enables you to serve both internal and external content to users using various Web services.

> The IIS 6.0 metabase is now a plain-text XML file, which greatly augments backup and restore. This makes it easier to restore the metabase and repair a Web server that is experiencing problems.

Installing Internet Information Service 6.0

Before you install IIS on a server, you should keep in mind a couple of security-related issues. First, you should definitely install IIS on a NTFS volume, which enables you to secure IIS resource files with the stronger permissions provided by NTFS. You might also consider installing IIS on a standalone member server that does not provide any other services. This helps control the work load placed on the server if it is receiving a large number of Web hits and then also has to provide other important network services. Running other services on the IIS server can also potentially lead to security leaks on the server that could compromise the Web server and the entire network.

IIS 6.0 can be quickly added to a Windows server's configuration using the Configure Your Server Wizard. To configure a computer as a Web server, follow these steps:

1. Start the Configure Your Server Wizard (Start, Administrative Tools, Configure Your Server Wizard). Click Next to bypass the initial wizard screen.

2. You are prompted to connect cabling and turn on all peripherals. Click Next. The Server Role list appears. Select the Application Server (IIS, ASP.NET) role and then click Next.

3. On the next wizard screen, you are given the option of installing the FrontPage server extensions and enabling ASP.NET. If you will use Microsoft FrontPage to build Web pages on the server, select the FrontPage Server Extensions check box. If ASP.NET Web-Based applications are going to be provided on the server, you can enable the ASP.NET service on this wizard screen. After making your selections, click Next to continue.

4. A summary screen of the components that will be installed is listed on the next wizard screen. Click Next to continue. The Windows Component Wizard appears, and IIS is installed on the server.

5. The final wizard screen appears, letting you know that the server is now an application server. Click Finish. The Manage Your Server window appears, listing the Application Server role.

24

> IIS can also be added to a server's configuration using the Add or Remove Software applet in the Windows Control Panel. It is added as a Windows component.

When IIS is installed on the server, you can create a Web site. IIS is managed in much the same as other Windows Server 2003 services, using a snap-in. However, two snap-ins enable you to access the IIS Manager. You can open the Application Server snap-in via the Manage Your Server window (click the Manage This Application link to open the Application Server snap-in), or you can open the Internet Information Services (IIS) Manager via the Start menu (Start, Administrative Tools, Internet Information Services [IIS] Manager).

The IIS Manager is a subnode in the Application Server snap-in (see Figure 24.1). It is the main node in the IIS Manager snap-in. So, it's your choice of snap-in and probably depends on additional services that you might want to manage as you administer your Web server.

FIGURE 24.1

The Application Server snap-in can be used to configure and manage the various IIS components.

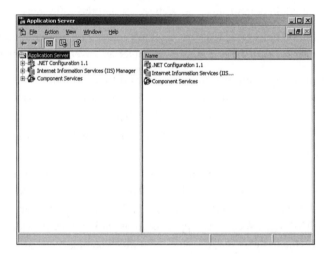

When you add the IIS service as a role using the Configure Your Server Wizard, you are provided with a fairly stripped-down installation of the various Web services, which is in sharp contract to earlier versions of the Windows network operating system platform (such as Windows 2000 Server). If you want to install features such as FTP or NNTP (which are discussed later in the hour), you need to add these components using the Windows Component Wizard.

So, if you want a more "robust" installation of IIS, you might want to use the route provided by the Add or Remove Software applet in the Control Panel rather than the Configure Your Server Wizard. We discuss adding FTP and NNTP to the installation later in the hour, to show you how the various components are categorized in the Windows Component Wizard.

Configuring the Web Environment

After you have installed IIS on the server, you can configure the various components that the service provides. One of the most commonly used components of IIS is the Web service. As already mentioned, you can access the various options for Web sites using the application server or the IIS Manager snap-in. For the sake of continuity, we use the IIS Manager in this section of the book as we discuss configuring the Web service.

To open the IIS Manager, select Start, Administrative Tools, then Internet Information Services (IIS) Manager. Expand the Server node (see Figure 24.2). The Application Pools, Web Sites, and Web Service Extensions folders appear.

24

FIGURE 24.2

The IIS configuration can be set in the IIS Manager.

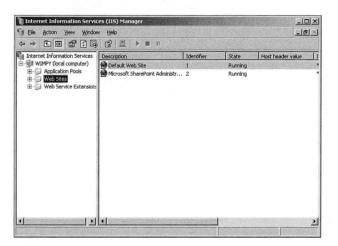

Two configuration layers are related to Web sites. There are the master settings that will affect all the Web sites created on the IIS server, and then there are configuration settings for each Web site that you create. Setting the master or Web site settings enables you to have the same base configuration for each site hosted by the server. If you want to fine-tune settings for an individual site, you can do that in the particular Web site's Properties dialog box (discussed later in the hour). Let's take a look at the master settings and then the settings for the default Web site that is created when you install IIS on the server.

Configuring Master Web Site Settings

To configure the global settings for your Web servers, right-click the Web Sites folder and select Properties. The Web Sites Properties dialog box opens (See Figure 24.3).

FIGURE 24.3

The Web Sites Properties dialog box.

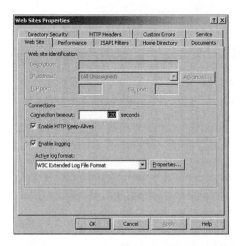

You will find that as you click the various tabs on this dialog box, some of the settings are not available. This Properties dialog box contains exactly the same tabs that you find when you open the Properties dialog box for a specific Web site, such as the default Web site. Certain settings (such as the Web site investigation information) are reserved for individual sites.

So, to make a long story short, a number of the settings that we discuss in this section related to global configuration of Web sites can also be set on a per–Web site basis. Let's look at some of the master settings that you might want to adjust.

Settings made in the Web Sites Properties dialog box are inherited by each Web site that you create on this server. If you require more flexibility for each Web site, configure the properties on a per–Web site basis.

Configuring the Performance Tab

The Performance tab (see Figure 24.4) is used to control bandwidth throttling and the total number of connections allowed on your Web sites (on this server). By default, the bandwidth available for the Web sites on the server is not limited. The number of connections is also unlimited. Click the option Limit the total network bandwidth available for all Web sites on this server to set the bandwidth using the Bandwidth spinner box.

To limit the number of connections, click the Connections limited to option button and use the spinner box to set the number of connections allowed. This setting affects all Web sites on the server.

FIGURE 24.4

The Performance tab enables you to set bandwidth and connection limitations.

Adding ISAPI Filters

The ISAPI Filters tab enables you to add or remove ISAPI filters for all the Web sites on the server (ISAPI stands for Internet Server Application Programming Interface). An ISAPI filter is a program that runs as part of the server process and responds to HTTP requests (the filter directs requests to the application). ISAPI filters are beyond the scope of this book, but be advised that, by default, the ASP.NET ISAPI filter is installed on the master Properties dialog boxes' ISAPI Filters tab. This means that it is available for all the Web sites on your server. Thus, your Web sites can include Active Server Pages (ASP) as part of their content.

Additional filters are added by clicking the Add button and then browsing for the .dll file that represents the filter. Custom ISAPI filters can be created, and ISAPI filters can be set at the Web site level.

Using the Documents Tab

The Documents tab enables you to specify the type of pages that should be recognized as the default content page or home page for your site when it is contacted by a Web browser. You can specify pages such as default.htm or index.htm and order them in the content page list.

You can also enable a document footer on this tab. This appends an HTML-formatted text string to the footer of every document that is returned by your Web server. This enables you to put your company name or other information at the bottom of each Web page. Documents' tab settings can also be configured at the Web site level using the Documents tab on a particular Web site's Properties dialog box.

Configuring Directory Security

The Directory Security tab enables you to configure authentication control and determine whether you will allow anonymous access. You can also grant or deny access to your Web sites based on IP addresses or domain names.

To configure anonymous access, click the Authentication and Access Control Edit button. The Authentication Methods dialog box opens (see Figure 24.5). You can enable (by default) or disable anonymous access, and select the user name and password that will be used for anonymous access.

FIGURE 24.5

The Authentication Methods dialog box controls anonymous access and the authentication scheme.

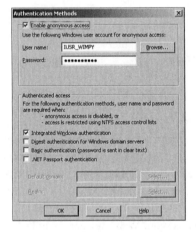

In the Authentication Access section of the dialog box, you can set the type of authentication used to access the Web site. You can use Windows authentication or other authentication methods, such as clear-text basic authentication or Microsoft .NET Passport authentication.

The other settings that are controlled via the Directory Security tab include whether to grant or deny access to your Web sites based on IP address or domain name. To access the IP Address and Domain Name Restrictions dialog box, click the IP Address and Domain Name Restrictions Edit button. In the IP Address and Domain Name Restrictions dialog box (see Figure 24.6) use the Granted Access or Denied Access buttons to determine the default setting for access to your Web sites.

FIGURE 24.6

Use the IP Address and Domain Name Restrictions dialog box to grant or deny access to the Web sites.

You can then use the Add button to either deny or permit access to a single computer, a group of computers, or a particular domain name. Add IP addresses (for individual computers), network IDs (for groups of computers), or a domain name to restrict (or permit) computers in a particular domain.

> If you are granting or denying access based on domain membership, reverse lookup must be available on the DNS server.

Configuring Custom Errors

The Custom Errors tab of the Web Sites Properties dialog box enables you to configure custom error messages for HTTP errors. You can select a particular HTTP error and then edit it by selecting the Edit button. To specify the location of the file that will appear when a user experiences this particular HTTP error when accessing your Web sites, select File as the message type and then specify the path for the file.

Using the Service Tab

The Services tab of the Web Sites Properties dialog box enables you to run your Web sites in IIS 5 isolation mode for backward compatibility with older ISAPI applications, and to set file compression for application and static files on your Web sites. To run the Web sites in IIS 5 isolation mode, select the Run WWW service in the IIS 5.0 isolation mode.

If you want to use HTTP compression on the Web sites, which provides compressed files to compression-enabled Web clients, select the check boxes Compress Application Files or Compress Static Files. You can also set the temporary directory where the compressed files will be held and specify the size allowed for the temporary directory.

Configuring Web Site Settings

Although the different global IIS settings that we looked at in the previous sections can be also set per Web site (using the Properties dialog box for a particular Web site), in many cases you will want to configure global settings for all the sites on a server; this provides you with a certain level of consistency. However, certain settings are best configured for each Web site. These includes settings that can be configured only at the Web site level, such as Web site identification.

These settings are controlled using the Properties dialog box for each specific Web site that you are running on the IIS server. Select the Web Sites folder in the IIS Manager snap-in tree and then right-click any Web site in the Details pane (such as the Default Web Site) to access the Properties dialog box.

> You might see other tabs on your Web Site Properties dialog box if you have done an upgrade from a previous version of IIS or added other server extensions to the server.

Choosing the Addressing and Log Settings for a Site

The Web Site tab of a Web site's Properties dialog box (see Figure 24.7) is used to configure the friendly name for the Web site (which appears in the snap-in), the IP address for the Web site, and other settings, such as the TCP port and the connection timeout.

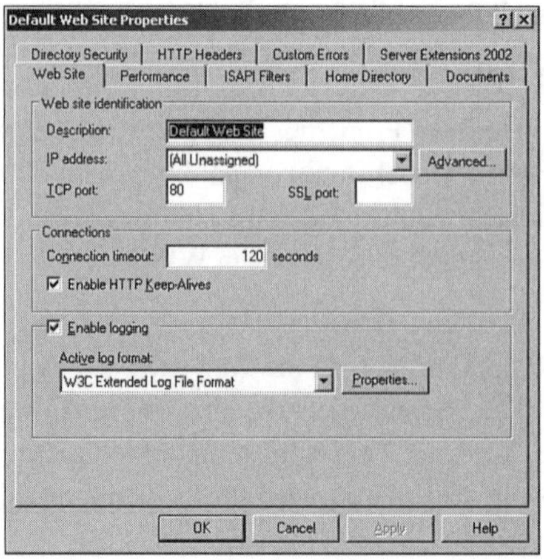

FIGURE 24.7

The Web Site tab enables you to set a friendly name and IP address specific to a Web site.

To change the description of the Web site, enter a new name in the Description box. If you want to assign a specific IP address to the server, click the IP address drop-down box and select the IP address. By default, all the addresses assigned to the computer are also assigned to the Web site.

You can also change the TCP port for the server (the default is 80). You can use any unique TCP port number for the port. However, you must make sure that you make your clients aware that the TCP port number has been changed so that they can configure their Web browsers to request the new port number for a connection.

This tab also enables you to configure the connection timeout (the amount of time that an inactive user's connection is kept), and you can choose the log type if you want to enable logging (it is enabled by default). You can select from different ASCII file formats for the log file, such as Microsoft IIS, NCSA Common format, and W3C Extended (this is a customizable ASCII file format) file types, or you can use the ODBC format to create a log file that is database compatible. You select the log file type using the Active Log Format drop-down box.

24

> To set the log schedule and log location for the Web log, click the Properties button on the Web Site tab. You can set the schedule for the log (such as daily or weekly), and you can specify the name and location of the log file.

Configuring Server Extensions

The Server Extensions tab of a Web site's Properties dialog box enables you to configure the properties for extensions such as the FrontPage Server 2002 Extensions. To configure the settings related to an extension family, select the Server Extensions 2002 tab and then click the Settings button. Internet Explorer opens with the Front Page Server Extensions page.

This page allows you to enable authoring on the Web site and set the mail settings to be used by the FrontPage Server extensions. You can also set performance settings for the Web site. You can select the size of the Web (in pages) and then set the specific size of the different caches and search index size. Select Submit in the browser window to save your setting changes. When you close the browser window, you are returned to the Web site's Properties dialog box.

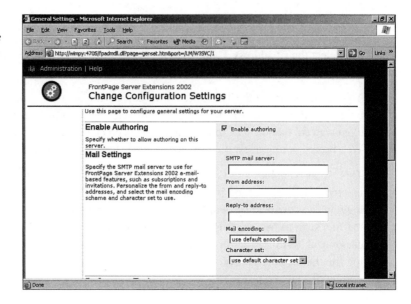

Enabling Web Service Extensions

Another aspect of configuring your Web environment is specifying the Web Service extensions that will be enabled on the IIS server. Web Service extensions are request handlers that allow your Web server to provide dynamic content, such as the content provided by a server configured for FrontPage extensions or ASP (as well as other dynamic content extensions).

To enable or disable available Web Service Extensions, follow these steps:

1. In the IIS Manager, select the Web Service Extensions node in the snap-in tree. The Web Service Extensions appear in the Details pane (see Figure 24.9).

2. Select a service in the Web Service Extensions list, and then select Allow or Prohibit as needed.

3. If you want to view the properties for an extension, select the extension and then Properties. The Properties dialog box for the extension opens. You can view the files that are required for the extension to function on the Required Files tab of the dialog box.

You can also add new extensions to the server by clicking the Add a new Web service extension link. Enter the extension name in the New Web Service Extension box that appears. You must then use the Add button to specify the file location and name for the files that enable the extension to run.

FIGURE 24.9

Extensions that provide dynamic content on the Web server can be enabled or disabled.

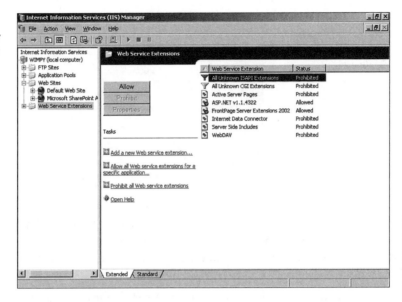

Creating a New Web Site

You can host multiple Web sites on an IIS server. This means that you can add Web sites to the IIS server's configuration (you can also delete Web sites that are no longer needed).

To add a Web site to the server, follow these steps:

1. Expand the Server node in the IIS Manager tree.

2. Right-click the Web Sites folder and then point at New on the shortcut menu. Select Web Site.

> You can also import Web sites from other Web servers (or locations on your network). Use the Web Site (from File) selection on the New shortcut menu.

3. The Web Site Creation Wizard opens. Click Next to bypass the initial wizard screen.

4. On the next screen, type a description of the Web site and then click Next.

5. On the next wizard screen (see Figure 24.10), specify the IP address for the site, the TCP port for the site (if you are running multiple sites on the server, you must choose a port other than 80), and a host header for the site. Click Next to continue.

FIGURE 24.10

Specify the IP address, port, and host header for the site.

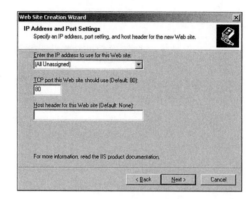

6. On the next screen, provide the path for the Web site files. By default, the site allows anonymous access. Deselect Allow Anonymous Access to This Web Site if you do not want to allow anonymous access. Then click Next to continue.

7. On the next screen (see Figure 24.11), set the access permissions for the site. By default, the Read and Run scripts permissions are enabled. You can also allow the Execute, Write, and Browse permissions.

FIGURE 24.11

Set the access permissions for the new site.

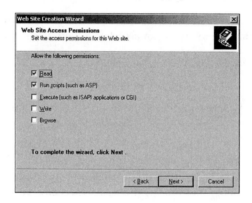

8. After setting the permissions, click Next. The final wizard screen appears. Click Finish.

To view the properties of the new site, right-click the site and select Properties. You can adjust any of the site properties, as discussed earlier in the hour.

Adding Content to the Web Site

One aspect of administering a Web site is supplying the Web pages that make up the site. A number of Web design tools exist; the tools employed and the overall look and feel of the Web site depend on the purpose of the site.

Web content must be placed in the home directory of the site. The default Web site's local path is c:\inetpub\wwwroot. You place or publish (if using Microsoft FrontPage) the content for the site in this directory.

You can preview Web content locally using your Web browser and the IP address or NetBIOS name of the server. For example, the content on a Web server named wimpy could be accessed using the command http://wimpy.

Administering the Web Site Remotely

We've already discussed that you manage and administer your Web sites using the IIS Manager snap-in. Content can be added to Web directories using Windows Explorer or by selecting Explore from the shortcut menu of any Web site in the IIS Manager. Another option for managing your Web sites is the Remote Administration Web Interface.

> Remote Administration for your Web sites is not supported on a domain controller.

To install Remote Administration, follow these steps:

1. Select Start, Control Panel, then Add or Remove Programs.
2. In the Add or Remove Programs window, select the Add/Remove Windows Components icon. The Windows Components Wizard appears.
3. Select Applications Server in the Components list and then click Details.
4. Click the Internet Information Services (IIS) subcomponent and then click Details.
5. Select World Wide Web Service and then click Details.
6. Select the Remote Administration (HTML) check box and then click OK. Click OK two more times to return to the wizard's main screen.
7. Click Next to begin the installation of the Remote Administration component.
8. Click Finish when the process is complete.

After Remote Administration is installed, you can connect to a remote Web server. Follow these steps:

1. Click the Start button and then select Run.

2. In the Run dialog box, type **https://server name: 8098**, where server name is the DNS name of the server.

3. Then click OK.

4. Internet Explorer opens, and a username and password dialog box appears (see Figure 24.12). Enter a username with administrative privileges and an appropriate password.

5. Then click OK.

The Web Remote Administration welcome page opens. The Web interface provides links to a number of administrative tasks at the top of the page (see Figure 24.13) .

Table 24.1 provides a list of the tasks found under each Web link on the administration page.

TABLE 24.1 Remote Administration Pages

Administration Web Page	Tools
Welcome	Links are available to set the Administrator password, the server name, and the default page for the server.
Status	Alerts related to the site are shown on this page. For example, alerts might be related to features not configured, such as email alerts or configuration of a certificate for the server.
Sites	This page lists the sites on the server and enables you to start and stop the service. You can also create new Web sites from this page.

Administration Web Page	Tools
Web Server	This page enables you to configure the server's general settings, such as the root directory and the number of maximum connections. Links to Web and FTP logs are provided. Links to FTP settings include FTP messages and FTP master settings (if FTP is installed on the server) .
Network	You can set the server name and domain membership and configure the network interface properties on the server. You can also configure the IP address that will be used for remote administration of the server.
Users	This page enables you to manage local users and groups on the server.
Maintenance	This page enables you to set the date and time on the server, view log files, and set the alert email for the server. You can also shut down or restart the server manually or by creating a schedule.
Help	This page provides a list of help topics for using the Web interface for Web server administration.

24

FIGURE 24.13

The Web Remote Administration page.

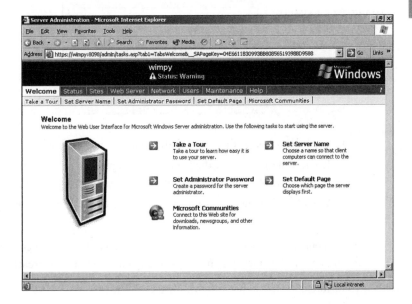

Many of the common tasks for managing the Web server are found on the various administration pages. The Administration Web page provides a way to quickly manage some of the basic settings related to your IIS server and your Web sites on the server, but it cannot perform all the tasks found in the IIS Manager snap-in. For example, you cannot set all the global or Web site settings discussed earlier in the hour. You also cannot back up or restore the metabase for the Web server; this is discussed in the next section.

Backing Up and Restoring the Metabase

An important aspect of managing your Web server is maintaining the integrity of the IIS server's metabase. The metabase is the file that contains all the configuration settings for the IIS server.

By default, the metabase is automatically backed up. But you can create a backup using a particular filename. To back up the metabase, follow these steps:

1. Right-click the Server node in the IIS Manager snap-in tree.
2. On the shortcut menu, point at All Tasks and then select Backup/Restore configuration. The Backup/Restore Configuration dialog box appears.
3. Click the Create Backup button. The Configuration Backup dialog box appears (see Figure 24.14).

FIGURE 24.14

Provide the name and password for the configuration backup.

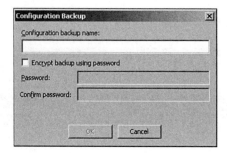

4. Type the name of the configuration backup in the Configuration backup name box.
5. If you want to encrypt the backup with a password, select the Encrypt backup using password check box. Then press Enter and confirm the password.
6. Click OK. The new backup appears in the Configuration Backup/Restore dialog box.

If the metabase file becomes corrupt, you can restore a backup copy of the file. You can restore any of the automatic backups or any backup that you create.

To restore a metabase backup, follow these steps:

1. Right-click the Server node in the IIS Manager snap-in tree.
2. On the shortcut menu, point at All Tasks and then select Backup/Restore Configuration. The Backup/Restore Configuration dialog box appears.
3. Select the backup that you want to restore, and then click the Restore button.

4. A message appears letting you know that the restore process will delete all current settings and stop the IIS services during the restoration (the service will be started after the metabase is restored). To continue, click Yes.

5. If you password-protected the backup that you are restoring, the Backup Password dialog opens. Supply the password and click OK.

6. When the restore is complete, a message appears letting you know that the operation was completed. Click OK. You can also close the Configuration Backup/Restore dialog box.

Creating FTP Sites

Hosting an FTP site on your IIS server can be a great way to provide the users on your network with either files that they need or a place to store files that are shared as part of a particular project. Supplying a repository of downloadable files might also be important to your company as a service that you provide to your public Web users. As with the Web server service of IIS, the FTP service can be used on the public Internet or for your private corporate intranet.

To add the FTP service to the IIS server, follow these steps:

1. Select Start, Control Panel, Add or Remove Programs.

2. In the Add or Remove Programs window, select the Add/Remove Windows Components icon. The Windows Components Wizard appears.

3. Select Applications Server in the Components list and then click Details.

4. Click the Internet Information Services (IIS) subcomponent and then click Details.

5. In the subcomponents list, select the File Transfer Protocol (FTP) Service check box. Then click OK twice.

6. To complete the process, click Next. When the component is installed, click Finish.

The FTP service is managed using the IIS Manager snap-in. You can set global settings for FTP sites or settings for each FTP site using the FTP Sites Properties dialog box or the Properties dialog box for a specific site. A default FTP site is created when you install the FTP service. Table 24.2 provides an overview of the tabs found on the Properties dialog boxes for both the global and specific settings (the tabs are very similar on the two different Properties dialog boxes).

24

TABLE 24.2   FTP Properties

Property Dialog Box Tab	Settings
FTP Site	Enables you to set the description for the site, the IP address, and the TCP port. It also enables you to set the number of site connections and the log format.
Security Accounts	Allows you to enable or disable anonymous logon and select the user account used for anonymous logon.
Messages	Enables you to set the Banner, Welcome, and Exit messages displayed when users log on to the FTP site.
Home Directory	Used to specify the content directory, the local path for the FTP directory, and permissions (Read, Write, Log visits) for the site. You can also specify whether directory listings should be in UNIX or MS-DOS format.
Directory Security	Enables you to deny or permit access based on IP addresses. By default, all computers are granted access.

You can quickly populate the FTP site using Windows Explorer. The FTP root folder is c:\inetpub\ftproot. Any files placed in this folder (just copy them to the folder using Windows Explorer from anywhere on your network) will be available to your users. The default permission, Read, gives them the capability to download files from the site.

If you also want to enable users to upload files to the site using their Web browser or an FTP client, you must enable the Write permission on the site. You can do this in the FTP site's Properties dialog box.

Right-click the site in the Details pane and then select Properties. Select the Home Directory tab (see Figure 24.15) .

FIGURE 24.15

Enable Write capabilities on the FTP site.

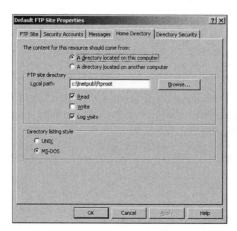

On the tab, select the Write check box. Then click OK.

Links to the FTP site can be placed on Web pages provided by the IIS server, making it easy for users to download or upload files to the server.

Summary

In this hour, you learned how to install and configure IIS 6 on a Windows server. You worked with both global and specific settings for Web sites created on an IIS server using the IIS Manager snap-in. You also became familiar with installing and using the Web Remote Administration for an IIS server. Finally, you learned how to install the FTP IIS component and configure a FTP site.

24

Q&A

Q As far as security and administration, should you install IIS 6 on a member server or a domain controller?

A It is a best practice to install IIS 6 on a member server. This helps protect the Active Directory from security hacks that might originate via the Web server component of IIS. Web Remote Installation of IIS is also not supported on a domain controller, again making the case for IIS installation on a domain member server.

Q How do you set global settings that will affect all the Web sites hosted on an IIS server?

A Use the Web Sites Properties dialog box to configure global settings such as directory security, performance settings, and logging settings for all the Web sites hosted on an IIS server.

Q How do you enable additional Web service extensions for Web sites?

A Select the Web Service Extensions folder in the IIS Manager tree. You can then allow (or prohibit) Web service extensions installed on the server and add new Web service extensions.

Q How do you add the FTP service to the IIS server?

A Use the Windows Component Wizard to add additional components to your IIS server, such as the FTP service. The service (such as FTP) can then be configured and managed using the IIS Manager snap-in or the Remote Administration Web interface.

INDEX

J-K

Kerberos, 22-24
Kerberos Policy node, 23
kernal-mode drivers,
  HTTP.SYS, 502
key distribution center,
  Kerberos, 22
keyboard hotkeys, 410
keys, hotkeys, 410

L

L2TP (WAN Miniport),
  450-451
LAN network protocols,
  121-123
LAN Routing check box,
  381
languages, WSDL (Web
  Services Description
  Language), 10
LANs (local area networks),
  NAT configurations, 480
launching
    Active Directory tools, 77
    Users and Computer snap-
      in, 77
layers, OSI model, 120-121
lease duration, scope
  (Dynamic Host Configu-
  ration Protocol), 327
Lease Duration screen, 327
leases
    DHCP (Dynamic Host
      Configuration Protocol),
      monitoring, 336
    IP addresses, 325

legacy clients, NetBIOS
  names, 146
legacy devices, installing,
  363
legacy versions, Windows,
  208
Let Me Choose What to
  Back Up option, 111
Let Windows Choose
  What's Best for My
  Computer option, 61
levels
    access, 18, 25
    domain functional levels,
      176-177
    domains, DNS (Domain
      Name Service), 302
    forest functional levels,
      176
    functional, domains, 153
    RAID (Redundant Array
      of Independent Disks),
      97-98
    share permissions, 257
License command, 36
licenses
    client access, 396
    External Connector, 36
    User Client Access, 36
licensing
    methods, clean installa-
      tions, 42
    servers, 34-36
    Terminal Server Licensing
      service, 396-400, 405
Licensing Agreement
  screen, 44
Licensing option, 405
Licensing snap-in, 35-36
Link Name box, 250

linked, GPO (Group Policy
  object), viewing, 224
Linked Group Policy
  Objects tab, 224
links
    Active Directory sites,
      181-182
    Add a New Web Service
      Extension, 512
    Add or Remove Role, 234
    Add Role, 396
    Configure Shadow Copies,
      244
    DFS (Distributed File
      System), 250-251
    Group Policy, 184
    Manage This Application,
      504
    Other Search Options, 287
    Remove role, 396
    Send Console Message,
      241
    User Accounts, 194
list disk command,
  DiskPart, 105
List Folder Contents per-
  missions, 260, 265
List Folder/Read Data permission, 267
List in the Directory check
  box, 287
list volume command,
  DiskPart, 104-105
lists. *See also* drop-down
  lists
    Access Control List, 260
    Applications Server in the
      Components, 515
    certification-revocation list
      (CRL), 494

Performance Monitor console, 430-434

System Monitor, 419, 431

Move dialog box, 191

MS-CHAP (Microsoft Challenge Handshake Authentication Protocol), 368

MS-CHAP v2 (Microsoft Challenge Handshake Authentication Protocol Versions 2), 368

MS-DOS clients, configuring as WINS, 353

multicast groups, Class D (IP addresses), 128

multicast messages, RIP (Routing Information Protocol), 385

Multicasts per Second, 441

Multicasts Sent column (Station Statistics pane), 442

multidrives, 100

multihomed computers, 449

multihomed servers, 200, 379

Multihomed static mapping type, 350

multiple DFS roots, hosting, 250

multiple installations, 44

multiple RIS clients, 205

multiple users, security, 66

MX (Mail Exchanger) resource record, 312

My Computer, 50, 107, 196

My Use Only button, 455

N

Name Not Found dialog box, 259

Name Resolution tab (NAT Properties dialog box), 483

Name Server (NS) resource record, 312

names

ARC (Advanced RISC Computing), 100-101

Country names (top-level domain), 300

domains, Web sites, accessing, 508

logon, 155

NetBIOS (Network Basic Input/Output System), 146, 342

principal, 155

resolutions, 342-343

usernames, 155

namespaces

domains, DNS (Domain Name Service), 299-300

defining, 302-303

naming

backups, 112

computers, clean installations, 42

DFS roots, 249

DNS zones, 307-309

domains, 299

groups, 174

shares, 237

naming conventions

Active Directory, 142

client computers, RIS (Remote Installation Services), 203-204

NAT (Network Address Translation), 80, 477

configuring, 478-483

DHCP Allocator, 478

private addressing, 483

troubleshooting, 483

NAT Properties dialog box, 483

NAT/Basic Firewall icon, 480-481

native modes (Windows 2000), 176

NBMA Neighbors tab, 386

NBTSTAT -c, 356

NBTSTAT -rr, 356

NBTSTAT -s, 356

NBTSTAT command, 343

NBTSTAT command-line tool, 355-356

NCP (NetWare Core Protocol), 122

neighbors, RIP (Routing Information Protocol), 385

Neighbors dialog box, 387

Neighbors tab, 385

nesting

Active Directory groups, 170

groups, 176

net (top-level domain), 299

NetBEUI, 121-122

NetBIOS (Network Basic Input/Output System), 341

Active Directory, client computers, 190

broadcasts, 342-343

LMHOSTS files, 343

name-resolution, 342-343

names, 146, 342

node types, 344

Software Installation policy, 216

Software Settings, GPO (Group Policy object), 216

Source tab, 431

space, volume space, 98

spanned volumes, 94

SPAP (Shiva Password Authentication Protocol), 368

special NTFS (NT File System) permissions, 266-268

Special Permissions, 403

Specify Computers for Logon option, 18

Specify Users with Dial-Up and VPN Connection Rights option, 18

speed, ICS (Internet Connection Sharing) connections, 472

SPI (security parameters index), 460

spin boxes
Metric, 382
Replicate Every, 183

spinner boxes, Bandwidth, 506

split-horizon processing, 385

SPX (Sequenced Packet Exchange), 122

SRV (Service) resource record, 312

stacks, protocol stacks, 120

standalone member server, IIS 6.0 (Internet Information Service 6.0), 503

Standalone root CA, 489

Standalone subordinate CA, 489

standard roaming profiles, creating, 229-230

Standard Server, 11

Standard User button, 194

Start command (Capture menu), 441

Start menu, 50

Start menu commands, Administrative Tools, Licensing, 35

Start Menu tab, 50

Start of Authority (SOA) resource record, 312

starting
Backup utility, 111
DiskPart, 104
WINS (Windows Internet Naming Service), 346

static entries, databases, 354

static IP addresses, 345, 371

static IP routing, 381-383

Static Mapping dialog box, 350

static mappings, WINS (Window Internet Naming Service), 346, 350

Static Route dialog box, 382

Static Routes node, 382

Station Statistics pane, 442

statistics, WINS (Window Internet Naming Service), 347

status
devices, 60
VPN (virtual private network) ports, 457

Status box, 457

Status page (Remote Administration), 516

Stop command (Capture menu), 443

storage
basic, 87
dynamic, 87
IPSec (IP Security Protocols), 458
mandatory profiles, 228
roaming profiles, 228
user profiles, 228
zones (Active Directory), 306

Storage tab, 493

Store Usernames and Password applet, 10, 63

striped volumes, 94

striped volumes with parity, 94

stub zones, 306-308

subdomain names, DNS (Domain Name Service), 302

subdomains, 300

subfolders, Replication Partners, 348

subnet calculators, 133

subnet masks, 129, 132

subnets
Active Directory sites, 181
IP, 154, 179

Subnets folder, 181

subnetting, IP subnetting, 129-133

subnodes, IIS (Internet Information Services) Manager, 504

How can we make this index more useful? Email us at indexes@samspublishing.com

X-Z

Your Guide to Computer Technology

www.informit.com